The
Murder of
Tutankhamen

ALSO BY BOB BRIER

Egyptian Mummies:
Unraveling the Secrets of an Ancient Art

Ancient Egyptian Magic

Encyclopedia of Mummies

The Murder of Tutankhamen

A True Story

Bob Brier, Ph.D.

G. P. PUTNAM'S SONS
NEW YORK

G. P. Putnam's Sons
Publishers Since 1838
a member of
Penguin Putnam Inc.
200 Madison Avenue
New York, NY 10016

Library of Congress Cataloging-in-Publication Data

Brier, Bob.
The murder of Tutankhamen : a true story / by Bob Brier.
p.   cm.
Includes bibliographical references and index.
ISBN 0-399-14383-1
1. Tutankhamen, King of Egypt—Biography.   2. Tutankhamen, King of
Egypt—Death and burial.   3. Egypt—History—Eighteenth dynasty, ca.
1570–1320 B.C.   4. Pharaohs—Biography.   I. Title.
DT87.5.B667   1998
932'.014'092—dc21
[B]   97-49193 CIP

Printed in the United States of America

1   3   5   7   9   10   8   6   4   2

This book is printed on acid-free paper. ∞

BOOK DESIGN BY AMANDA DEWEY

Acknowledgments

In Egyptology it is normal to have a team of specialists working on a single project; this book is no exception. When knowledge failed me, which was often, colleagues always were there, ready to help.

On the medical-forensic front I have been doubly fortunate in that many of the experts are close personal friends and I often called on them at strange and inconvenient times. Dr. Gerald Irwin, head of Radiology at Winthrop University Hospital, was the first to suggest that Tutankhamen may have survived for quite a while after receiving a blow to the back of the head, and remained a close consultant throughout the writing of this book. Dr. Michael R. Zimmerman, director of Clinical Laboratories, Maimonides Medical Center, Brooklyn, New York, read an early draft of the manuscript and made important suggestions about the actual cause of Tutankhamen's death following the blow. Dr. Michael Perry, chief of Trauma Radiology, School of Medicine, Univer-

Acknowledgments

sity of Maryland, also made important suggestions about how to determine if Tutankhamen did indeed linger before death. As always, I have benefited from discussions with Ronald Wade, director of the State Anatomy Board, Maryland. In Egypt, Dr. Fawzi Gabella, head of the Department of Anatomy, Kasr el Einy Hospital, kindly permitted me to examine the two human fetuses discovered in Tutankhamen's tomb. Dr. Nasri Iskander, Curator of Mummies, Egyptian Museum, Cairo, was most helpful in making available to me the mummy of Tutankhamen's grandfather, Amenhotep III. I must also thank my colleagues in the Paleopathology Association who were always willing to discuss the medical aspects of the case.

On the Egyptological front, my colleagues have been equally helpful. Dr. Ali Hassan, former Secretary General of the Supreme Council of Antiquities, permitted me repeated access to closed tombs. Dr. Mohamed Sallah, director of the Egyptian Museum, Cairo, kindly gave permission to examine objects in storage in the museum. In Germany, Dr. Dietrich Wildung, director of the Ägyptisches Museum in Berlin, allowed me to examine and photograph the finger ring indicating that the Vizier, Aye, married Tutankhamen's widow. I will never forget the day when Dr. Hannelore Kischkewitz, curator at the museum, placed the ring in my hand. Thanks are also due to Diana Magee of the Griffith Institute, Ashmolean Museum, Oxford, for supplying a photocopy of Percy Newberry's letter to Howard Carter describing the ring. Closer to home, I would like to thank Dr. Dorothea Arnold, curator of the Egyptian Department, Metropolitan Museum of Art, New York, for granting access to the funerary collars worn at Tutankhamen's burial meal, and for permission to reprint Harry Burton's 1920s photographs of Tutankhamen's mummy. I would also like to thank Dr. Rita Freed, curator, Department of Egyptian and Nubian Art, Museum of Fine Arts, Boston, for the discussions about what daily life at Amarna must have been like.

Special thanks are due the administrators at Long Island University, who made it possible for me to reduce my teaching load and reschedule classes so that I could research this book. My colleagues in the Philosophy Department were both supportive and understanding when their chairman was away, crawling through tombs in Egypt.

I am very appreciative of everyone at The Learning Channel. When I first agreed to make a documentary about the murder of Tutankhamen I must admit, I had misgivings—that they would ask me to say things that I didn't want to, that there would be limitations on what I did say, etc. I was delighted to discover how wrong I was. If anything, when my enthusiasm got the better of me, my director, Peter Spry-Leverton, was there saying, "Now, Bob, are you sure you can say that?" When it became crucial to see the ring in Berlin, or go back to the Egyptian Museum to check an object, The Learning Channel was always agreeable. In the end, I viewed it as private industry supporting research.

In the preparation of the manuscript I have been very fortunate. My wife, Pat Remler, spent many long hours on the computer, improving the manuscript. I may not have always been happy to hear "Brier, this doesn't make sense," but it certainly helped the book. My friend and colleague at the C. W. Post Campus of Long Island University, Dr. Hoyt Hobbs, read many drafts, made essential suggestions—both Egyptological and structural—and was a one-man support team throughout the revising of the manuscript. Also on the editorial front, Elizabeth Himelfarb was always there, ready to do what was needed. Above all, I would like to thank Liza Dawson, my editor at Putnam. I am sure she never knew what she was getting into when she first became involved in *The Murder of Tutankhamen*. It is her unerring vision of what the book should be that has made it as coherent as it is. If this book succeeds in telling the story of Tutankhamen, it is largely due to Liza's efforts.

For P. S.-L.

Tutankhamen and Ankhesenamen
Painting by Winifred Brunton

Contents

Introduction

Pointing to a cranial X ray, Dr. R. G. Harrison, head of the Anatomy Department of the University of Liverpool, was explaining a density on the film. His opinion was that it was

> within normal limits, but in fact it could have been caused by a hemorrhage under the membranes overlaying the brain in this region. And this could have been caused by a blow to the back of the head and this in turn could have been responsible for death.[1]

His patient, the pharaoh Tutankhamen, had been dead for 3,000 years.

Dr. Harrison was part of yet another television special on King Tut, another of the spasms of Tutmania since the discovery of the young king's tomb in 1922. I really wasn't that interested in Tutankhamen. I had seen his treasures in the Egyptian Museum in Cairo, knew the story of the tomb's discovery, and hadn't thought much more about him.

I don't know why I watched television's latest addition to the Tut glut, but as I was about to turn it off, it struck me that Dr. Harrison actually had something novel. On the screen came X rays of Tutankhamen's chest, the long bones of the legs and arms. I was riveted. The X rays contained new forensic evidence about Tutankhamen possibly being murdered. An idea began to percolate, an idea I couldn't dismiss.

There was such a tremendous amount of information to be found in the mummy of Tutankhamen. What if I cast a fresh eye on all of it? The mummy had never been examined with an eye to answering basic questions about a murder victim. Did he die immediately from the blow to the back of his head or did he linger? Was he robust and healthy when he died or had he been ill? What was his last meal? How soon after he ate it did he die? I knew I would probably never be granted permission to examine Tutankhamen's mummy—it was sealed in the Valley of the Kings—and the Supreme Council of Antiquities, Egypt's Antiquities Organization, wasn't about to give permission to remove Tutankhamen for an autopsy. But there were still the X rays, photographs of his internal organs, and the reports of the 1925 examination of the body. There was plenty that could be investigated. The last word on the death of Tutankhamen had not been written.

Dead bodies fascinate me, professionally speaking, of course. My specialty is mummies, with a particular interest is paleopathology—diseases of ancient man. What illnesses afflicted the ancient Egyptian? What were his chances of recovery? How did he cope with his disease? Mummies hold the answers. A modern, high-tech autopsy of an Egyptian mummy can reveal what he ate, when illness struck, and, if we're lucky, the cause of death. Beyond the information gained from mummies, there is an immediacy and intimacy when I look at the face of a mummy that I just don't get with artifacts. I am face-to-face with a person who lived 3,000 years ago.

I remember working with Michael Silva, a third-generation silversmith from Spain. We were trying to figure out exactly how ancient Egyptian craftsmen made their amulets. Using 3,000-year-old terracotta molds, Michael was going to recreate the process and make replicas of the amulets. On the back of one of the molds could be seen the ancient craftsman's thumbprint where it was pressed into the moist clay. Understandably, Michael was moved by this link with ancient humanity he was touching—a ghostly trace left by the man who held that clay 3,000 years ago. In my work, I touch the actual fingers. But other types of Egyptologists are just as passionate about their work, and many have contributed to the evidence I'm going to be presenting here.

We "Mummy People" are called to excavation sites when human remains are found. Wrapped mummies are rare. Far more often, a tomb was looted in antiquity, the mummy ripped apart by robbers searching for jewelry, and its bones scattered by the looters. Mummy People eye the tangle of bones to reconstruct what's left. The density and quality of bones reveal the social status and occupation of a person. For instance, manual labor increases muscle size which causes bone to thicken, so a single arm can tell us if the dead man was a laborer or a man of leisure. Recently I examined the remains of a queen from 4,000 years ago. I had never seen such delicate bones; it was as if she had never lifted her hand and traveled everywhere in her sedan chair. On the other end of the spectrum, the cemetery of the workmen who built the pyramids at Giza held the bodies of men who moved heavy loads. Their spines were severely deformed, especially the lumbar vertebrae which ultimately bore most of the stress. With enough experience and a dollop of imagination, a Mummy Man can discover remarkable things.

My approach to Egyptology has always been an experimental one— a hands-on approach. A couple of years ago I mummified a human cadaver in the ancient Egyptian manner. I was trying to figure out exactly how the ancient embalmers did it. Again, Michael Silva made replicas, this time of ancient bronze and copper tools, so that when I removed the internal organs I would be using the same kind of tools the ancient embalmers used. My colleague in this project was Ronald Wade, director of the Maryland State Anatomy Board. Ron was also a licensed mortician and had been interested in mummification since he was a kid—he mummified a rat for his high school science project. When we began the modern mummification and I made the incision in the deceased's abdomen, Ron and I both had goosebumps. We knew it was the first time in 2,000 years that an Egyptian style mummification had been performed.

As we removed each organ—spleen, stomach, intestines, liver—we knew this was the order in which the ancient embalmers must have removed them. It was almost as if we were watching rather than performing a mummification. Removing the brain through the nasal passage proved to be the most difficult part of the experiment. We really weren't sure we could do it. All we had to guide us were X rays of mummies.

When I presented a slide lecture of what we'd done, one colleague let out a *very* audible gasp. Several others apologized that they were so uncomfortable watching the National Geographic television special on the project that they had to turn it off. Human cadavers, even when mummified, just put some people off.

Consequently, we Mummy People have our own conference, The International Mummy Congress. (I've often thought it should be called "Mummies 'R' Us.") We come from different backgrounds. Many of us have attended medical school, and quite a few are practicing physicians who bring their skills to the study of mummies. Others are physical anthropologists with extensive training in anatomy and physiology.

A few years ago at the Mummy Congress in Cartagena, Colombia, I listened with admiration as a colleague described how she traced trade between ancient Peruvians living on the coast with those living higher up on the Altiplano. It was great detective work based on the principle "you are what you eat." Protein from fish differs from protein from vegetables or terrestrial animals, so by analyzing carbon isotopes from mummies' bones she determined their diet. Naturally the bones of populations that had lived and died on the shore indicated high marine protein, but the inland inhabitants of the Altiplano also showed marine protein, which meant they traded with the shore dwellers for dried fish.[2] If you can figure out dietary habits and trade routes from a mummy's elbow, think what you might learn from a pharaoh like Tutankhamen whose history we know.

This is why I was glued to the television when Dr. Harrison paraded his Tutankhamen X rays. Despite my original lack of interest in Tutankhamen, I now found myself thinking about revisiting the X rays to solve an ancient puzzle. Of course, information from other specialists would be crucial to my investigation, but the key to unlocking the riddle of the cause of death would be the mummy. I just wanted to see if I could figure out how he died; it was to be an academic exercise. At the time I didn't think about murder—or who the murderer might have been.

The past two years have been an adventure. Over dinners at home, and inside several Egyptian tombs, colleagues and I discussed clues, translated hieroglyphs, peered at X rays and photographs of young Tutankhamen and his relatives and argued considerably. When all the facts relating to the boy-king's untimely death were examined, after I'd looked at a frantic letter written by his widow, after I'd held an ancient ring, when I considered the violent, unstable times Tutankhamen ruled in, and examined the forensic evidence with the help of several trauma specialists, murder and intrigue emerged as the best explanation. I must admit, however, that at some point the project ceased to be academic. I was unexpectedly moved as I looked at and handled objects buried with Tutankhamen—the board games he played, the bows he used when hunting in the marshes, the fetuses miscarried by his young bride—a 3,000-year-old death became a personal tragedy. For so many years Tut, in my mind, had been synonymous with treasures and so I'd been aloof from his charms. Somewhere along the way I grew enormously fond of the boy. As the dossier of clues grew, I began to hate the prime suspect. I was delighted to discover that his portraits in the museums in Berlin and Cairo were decidedly sinister. Still, in spite of these clearly nonobjective feelings, I believe my presentation of the facts is undistorted, that murder and political intrigue provide the most reasonable explanation for a tragic event that occurred 3,000 years ago.

Introduction

What follows is an account of the circumstances that led to Tut-ankhamen's unexpected death at the age of nineteen, the political and religious turmoil that made it possible and the bold, almost successful attempt to cover it up. It is the story of the life—and death—of Tut-ankhamen. An army general, high priests, and senior government offi-cials all were involved. It was a unique and fascinating time in Egypt that led a commoner to believe that he could become a king.

Tutankhamen Time Line

✦

Early Dynastic Period
3150–2686 B.C.—Dynasties 0–II
Narmer—First king of Egypt unites Upper and Lower Egypt

The Old Kingdom
2686–2181 B.C.—Dynasties III–VI
Zoser builds the Step Pyramid
Pharaoh Khufu builds the Great Pyramid;
Pharaoh Khephren has the Sphinx carved with his features

The First Intermediate Period
2181–2040 B.C.—Period of anarchy and chaos

Middle Kingdom
2040–1780 B.C.—Dynasty XII
Pharaoh Mentuhotep II restores order to the land

The Second Intermediate Period
1780–1570 B.C.—Period of weak rulers and invasion by the
Hyksos ruling in the north

The New Kingdom
1570–1070 B.C.—Egypt's Golden Age

Dynasty XVIII—1570–1293 B.C.

1570–1546 B.C.—Ahmose I—Hyksos are expelled from Egypt

1551–1386 B.C.—Pharaohs Tuthmosis III, Hatshepsut, and
Amenhotep III increase Egypt's wealth and
power

1386–1349 B.C.—Amenhotep III (Tutankhamen's grandfather)

1350–1334 B.C.—Amenhotep IV (Akhenaten) (Tutankhamen's
father)

1336–1334 B.C.—Smenkare (Akhenaten's son and
Tutankhamen's brother?)

1334–1325 B.C.—Tutankhamen

1325–1321 B.C.—Aye

1321–1293 B.C.—Horemheb

Dynasty XIX

1297–1212 B.C.—Ramses the Great—probable pharaoh of the
Exodus

The Third Intermediate Period

1069–525 B.C.—The power of the pharaoh weakens

The Late Period

525–332 B.C.—Persian kings rule Egypt

The Graeco Roman Period

332 B.C.—Alexander the Great conquers Darius III, ruler of
the Persian Empire
Egypt hails Alexander as a divine being and a savior

50 B.C.—Cleopatra VII becomes queen of Egypt

30 B.C.—Cleopatra VII dies and Egypt becomes the private
estate of the Roman Emperor Augustus

The
Murder of
Tutankhamen

The King Must Die

Stay away from hostile people,
Keep your heart quiet among fighters.

—The scribe Ani
circa 1400 B.C.

We possess a remarkable amount of evidence about Tutankhamen—
enough to re-create what his last days may have been like. So let's
start with a fictional account, but one that is probably very close to the truth.

Sometime in late autumn, during the eighteenth year of his life,
Tutankhamen went to bed alone. Although peasant husbands and wives
slept in the same room, Egyptian pharaohs lived in separate palaces
from those of their queen and the ladies of the harem. Conjugal visits
were one thing, sleep was another. Tutankhamen reposed in a large
room, sparsely furnished—a few stools, tables, and a single wood bed
with feet shaped like lion's paws. Fish, ducks, and marsh grasses painted
on the room's plastered walls glowed spectrally in the dim light.

In the depths of this night the door slowly, silently opened, just
wide enough for a single man to creep through before closing it behind

him. Somehow he had slipped past the sentries. Had they been told to look the other way? Stealthily the night intruder made his way to Pharaoh's bed, the sound of his steps perhaps obscured by the drip, drip of a water clock. He found the king sleeping on his side, his head supported by an alabaster headrest. From under his clothes the man drew out a heavy object, possibly an Egyptian mace that joined a solid three-inch stone to the end of a substantial two-foot stick. After a single deep breath, he swung the heavy object at Tutankhamen's skull.

Waiting just a moment for the sudden sound in the night to be forgotten, the intruder retraced his steps through the Royal Bedchamber, out the door, and stole through the palace to the safety of night.

The next morning servants discovered the unconscious, but not yet dead, pharaoh and quickly summoned the vizier, Aye, and Tutankhamen's wife, Ankhesenamen. A priest-physician skilled in head injuries was ordered from the temple. The physician has seen many trauma injuries. Blocks of stone sometime fell on workmen during construction; infantrymen received blows to the head. But this was the pharaoh; the physician must be very careful what he does and says. He instructed his assistant to shave Pharaoh's head so a proper diagnosis could be made. As the bronze blade removed the fine dark hair, the surgeon was already thinking about the consequences of treatment—both for the pharaoh and for his own career. If he took decisive action and Tutankhamen died, he could be blamed. Now the head was shaved, revealing one wound, a large, warm swollen mass. It was in an unusual place for such an injury, at the back of the head where the neck joins the skull. The great surgical papyrus did not describe how to treat such an injury.

The blow has caused unconsciousness, but only a slight fracture to the skull. There are no bone fragments that must be removed. Relieved, the surgeon replaces his bronze probe and tweezers in their wooden case. Still, blood is oozing from the pharaoh's nostrils, a sign that the meninges, the skin enclosing the brain, has been damaged. Aye, the prime minister, stands silently next to the bed, calm, weighing what the pharaoh's death will mean to Egypt and himself. Ankhesenamen, frightened, looks to the physician for his prognosis. He has been trained to give one of three responses: 1) "this is an ailment which I will treat," 2) "this is an ailment with which I will contend," and 3) "this is an ailment not to be treated."[1] If he says the ailment can be treated, he implies that the treatment will be successful. If he instead says he will merely contend with it, he implies an uncertain outcome.

The physician quickly evaluates the situation. With no splinters to remove, no bones to set, there was little he could do physically for the king. To say that he will treat the ailment asserts that the king will survive, and of this he is not sure. Should Tutankhamen die, the physician will be blamed. There are only two real alternatives, and given the importance of the patient, it is safer to say that this is an illness not to be treated. Better to hand the fate of the king over to the gods.

The predicament faced by this priest-physician was no different from modern physicians called to treat a famous patient. Doctors in emergency rooms around the world have observed and named it the "famous-patient syndrome." When confronted with a famous patient, medical personnel are afraid to act quickly, to do instinctively what they have been trained to do. Junior staff members defer to senior staff members, discussions take place before actions are taken. Tutankhamen was probably not the first ruler to suffer the consequences of his exalted position, and he was certainly not the last.

Abraham Lincoln may have died because of his fame. After the President was shot in the head, the young surgeon attending him at Ford's Theater did everything right. He examined the entry hole with his finger, determined there was no exit hole, and let the president rest. Then the Surgeon General was summoned, while President Lincoln was removed to a nearby boardinghouse. The Surgeon General was a bureaucrat who had not treated a patient for years, but he immediately took control of Lincoln's treatment. He inserted a probe into the entry hole and slid it in, almost up to Lincoln's eyes. The Surgeon General did not know that the latest medical wisdom, taught in medical schools, was not to probe—the brain is so soft you can't tell if you are following the path of the bullet or causing additional damage. Recent reevaluation of the case suggests that Lincoln might have survived with the bullet lodged in his brain. He was a victim of famous-patient syndrome.

So the surgeon-priest turned to Ankhesenamen and spoke the very words she feared: "This is an ailment not to be treated." As Ankhesenamen sobbed, the surgeon's assistant was instructed to clear the king's nostrils of blood. The pharaoh breathed more easily now, lying peacefully on his low bed. Magician-healers would be called to assist the king.

By afternoon the healers had gathered the ingredients for their poultice: equal parts of berry of coriander, berry of the poppy plant, wormwood, berry of the *sames*-plant, berry of the juniper plant. Mixed with honey, it formed a paste that they spread on the wound and covered with a square of finely woven linen on which had been drawn the Eye-of-Horus symbol. Horus the falcon god had lost his eye in the battle with Seth, but it was magically regenerated by Toth, god of magic. The markings around a falcon's eye became a sign for healing.

For the first few days there was optimism. Tutankhamen briefly regained consciousness and was able to eat. Ankhesenamen brought him chopped figs mixed with eggs because eggs had regenerative properties. The magician-healers placed "flour of egg"—powdered egg shells—in Tutankhamen's wine, so the damaged skull would knit smooth, like an eggshell.[2] Yet, as days became weeks, the pharaoh, drifting in and out of consciousness, weakened. His vision blurred and the pain in his head became almost unbearable, as if something were pressing on every part of his skull. To dull the pain, Ankhesenamen brought more and more of his favorite wine, made from grapes from his own vineyards. When winter came, Tutankhamen lapsed into final unconsciousness and could receive tiny amounts of wine through a straw only with difficulty.

The wailing started with Ankhesenamen, who was with Tutankhamen when he died, spread through the female servants in the palace, then across the river to Thebes, uniting rich and poor in the primal ritual mourning cry that told Osiris, god of the dead, to expect another Westerner. Within a few hours of the shock, Aye began the plans to prepare Tutankhamen's burial.

Our account above of Tutankhamen's death is fiction, but is based on evidence that has survived 3,300 years since his death. We are in an even better position to reconstruct his burial.

The tomb that Tutankhamen had been preparing for himself, next to his grandfather's in the western spur of the Valley of the Kings, was far short of completion when the boy-king died. There was, however, a nearly complete tomb in the main valley that had not been used. Originally intended for a private person, a rare but not unprecedented honor, Aye decided to appropriate this small tomb for his pharaoh. Artists commenced painting appropriate scenes on the walls immediately; there was no time to carve the scenes. As the tomb was being readied, embalmers prepared Tutankhamen's body for eternity.

Mummification was primarily a physical process, but every stage of the embalming was accompanied by religious rituals. The most important step was to remove all moisture from the body as quickly as possible. Bacteria need moisture to destroy tissue; if there is no water, the body will not decay.

Both the brain and the internal organs are extremely moist, so to avoid putrefaction, they had to be removed soon after death. When Tutankhamen's body was brought to the royal embalmers, it was placed on an alabaster mummification table, inclined so that as work proceeded on the body, the fluids would run off into a basin below. The brain was removed by inserting a long wire into the nostril, breaking through the ethmoid bone into the cranium. The wire was then rotated—used as a whisk—to break down the brain tissue into a semi-liquid state that would drain out through the nostrils when the body was turned upside down. The embalmers preserved almost every part of the body so Tutankhamen would be complete when he resurrected in the next world. However, they discarded the brain, unaware of its function. Egyptians believed that you thought with your heart, not your brain, since it is the heart that beats rapidly when someone is excited, not the brain. In the Bible when pharaoh stubbornly refused to let the Israelites go, we are told "pharaoh's heart was hardened."

After Tutankhamen's brain was removed and discarded, an incision was made in the lower left side of his abdomen so the internal organs could be reached. The stomach, liver, intestines, and kidneys were carefully removed and placed in shallow bowls. Later the desiccated organs were deposited in four miniature gold coffins in preparation for the day the king would resurrect in the next world. Only his heart was left in the body, so that he would be able to remember and recite the magic spells that would reanimate his corpse.

Even after the brain and internal organs were removed, considerable moisture still remained locked in the body's soft tissues. To eliminate this, the embalmers covered Tutankhamen's body with natron, a naturally occurring compound of sodium carbonate, sodium bicarbonate, and sodium chloride—basically baking soda and salt. After the body had rested for thirty-five days in natron almost all its water had been leached out. The mummy now weighed less than fifty pounds and was ready for wrapping. As each bandage was applied, a priest wearing the mask of Anubis the jackal, the god of embalming, read magical spells that would ensure Tutankhamen's preservation and resurrection. The priests placed more than one hundred and fifty pieces of jewelry and magical amulets within the linen bandages to ensure the boy-king's immortality.

As the embalmers practiced their art, master craftsmen throughout the land worked to prepare his funerary goods. There were wooden shrines to be carved and gilded, a gold mask and coffins to be fashioned, furniture, linens, clothing, and jewelry to be assembled. Preparation of the ushabtis figures alone was a major undertaking. These hundreds of little servant figurines were expected to magically come alive and serve Tutankhamen in the next world, each one an individual sculpture in wood or stone carved in the likeness of Tutankhamen (fig. 20). The figures were mummiform in shape, the image of Osiris, the god of the dead. Because Egypt was an agrarian society, the work in the next world would be farming, so the ushabtis held agricultural implements in their hands. Tutankhamen had 413 ushabtis, 365 workers, one for each day of the year, 36 overseers—one for each gang of 10 workers—and an additional twelve monthly overseers.[3] There must have been panic in the workshops of Egypt as craftsmen worked in teams through the night to prepare for the burial of the pharaoh.

Maya, the treasurer, commissioned a beautiful miniature wooden sculpture of Tutankhamen on a funerary couch holding a tiny gold crook and flail, so the gods would know he was a great king. Along the side of the sculpture an inscription proclaimed Maya's devotion to his young pharaoh: "Made by the servant who is beneficial to his lord, doing what he says, who does not allow anything to go wrong, whose face is cheerful when he does it with a loving heart as a thing profitable to his lord."[4]

At some point in the preparation of Tutankhamen's funerary goods, time ran out. The seventy days had elapsed, the embalmers' work and all the coffins were complete, but other ritual objects simply couldn't be finished on time. So the tomb of Tutankhamen's brother, Smenkare, was opened and the miniature coffins that held his internal organs were reused for Tutankhamen. Inside each coffin, inscribed in gold, is a prayer from the *Book of the Dead,* a collection of about 200 spells, incantations, prayers, and hymns. The prayers inside refer to Tutankhamen, but beneath his cartouche are traces of the name Smenkare, his brother.

Seventy days after Tutankhamen's death, the funeral procession gathered on the west bank of Thebes to conduct his mummy to its house of eternity. The body was placed on a sled and a wooden shrine draped with garlands was placed over it. Across the top of the shrine two rows of beautifully carved and painted wooden cobras reared up to protect Tutankhamen on his journey to the netherworld. The sled was pulled by the palace officials. Pentu and Usermont, the ministers of Upper and Lower Egypt, wore the distinctive robes of their office, and were joined by ten other officials, all wearing white mourning bands around their heads. As the procession slowly made its way over the barren land toward the Valley of the Kings, the women wailed, tore their garments, and threw sand on their heads in the traditional gestures of mourning. Among them, but feeling very alone, was Ankhesenamen.

When the pallbearers reached the tomb, the procession paused. In the course of wrapping the mummy Tutankhamen's mouth and nose had been covered. Now, before he entered the tomb for eternity, a ceremony was performed to magically open his mouth so Tutankhamen would be able to breathe and say the magical spells of the *Book of the Dead.* The pallbearers, joined by the priests and members of the funeral procession, performed the opening-of-the-mouth ceremony for Tutankhamen.

More a mystery play than a religious ritual, a dozen participants were required for the performance.[5] The officiating priest held a papyrus describing how things should proceed. A small group of the officials played roles of the guards of Horus, who would help Tutankhamen be resurrected like Osiris in the next world. The area in front of the tomb where the play was to be performed was purified with water from four different vases, each representing one of the four corners of the earth. Four burners holding incense were lit, and various gods were invoked. A ritual slaughter was performed, commemorating the battle in which Horus avenged Osiris's death.

In the myth, Seth's conspirators, after dismembering Osiris's corpse, attempted to escape Horus by changing into various animals, but Horus caught them and cut off their heads. Thus, at the opening-of-the-mouth ceremony various animals were ritually killed—two bulls (one for the south and one for the north), gazelles, and ducks. When the bull of the south was slaughtered, one of the legs was cut off and, along with the heart, offered to the mummy. By sympathetic magic, Tutankhamen became Osiris: The sacrificial killing of the animals represented the conspirators who tried but failed to destroy the body of Osiris, and assured that the body of Tutankhamen would remain safe from such an attack. The slaughtered animals provided food for Tutankhamen's long journey.

The high priest touched the mouth of the mummy with the leg of the bull, and then an assistant came forward with a ritual instrument shaped like an adze. Touching the mouth of the mummy with this implement, the priest recited:

Thy mouth was closed, but I have set in order for thee thy mouth and thy teeth. I open for thee thy mouth, I open for thee thy two eyes. I have opened thy mouth with the instrument of Anubis, with the iron implement with which the mouths of the gods were opened. Horus, open the mouth! Horus, open the mouth! Horus hath opened the mouth of the dead, as he in times of old opened the mouth of Osiris with the iron, which came forth from Set, with the iron instrument with which he opened the mouths of the gods. He hath opened thy mouth with it. The deceased shall walk and speak, and his body shall be with the great company of all gods in the Great House of the Aged One in Annu, and he shall receive the ureret crown from Horus, the lord of mankind.[6]

While this ritual was being performed, Tutankhamen's body was resting inside the shrine on the sled, so a statue of Tutankhamen—one of the two life-sized guardian statues almost exactly the height of Tutankhamen—was used instead.

At the conclusion of the ritual, the priest raised the adze and touched it to Tutankhamen's mouth, uttering the spell that would give the young king breath in the next world. *"You are young again, you live again, you are young again, you live again, forever."* He was now ready for immortality.

The pallbearers carried the body of Tutankhamen-Osiris—he was now a Westerner like Osiris—down the thirteen steps leading to the tomb. At the bottom they turned right toward the burial chamber. On their left side they could see three five-foot-high ceremonial beds on which various rituals had been performed for Tutankhamen during the seventy days of mummification. At the corners of the head end of one bed were two beautifully carved hippopotamus heads covered in gold, the second bore the head of a cow with a sun disk between its horns, the third lion heads. These were the gods who controlled whether Tutankhamen could enter the next world. As the pallbearers slowly carried the mummy to the burial chamber, they took quick sideways glances, trying to take it all in—the burial treasures of a king.

Waiting for them in the burial chamber was a rectangular stone sarcophagus containing three coffins, one inside the other like Russian dolls. Their lids lay on the floor. The pharaoh was placed inside the innermost one. While the lector priest recited prayers, unguents were poured on the body to perfume Tutankhamen's way to the next world. Then the lid of the innermost coffin was placed over Tutankhamen, sending him into darkness, the last time anyone would see his face for thirty-three centuries. The lid to the middle coffin was placed on its lower half, and finally the outermost coffin lid was lowered into place. Each coffin bore a likeness of the boy-king. Once the final lid was in position, Ankhesenamen placed a miniature wreath—the "Wreath of Victory"—around the sculpted vulture and cobra protecting her husband's forehead. The tiny wreath commemorated the god Osiris's victory over his enemies. As the wreath was positioned, a priest recited:

> Thy father Atum binds for thee this beautiful wreath of vindication on this thy brow. Live, beloved of the gods, mayest thou live forever.[7]

With that, heavy the heavy stone lid of the sarcophagus was slid into place. The sad party of mourners walked slowly up the steps of the tomb into the blinding sunlight. As soon as the mourners left the tomb, a team of workmen hurried into the burial chamber to assemble the panels of three nested shrines around the sarcophagus, as an overseer watched. When their work was completed, they were replaced by masons who constructed a plaster wall sealing the burial chamber from the rest of the tomb. The statue used for the opening-of-the-mouth ceremony and its twin were placed in front of the wall, guarding their king. The last objects for the tomb—chariots, chests of linen, ebony foot stools—were quickly carried into the antechamber by servants, watched all the while, lest the pharaoh's treasures be stolen from him. Now the antechamber was sealed by the masons, the wet plaster stamped with the seal of the Royal Necropolis, a jackal over nine bound captives, the nine traditional enemies of Egypt. Even in death, Tutankhamen was victorious.

Ankhesenamen's long day was not yet over. A ritual last meal in honor of Tutankhamen's victory over death had to be eaten at the entrance to the tomb. The participants wore brightly colored pectorals made of flowers and beads sewn onto a papyrus collar (fig. 16). Normally the meal was eaten by the family of the deceased, but in this instance Ankhesenamen, Tutankhamen's last living relative, was joined by the palace officials—Pentu, Usermont, Aye, Aye's wife, Tey, and General Horemheb. The servants brought a banquet of sheep, four different kinds of duck, three different kinds of geese, all washed down by considerable quantities of wine poured from an elegant long-necked vase painted with blue lotus petals. But none present were thinking about the meal. They pondered their futures. Who could have known that two of the men eating together would become kings of Egypt, and, within a very short while, one of the two women would be dead.

When the meal was completed, servants ritually broke the dishes, cups, and beautiful wine jar, and placed the fragments, along with the bones of the meat and fowl, inside large storage jars. They then swept the area with brooms and placed the brooms in the jars. The jars were sealed, carried to a nearby pit that had been dug, and buried. The funeral was over.

We actually have the broken dishes, collars, and brooms from the last meal. They are in the Metropolitan Museum of Art in New York. There is indeed a surgical papyrus that instructs physicians whom to treat and whom not. Painted on Tutankhamen's tomb wall are scenes of the funeral procession and the opening-of-the-mouth ceremony. Of course, we have the treasures from Tutankhamen's tomb, but we also have X rays of his skull.

But before we can get to the evidence of his murder, we must first understand what brought him to this moment. We must understand the evolution of Egyptian society, religion and its pharoahs. The next chapter is Egypt 101—a crash course in the history of Egypt that made the murder of a pharaoh possible. Stick with it and you will see the forces develop that bent Egypt until it snapped.

2

Egypt Before Tutankhamen

The wealth of an army is its leader.

—Instruction of Ankhsheshonq
circa 300 B.C.

Two thousand years before Tutankhamen was born, three distinct forces were set in motion that would determine the course of Egypt's social organization and which would ultimately lead to his death. Egypt would get its first king, a national military would be established, and a priesthood would develop. Over the centuries these power bases grew strong and rich; they became so essential to Egyptian society that to change any one of them could bring disaster. Thus for centuries and centuries Egypt presented a seemingly static face to the ancient world. Internally Egypt was a wealthy, well-oiled machine, with each of the three powers supporting the others. Tutankhamen had the unfortunate distinction of being alive when there was a dramatic, revolutionary effort to change all three simultaneously. To understand how shockingly different the times Tut grew up in were, we first have to understand how and why the country had enjoyed such an unparalleled period of stability. Before we get to play detective, we have to do our history lessons.

EGYPT BEFORE KINGSHIP

The concept of a pharaoh in many ways defines our notion of ancient Egypt, but of course Egypt did not always have a king. Let's look back to Egypt around 4000 B.C. when the verdant Nile Valley was dotted with small villages stretching for a thousand miles along the Nile. We don't have written records from this period, but there seem to have been two independent political entities, Upper and Lower Egypt, each governed by its own chieftain. All indications are that life along the Nile was safe and satisfying, partly because Egypt was relatively inaccessible to the rest of the world and thus had few marauding enemies to fear and partly because the river provided economic bounty.

Each year the Nile overflowed its banks, depositing fresh rich topsoil on the flat plains that spread to either side of the river, enabling Egypt to grow an abundance and variety of crops. Other countries relied on unpredictable rain that only during certain seasons fell in sufficient quantity to irrigate fields. Even if rainfall were spread perfectly throughout the year, fields would soon be exhausted of nutrients if they were planted more than once a year. Egypt's great good fortune was to have a river that renewed the topsoil annually and flowed in sufficient volume to water the crops. Every year Egypt harvested a variety of crops, while other countries thanked the gods when when they produced one. No wonder the ancient Greek traveler Herodotus called Egypt the "Gift of the Nile."

The annual inundation amazed the Egyptians, who had no explanation for its sudden great growth, nor the fact that its color changed to red and then to green. It was a natural occurrence, of course, but it must have provided the equivalent mystery and pyrotechnics of a Las Vegas magic show. Today we know that torrential spring rains in Ethiopia, far south of Egypt, ran off granite bedrock to swell the Nile. The oversized

Nile rushed north from sub-Saharan Africa, arriving in Egypt almost twenty feet above its normal level. It was red in color from all the runoff soil suspended in the water, but as it overflowed and the soil settled, its color changed to the green of the floating vegetation. The annual show provided by the Nile was surpassed only by the dazzling daily performance put on by the sun. Each day it rose in the east, traveled across a cloudless, jewel-like sky, and descended in a fireball of colors in the west, constant and predictable, like the Nile.

The population of the Nile Valley was probably less than a million. Although Egypt was a vast country, 95 percent of the population lived on the 5 percent of the land that hugs the Nile. The Nile was the heart of the country—even the seasons of the year were determined by the Nile. Our 365-day calendar comes from the Egyptians, but they counted only three seasons: 1) *Inundation*, when the Nile overflowed and flooded the land; 2) *Emergence*, when the waters receded; and 3) *Summer*, the dry season. Each season had four months of thirty days each. At the end of the year, "5 extra days" were added to make 365 days in the year. Inundation was Egypt's most unusual season for it was a time for relaxing—the fields were underwater and little agricultural work could be done. During these weeks, plows and implements were repaired, future crops were discussed, and plans for the future were made. Emergence was the season for planting, in Summer crops were harvested.

The food staple of the farmer was bread and beer, a phrase that became synonymous with "food"—our "meat and potatoes." A common funerary prayer begins, "May the king make an offering to Osiris, Lord of the West. May he give bread and beer, cattle, geese, and oxen and all things good and pure upon which the gods live." The long growing season allowed the Egyptians to raise a variety of crops—the most important being emer (wheat) and onions. Meat was reserved for the upper classes, but the farmers had fish from the Nile and perch was the favorite, but whatever the Egyptians ate, it was accompanied by onions. Year after year Egypt's crops were reassuringly plentiful and inevitably a sense of security arose along the banks of the Nile, a feeling that nature and the world would not present any horrifying surprises.

This feeling was encouraged by Egypt's geographical isolation from her neighbors. To the west of Egypt spread endless miles of desert. In order for ancient peoples to cross, wells had to be dug, provisions stored; in all, tremendous organization and careful planning were required. From Libya, for example, the journey to Egypt would be across more than four hundred miles of arid shale. Six centuries after Tutankhamen, when the mighty Persian king Cambyses sent an army of 20,000 men across this wilderness, they disappeared without a trace.

Egypt is bordered by the Red Sea on the east, backed by one hundred miles of inhospitable sand. (Incidentally, the camel, "the ship of the desert," did not arrive in Egypt until the Roman occupation, more than a thousand years after Tutankhamen.) To the north, hundreds of miles of the Mediterranean formed a third natural barrier, even if it was more psychological than real. Egyptians had developed their navigational skills on the smooth-flowing Nile, and they remained river sailors, not tempted by the lure and dangers of the open sea. The south offered a river-borne ingress into Egypt, for the Nile stretched far below Egypt's southern border. Since the current flows from south to north and the prevailing winds are from north to south, travel in either direction was easy. Going north, sailors floated with the current, steering with oars; for the southward journey they hoisted sails and followed the wind. Boat travel was easy except at Egypt's southern border where huge river boulders create a cataract. Although it was possible to travel south past this barrier, navigation was quite difficult and laborious. The crew had to haul the boats out of the river and drag them around the boulders or use ropes to guide them through the rapids. It was not an easy journey.

In later centuries, Egyptians would wander to other lands and would bring back riches, but it was always clear to them that they were living in paradise, that it existed in this time, in this place, and nowhere else in the world.

KINGSHIP COMES TO EGYPT

Ancient Egyptians revered their pharaoh, not simply as a leader, but as the embodiment of the country itself. Egypt's first pharaoh, Narmer, early in the third millennium B.C., created a nation from two independent states. Ever after, Egyptians referred to their country as "The Two Lands" whose continued unification depended entirely on the pharaoh.

The Narmer Palette, one of the most significant objects in all the priceless collection of Cairo's Egyptian Museum, depicts Narmer's conquest that resulted in the unification of Egypt and celebrates the importance of this achievement.

Nearly three feet high and carved from a slab of stone, the mammoth Narmer Palette introduces Egypt's first pharaoh, King Narmer. From early times Egyptians had used small slate palettes to grind ingredients for eye paints (a little bit of fat, a little pulverized malachite and you had green eye shadow). To commemorate important events, large ceremonial palettes were carved.

On one side of the palette King Narmer is shown wearing the traditional white crown of Upper Egypt as he strikes his enemy, presumably the ruler from the north, whom he grasps by the hair. The other side shows him walking in a procession and wearing the red crown of Lower Egypt (the north). He is now king of both the north and the south, the first king of the First Dynasty. This unification took place around 3200 B.C., nearly 2,000 years before Tutankhamen became King of Upper and Lower Egypt, but when the boy-king ascended to the throne, the concept of kingship was virtually unchanged since the time of King Narmer. Egypt would for the next 3,000 years be ruled by kings with absolute power, who were accepted as gods on earth and personally responsible for Egypt's well-being. Each pharaoh was pope, president, king, and commander-in-chief—all in one.

Soon after Narmer unified the northern and southern territories, the country's isolationism ended; Egypt became an aggressive international force led by the pharaoh. Egyptian armies ventured outside the borders of Egypt in search of lands to conquer and of gold to claim.

RISE OF THE MILITARY

There are no extant military records from the first few centuries after Narmer, but the origins of Egypt's army are to be found in this period.[1] With a centralized government under a single king the organization of an army was inevitable. A pottery fragment inscribed with Narmer's name found at Tell El-Mayshieh in southern Palestine suggests Narmer may even have ventured outside of Egypt with his army.[2] We do not know how large these early armies were, but excavations have shown that their main weapons were the mace, spear, battle ax, and dagger. Warfare in the ancient world was mostly hand-to-hand combat, soldiers were face-to-face with the enemy they killed. In today's military, generals make decisions at a distance, which are then carried out by the troops on the battlefield. In ancient warfare the generals were in the front lines, leading by example. The military man soon became intimately acquainted with killing.

Egypt could support an army because of the Nile. With the ability to grow more food than a farmer's family could consume, specialization of work developed among the Nile Valley dwellers and so a professional standing army could be maintained. As the army grew bolder, its expeditions moved further and further from Egypt's borders. Seven centuries after Narmer, the pharaoh Sneferu was able to boast that he had subdued the Bedouin tribes and made the Sinai safe for his turquoise miners.

With kingship there also came a desire and ability to focus national attention on huge projects such as irrigation canals. Digging and dredging irrigation canals required the organization of gangs of men working toward a common goal, possible only after central organization and authority were in place. Men could be coordinated to dredge and channel, coaxing flood waters further and further inland. This created more arable land, raising agricultural productivity ever higher.

Central coordination also produced, as a side effect, the beginnings of astronomy. Advance warning before the floods arrived was required to allow the time necessary to refurbish increasingly extensive canal systems. Timing was critical. Fix the old canals too soon and the hot Egyptian sun would turn them to dust blown away by the wind; fix them too late and the floods would arrive before the system was finished. Fortunately, Nile inundations were quite regular, occurring within the same five- or ten-day period each year. Needing to know when that time of year was coming before it happened prompted astronomer priests to observe the heavens and learn how to predict the time of the year from the stars, one of the earliest examples of serious astronomy. Mathematics, too, had to be improved to accurately measure fields whose boundaries were washed away each year by the Nile.

So fundamental were the pharaohs to Egyptian society that ancient Egyptians reckoned their history, not as a sequence of events, but as a series of reigns of kings during which events occurred. Instead of numbering years consecutively—as our 1999 follows 1998—when a new king was crowned, a new calendar began with day 1, year 1 of the reign of King X. If one king died, the next king started another calendar: day 1, year 1, King Y. This has proven a great help to modern Egyptologists in determining the length of each pharaoh's reign. But it also shows that ancient Egyptians saw no unity, even of time, without their pharaoh.

In addition to placing all central authority solely with their pharaoh, they viewed him as a god necessary for their safety. The pharaoh's protection is described in one of the oldest myths of Egypt. The story tells how the god Re once appeared on Earth in human form to rule as the original pharaoh. During his reign the country flourished as a kind of Eden, without want, suffering, or disease. Re's subjects lived such carefree lives that they gradually forgot to pay him homage and respect for the paradise he created. This angered Re, who created a bloodthirsty demon in the form of the lioness Sekhmet and loosed her on his errant subjects to teach them a lesson they would not soon forget. When she wantonly slaughtered hundreds of people, the frightened survivors became respectful again. But crazed by all the blood, Sekhmet nonetheless continued killing, despite Re's order that she stop. Re called all the gods together to agree to a scheme to save humnanity. Sending some to produce vast quantities of beer and others for red dye to color it, he ordered that the mixture be spread over the ground. When Sekhmet arrived the next day to begin her round of slaying, she saw the beer and, thinking it was blood, drank until she fell, intoxicated, into a deep sleep. Thus did Re, the pharaoh's prototype, save humanity. In time, however, Re grew weak and returned to the netherworld, sending his son Horus, the falcon, to rule in his place.

To his subjects, pharaoh was Horus incarnate, and each ruler took as one of his names "The Horus so-and-so." Through his father Re, Pharaoh preserved the human race, but he also had the power to destroy it. The message was understood by every subject—only by obeying and honoring Pharaoh would unimaginable evils be kept at bay. As long as Egyptians believed that, it would be hard to imagine anyone lifting a hand against a pharaoh.

THE AGE OF THE PYRAMIDS

The pyramids are the ultimate testament to just how important the concept of kingship was in ancient Egypt. Five hundred years after Narmer's unification of Egypt, the pharaoh was stronger and more powerful than any other ruler on earth. Understood to be a living god, the pharaoh required a resting place for eternity that had to be a monument worthy of a god. When the pharaoh's days on earth were over, his mummy was placed in his pyramid till the time he would ascend to the heavens. Built more than a thousand years before Tutankhamen, the pyramids reflected the role of kingship in Egypt, a role Tutankhamen would have to assume as a boy.

As a kid, I watched Charlton Heston on television and wondered about the slaves hauling huge blocks while a cruel overseer whipped them mercilessly. I always wondered why all the slaves didn't jump the overseer; they certainly had him outnumbered. The answer is that such a scene never happened. The pyramids were built with free labor, paid for by the pharaoh. When Menachem Begin, the Prime Minister of Israel, visited Egypt, he mentioned that his ancestors built the pyramids. He had it all wrong. Not only were they not built by slaves, the pyramids were completed more than a thousand years before Moses and the Israelites were in Egypt. The pyramids were built at the beginning of Egypt's long history; they were ancient by the time of Tutankhamen. Even as a young nation, Egypt was very sure of itself. Think about what was involved in pyramid building.

There are more than seventy pyramids in Egypt, and to construct something like the Great Pyramid at Giza thousands of laborers had to be coordinated in teams that worked for twenty years on one structure. Quarrymen cut and shaped 2½ million blocks of limestone, each weighing an average of five tons. Transportation men floated the blocks across the Nile from the quarry to Giza. When the blocks were off-loaded from the barges they were pulled on wooden sleds by gangs of workers to their final position in the pyramid. All of this was without the use of the wheel, which would sink into the sand under heavy loads. To build the Great Pyramid, a new block was put into place an average of every three minutes, day, and night, for twenty years. Today, it is difficult to imagine a single building project of such enormity continuing for twenty years. Only a society of great wealth and stability led by an absolute ruler could sustain such a project. The pharaoh's word was law; so it was said, so it was done.

With a divine king and a strong military, two of the three forces that would lead to Tutankhamen's death were in motion. It is now time to talk about the third force, religion. No other people have ever been so focused on religion and have had such concern with life after death as the ancient Egyptians. This too may result from Egypt's unique geography.

During prehistoric times Egyptians were buried in sandpits in the desert, cultivated land being too precious to use for cemeteries. This was fortunate, since the moisture and high mineral content of the soil would have destroyed cadavers. On the other hand, simple desert burials, with no coffins enclosing the deceased, allowed hot, dry sand to quickly dehydrate bodies. Without moisture bacteria do not act on soft tissue, so Egypt's dead were naturally preserved.

Because these graves were shallow, occasionally the sand would blow away, revealing a dead body that had retained its flesh and hair—a still recognizable individual. Whether such events gave rise to the idea of eternal life or whether they merely reinforced an existing religious belief in life after death, we will probably never know, but what is clear is that their own eyes told the ancient Egyptians that a dead person did not vanish from existence altogether.

Soon after Narmer, Egyptian burials grew more complex. Shallow pits became brick-lined tombs; bodies were covered with animal skins and placed upon woven mats. As time passed, the brick structures became more elaborate depending on the social status and wealth of the deceased. The woven mats were extended to cover the whole body like a crude coffin. But these early funerary practices threatened the natural preservative process. All these changes removed the bodies from the natural drying process in the hot sand. The longer body fluids are retained the more its soft tissue decomposes. Ironically, the tombs intended to preserve the bodies led to their destruction, forcing the Egyptians to devise means of artificially preserving the dead—mummification.

Egyptian religion required mummification. Contrary to what many modern occultists claim, the ancient Egyptians did not believe in reincarnation—the idea that a soul returns to earth after a person dies to inhabit a different body, and that this cycle of birth, death, and rebirth is repeated many times. Mummification would not have been necessary had the Egyptians been reincarnationists; because the soul of the deceased could inhabit a new body, it wouldn't need the old one. The ancient Egyptians believed in *resurrection*—the belief that people exist just once, and that their earthly bodies would reanimate, would get up and go again, in the afterworld. It was a belief that would dominate Egyptian society for thousands of years and remain virtually intact for centuries after Tutankhamen.

To understand the nuts and bolts of the ancient religion and the belief in life after death, you have to understand Egypt's oldest myth: the story of Isis and Osiris. Isis and Osiris were both brother and sister and husband and wife. Osiris brought civilization to Egypt, introducing farming and cattle-raising, thus freeing the early inhabitants of the Nile Valley from misery. Then Osiris left Egypt to bring civilization to the rest of the world, leaving Isis, the powerful goddess of magic, to keep their evil brother Seth in check.

Upon Osiris's return, Seth obtained his brother's exact bodily measurements by trickery, and constructed a wooden chest to fit him precisely. During a banquet Seth offered the magnificent chest as a gift to whoever could fit into it, but guest after guest tried and failed. Of course it fit Osiris, but as soon as he settled inside the chest, Seth sealed the chest, poured molten lead over it and threw the chest into the Nile where Osiris died. A violent storm subsequently carried the chest to Byblos, in Lebanon, where it washed up in the branches of a tree. In time the tree grew to extraordinary size, its trunk enveloping both the chest and Osiris inside it. In the course of building his palace, the king of Byblos cut down the tree for one of the pillars

As soon as Isis learned what had happened to her husband (don't ask how, it's a *very* long story), she set out to recover his body. Enlisting the aid of the queen of Byblos, Isis had the pillar cut open so she could recover the body and bring it back to Egypt for proper burial. When the body was returned to Egypt, Seth discovered it, hacked it into fourteen pieces, and scattered them throughout Egypt. Isis eventually recovered every piece, except one, the phallus, which had been thrown into the Nile and eaten by fish. She reassembled her deceased husband, fashioned an artificial phallus for him. Transforming herself into a bird, she hovered over Osiris's body, and brought him back to life by reciting magical words. And shortly thereafter, their son Horus, the falcon-headed god, was born. (Yes, this is the same Horus as in the Re myth; the Egyptians didn't seem to notice or care that he had two fathers.)

Almost all of Egypt's funerary beliefs are derived from this myth. Isis's search for all the pieces of her deceased husband's body and the fashioning of an artificial phallus emphasize the importance of an intact body. Isis hovered over a *complete* body. Osiris retains the same body he had inhabited while alive. Finally, and most important, she speaks the proper words and he is resurrected. Mummification thus becomes essential to immortality; the body must be preserved for the afterlife and the proper rituals performed. The chest that exactly fit Osiris was the precursor of the anthropoid coffin, shaped like the deceased and intended to protect his body.

Myths furnish insights into the nature of society, and the Isis and Osiris myth not only tells us about immortality but also suggests that there is justice in the world. In the story's final twist, Horus the falcon god fights an elemental battle to avenge the death of his father, and defeats his uncle Seth.

It is not surprising that the world's first concept of justice comes out of Egypt. To have justice, there must be a sense of order, a belief that there are rules governing behavior. This sense of order permeates every aspect of Egyptian society. The Egyptian believed that when he died he would be called upon to appear in the Hall of the Double Truth, a court presided over by the gods of Egypt. There he would make his pleas as to why he should be admitted to the next world. If found worthy, he was declared "true of voice." In a second judging his heart would be placed on one side of a balance scale and on the other side a feather, the hieroglyphic symbol for the Egyptian word "maat"—truth, divine order. If the scales balanced and his heart was as light as the feather, uncluttered with evil deeds, he could proceed to the netherworld. If his heart was found to be heavy with evil, it was thrown to a creature with the body of a crocodile and the head of a hippopotamus who was called the "devourer of hearts." Once the creature ate your heart you ceased to exist. When western legal systems adopted a symbol of justice, it was the balance scale of the Egyptians. In the myth of Osiris, Seth who represents evil poses a constant threat to divine order because he was not killed in the battle, he was merely defeated. So Egypt had to remain ever vigilant;

evil emanating from Seth was always lurking, waiting to upset "maat," divine order.

Ultimately it was the pharaoh's responsibility to establish and maintain divine order in the land, and once each year the king sailed up the Nile on his royal barge and took part in a kind of mystery play that ensured that good would triumph over evil throughout the land. The play, based on the myth of Osiris, is the oldest written drama in the world. Inscribed on the walls of the Horus Temple at Edfu in the south of Egypt, it is called "The Triumph of Horus." Pharaoh played the part of Horus.

THE PRIESTHOOD

As Egypt grew, the pharaoh, occupied with the administration of a growing government, could no longer journey to each temple to make the necessary offerings and recite prayers pleasing to the gods, and there were plenty of them. Each town had its patron deity—Sobek, the crocodile god; Thoth, the Ibis-headed god; Horus, the falcon god. Hundreds of Egyptian gods in temples up and down the Nile competed with each other for prominence in the hierarchy.

Someone was needed who could stand in for the pharaoh at the shrines of the gods, who could make offerings, recite the prayers that ensured the sun a successful journey through the night. Thus, early in Egypt's history, a group of men were selected to recite the words and perform the rituals in place of the king. These were the priests of Egypt. They performed an important religious function, but the priests did not contribute to the nation's economy. The priests were a luxury, and a sign of Egypt's prosperity. These substitutes for the pharaoh set the pattern of the priesthood for thousands of years.

Because the priests were merely acting as representatives of the pharaoh, they were not required to hold deep religious convictions. Their duty was to perform a task, to place the proper offerings upon the altar, utter the appropriate prayers in the prescribed manner, to honor and please the god, so the god would in turn favor Egypt with prosperity. Priests were not required to be devoted to the god they served and this was not unusual in the ancient world. In the Old Testament there is little said about what the followers of Yahweh must believe. One had to follow the law, but none of the Ten Commandments says that you must believe. It was not until Christianity that there was an emphasis on what was "in your heart." So when we think of the priests of Egypt we should not think of purely spiritual servants of the gods. These were men who could be ruthless, who were capable of evil, and in a large bureaucracy there was plenty of opportunity.

The role of high priest in a temple was usually hereditary; we have autobiographies from priests who say they held the same position as their fathers and grandfathers—Prophet of the god Min, First Priest of Amun, etc. With such a huge priesthood, there were plenty of opportunities for capable and ambitious men to rise to the top. The high priest of each temple controlled the temple's fields, orchards and cattle—it was an administrative position that led to great personal wealth and power. Along with the position of high priest came estates, servants, gifts, bribes, and all the trappings of nobility. Beneath the high priest were the second and third prophets of the god, and beneath them were endless ranks and casts of priests, a hierarchy that would rival any modern corporation.

The different branches of the priesthood were fiercely competitive, each claiming priority for their god, seeking the pharaoh's special patronage and the rewards that it would bring. At Memphis, near modern Cairo, the patron god, Ptah, who created the universe was proclaimed to be the foremost of all the gods. But every city claimed its patron deity was the foremost. Thrusting your patron god to the forefront didn't just earn you theological brownie points; it was a struggle for wealth and status, something the priests of ancient Egypt knew very well.

One could succeed in the priesthood by merit and often scribes rose through the ranks to high office. Each temple had its own hierarchy of priests, each group performing specific duties, each holding special privileges. The temple scribes kept careful records of the gifts bestowed on the temple by the pharaoh, and they recorded the yield of the temples' lands, inventoried the storerooms—the grain, wine, linen, and gold. They copied sacred prayers on papyrus scrolls so the lector priests who read the prayers would have clear copies. Other scribes were temple librarians, organizing the papyrus scrolls so they could be easily located and consulted. Besides the religious texts, the temples kept medical texts for the priest physicians and books of dream interpretations to be consulted by those who wanted to know what their dreams meant.

The "stolists" were priests who attended the statues of the gods. They followed a precise routine of devotion to maintain the god's continuing good will. Each day at the prescribed time the stolist priests entered the "holy of holies"—the innermost sacred room in the temple, withdrew the statue of the god from its shrine, and performed the morning rituals. The "god" was anointed with fragrant oils, placated with incense, presented with the choicest foods, then wrapped in pure white linen, and replaced in the holy shrine. As the doors were closed and bolted, prayers and incantations were chanted.

Many of the priests holding lesser positions were married, had families, and held jobs outside the temple. They were carpenters, teachers, and scribes who would, at regular intervals, serve thirty days in their temple, a kind of religious national guard, and then return to secular life.

When pharaohs conquered foreign lands and returned with gold and captives, they donated a portion of the tribute to the temples, to thank the gods for looking upon them with favor in battle, and to ensure their continued goodwill. Foreign captives became a sizable source of manpower and maintained the temples, as well as the fields and orchards owned by the temples. Pharaohs often gave large tracts of land to the temples so the cattle and produce could provide a continuing annuity. As each succeeding pharaoh tried to surpass his predecessor's generosity, temples grew incredibly wealthy and the priests numbered in the tens of thousands. In the years just before the birth of Tutankhamen, the priesthood of Egypt had swollen to the largest bureaucracy the world had ever known, a powerful force, second only to the pharaoh.

It is interesting that although pharaohs conquered foreign lands, Egypt never became a true empire. The gods of Egypt were the gods of only Egypt, the pharaoh was king of Upper and Lower Egypt, not of the world. Life on the banks of the Nile was too good to want to live elsewhere—to colonize and live in foreign lands. If you died on foreign soil, far from the Egyptian embalmers, your body might not be mummified and all chance of immortality would be lost. Better to live in Egypt. So when the pharaoh rode out with the army each year to conquer his neighbors, the troops always returned home to Egypt. For the Egyptians, the center of the universe was Egypt, and at the center of Egypt was the pharaoh.

Much of our understanding of ancient Egypt comes from the ancient Egyptians' belief in life after death. Because they believed you could literally take it with you, tombs were filled with furniture, food, clothing, even games to amuse themselves in the next world. There were items of luxury, practicality, and whimsy. It was as if they were packing for a trip to a place they had never visited and weren't sure what to bring, so they brought everything. Tombs are windows into daily life in ancient Egypt. Their contents weren't carefully arranged like mini-apartments; objects were piled on top of each other and crammed into every small space. On top of a bed might be the toiletry objects of the lady of the house—her favorite scents and oils still in delicate alabaster jars, her eyepaint in slender ceramic tubes. Next to this might be stacks of fine linens, clothing, and food, breads, and sweets of all kinds, and wine jars of a favorite vintage sealed for eternity, joints of meat, roast ducks—it was the ultimate picnic. This is how we know what the Egyptians ate and drank at banquets, what they wore, and what kind of furniture they had. Sometimes, the scenes painted on the tomb walls are just as revealing.

Every ancient Egyptian wanted immortality and the chance of attaining it was directly tied to his wealth and status. The kind of tomb you prepared for your afterlife depended on what you could afford. The beautifully painted tombs that we see in art books were prepared for Egypt's aristocracy. The nobility invested as much as they could afford in their tombs, and sometimes as a special favor, the pharaoh would grant a member of the court a prime location. For most Egyptians—the farmers, the craftsmen, and the laborers—there were no beautiful tombs packed with furniture, food and luxuries. When his time came, the common man was wrapped in a sheet, perhaps from his own bed, and placed in a mass burial site for the poor. There, surrounded by hundreds of his deceased neighbors, he awaited resurrection. Since most commoners couldn't write, they left no literature, no records of their hopes and concerns, no stories of their lives. Most of what we know about ancient Egypt comes from the privileged few.

The idea of decorating tomb walls with scenes from daily life was based on a principle of ancient Egyptian magic: if you showed it, it would happen in the next world. Egyptian tomb walls are covered with scenes of the deceased feasting, hunting, fishing, overseeing the work in his fields on his estate. The whole family was almost always portrayed—the wife, kids, and pets—so the deceased would have company in the next world. When I look at the paintings in an Egyptian tomb, I get the feeling they thought the next world was just like this one, only better, maybe with air-conditioning. You never see an unhappy camper on a tomb wall. They may be working in the fields, but they're wearing their finest linen robes.

Sometimes a high official would write his autobiography on his tomb wall, chronicling his accomplishments. Military men often gave vivid accounts of their campaigns, royal scribes related their duties in the palace, and governors listed the territories under their jurisdiction and the taxes they collected for the king. Sometimes the vizier, the equivalent of prime minister, listed his official responsibilities. Each tomb was a miniature world revealing the life of the deceased. Preserved by Egypt's dry climate, the tombs form a three-dimensional encyclopedia of ancient Egypt.

As the custodians of writing, priests were often the keepers of records, an essential part of any bureaucracy, and as Egypt grew, so did the numbers and importance of the record keepers. Because the fertile land along the Nile produced a surplus of crops, the pharaoh collected the excess (the origin of taxes) to pay the army and the priests. When taxes were collected up and down the Nile, accountants were needed to tally the crops grown by each farmer and to record how much was deposited in the pharaoh's granaries. Egypt's booming economy produced an army of bureaucrats, and becoming a scribe was a sure path to upward mobility.

Ancient texts urged the youth of Egypt to learn how to write. *"You won't have to march in the army, your robes will be clean, you won't have to work the fields in the heat of the day, . . ."* Once you could write, you were on your way up. There were all kinds of scribes. Some spent their days listing inventories in temple storerooms and had titles like "Scribe of Amun," others wrote religious texts and were called "Keepers of the Secrets." If you showed ability, you might become a "Royal Scribe" attached to the palace, perhaps answering correspondence, or composing inscriptions to be carved on the temple walls.

As Egypt became prosperous, the country was divided into administrative units called nomes, almost the exact equivalent of our states. There were forty-four nomes, each with a nomarch, or governor, and under him were other officials, the mayors of the towns, overseers of construction, overseers of the scribes, overseers of the stables. All of these officials were selected from the ranks of the scribes. No wonder parents were always urging their children to "Be a scribe." This was the middle class.

There were books that told you how to move quickly up the ranks—*"Don't indulge in drinking beer, lest you utter evil speech." "Study the writings, put them in your heart, then your words will be effective." "Attend to your position, be it high or low; it is not good to press forward, step according to rank."* It was practically a Dale Carnegie course for ancient Egyptians.

What made the whole thing possible was the growing population of farmers. There were no hungry mouths. Each new arrival could be fed, and still there was a surplus. Luxury industries could be supported. Artists were hired to decorate tomb walls, jewelers and craftsmen were paid for their creations, and it was all the gift of the Nile.

By the time Tutankhamen came to power the three major forces of Egyptian society—kingship, the military, and religion—had been in place for centuries and were growing stronger, more demanding, and independent. The pharaoh could not maintain Divine Order without the priesthood and the military. The priests were eager for donations from the pharaoh and for booty from the military. The military, strong in their own right, still asked for the god's favor for successful campaigns, and it was politic to have the support of the priests. It was a delicate balance among them, for each of the three institutions had grown so strong that it was almost unstoppable. But the notion of divine kingship remained central to it all and Egypt without a pharaoh was unthinkable.

Kingship was the foundation of civilization throughout the ancient world. Every great nation had a leader without whom there would be chaos, but Egypt alone perceived its king as divine—the pharaoh was the son of Re, the sun god. Other nations were led by mere mortals; in Egypt a god was at the helm.

Of the 170 or so kings whose reigns were recorded, most followed and upheld the traditional role of kingship. They led the army, built monuments, and made offerings to the gods. Under the pharaoh's guidance, divine order prevailed and Egypt prospered, but the line of succession from Narmer to Tutankhamen was not without its breaks.

There is a tendency to think of Egyptian history as perfectly seamless, but there were times when the fabric of Egypt tore. The point to be made is that when such rare events occurred, the society was so well established that it could right itself again. There may have been brief periods of chaos, but the infrastructure was still there, the land still produced, the priests still had wealth, the concept of kingship was unchanging, and the military was in the wings. For example, the pyramids were built during the Old Kingdom (2686–2181 B.C.), but by 2200 B.C. Egypt had descended into anarchy and the era of pyramid building was over. We are not sure why Egyptian society collapsed; there are few records. One theory is that the last pharaoh of the Old Kingdom lived too long. Pepi II became pharaoh as a child and reigned for more than ninety years, the longest reigning monarch in the history of the world.

Unlike modern England, where the monarch is a figurehead, Egypt's pharaoh actually led the army into battle. As Pepi grew older and older, perhaps he was unable to govern, the army was not maintained, and Egypt grew weak. Egypt was tumbled by its greatest strength, a strong central government built around its king as absolute ruler. If the pharaoh was weak, Egypt suffered. Tutankhamen would learn this lesson firsthand.

For more than a century after Pepi, Egypt was without a true king as local governors fought for supremacy. Even in this period of weakness, Egypt was not invaded. Its natural barriers of sand and water held. Finally a local ruler, like King Narmer, unified the land, and Egypt had its pharaoh. Like a boat righting itself after capsizing, Egypt had returned to exactly the same position that had served it so well. With a single absolute ruler leading a strong military and priesthood, divine order had returned to the land. But we are still eight hundred years away from Tutankhamen's reign, and we have talked only in terms of "political forces," "kingship," and "the priesthood." It would be an oversimplification to view Egypt only as a vast mechanical system, totally determined by the laws of physics. It was also the personalities that made Egypt great. It is time to meet Tutankhamen's family.

Tutankhamen's Ancestors
The Glorious Eighteenth Dynasty

Respect the nobles, sustain your people.
Strengthen your borders, your frontier patrols.
It is good to work for the future,
One respects the life of the foresighted.

—*King Khety Nebkaure*
circa 2150 B.C.

Egypt believed its rightful place in the world order was on top, dominating her neighbors. The history of Egypt can be viewed, in fact, as a series of conquests; it was the natural order of things. To maintain supremacy, the pharaoh repeatedly led the army out of Egypt, smashed some foreign country, then returned home with anything of value that wasn't nailed down. The subdued country was expected to send annual "tribute" or the pharaoh would return. Today we would view this as unprovoked aggression, which it was, but it was also the way of life in the ancient world. No pharaoh ever boasted, "There were no battles in my reign."

Annual invasions were necessary because the Egyptians never colonized. Once they conquered a foreign territory, that was it; they went home and waited for the yearly tribute. But with the army far away in

Egypt, there wasn't much incentive for foreign countries to send tribute, so the pharaoh would ride out with his army again, repeating the cycle. War was the natural order of things in Egypt.

Tuthmosis I, one of the early pharaohs in Tutankhamen's dynasty, is best known for his military exploits, but he is also significant because he is the reason that the pharaohs of the New Kingdom are buried in the Valley of the Kings and not in pyramids. An autobiographical inscription in the tomb of Tuthmosis's Overseer of the Works, Ineni, describes how the first tomb was constructed.

> I inspected the excavation of the cliff-tomb of his majesty, alone, no one seeing, no one hearing . . . It was a work of my heart, my virtue was wisdom; there was not given to me a command by an elder. I shall be praised because of my wisdom after years, by those who shall imitate that which I have done.[1]

Secrecy was indeed crucial if Tuthmosis's body was to be protected. Soon after the collapse of the Old Kingdom the pyramids of Giza were plundered by tomb robbers, and all the bodies destroyed. When the government was finally stabilized, the pharaohs of the Middle Kingdom resumed building pyramids, but a diminished work force and reduced resources resulted in interiors being constructed of mud brick with only a thin stone casing skimming their exterior surfaces. These pyramids were also plundered, so Tuthmosis's secret tomb carved into the cliff of a desolate valley was meant to outsmart tomb robbers. Eight generations later, Tutankhamen would join his august ancestor in this place that became known as the Valley of the Kings. Those generations included some of the greatest monarchs ever to rule Egypt.

Tutankhamen's ancestors, the kings of the Eighteenth Dynasty, elevated the concept of the warrior-pharaoh to heights never before seen. The pharaoh Tuthmosis created an army of thousands of well-trained, well-equipped career soldiers. It was totally unlike the small corps Narmer had organized, and it had an advantage that Narmer couldn't have imagined—the chariot.

Two horses pulled these chariots that carried two men, a driver and an archer. Chariots were constructed from imported wood—elm wheels for its suppleness, and ash as the body because of its strength. The floor was woven from leather thongs and covered with a leather flap, acting as a shock absorber, providing a relatively stable platform from which the archer could shoot his arrows. It was a light body with a lot of engine.

Supporting the charioteers were the infantry. Each soldier carried a leather shield, spear, battle ax, and dagger. The infantry marched fifteen miles a day. By the time Tuthmosis was through with his campaigns Egypt was master of the seven hundred miles between Egypt and the Euphrates river. On the banks of the Euphrates, Tuthmosis erected a stela—a large round topped stone, resembling a giant tombstone, that served as an ancient Egyptian bulletin board. If you wanted to announce something, you carved it on a stela and Tuthmosis proclaimed that this was Egypt's northern territory.

The only surviving child of Tuthmosis and his queen was Princess Hatshepsut. There is no word for "queen" in ancient Egyptian. The phrase we translate as "queen" is actually "king's great wife." Had Hatshepsut been a son, the royal crown would have passed directly to him, but she was a girl and this created a problem. It is not always clear how the successor to the throne was chosen. It wasn't as simple as in England—where the laws of primogeniture decreed that the throne was passed down through the king's eldest son, with specified contingencies for all possibilities. In Egypt, the pharaoh had several wives and could also marry his sisters, so the lines of succession for his children could be rather complex. Overall, the rule known as the "Heiress Theory" covered most cases: whoever married the eldest, most royal daughter became pharaoh.

When Tuthmosis died, his son Tuthmosis II by a minor wife was married to his half sister Hatshepsut, the eldest daughter of the pharaoh and his great wife. Marriage to Hatshepsut established Tuthmosis II's right to the throne. The couple had a successful, uneventful twenty-year reign. When Tuthmosis II died he left two children, a daughter by Hatshepsut, and a young son, Tuthmosis III, by a minor wife. Hatshepsut ruled as regent for the young boy for about seven years. Then, suddenly, one of the most incredible events in Egypt's long history occurred: Hatshepsut changed her royal title from "Queen" to "King" and had herself portrayed in full male royal regalia, complete with a beard. This was unheard of in conservative ancient Egypt. By wearing the false beard and the royal kilt of the pharaoh, Hatshepsut was attempting to stay within the traditional boundaries of Egyptian kingship—she was the king who happened to be a woman. The only reason Hatshepsut pulled it off was that she was a good administrator, and her reign brought prosperity throughout the land. That she chose to be represented as king posed several challenges for the artists and scribes in Hatshepsut's court. Was the pharaoh to be referred to as "his majesty" or "her majesty?" (They did it both ways.)

When Hatshepsut died on the 10th day of the 6th month in the 22nd year of her reign (February 1482 B.C.), Tuthmosis III became sole ruler of Egypt and through his conquests went on to become the greatest military leader Egypt had ever seen. In the sixteen years following Hatshepsut's death, Tuthmosis III led fourteen military campaigns north of Egypt, causing Egyptologists to dub him the "Napoleon of Egypt." In year 33 of his reign, Tuthmosis battled his way to the Euphrates river, defeated the King of Mitanni, and erected his own stele alongside his grandfather's, and another one across the river.

A generation after her death, Tuthmosis had Hatshepsut's name erased from all her monuments in an official attempt to remove any trace of her from the records of Egypt. It was too revolutionary to admit that a king of Egypt had been a woman. This erasure of a pharaoh's name and memory established an ominous precedent. A hundred years later, a similar purge would sweep through Egypt. This time Tutankhamen would be the target.

When Tuthmosis III died after fifty-four years as king, Egypt was the military power feared by all in the Middle East. He was Tutankhamen's great-great-great grandfather. The remaining pharaohs between Tuthmosis III and Tutankhamen maintained the grand tradition of their ancestors. They elevated the Eighteenth Dynasty above all previous and subsequent eras of Egypt's glorious history.

Now Tutankhamen's direct ancestors begin to emerge. Twenty-five years before his birth, Egypt was ruled by his strong-willed, decisive grandfather, Amenhotep III, a man whose probity and strength would echo loudly through the lives of succeeding pharaohs. Secure in his claim to the throne because his father had publicly nominated him as his successor, Amenhotep was able to marry a commoner; his wife did not have to be of pure royal blood to establish his right to rule. To commemorate his marriage to the Lady Tiye, he sent the ancient Egyptian equivalent of a telegram, a carved stone in the shape of a scarab (beetle), a symbol of good luck. On the base of the scarab was the inscription:

> . . . *the king's great wife, Tiye, may she live,*
> *The name of her father is Yuya*
> *The name of her mother is Tuya*
> *She is the wife of a mighty king.*

Anyone reading between the lines would get the message: Tiye is a commoner, but you had better accept her as my wife. All indications are that it was a successful marriage. Statues of the king show Tiye next to him, represented almost equal in size—a great honor to his queen. Royalty was always shown as idealized, but Tiye's portraits often convey a sense of the person. The beautifully sculpted head of Queen Tiye in the Berlin Museum is that of a mature woman with handsome regular features, a strong woman who got whatever she wanted.

Tiye bore the king six children—four daughters, and two sons. The princesses were given important titles. One daughter, Sit-Amun, was called "The King's Wife," which suggests to some Egyptologists that she married her father. Often sisters married their own half brothers, but it was rare for a pharaoh to marry his own daughters. The oldest son, named Tuthmosis after his ancestor, was groomed for the throne by being given the important position of high priest of Memphis, one of the two capitals of Egypt (along with Thebes). This was a shrewd maneuver on the part of Amenhotep III. It was always politic to honor the gods of Egypt, and he now had a loyal family member inside the powerful priesthood. The younger son, Amenhotep, was named for his father, but he was mentioned in no royal inscriptions, is not shown in any statues, and his name appears only on one broken wine jar. Such were the inauspicious beginnings of Tutankhamen's father, a prince who appeared to have no future. We will look closely at this enigmatic figure in the next chapter.

The reign of Amenhotep III was as close as Egypt, or almost any other country, ever got to paradise. Never did precious unguents and oils flow so freely, turquoise, lapis lazuli, and gold adorn more necklaces, or rich, aromatic cedar form more temple doors. Food was abundant and there was peace. Thanks to Amenhotep's predecessors, Egypt now firmly controlled the area from northern Syria to the Fifth Cataract of the Nile (the center of the Sudan). The military rarely had to demonstrate its might by fighting, so firmly had all the earlier invasions driven the lesson home. A steady flow of gold from Nubia (Sudan) and the western desert kept Egypt's economy strong, prompting a foreign king corresponding with Amenhotep III to observe: "Gold is like dust in your country, one has only to pick it up."[2] From Kush, in the south, came elephant tusks, giraffe skins, and ebony wood for palace furniture. From Afghanistan came lapis lazuli to be carved into amulets of the gods, and used as inlays in jewelry. By now foreign traders were regularly plying the Mediterranean. From Crete came exotic jars for palace use; Cyprus contributed copper ingots. Amenhotep had favored the gods, and the gods had favored Egypt. It was good business all around.

Amenhotep and Queen Tiye led a cosmopolitan life, successfully integrating both halves of the country. They traveled frequently between Memphis and Thebes. Memphis, the northern capital, was situated where the Nile began to branch out into the delta fan on its way to the Mediterranean. It was the administrative center of Egypt where the king resided to control the country; it held the national archives and accommodated thousands of bureaucrats. Little remains of Memphis today, because of a rising water table at the site. A colossal statue here, a massive column there, evoke what must once have been the busiest city in the world. Sadly, the office complexes that composed the city were constructed of sun-dried bricks that time and rising water have returned to the mud they came from. The palace suffered the same fate. All the precious documents from the archives disintegrated and rotted away, the fate of wet papyrus. Glorious temples have sunk out of sight into the moist ground.

The 400-mile journey from Memphis south to Thebes took the royal barge about three weeks, sailing against the current. The boat was a huge lumbering craft, probably two hundred feet long, built for comfort on river voyages. Along the way Amenhotep stopped to perform rituals in the temples, events that would be remembered by generations of priests who would fondly recall their brush with a living god.

If Memphis was like Washington, filled with records and preoccupied with business, then Thebes was like Paris, wealthy, glamorous, and alluring. Thebes was a city of edifices built for the glory of gods, not of functional office buildings. With every military conquest, Amenhotep's ancestors had heaped large portions of their plunder on Thebes's temples in gratitude for their success. Coffers overflowed with gold, storehouses burst with endless bolts of white linen—the priestly cloth—and produce arrived in endless streams from thousands of acres of donated farmland. The priests were rich and on their way to becoming independent—their land produced wheat, cattle, vegetables, everything they needed plus a surplus that could be sold.

So when the royal barge finally docked at Thebes, Amenhotep and Tiye would have been met by a thriving, prosperous priesthood. Homer called the city "Hundred-Gated Thebes" because of the countless huge pylons that formed the entrances to temple upon temple. And indeed Thebes had temples to many gods, but the reason for the city's importance was the patron deity Amun, the "hidden one." To this god Egyptians attributed the resurrection of their country from the anarchy and foreign domination that followed the Old Kingdom. By Amenhotep's time almost a thousand years of pharaohs had taken Amun as their special patron and pledged donations for his support, making Thebes more splendid with every gift. Amun had eclipsed even the old god Re, incorporating that former preeminent god in one of his titles, Amun-Re. Represented as a man with a tall crown surmounted by two ostrich plumes, Amun was married to the goddess Mut. With their son Khonsu, they formed the trinity, the holy family of Thebes.

Amenhotep's own name meant "Amun is pleased." He proceeded to outdo every other pharaoh in ensuring that god's continued satisfaction. Perhaps urged on by the priests, Tutankhamen's grandfather embarked on the most massive building ever to honor the patron god of Thebes and himself. He seems also to have had genuine beliefs of his own. After all, he named his oldest son Tuthmosis, "Toth is born," in honor of Toth, the god of writing. His second son was named for Amun, as was Amenhotep himself, and his eldest daughter was named for that god as well.

The pharaoh began his homage to Amun at the great temple of Karnak, the largest religious structure ever built. It was not really a single cathedral but a complex of temples and shrines sprawling across acres of land in no particular order. Like Topsy, it just grew as over the centuries each pharaoh dedicated his particular monument to the gods. When Amenhotep began his addition to the Great Temple of Amun at Karnak, the pylons of Tuthmosis I and his daughter Hatshepsut were still standing. People still marveled at Tuthmosis's obelisks, the first to be erected in Karnak Temple.

First, Amenhotep constructed a pair of grand entrance pylons (the Third Pylon) in front of all the other buildings at Karnak, so that these largest, most magnificent gates would be the first anyone would see. Their cornices were brightly painted and festooned with colorful pennants that flew from sixty feet high; shining electrum (a gold-silver alloy) covered poles. The imposing structure was dedicated to Amun.

A mile and a half from Karnak, in central Thebes, stood another temple of great importance. Once each year, shaven-headed priests bore the weighty gold statue of Amun to a special divine barque while others carried the statue of his wife Mut to her ship to form a convoy that sailed to this temple. Priests in their finest white robes joined important dignitaries adorned in silver and gold to trail the vessels in a procession called the "Beautiful Festival of the Harem," the most festive, most important holiday of Thebes. The celebration re-created the wedding of the two gods and of the conjugal bliss that followed. It took place in the "Harem of the South," a smallish temple used just once each year. Amenhotep directed his architects to replace the old temple with a beautifully proportioned, more imposing substitute. They produced a colonnade hall of seven pairs of majestic lotus columns leading into an open court. Two sides of the court were flanked with a double row of papyrus-bud columns roofed by slabs of stone, creating a shady spot beside an open yard prefaced by a forest of columns. Past the court, at the far end of the temple, a double sanctuary was constructed—the holy of holies—that housed the gold statues of Amun and Mut. Amenhotep had outdone himself in this tribute to the great god. It was the largest temple ever built by a single pharaoh.

Amenhotep took such interest in these projects that he built a palace across the river, where open land was still available, so he could reside in comfort, near enough to oversee the construction. Only a few walls of this palace have survived, since such buildings were intended for the lifetime of just one pharaoh and were constructed of impermanent mud bricks. Enough remains, however, to show it was a splendid affair. Floors were brightly painted with scenes from nature, walls with colorful decorative borders. Rather than a single large building, it was a compound with a separate building for the king and his staff, another for the queen and her court, another to serve as the kitchen, and still others to house the palace guard. In addition, there was a large auditorium, or festival hall, in which Amenhotep celebrated special jubilees celebrating his long rule. Life must have been sybaritic here. It seems that, despite proximity to the Nile, Amenhotep constructed an artificial lake behind the palace large enough for Queen Tiye to sail her barge.

As time passed, Amenhotep's personality mingled more and more with the glory of the city. He ordered a pair of the largest statues ever carved of himself, seated in seventy-feet-high majesty, to lead the way to a new temple dedicated to his memory. Nothing of this temple survives today, but the massive seated statues of Amenhotep still gaze eternally toward Thebes. These are the famed colossi of Memnon that amazed visitors in antiquity. The unparalleled building spree of Amenhotep must have energized the city to an unprecedented frenzy. He provided steady work for thousands of workers quarrying, cutting, dressing, and transporting tons of stone. Hundreds of artists carved and painted scenes on gleaming new temples and the luxurious palace. Riches flowed into Thebes as never before. A magic grew about Thebes that captured the hearts of poets. "She is called 'The City,'" says a late New Kingdom hymn in her praise; "all others are under her shadow, to magnify themselves through her."[3]

Soon the banks of the Nile were dominated by magnificent architecture, presenting a rich facade that hid a less than perfect interior. The houses and shops of the mortals sprawled in confusion behind the temples, forming a maze of dirty, narrow winding streets. It was a noisy city filled with the sounds of horses, penned ducks and pigs, and people busy at their work and at surviving. Although they resided in the greatest city in Egypt, life remained hard for the common people. Clouds of dust hung over their houses from the continuous cutting and polishing of stone for all the construction. Overpoweringly pungent odors emanated from all the animals and crowded conditions, and flies, lice, and fleas were ever-present.

Despite its face of splendor and energy, or maybe because of it, Thebes began to question itself. Many in the upper class believed that the priesthood of Amun had become too rich, too materialistic, and too powerful. Although the king and the nobles of the city continued to pay tribute to Amun, as time passed, some of the faithful added an interest in other cults. Amenhotep led the way when he took the new title, "Dazzling Sun Disk of All the Land." It became popular at the court to contemplate the nature of the sun-disk, the Aten, an interest not confined to the king alone, for Queen Tiye named her pleasure boat *The Aten Gleams*. People in the highest places were thinking about religion now, instead of merely going through the old motions. This profoundly affected the mind of Amenhotep's ignored second son, who would ascend the throne before long.

For his final resting place, Amenhotep selected an isolated wadi west of the Valley of the Kings that had never been used before. Why he chose not to be buried near his august ancestors of the Eighteenth Dynasty we will never know. Amenhotep III had a mind of his own.

Then tragedy struck the elderly king and his wife—their eldest son, Tuthmosis, the high priest Ptah, died. This was the son groomed to succeed his father. Their grief must have been intense, compounded by the fact that all of Amenhotep's plans for the future, for Egypt after his own passing, died with his boy. Now there was the real question of who would succeed the pharaoh. There was the second son, named Amenhotep for his father, but there probably was a reason he had been so rarely mentioned. He may have been afflicted with some very strange disease. No doubt there were other contenders for the throne, perhaps sons by Pharaoh's minor wives, some of whom were princesses of foreign countries, but only one was Tiye's child. She must have schemed successfully in his behalf, because, with all his problems, he became the heir and more. In what seems a surprising move, the aging king appointed his younger son, Amenhotep, to be coregent, which meant that they would rule together. There could be no controversy as to who ruled Egypt when the king died. The question is why did Amenhotep III, the energetic and powerful ruler, agree to share his power?

The answer can perhaps be found in Amenhotep III's mummy, which was discovered in 1898 under strange circumstances by a very nervous Egyptologist. Victor Loret, a Frenchman, served for a short time as head of the Egyptian Antiquities Service. High-strung and unsuited for his high administrative position, Loret managed to antagonize both European and Egyptian authorities, and consequently lasted only two years. He had barely time to undertake the first systematic excavation in the Valley of the Kings, discovering the robbed tombs of Tuthmosis I and Tuthmosis III, Egypt's Napoleon. He also found the tomb of Amenhotep II, in which lay the answer to our question.

This, too, was a plundered tomb. Broken bits of blue ceramic and wooden funerary objects with Amenhotep II's name littered the entrance passage when Loret uncovered it. Crawling through the passageway, Loret came to a square shaft, or "well," designed to catch water so that the burial chamber would remain dry during the rare cloudbursts that occurred in the Valley of the Kings. Placing a ladder across the well, Loret crossed into a square-pillared antechamber and saw broken funerary boats, models of what the pharaoh would need in the next world, gilded images of the king, and broken ushabti servant statues that were supposed to come to life in the next world and perform any tasks needed. It was now late into the night, Loret was tired, and with only his candle to illuminate the scene, his imagination started to take over. Then the candlelight fell on something for which he was not prepared.

> I went forward (between two columns) with my candle and, horrible sight, a body lay there upon the boat, all black and hideous, its grimacing face turned towards me and looking at me, its long brown hair in sparse bunches around its head. I did not dream for an instant that this was just an unwrapped mummy. The legs and arms seemed to be bound. A hole exposing the sternum, there was an opening in the skull. Was this a victim of human sacrifice? Was this a thief murdered by his accomplices in a bloody division of the loot, or perhaps killed by soldiers or police interrupting the pillaging of the tomb?[4]

What Loret had seen was the mummy of a prince, disturbed so soon after his burial that the oils and resins used in embalming were still liquid. The robbers had placed the body in one of the model boats, where the oils solidified and glued the mummy to it. Regaining his composure, Loret continued his descent, eventually arriving at a burial chamber containing a lidless stone sarcophagus. Peering over the top, Loret saw a coffin with a garland of flowers at its head and a wreath at its foot. He had found the mummy of Amenhotep II.

Loret's long evening was not over. Examining the four side chambers off the burial chambers he found statues of the pharaoh, vases for the seven sacred oils the king would need, meat and fruits to sustain him in the next world, and wooden models of boats for his journey to the netherworld. It was in one of these side chambers that Loret received his next shock:

> We passed to the rooms to the right. In the first one we entered, an unusually strange sight met our eyes: three bodies lay side by side at the back in the left corner, their feet pointing toward the door. The right half of the room was filled with little coffins with mummiform covers and funerary statues of bitumen (resin-painted) wood. These statues were contained in the coffins that the thieves had opened and rejected after having searched in vain for treasures.
>
> We approached the cadavers. The first seemed to be that of a woman. A thick veil covered her forehead and left eye. Her broken arm had been replaced at her side, her hands in the air. Ragged and torn cloth hardly covered her body. Abundant black curled hair spread over the limestone floor on each side of her head. The face was admirably conserved and had a noble and majestic gravity.
>
> The second mummy in the middle was that of a child of about fifteen years. It was naked with the hands joined on the abdomen. First of all the head appeared totally bald, but on closer examination one saw that the head had been shaved except an area on the right temple from which grew a magnificent tress of black hair. This was the coiffure of the royal princes (called the Horus lock). I thought immediately of the royal prince Webensennu, this so far unknown son of Amenophis II, whose funerary statue I had noticed in the great hall, and whose canopic fragments I was to find later. The face of the young prince was laughing and mischievous, it did not at all evoke the idea of death.
>
> The last corpse nearest the wall seemed to be that of a man. His head was shaved but a wig lay on the ground not far from him. The face of this person displayed something horrible and something droll at the same time. The mouth was running

45

obliquely from one side nearly to the middle of the cheek, with a pad of linen whose two ends hung from the corner of the lips. The half-closed eyes had a strange expression, he could have died choking on a gag but he looked like a young playful cat with a piece of cloth. Death which had respected the severe beauty of the woman and the impish grace of the boy had turned in derision and amused itself with the countenance of the man.

These three corpses, like the one in the boat, had their skulls pierced with a large hole and the breast of each one was opened.[5] The condition of the three mummies in the side chamber and the one in the boat was caused by methodical tomb robbers. In their search for jewelry, they had hacked at the wrappings on the heads first, quickly stripping the outer linen; they then hacked at the chest searching for more jewelry, damaging the royal bodies.

Loret had no idea of the identities of the four mummies, and his judgment was certainly confused that night. The third mummy in the side chamber that he described as a man is clearly that of a young woman. To this day the identities of most of these bodies remain uncertain. One identification was made almost a century later and required both modern technology and a find in Tutankhamen's tomb, but more about that later. The four mummies that so moved Loret were not the only ones he found that night. One of the side chambers had been sealed with limestone blocks, with only a small opening near the ceiling. Loret climbed to the top and with his flickering candle was barely able to make out nine coffins, neatly arranged—six against the wall and three in front of them. That was all he could see, and he realized that the wall would have to be taken down before the coffins could be studied. But first the tomb had to be cleared.

Loret mapped the tomb, superimposing a grid to record the positions of more than 2,000 objects. Only after all this was he finally able to examine the nine coffins behind the wall. Loret had discovered the mummies of eight kings of Egypt and an unidentified woman. These mummies had been rescued from their plundered tombs by a Twenty-first Dynasty king in order to protect them from further desecration. Written on the bandages of the mummy of Seti II was the sad story of how the convention of kings came to be held in the tomb of Amenhotep II. On the sixth day of the fourth month of winter, in the twelfth year of the reign of Pinedjem I, the king had collected despoiled royal bodies, rewrapped them, and placed them in the tomb of Amenhotep II for safekeeping, where they remained until Loret's discovery.[6] Among the mummies was Tutankhamen's grandfather, Amenhotep III.

The mummy of Amenhotep III along with the others was taken by boat to Cairo where it remained till it was unwrapped on September 23, 1905.[7] The mummy of the father provided the clue as to why his son, Amenhotep IV, became co-pharaoh with his father. The king was fat and in very poor health when he died.

When I examined the mummy in the Egyptian Museum in Cairo, it was clear that Amenhotep must have been in great pain toward the end of his life. He suffered from horrible abscesses on his right lower incisors and his upper right canine. I could tell that he had lost the incisors some time before death as the sockets had filled in with new bone growth. Dental disease was common in ancient Egypt for kings and commoners alike, not from eating too much sugar as it is today, but from their daily bread. All grains in Egypt were stone-ground, which meant that along with your bread, you ate a considerable portion of sand and grit. Years of eating Egyptian bread wore down the teeth, exposing them to decay. Skilled as the Egyptian physicians were, they did not practice dentistry.

With the severe deterioration of his teeth, Amenhotep III must have been in constant pain. He may have been sedated with wine or even the new wonder drug of the Eighteenth Dynasty imported from Cyprus—opium. Cypriot physicians collected the sap that oozed from slits in the poppy's capsule, then dried the sticky mass for easy application. Applied directly to a wound or tooth, it may have had about the same effect as a modern-day injection.[8] Amenhotep would have found it difficult to carry out the affairs of state as his health deteriorated and may have been so sedated that he was in no condition to make decisions. Under these circumstances it would have been easy for the determined Queen Tiye to convince her husband to share the duties so difficult for him in his pained state with their son, Amenhotep IV. As coregent, her son was assured the throne when the old king died.

When the young king finally came to power after his father's death, one of the first changes he seems to have made was to approve a new technique for the mummification of his father. The embalmers injected tree resin and salts under the skin of the arms, legs, and neck to fill them out and to give the body a more lifelike appearance. It was a small break with tradition but one that foretold dramatic changes to come.

THE HANDWRITING ON THE WALL— WHAT THE TEMPLES TELL US

Temple walls are a crucial source of information for Egyptologists. They provided huge surfaces for pharaohs to boast of their deeds, and, because the walls were made of stone, they have survived. If a king wanted to announce how much land he dedicated to the temple, it was carved on the wall. When a pharaoh returned from a victorious military campaign, the triumph was recorded in full detail for all to see and marvel at the bravery of their pharaoh. There were glorious scenes of the pharaoh charging into battle in his war chariot, killing his enemy with arrows, and returning victorious with bound captives. Invariably, at the end of the panorama, are the scribes, counting piles of severed human hands—the Egyptian method of tallying the number of enemies killed. Actually two versions of the story were carved on the walls, one in words and one in pictures. When Napoleon invaded Egypt in 1798, hieroglyphic writing hadn't been decoded yet so they couldn't read the inscriptions. Because so many of the scenes were of battles, they assumed that temples were palaces. They couldn't imagine putting such violent scenes in a place of worship. But to the ancient Egyptian it was all connected. Conquering foreign territories was part of the divine order, something assisted by the gods. Every war was a holy war. If Napoleon's men could have read the inscriptions, they would have realized that these were temples and they could have read the dates of the battles, numbers killed, and even the names of the king's horses.

If you can read a temple wall you can learn a lot about Egyptian history. The wall paintings in the tombs of the nobles and the funerary objects found inside them have given us rich details about the people's daily lives. It's in the temples, however, where we find the official party line history of Egypt, but because most of the official records and temples from the northern capital, Memphis, have sunk into the mud, what records we do have really only give Egypt's southern party line.

Thebes rarely saw rain or high humidity so the temples and tombs are well preserved, the papyri they housed still legible. During the reign of Amenhotep III and his Eighteenth Dynasty ancestors, the information from Thebes is rich with detail. We have Amenhotep's temples and we have his tomb, but suddenly the records break off with the king's death.

The first clues as to what happened after Amenhotep died came from inside the walls of Karnak Temple. By the turn of this century, some of Karnak's great pillars had fallen, its huge gateways were crumbling, and major restoration was needed. In 1926, French Egyptologist Henri Chevrier began reconstructing the second pylon at Karnak (built by the pharaoh Horemheb). The crumbling pylon had to be completely dismantled and each block numbered for reassembly like a huge Lego project. As the blocks were being taken down Chevrier discovered, inside the pylon, blocks from the mysterious time right after Amenhotep III's reign.

The Amarna Talatat

The blocks found at Karnak Temple became known as "talatat," from the Arabic word *talata* meaning "three," because the blocks measured three handspans wide. These newly found blocks were decorated with the cartouches (oval shapes encircling royal names) of Amenhotep IV. They were from an entrance gate at Karnak built by Amenhotep III just before he died and completed by Amenhotep IV after his father's death. A picture began to emerge: Amenhotep IV ruled for a time with his father, and when the old king died, it looked as though his son completed his father's pylon in the usual Egyptian style.

As more talatat were uncovered it was noted that they were actually decorated in two different styles. Some were traditional, others came from a temple built by Amenhotep IV and on these the art changed. He and his wife and children are shown as grotesque and deformed. There were scenes of the pharaoh worshipping the solar disk, its long rays terminating in hands holding an ankh, the symbol of life, extending toward the pharaoh. Such scenes had never been seen before. The excavators realized that Amenhotep IV had built a temple to the sun disk, the Aten, in Karnak Temple, which was ancient Egypt's equivalent of the Vatican. A previously obscure god was being thrust into prominence inside the national church. As more and more blocks were discovered, it became clear that this was more than a new style of art; it was a full-blown religious revolution. On many blocks the faces of the king and queen had been hacked out, the hands at the ends of the Aten sun disk had been slashed. Amenhotep IV may have started a new religion, but clearly at some point it was rejected.

The Reconstruction of the Talatat

Over the years, more than 40,000 blocks were found and kept in large storehouses for the day when sense could be made of them. Far too many blocks were missing to reconstruct the temples from which they came, but in 1965 Ray Winfield Smith, an American businessman, conceived of a plan to re-create on paper what couldn't be put together in stone.[9]

His idea was to photograph every single talatat—not just those in Egypt, but even blocks that had over the years found their way into museums and private collections around the world. Every block was photographed on the same scale, creating pieces for a giant jigsaw puzzle. Then, with the aid of a computer, the temples could be reconstructed on paper.

A detailed description of each block listing all significant features was entered into the computer. If a piece had the head of a pharaoh that was broken off at the neck, that was recorded so the computer could search through the thousands of talatat for the blocks that had the body of a king beginning at mid-neck. When the computer found blocks that were possible joins, the photos were located and fitted together to see if there was a match. As the six-year project continued, it became clear that the talatat came from not one but several different temples built by Amenhotep IV during the early years of his reign.

Chevrier also found colossal statues of Amenhotep IV that once stood in front of his temple called *Gem-Pa-Aten—"The Aten is Found."* One of the statues, sculpted in the nude, shows the king almost as a hermaphrodite with wide hips and breasts but no genitalia. One can only wonder what the people of Thebes thought of these statues of their king. There is not a single contemporary account of how the man in the street felt about his new pharaoh.

Probably there was general acceptance in the beginning; after all, the new king buried his father, the revered Amenhotep III, completed his father's gateway at Karnak, and then began building his own temple, just as expected. Perhaps even the unusual representations of the royal family were quietly endured, but there must have been murmuring in the street when the bizarre statues of the king were matched by even stranger representations of Amenhotep IV inside the temple.

The main decoration of the temple was a depiction of the *Sed* festival, traditionally celebrated when a pharaoh had ruled for thirty years.[10] Amenhotep IV celebrated his *Sed* festival only four years or so after he became pharaoh. During a traditional *Sed* festival, just as Narmer had done centuries before, the pharaoh wore the white crown of Upper Egypt and the red crown of Lower Egypt to assert his dominion over the Two Lands. He would demonstrate his strength and vigor by running a racecourse and shooting arrows. Then the king would visit the shrines that housed the statues of the gods from different localities that had been assembled for the festival. But Amenhotep's was no ordinary *Sed* festival. There were no statues of Amun, Osiris, Ptah, Isis, and the other gods. All the shrines held statues of Amenhotep IV. All the familiar gods of Egypt had been banished in one broad sweep!

Now a young man in his early twenties, Amenhotep IV married Nefertiti. Little is known about her background before the marriage, but her looks alone made her a remarkable woman. Nefertiti was the king's great wife and the queen who would be remembered into the twenty-first century both as an icon for femininity and beauty and as a symbol of Egypt. Nefertiti's reputation as a great beauty is based primarily on a single statue, the famous "Nefertiti Bust," now in a Berlin museum. Her regular features, long graceful neck, and wide-set eyes are classic. I suspect that it is an accurate likeness of the Queen.

But this is not the way the queen was shown on Akhenaten's new temples at Karnak. Nefertiti, Akhenaten, and their two daughters all appear to be deformed with wide hips and elongated heads. Most peculiar of all was Akhenaten himself, shown with an elongated jaw, thin neck, spindly arms, fullness of breasts, sagging abdomen, and bulging thighs; the people of Egypt had never seen anything like this—neither had the Egyptologists.

In the fifth year of his reign Amenhotep IV changed his name to Akhenaten, "it is beneficial to Aten," which is the name the world knows him by today. We will talk about the importance of his name change later in the chapter. Akhenaten (Amenhotep IV) is the most discussed pharaoh in Egyptology and the discussion invariably turns to what he looked like. Some investigators believe he may actually have been normal, that the physical distortions were merely an artistic convention portraying the pharaoh as both male and female—he was everything. Others are convinced that he was grossly deformed and that it became an artistic convention to portray the members of the royal family with the same deformities as the king, something like the situation in seventeenth-century Spain, when the king of Castile lisped and all the courtiers affected a lisp.

Early investigators looking for the cause of the deformity offered a medical diagnosis. It was suggested that Akhenaten suffered from Froelich's syndrome, a malfunction of the pituitary gland that causes symptoms matching the unusual physical features in the Akhenaten portrayals. But the entire royal family was shown with the same unusual physical shapes. All the princesses are depicted with elongated heads, and Nefertiti is often indistinguishable from Akhenaten. Could every member of the royal family have been afflicted with Froelich's syndrome? Surely not.

One problem with the Froelich's syndrome explanation is that it always causes undeveloped genitalia and sterility in males. Akhenaten and Nefertiti eventually had six daughters. The symptoms of Froelich's syndrome so clearly match Akhenaten's appearance, however, that some Egyptologists believe Akhenaten did not father the six daughters. Yet, if the six princesses are not Akhenaten's children, why do they have his unusual physical characteristics?

I have always been convinced that there was something physically wrong with Akhenaten, but that it wasn't Froelich's syndrome, because there are all these children. Recently, a suggestion has been put forward that seems far more likely—Marfan's syndrome. This illness was first diagnosed in 1896 by Antoine Marfan, a French pediatrician who was examining a five-year-old girl with long thin fingers and toes, and a curved spine. As the symptoms were recognized by other physicians it was noted that they were often accompanied by eye problems, elongated faces, and deformed rib cages. Because the various symptoms tend to accompany one another, they constitute a "syndrome." Many of the features of Marfan's syndrome can be seen in Akhenaten and members of the royal family. For example, the thin slanted eyes in the colossal statues of Akhenaten (fig. 1) could easily be the result of Marfan's syndrome. About half of those suffering from Marfan's have the lenses of their eyes dislocated—off-center—which gives an unusual appearance.[11]

Akhenaten and the entire royal family are shown with extremely long fingers and toes, spindly arms, narrow chests—the precise symptoms of Marfan's syndrome. But could they all have had the same condition? Was it contagious?

Although the syndrome was identified in the nineteenth century it wasn't until the middle of this century that the cause was understood to be genetic. The condition results from a mutant gene that controls the development of the body's connective tissue. All the symptoms associated with Marfan's syndrome are caused by defective fibrillin, a protein responsible for holding our muscles and bones together.[12] Although not contagious, Marfan's syndrome is passed on genetically. Our bodies have between fifty thousand and one hundred thousand different genes, the basic unit of heredity. Genes usually come in pairs, one from each parent, and they are the cause of Marfan's syndrome. If the DNA in your body mutates in the gene that controls fibrillin, you will be the first in your family to have the syndrome. You can also inherit it from a parent who has the gene.

Of the many statues of Akhenaten's parents, Amenhotep III and Queen Tiye, not one shows any sign of Marfan's syndrome. Akhenaten was apparently the first person in his family to exhibit any of the characteristic features of Marfan's syndrome, so his condition was probably the result of a mutant gene. About 25 percent of Marfan's sufferers acquire the syndrome by a gene mutation.

The trait is dominant, which means that only one parent need be afflicted for the children to inherit the defective gene. Each child of a Marfan parent has a 50 percent chance of inheriting the Marfan gene. Thus, the six daughters of Akhenaten each had a 50 percent chance of having the Marfan gene passed on to them. This may explain the appearance of the Amarna princesses, long fingers (the medical term is *arachnodactyly*—"spider fingers"), and thin spindly arms and legs. Some of the daughters may have inherited the gene, and this could explain the curious depiction of the royal family.

If Akhenaten did, indeed, suffer from Marfan's syndrome, it still leaves the question: why did he permit the court sculptors to show his physical characteristics? For more than a thousand years pharaohs had been portrayed as young, well muscled, and perfect, no matter what they looked like. Akhenaten could have stayed with the traditional art style and been portrayed slim and well muscled like his ancestors before him. He chose not to and the entire royal family followed suit. Why?

I think the answer is a psychological one. But how do you confirm a psychological theory about someone who has been dead for 3,000 years? I thought that if I talked to people with Marfan's syndrome I might see how it affected their lives. How did they feel growing up different? Did they feel left out? Were they shunned? A geneticist colleague[13] working on Marfan's syndrome suggested I talk to a New York chapter of people with the syndrome. I called the organizer of the group, Julie Kurnitz, to see if I could attend their meeting and try out my theory on them. I would give a brief slide lecture about Akhenaten and ask for the group's reactions.

Most of the people who attended the meeting were women, many would blend in with any crowd; their physical characteristics were not extreme. But some could have been sisters of Akhenaten. Julie has classic Marfan features; she is tall with an elongated chin, narrow eyes, long thin arms, fingers, and toes, unusual features but not freakish. If anything, Julie is a handsome woman. Even before talking with the group, I revised my view of Akhenaten: he wasn't a freak. You can look different without looking freakish. None of the women in the group had physical features that were shocking.

Julie introduced me to the group and I began talking about Akhenaten and showing slides. After the second slide, I began to hear a lot of "Yups," and "Wows." As I continued with slides of the elongated hands and feet of the royal family, there were even more exclamations—"Marfan toes!" They had found a kinsman from ancient Egypt. After my talk I asked if any of the women had been treated differently when they were growing up, felt left out, had been shunned. And if so, how they had reacted. One woman said as a child she was always told to stand in the back to hide her long hands when a family photo was taken. Another young woman with close-cut hair and wire-rimmed glasses told a similar story and then provided the insight I was looking for. She said she rebelled and did everything she could to accentuate her appearance, wore capes and strange clothing and bizarre makeup. Who knows what she would have done had she been king of Egypt. The group understood

Akhenaten, it seemed perfectly reasonable for him to have colossal statues, to validate himself, to assert himself. It would have been a great catharsis after having been shunned and ignored for so long.

They were a group of wonderfully open people eager to share their experiences. When it became obvious that I was an Akhenaten fan, they removed their shoes and compared their feet with the pictures I had of the king's feet. Julie tried to extend her extremely long fingers into the position of the Amarna hands with the fingertips turning slightly upward. It was a very touching experience to meet with this group and at the end they asked for copies of the slides I had shown. Akhenaten will become a poster boy for the Marfan Association in their effort to reach out to others with the disorder. He never knew what made him different.

The Move to Akhetaten—Amarna

If Akhenaten was reacting to his lonely childhood, he went at it full steam. He placed a proclamation on the temple wall declaring his rejection of the gods of Egypt, saying that the old gods ceased to exist, and that a single new god had been embraced. In the early stages of the change, the new god took the form of the traditional sun god, Re-Horakty—"Re the Horizon Horus," appearing as a falcon-headed man wearing a royal kilt. This version first appeared on the southern gate at Karnak, which was completed by Akhenaten. But the "Re-Horakty" form of the god did not last long. In the third year of Akhenaten's reign the falcon-headed god was replaced by a disk, the Aten. The sun disk was an ancient symbol in Egypt—the word "aten" means "disk"—which first appeared a thousand years earlier during the Old Kingdom. The sun god is a central theme in Egyptian religion. The word for sun was "re," which was the same as the word for sun god, although they were not written the same way in hieroglyphs. The role of the sun god changed over the centuries, rising and ebbing in importance. Re was the patron deity of the northern city Heliopolis—literally "sun city." Although Amun, Mut, and Khonsu were the patron gods of Thebes, interest in the sun cult was growing. Amenhotep III, for example, was called "the Sun King." Still, the Aten, an aspect of the sun, was a minor god. But Akhenaten changed that. Inscriptions found on the Karnak blocks showed that in the fifth year of his reign Amenhotep IV changed his name to Akhenaten, "it is beneficial to Aten."

Names held a special significance in ancient Egypt. Often Egyptian children were given two names at birth—one known only to the mother, another for public use. The "real" name was the one only the mother knew, so if someone attempted a magical spell using the commonly known name it wouldn't work. Isis, the goddess of magic, was called "She who knows all the names"—no one was beyond her magic. Akhenaten's name change was not just the whim of an adolescent, it was a statement about things to come.

At about the same time he changed his name, Akhenaten announced that he would move his capital from Thebes to a remote site in Middle Egypt. It was here in an isolated city that Tutankhamen would be born. Akhenaten's revolution had evolved over a period of four or five years, what seems like an instant in Egyptian history, but there was plenty of time for tensions to develop. The strange depictions of the king and his family hurt no one; even the elevation of the new god Aten to a place of prominence at Thebes might have been acceptable to some, but when Akhenaten declared the Aten the sole god of Egypt, the battle lines were drawn. It meant that no longer would royal donations of gold, linen, wine, grain, cattle, captives, and land enrich the temples of Amun, Mut, Khonsu, and all the other gods up and down the Nile. Akhenaten was a god against the gods.

If the priesthood of Amun had been weak and unsupported, the temples would have closed, perhaps eventually to be replaced by priests of the new religion. But the powerful priesthood at Thebes had its own lands, its own revenues, and didn't require Akhenaten's patronage for survival. The priests must have been furious. The pharaoh had decreed their gods were false, had withdrawn support of the temples, and was abandoning them. The tension between Akhenaten's court and the tens of thousands of priests must have been incredible. The release valve was Akhenaten's decision to leave Thebes. But who would stay, and who would accompany him?

What must it have been like at Thebes at the time of the big move? The older people probably clung to their gods and said, "Let him go . . ." Thebes was prosperous, life was good for the upper classes who had no desire to leave the comforts of their homes. Officials like Ramose, the mayor of Thebes, stayed behind. His dilemma is reflected on the walls of his tomb in the Valley of the Nobles near Thebes. Ramose had completed two walls of his tomb, showing him with his beautiful wife and family in the traditional art style. Everyone wears his finest garments, every curl of his wig is in place, everyone is perfect— just the way he wanted to be for eternity. Then Akhenaten changed the style of art. Caught in the middle and desperate to be politically correct, Ramose completed his tomb decoration in the new style, featuring Akhenaten with his misshapen body preaching to his followers, and showing Akhenaten and Nefertiti in their "Window of Appearances" giving an audience. Ramose was also careful to show himself wearing gold collars—his reward for switching to the new god—or was it a bribe for seeming to do so? Ramose died before his tomb was completed. The funeral procession that buried him was quickly painted on the wall. Ramose had one foot in the old religion and one in the new. I wonder what he thought would happen to him in the next world?

This was the first religious revolution in recorded history and it must have been an exhilarating time for the followers of the Aten. There may have been some who had been wronged by the priests, who were unhappy with their lives, or who simply wanted to be part of the great adventure. When I think about Akhenaten's move to Amarna, I am reminded of the communes of the 1960s. Their members were rarely the overachievers of society, they were often the ones who hadn't quite found their niche. Unhappy with society, they were "dropping out," hoping to make a better life. What's amazing about Akhenaten's "cult" is that its leader was the king of Egypt. They were all dropping out with the pharaoh!

So when Akhenaten left Thebes to start his utopian community, I don't think many of the Theban establishment followed him. They would have had to give up too much. The names of the nobles of Amarna are not ones known at Thebes. The boats full of people that traveled to Amarna must have been like the pilgrims who came to America. They were not aristocracy, they were simple people hoping to better their lives. Hundreds of craftsmen were need to build an entire city; they were probably offered incentives to follow the king on his holy quest.

There are no records of what the trip was like. Boat travel was usually reserved for the upper classes, the poor rode donkeys. But since the pharaoh was their leader, perhaps everyone went by boat. Sailing north with the Nile current, the one-hundred-fifty-mile trip would have taken a week, and the convoy of boats must have been buzzing with excitement about their wonderful new city presided over by a single god. There must have been a joyous feeling of optimism. Life will be good. We can do anything, the pharaoh is our leader.

4

Amarna—The Holy City

I am your son who serves you, who exalts your name;
Your power, your strength, are in my heart.
You are the living Aten whose image endures.

—*Akhenaten*
circa 1340 B.C.

W hen Akhenaten and his pilgrims landed at the site of their new city, they were met only by barren desert. The modern name for the site is Tell el Amarna, Amarna for short, named for the bedouin tribe inhabiting the site when excavators arrived centuries later. No one lived there when Akhenaten selected this spot for a new capital. He had chosen virgin territory, unsullied by shrines and temples for other gods, like Joseph Smith leading the Mormons into the unknown Utah desert. Probably a few thousand hearty people made the initial exodus, setting up tents and temporary shelters to watch a city rise before their eyes. The logistics of organizing and feeding them must have been complex. The tent city would have been coordinated like a military camp, with a quartermaster in charge of supplies. Crops could not be planted immediately, for there were no fields or irrigation canals; fortunately, plenty of fish and birds were available. First, they must have built a brewery and bakery to produce the two staples of the Egyptian diet. They would have been positioned next to each other because both depended on the same vital ingredient—yeast.

The workmen were the real heroes of the new city. While the stone masons freed blocks from quarries with bronze chisels and wooden mallets, brickmen formed the millions of bricks needed to build an entire city. Brickmaking was a simple matter. Nile ooze was placed in a rectangular wooden mold; the mold could then be removed to leave the future brick to dry in the burning Egyptian sun. Artists and craftsmen worked frantically to decorate the new houses and government buildings as courses of bricks rose higher and higher. Probably they sent word back to their friends in Thebes to come and join them, for there was plenty of work. There was no time to waste. Brightly colored ceramic tiles and inlays in the shapes of rosettes and flowers needed firing in pottery kilns to lend accents to painted murals on the walls.

The two essential building materials in ancient Egypt were readily available at Amarna: stone and Nile mud. Temples in ancient Egypt were built of stone blocks because they had to last for eternity. Houses, however, even the royal palaces, were built with a core of mud brick plastered then painted over. There must have been a constant haze over the city from the dust and sand stirred up by all the construction as the stone blocks were cut and dragged from the quarries to the temple sites. Living on a construction site, however, must have fascinated the city's children as they watched in awe as a new temple materialized. When the walls reached six feet or so, mud brick ramps had to be added so blocks could be hauled on sleds to the top. Five or six major buildings went up simultaneously, providing continuous excitement. In the early days at Amarna, every child probably dreamed of growing up to be an architect. It is curious that with all the building activity in Amarna and in the rest of Egypt, not a single architectural papyrus has ever been discovered. There is no written record that tells us how to build a pyramid, design a temple or, even, build a wall. It may be that they once existed and have all perished, but I don't think so. I suspect that such information was a trade secret, passed down from father architect to son. We have plenty of literary and religious papyri, but not one on any of the trades.

The plan of the city was dictated by the geography formed by the Nile on the west and by abrupt cliffs on the east. Space for the main city lay between these borders, a crescent about three miles wide by eight miles long. A "Royal Road" ran north and south, splitting the length of town. At more than 125 feet wide, it composed perhaps the greatest thoroughfare in the ancient world. Designed originally for grand chariot processions of the royal family, it came to serve as a commuter road along which administrators rode on donkeys from homes in the suburbs to their central city offices.

Running from east to west, two dried river beds, on which nothing was built for fear of flash floods, divided the city into three sections: the central city and the north and the south suburbs. The complete city sprawled—seventeen miles north to south—including suburbs at each end, each with bright new workshops, temples, and homes. Beyond the northern suburb a village was set aside for the workmen, crammed with tiny houses. The estates of the rich and famous of Amarna were mansions that followed similar designs. A large entrance hall supported by slender wooden columns brightly painted with lotus motifs led into a large living room dominated by four massive columns. Bedrooms, bathrooms, and guest rooms ran off from this communal room. Behind the main house were servants' quarters, granaries, storerooms, kitchens and stables. All these grand houses were built quickly at the same time—an ancient, upper-class housing development.

The central city, called "Island Exalted in Jubilees," was the administrative heart of the new capital. Here the foreign office filed correspondence between Akhenaten and the rulers of Asia in a building known as the "Place of Pharaoh's Dispatches." Also, Akhenaten stored all the old correspondence from his father's reign: letters and trade agreements between Amenhotep III and his foreign emissaries. Someone had thought to bring the files with him when they moved. Near the Records Bureau was the police station with dormitories, training grounds, and stables for the police cars of the day—chariots. Even in a theocratic city there would be thieves to apprehend, marital spats to resolve and, as soon as they were constructed, tombs containing great wealth to protect. Nearby was the university, known as the "Per-ankh," "house of life," where future priests were educated. But a new curriculum was taught, most likely designed by Akhenaten himself. Young priests in training were no longer called upon to recite the myth of Isis and Osiris or chant the "Hymn to Re" until they were committed to memory, since all these gods had ceased to exist. A new liturgy of prayers and hymns had been written by Akhenaten, who, it seems, not only provided the revelations for the new religion, he composed its hymnal.

What an exciting time it was for the initiates of the Aten. This was radical theology. No country had ever reduced its pantheon to a single, all-powerful deity. Here was a heady, powerful concept whose details would have to be developed. With their leader, the pharaoh, they expected to do so, then they would change the world. The students were supervised by Meri-Re, the high priest of the Aten. Since his name means "Beloved of Re," perhaps he was a minor priest from Thebes who had switched his allegiance to Akhenaten's new theology early on and accompanied him to Amarna in the first wave of pilgrims.

Dominating the central city was the royal residence, perhaps the largest in the ancient world at this date. It was a huge, rambling, elaborate maze of audience halls, open courts, private apartments, nurseries, kitchens, and huge storage rooms. Fronted by three terraced gardens of exotic plants, the palace faced the Nile to benefit from its cool breezes. Most unusually, the compound straddled the main road, with an overpass—an innovation in architecture—joining the east to the west wings. This overpass became the most notable feature of the palace and of the city. It was called the "Window of Appearances," for it was here that Akhenaten and Nefertiti made an appearance, often accompanied by the princesses, to give audience to assembled dignitaries in the road below.[1] From this window, too, they handed out collars of massive rings of gold as rewards to the faithful. Religion has its own strong attractions, but a few ounces of gold must have amplified those attractions considerably.

A private temple, "Castle of the Aten," near the palace provided a sanctuary where the royal family worshipped privately and were rejuvenated by the Aten's rays. For ordinary citizens a great swathe of a city temple soon rose to challenge even the unparalleled Karnak in area. Measuring almost two hundred yards in length by fifty wide, nothing like it had ever been seen. Egyptian temples were, for the most part, dark mysterious places, roofed over by stone slabs that left only small slits cut in the stone to admit shafts of light into a murky interior. Traditional temples mirrored our railroad flats—one section simply led into the next in line. First came an open court, a large area where the common people could pay their respects to the gods. A ramp at the back of the open court led to a second, more secluded, court covered with a roof. This second chamber was reserved for the nobility. As you moved deeper into the temple, rooms became smaller and more intimate as the floor rose and the roof lowered, creating the atmosphere of a special sacred space. The third section, the "holy of holies," was the precinct of the priests alone who attended the gods. Oracles resided in the "holy of holies," cult statues used for forecasting the future and obtaining divine guidance. Normally, they remained in their shrines of stone, though on special festival days they were carried around the town in portable shrines of gilded wood that resembled the sacred barks of the pharaoh.

Akhenaten swept all this aside in designing his new cathedrals. Since there were no statues of the Aten, and all the old gods had been banished with their idols, there was no need for a "holy of holies." Because the solar disk was the object of all the worship, darkened passageways and even a roof would be entirely out of place. The new temple of the Aten was designed to be an open-air affair, full of light and sun. Essentially, it consisted of a rectangular perimeter wall that defined an open court two football fields in size. Inside was nothing but the sweep of space and rows of offering stands, one for each day of the year, at which the Aten received daily food offerings. Akhenaten's other temples varied only slightly from this design. Some were smaller, more like a kiosk, but all were light, airy, and open to the sky. I think of Akhenaten and his followers as like California sun worshippers, every one with a perpetual tan.

The new temples, however, did retain one architectural feature of Theban temples, probably because it was too dramatic to omit. Massive entrance pylons, like those found at Karnak and Luxor temples, separated the outer precincts from the inner temple. Poles mounted on the pylon's face flew long streamers fluttering in the breeze to symbolize the breath of life.

All this knowledge of Amarna comes from a series of extraordinary excavators who were intrigued by the enigmas of the lost city. John Gardiner Wilkinson, one of the first British Egyptologists, the son of a minister, attended Oxford but left, before obtaining his degree, for a career in the army. While stationed in Italy, Wilkinson learned of the attempts of Egyptologists to decipher hieroglyphs. Excited, he headed straight for Egypt where he remained for twelve years. Like all the pioneers of Egyptology, Wilkinson was self-taught, but his brief military experience prepared him for the spartan regime that was to become his life. After taking up residence in Thebes, Wilkinson first cataloged the tombs in the Valley of the Kings. It was a simple matter. With a can of paint in one hand and a brush in the other, he numbered each one. His numbers remain to this today.

Wilkinson traveled to Amarna in 1824. He found the remains of temples, palaces, tombs, houses, and broad thoroughfares, everything you would expect in an ancient city, but something was askew. The art—the wall paintings, carvings, and sculpture—differed from anything he had ever seen in Egypt. Like their images on the blocks that were found a century later at Karnak, the king and queen were portrayed as deformed. The king had wide hips and obvious breasts, an almost feminine figure. The body of the queen had equally wide hips and obvious breasts, though this was not notable for a woman. However, her neck was impossibly long and her arms were thin and spindly. Pictures of the princesses showed elongations at the backs of their heads. Accompanying these figures was a solar disk with its rays shining down upon the royal family, each ray terminating in a hand that held either an ankh, the symbol of life, or a scepter, the symbol of power. Who were these peculiar people? Wilkinson could not tell; their names had been erased.

Wilkinson couldn't decipher the hieroglyphs on the boundary markers that defined the limits of the city, but he was the first to observe what would later provide a crucial clue to Amarna's fate. The city hadn't merely been abandoned; it had been taken apart.[2] The palaces, temples, and houses had been razed to ground level, so that practically all that remained were their foundations and random blocks of stone. Only the tombs were intact, because they had been cut into mountains and couldn't be dismantled. The decorations on their walls would later provide further clues to the cataclysm at Amarna. Decades of speculation followed, but the first formal excavation of the site didn't take place until half a century later.

The French Archaeological Mission began excavating at Amarna in 1883 to attempt to solve the riddles of the family of royal misfits, their curious art, and the destruction of their city. Something unprecedented had happened here. The site was different from any previously investigated. Most excavations focused on single buildings, like Luxor Temple, or building complexes, like Karnak, but this was an entire city, although not much of it was left. All the French could see were mounds in the sand stretching for miles. It was not clear where they should begin. Because the city had been intentionally dismantled, this was a challenging excavation and there was little hope of finding treasures to bring home.

Nevertheless, the excavation proceeded, clearing the foundations of palaces, temples, and houses from sand. They discovered the suburbs and the wide road running through the city. In the east, where cliffs rose suddenly from the plain, they examined the rock cut tombs—one group to the north and one to the south. These were the tombs of the nobility and high officials of the city. In each, the unusual-looking king and queen and the sun disk were carved on almost every wall. The French were slow to publish their findings, so in 1890 Flinders Petrie, a young British archaeologist eager for answers to the questions raised by this unique site, began his own excavation.

In an era filled with colorful, adventurous Egyptologists, Petrie outdid them all. With a long white beard and ragged clothes, he looked like Charlton Heston's Moses from a Cecil B. DeMille production. Petrie thought nothing of walking sixteen miles to town to pick up the weekly wages for his crew, then walking back to camp.

Even in the early days of excavation there was a brisk market for antiquities. One of the problems on all early excavations was theft by the workmen of small objects found as they were digging. If a workman uncovered a fragment of jewelry and hid it in his robes, he could sell it for more than a month's wages. Petrie instituted a system of paying his workers a fair price for the objects they unearthed, when they turned them in, so he was the only excavator who got a fairly complete picture of finds from his site. Still, thievery from the outside remained a problem. Disreputable characters would lurk on the fringes of an excavation to see what they might pilfer under cover of the night. This didn't faze Petrie, who recorded his encounter with a thief:

> One man Quibell held down while I walloped him. He swore
> that he would go to the Consul; that I had broken his leg; I let
> him crawl off on hands and knees some way, and then, giving a
> great shout, ran at him, when he made off like a hare."[3]

These were the wild west days of Egyptology.

Petrie became intrigued by the new art style. For a thousand years the king of Egypt had been depicted as young and vigorous, well muscled, ready to stride into battle. The pharaoh always was victorious. But at Amarna there were no battle scenes, no pharaoh smiting the traditional enemies of Egypt. Even more surprising, there were no scenes of pharaoh making offerings to the gods, indeed, no recognizable gods at all. Instead, Petrie found scenes of the pharaoh and his family in which the king affectionately cradled his children on his lap, tender scenes of the pharaoh kissing a daughter or his wife, and scenes of the pharaoh and his queen worshipping the sun rather than any recognizable Egyptian god. Nothing like these pictures had ever before appeared in 2,000 years of Egyptian art.

This was an incredible departure from centuries of traditional Egyptian art in which not only the subject matter, but even the proportions of the figures and their relative sizes were carefully regulated. When artists began decorating a tomb or temple, the first thing they did was draw a red grid on the wall to guide proportions—two squares for the head, four squares for the shoulders, etc. They almost reduced wall decoration to paint-by-numbers. When it came to Akhenaten, all the old rules of proportion went out the window. The queen often stood just as tall as the pharaoh, his children were drawn in the same scale, even commoners seemed little shorter than their king. Petrie found Amarna art completely absorbing, an artistic breath of fresh air.

The more that was revealed about the mystery family as the excavation continued, the more Petrie became enamored. It seemed as if this pharaoh—whose name was eventually revealed to be Akhenaten—was a religious visionary! After centuries of worshipping a multitude of deities, the pharaoh banished all the others in favor of one god—the solar disk, the Aten. He had introduced monotheism to Egypt. "Living in Truth," the motto adapted by Akhenaten, seemed to Petrie to be the crux of the revolution. Akhenaten must have had a physical deformity, but in keeping with his motto, he permitted, or perhaps insisted, that he be portrayed realistically. The idea carried over to choices of subject, hence the intimate family scenes.

All in all, the art was lovely. In 1891 Petrie unearthed beautifully painted floors in what had once been the palace. Birds flying over marshes with animals cavorting below still glowed in their original, vibrant colors. Petrie copied 250 square feet of floor paintings himself for eventual publication. The floor was so spectacular that Petrie built a wooden walkway for visitors, so they could amble around the paintings without causing damage to them. Concerned that local carpenters might scratch the floors by dragging their materials across them, Petrie performed all the carpentry himself. For years after Petrie closed his excavations, tourists continued to flock to the wonderful paintings. Unfortunately, as there was no pathway from the river, visitors often cut across a farmer's fields and damaged his crops. One night the farmer hacked the pavements to bits.

Petrie was a religious man who saw the beginnings of his own faith in Akhenaten's monotheism. Like many early Egyptologists of similar background, he came to Egypt because it was a part of the Holy Land, the place of the Exodus, to find confirmation for the Bible. Still, aside from the religious aspect, Petrie was not far from the truth. Akhenaten is the first individual whose abstract ideas had a profound effect on his society; the first man in recorded history to speak of a single god. As Petrie put it:

> No king of Egypt, nor of any other part of the world, has ever carried out his honesty of expression so openly. Thus in every line Akhenaten stands out as perhaps the most original thinker that ever lived in Egypt, and one of the greatest idealists of the world. No man appears to have made a greater stride to a new standpoint than he did . . .[4]

Petrie had no formal training in translating hieroglyphs so he couldn't completely understand the inscribed material he found; nonetheless he realized how important the boundary markers for the city were, and hoped to make some sense of their inscriptions. Assigning a letter to each stela, he began assiduously copying their inscriptions, including one of the most inaccessible stelae that required viewing through a telescope![5] When his drawings were later translated by others, the fourteen standing stones Akhenaten had erected to define the area of his new city were told an amazing story.

The stelae, all carved within a four-year period, presented two versions of the same declaration. Akhenaten claimed that the Aten, himself, had led him to the site, and commanded him to build upon the spot where the Aten first manifested himself, where the world had come into existence. The pharaoh had been directed through a mystical vision to build a new city in the wilderness. He named the city Akhetaten—Horizon of the Aten. He assured any reader of the stela that

> His majesty appeared in his great chariot of electrum, like the Aten when he rises in his city horizon . . . Now, it is the Aten, my father, who advised me concerning it, Akhetaten. No official ever advised me concerning it; or people who are in the entire land ever advised me concerning . . . making Akhetaten in this deserted place.[6]

Perhaps, looking across the horizon, Akhenaten saw a line of cliffs broken only by a wadi (valley) and realized the landscape formed the shape of the hieroglyph for horizon $\bigcirc$. Perhaps this was his sign from the Aten. When I was staying at Amarna a few years ago, I rose early one day and looked out my window to see the sun rising in a notch in the cliffs across the Nile, just like the hieroglyph. I could not help but think, "Akhenaten really did see it."

After describing the buildings he would construct for "his father," the Aten, the stelae closes with a remarkable pledge:

> As for the southern landmark which is upon the eastern mountains of Akhetaten . . . I shall not pass beyond it toward the south, forever and ever . . . As for the middle landmark which is upon the eastern mountains of Akhetaten . . . I shall not pass beyond it toward the east forever and ever . . .[7]

Akhenaten vowed never to leave the city. I wonder if anyone at the time realized the effect that the pharaoh's pledge would have on Egypt. If the king remained in the city forever, he could not fulfill the traditional roles of a pharaoh. He could not lead the army against the enemies of Egypt, nor attend to any matter of state that required him to travel outside of this one city. This meant that the management of the country had passed from the king to civilian functionaries. Resignation of royal power left the more ambitious members of the court scrambling to pick up the pieces. Nor would Akhenaten have the opportunity to connect with the offended, yet still powerful, priests in Thebes and Memphis. The king had taken a throne that provided absolute power, then made the decision to abrogate all responsibility! Akhenaten wasn't just changing the religion, he was changing the role of the king. In tradition-bound Egypt, this was a revolution as stunning as his banishment of the old religion. It seems that Akhenaten's idea of kingship was to shepherd his people in their spiritual lives only.

One day Akhenaten gathered his followers in a worship service at the site of one of the boundary stelae and spoke to those assembled in a sort of "Sermon on the Mount":

> To the great and living Aten . . . ordaining life, vigorously alive, my Father . . . my wall of millions of cubits, my reminder of Eternity, my witness to what is eternal, who proclaims Himself with his two hands, whom no craftsman had devised, who is established in the rising and setting each day ceaselessly . . . He fills the land with His rays and makes everyone to live . . .[8]

This declaration contains an important phrase—"whom no craftsman had devised." The implication is subtle but clear: the Aten, the true god, is intangible and abstract. This announcement signaled the end of all cult statues—mythology and symbolism were gone. No longer would craftsmen sculpt figures of the gods. No longer would there be a familiar image for the faithful to focus on, no more "Books of the Dead" with their vignettes of the denizens of the journey to the netherworld. The new god was as elusive as the sun's rays.

The shift from visual gods to an abstract concept was perhaps the most fundamental change that Akhenaten instituted. Ancient Egyptians were advanced and sophisticated in many areas, but they were not abstract thinkers. They left no philosophical writings, such as would come from the Greeks a thousand years later. Egyptian mathematics was the best in the ancient world, but it was not abstract. They developed some geometry because they needed to resurvey farm boundary lines that were swept away each year when the Nile flooded the fields, but they did not inquire about the nature of space. All their thoughts were directed to specific, concrete needs. Akhenaten, it seems, thought in ways completely new to the Egyptians. When he moved his followers to Amarna, he carried them on a greater mental journey than any of them could imagine.

AKHENATEN THE DREAMER

The fullest explanation of the theology of the new religion comes from a hymn carved on the walls of several tombs at Amarna. The most elaborate version is incorporated in the west wall of the tomb of Aye, a favorite courtier of Akhenaten. All indications are that Akhenaten himself composed it. Although written centuries before the Old Testament, it has a similar tone. In fact, scholars find resemblances to Psalm 104.

Splendid you rise in heaven's lightland,
O living Aten, creator of life!
When you have dawned in eastern lightland,
You fill every land with your beauty.
Your are beauteous, great, radiant,
High over every land;
Your rays embrace the lands,
To the limit of all that you made.
Reign Re, you reach their limits,
You bend them (for) the sons whom you love;
Though you are far, your rays are on earth,
Though one sees you, your strides are unseen . . .

How many are your deeds,
Though hidden from sight,
O Sole God beside whom there is none!
You made the earth as you wished, you alone,
All peoples, herds, and flocks:

All upon earth that walk on legs,
All on high that fly on wings,
The lands of Khor and Kush,
The land of Egypt.
You set up every man in his place,
You supply their needs;
Everyone has his food,
His lifetime is counted.
Their tongues differ in speech,
Their characters likewise;
Their skins are distinct,
For you distinguished the peoples . . .

You are in my heart,
There is no other who knows you,
Only your son, Nefer-khepru-re (Akhenaten), Sole one of Re,
Whom you have taught your ways and might . . .[9]

Poetry shows Akhenaten at his best. The "Hymn to Aten" is one of the great intellectual achievements of the ancient world. By so elegantly stating the essential theological doctrine, this hymn must have been a great inspiration to his followers. Only one god—the Aten—is responsible for creation of the world and that god created the people of all nations, not just the Egyptians. Of course, if the Aten was the god of all people, then the Egyptians were no longer superior. By embracing all the people of the world, Akhenaten had undermined the justification for all of Egypt's previous military campaigns. The world no longer revolved around Egypt; it revolved around the sun.

The "Hymn to the Aten" reveals Akhenaten as a man of sensitivity, an inspired poet, while his speech on the boundary stelae shows a visionary, a mystic. The policies instituted and the changes made during his reign were so radical in their humanism and so divergent from tradition that they could only have been initiated by the pharaoh himself. From temple and tomb walls we discover a man devoted to his family.

From his city we observe the bold planning of a creative mind. From his art we discern his love of beauty, his belief in "living in truth."

Nefertiti, whose name means "the beautiful one has come," is always shown at his side making daily offerings to the Aten. They are together at every official function, affectionately holding hands in public and embracing in their chariot as they drive to the temple. The king refers to Nefertiti as "Sweet of Love" and " in the sound of whose voice the king takes delight." Each boundary stela includes a long preamble extolling the virtues of his beloved queen:

> And the Heiress, Great in the Palace, Fair of Face, Adorned with the Double Plumes, Mistress of Happiness, endowed with Favors, at hearing whose voice the King rejoices, the Chief Wife of the King, his beloved, the Lady of the Two Lands, Neferne-feruaten-Nefertiti (Good like the beauty of Aten—a Beautiful Woman Comes), May she live forever and always.[10]

Devoted to his young daughters, he is often shown holding one or more on his knee, kissing them tenderly. Akhenaten, a champion of family values, emerges from the ruins of Amarna as a man we can like, thoughtful and caring. We understand why Petrie was taken with the man.

It is tempting to look only at this side of Akhenaten, the man who preached love and peace, but there was another, darker side. Akhenaten was also an intolerant elitist. A second look at Amarna art reveals that the Aten shines only on Akhenaten and the royal family, not on the Egyptian people. The common man is never shown receiving the Aten's rays and the symbols of life and power. The Aten was Akhenaten's personal god; everyone else had to make do with secondary light reflected from Akhenaten.

An examination of the records found at Amarna show that the king was also inept and disinterested in ruling the country. The Egypt that he inherited from his father, Amenhotep III, was in its golden age, at the peak of its power. Taxes collected from her foreign territories flowed into Egypt each year, but, after Akhenaten took over, no one minded the store any longer. Revenue was only forthcoming as long as Egypt was strong with an army to enforce the collection of tribute. Akhenaten, unwilling or unable to attend to the affairs of the government, effectively turned over the administration of the country to his aides. Without a strong king at the helm, Egypt's tax revenue and lucrative trade agreements were allowed to lapse. The army received little support. While Akhenaten contemplated the Aten, the affairs of state disintegrated from neglect. He was the flower child of a wealthy man (Amenhotep III) who inherited, but ignored, the family business.

Under Akhenaten's disinterested control, Egypt's power in the Near East declined rapidly. Donald Redford, the Egyptologist who has devoted more than a quarter of a century to unearthing Akhenaten's scattered monuments, believes his findings reveal "one of the most displeasing characteristics of the way of life Akhenaten held up as a model, refined sloth."[11] As Egypt gradually lost its dominant position in the Near East, the residents of Amarna, although isolated, must have sensed that all was not well in the land. The new god, the abstract Aten, had not provided for the country and its people as well as the old gods of Egypt had. In the end, Akhenaten resorted to lavish rewards to keep the faithful true to his cause. Scenes carved on tomb walls show Akhenaten, Nefertiti, and the princesses standing at the palace's "Window of Appearances,"[12] while citizens of Amarna gather in the street below, reaching up to receive necklaces of gold handed down by the royal family. By the end of Akhenaten's reign, the distribution of gold necklaces may have been little more than a bribe to keep the people faithful.

With his control slipping, Akhenaten in a surge of fanaticism dispatched workmen throughout Egypt to chisel out the name of Amun, the Chief god of Thebes, wherever it appeared on monuments. Even the three hieroglyphs signifying "Amun" in his father's name (Amenhotep) were erased.

Akhenaten died in the seventeenth year of his reign, taking his vision of a new world with him. His body was never found; no inscription tells us what caused his death. We only know that a reign that began by preaching peace and beauty ended in a regime of intolerance.

Tutankhamen's Parents

God will attack the rebel for the sake of the temple,
He will be overcome for what he has done . . .
He will find no favor on the day of woe.

—*King Khety Nebkaure*
circa 2150 B.C.

Immediately after Akhenaten's death, messengers were dispatched to announce the news throughout the land. They traveled to Thebes in the south and Memphis in the north. Normally, such an announcement would cause the whole nation to grieve from both sadness and worry because it demonstrated Seth's triumph over Osiris, a disruption of the divine order. Akhenaten's death must have been different, eliciting a variety of emotions in different segments of society. Divine order had already been profoundly disrupted, by Pharaoh himself, during a reign marked by years and years of confusion. At least in private, there must have been great rejoicing among the priests of Amun in Thebes; their prayers had been answered, the pharaoh who chiseled out the name of their god had felt Amun's revenge. In Memphis, priests awaited the day when they could again worship Ptah, creator of the world, as they had for centuries past.

The military establishment, too, must have cheered. Nothing pained them more than to merely stand by watching Egypt's dominance ebb away. It had been decades since they made their last annual campaign to wrest tribute from the territories. First, Amenhotep III had focused all thirty-five years of his reign on building in Thebes, seeking immortality in temples rather than in the battles that tradition dictated. Thirty-five years of parades had been hard to endure, but at least the earlier drubbings of Egypt's vassal states had so cowed them that they remained loyal. It was the last fifteen years that had wrenched the army's collective heart. One by one, Egypt's foreign tributaries had fallen under the power of the hated Hittites or equally despised Mitanni, after plaintive letters from ambassadors for an Egyptian army had fallen on Pharaoh's deaf ears. The soldiers must have rejoiced more than anyone when news reached them of Akhenaten's death—now, their careers might begin again.

The citizens of Amarna would have been agitated by uncertainty and fear. What and where would their place be in a new universe? Their religion, which was the sole reason for Amarna, had been the vision of one man. With the prophet dead, who would take his place? What would become of his city and people? These questions soon would be answered, but first there was a funeral to prepare.

Traditionally, seventy days were required for mummifying a pharaoh and all the accompanying rituals, but along with everything else in his religion, Akhenaten had changed the concept of life after death. The old belief that the next world was a continuation of this one, only better, was too materialistic and worldly for the pharaoh who gave the world its first abstract god. Akhenaten believed the next life would be a shadow existence—the deceased, or at least his spirit, remained in his tomb and awoke each morning when the Aten appeared on the horizon. From broken fragments excavators found in his tomb, we know that Akhenaten was buried with ushabti statues. These traditional netherworld servants, in his case, did not hold farm implements for work in Elysian fields, they held ankhs, the sign of life.[1] We do not know what other new rituals or prayers would have honored Akhenaten's spirit, but I believe that the high priest, Meri-Re, must at least have recited the Hymn to the Aten.

Work began on Akhenaten's tomb when he first moved to Amarna, and continued until the time of his death. The desolate spot he selected for his eternal resting place lay six and one half miles from the city. The first time I traveled the forbidding landscape, I wondered, why here? The only way to reach the tomb is through a valley strewn with boulders, natural obstacles for transporting workers and supplies. Once there, though, I understood why Akhenaten had been drawn to the spot. It has the distinct feeling of the Valley of the Kings in Thebes. Similar white limestone cliffs rise above the valley floor. The plan of the tomb is like those in the Theban valley where Akhenaten saw his father, Amenhotep III, laid to rest. Perhaps Akhenaten, still suffering from childhood rejection, was seeking his father's acceptance at the end.

The royal tomb began with a twenty-five-foot-long descending passage cut into the floor of the valley. At the bottom and to the right, a level corridor led to an unfinished suite of six rooms. Ahead, the descent continued for another twenty-five feet to a second suite of rooms, also on the right. In one of these we will pick up the trail of Tutankhamen. The passage then ended in a cavernous room that contained the sarcophagus of Akhenaten. Reconstruction of the fragments found by excavators showed that Akhenaten abandoned tradition even in the design of his sarcophagus. He chose a simple granite rectangular box, whereas most of his ancestors had been buried in stone coffins shaped like cartouches, the sign of royalty. At each corner, traditionally, the figures of goddesses were carved whose outstretched arms protected the king. The goddesses were banished from Akhenaten's sarcophagus in favor of four images of his beloved Nefertiti.[2]

While the pharaoh's body was being prepared for burial (we have no records for this, so it is not known how, or even if, the bodies were mummified under the new religion), a matter even more pressing had to be settled. The country could not wait seventy days for a leader; a new pharaoh had to be crowned. There were few choices. As far as we can determine from inscriptions on the broken blocks at Amarna, Akhenaten's family was severely depleted. Nefertiti had died several years before him. Another shadowy member of the royal house who reached adulthood was a boy named Smenkare. He may have been Tutankhamen's brother, but is not mentioned as a child or shown with the other royal children, though he appears briefly as coregent with Akhenaten at the tail end of his reign. Smenkare, however, died after less than two years of sharing the throne, leaving Akhenaten alone until his death.

·Of the six daughters born to Akhenaten and Nefertiti, Ankhesenpaaten is the only one we hear of after her father's death. One other may have lived, but there is no solid evidence. Not only did infant mortality approach fifty percent of the birthrate in ancient times, but child mortality was also high. At the very least, four daughters had died; Ankhesenpaaten may well have been the only surviving member of the family with pure royal blood. The only other child with any royal blood at all was a young boy named Tutankh*aten*, who would later change the last part of his name to *-amen*. I believe he was the son of Akhenaten. Although many Egyptologists agree on this point, many do not. It is time to figure out who he was.

When Petrie began excavating the palace at Amarna, one of the first things he looked for were its rubbish mounds, a source for copious information about palace life. Royal objects—jars, dishes, lamps, cosmetic jars—were often inscribed with the owner's names, and, when broken, were discarded in the royal garbage heap. Petrie knew the value of carefully sifting through such debris, and put some of his diggers on the job. Hundreds of objects inscribed with the names of the royal family were found, including some with Tutankh*aten*'s name. It was clear to Petrie that this mysterious Tutankhaten, who at this time was a shadowy figure to Egyptologists, was in some way connected with the religious revolution at Amarna.

Fortunately, in Tutankhamen's day it was the fashion of the royal court to wear ceramic finger rings with the names of one member or another of the royal household. These bright blue ceramic rings, probably party favors, were fragile and broken easily. Among the royal trash Petrie found dozens of them with the names of Akhenaten, his queen Nefertiti, the six princesses, and Tutankhaten. It was clear that he was a member of the royal household, but who were his parents and why was he never shown with the princesses? One question may answer the other, so let's start with Tutankhamen's father.

If the temples and palaces at Amarna still stood, scenes from their walls might have supplied the missing details of Tutankhamen's parentage. There would have been thousands of blocks that once composed the great temples, all carved with inscriptions; surely they were not all smashed to dust. Where were they? Petrie seems not to have wondered about this. Years after he left Amarna, a German expedition working across the river from the ghost city of Amarna discovered that the blocks had been floated across the Nile for reuse in other temples at a later city called Hermopolis. These provided the first real clue about Tutankhamen's parents.

When the German expedition translated the Hermopolis blocks, as they later became known, they found the inscription *"King's son, of his body, his beloved, Tutankhaten."* Other objects presented Tutankh*aten*'s name in a cartouche which indicated that this Tutankh*aten*-amen was a king. The Hermopolis block established with certainty that this king was also the son of a king, but of which king?

Who Tutankhamen's parents were has been debated by Egyptologists ever since the Hermopolis block was found. Some believe he was the son of Amenhotep III and his Queen Tiye. I have never found this theory credible because of simple arithmetic. From other sources that I will talk about later, we know the year Tutankhamen died, and from a careful examination of his mummy we know he was about nineteen at the time of death. Working backwards from the time of death shows that he was born in the middle of Akhenaten's seventeen-year reign. Queen Tiye married Amenhotep, Akhenaten's father, early in his thirty-eight-year reign. Even if she were fifteen at the time, she would have been in her fifties when Tutankhamen was born, almost certainly beyond childbearing age. Also, Amenhotep and Tiye never mention a son Tutankhaten when their other sons are discussed. The records show they had six children, four girls and two boys. We know all their names. Finally, the name *Tutankhaten* is an Amarna name, associating him with the Aten, rather than with the god Amun or other traditional gods Amenhotep III named his children after.

The best candidate for Tutankhamen's father is Akhenaten himself. The problem, however, is that Tutankhamen is never shown with the rest of his family. The Amarna tomb walls show Akhenaten, Nefertiti, and six daughters, time after time—never a son. If Tutankhamen really was Akhenaten's son, why isn't he shown with the rest of the family? There are two good answers. The first is that royal princes in the Eighteenth Dynasty are rarely shown on monuments, only princesses. No one knows why. Perhaps pharaohs feared that pictures of sons would establish royal credentials for a competitor before the father was ready to give up his throne. Whatever the rationale, the omission of sons in royal family scenes, in this dynasty, in no way indicated that sons did not exist.

A second, more compelling reason, came to light in the 1960s when cosmetic vessels in both the British Museum and New York's Metropolitan Museum of Art were found to have the names and titles of a previously unknown Amarna queen named Kiya.[3] The Metropolitan's vessel had been purchased in 1920 from Howard Carter, before his discovery of Tutankhamen's tomb, during a time when he sold antiquities to make ends meet. The inscription, carved in the white stone and filled with blue pigment, gives Kiya's title: "Wife and great beloved of the King of Upper and Lower Egypt, who lives in truth, (Akhenaten) the beautiful child of the living Aten, who shall live forever, eternally, Kiya." The vase in the British Museum bears an almost identical inscription.[4] Once Egyptologists became aware that Akhenaten had a second wife, they searched for other traces of her.

Soon, blocks from the dismantled temples at Amarna were found with Kiya's name (fig. 2). Although she was not called the "King's Great Wife"—that was Nefertiti—Kiya was the king's second wife, still an important person of the court. The blocks recovered from Akhenaten's dismantled temples contain scenes of Kiya in the presence of Akhenaten, making offerings to the solar disk. Others show her worshipping the Aten in a temple built especially for her. She is never present, however, in any scene with the Great Wife, Nefertiti. They may have shared a husband, but certainly not the same prominence.[5]

Many of the blocks with scenes of Kiya came from the area of the city known as the Maru-Aten where her temple, called a sunshade, once stood. This "temple" was actually a large park enclosed with stone kiosks, probably closer to a meditation garden than a formal place of worship.[6] Kiya's sunshade was a place of beauty with a large central pool, pavements decorated with scenes of nature—marshes, water birds, plants and trees—everything that the Aten provided. The kiosk, inlaid with colored ceramics and stones, showed Kiya making daily offerings to the god.

Kiya's name ceased to appear on monuments around the ninth year of Akhenaten's reign, just about the time Tutankhamen was born, suggesting the possibility that she may have died while giving birth to the future king of Egypt. Soon after her death, her name was erased from her sunshade temple, replaced by that of the eldest Amarna princess. If Kiya were indeed Tutankhamen's mother, that would explain why the young prince did not appear in the official scenes of the royal family. Children of the king by a secondary wife occupied a lower status than children of "the Great Wife." Tutankhamen would not have been displayed with his more exalted half sisters.

All of this was merely abstract theory until some confirmation that Akhenaten was Tutankhamen's father was discovered in his isolated tomb at Amarna. From the era of the pyramids on, the tombs of the kings were rarely completed by the time of their burial. I think the idea was that it was bad luck to complete a tomb before the king died, and there generally was not enough time to finish it during the interval between death and entombment. So Akhenaten's tomb is incomplete, but wall decorations had been finished in several rooms. The scenes were like nothing ever found before in a pharaoh's tomb. Because of his religious beliefs, these were not scenes of gods welcoming pharaoh into the next world. Tradition had been replaced with intimate glimpses and tender moments from Pharaoh's private life. It had been known to Egyptologists[7] for a long time that one wall presented a touching scene of Akhenaten and Nefertiti mourning the death of their second daughter, Meketaten. The puzzle was that there are actually two such scenes in the tomb, remarkably similar, one in room Alpha and another in room Gamma. Both show a dead woman on a bed, Akhenaten and Nefertiti in attitudes of mourning, and an infant held in a nurse's arms. Most experts supposed that both recorded the death in childbirth of Meketaten. But why would there be two scenes of the same event? In the 1970s, Professor Geoffrey Martin of University College, London, in the course of making an accurate record of everything that remained on the walls of the tomb, found the confirmation that Akhenaten was Tutankhamen's father.

Martin noticed that, although the two mourning scenes are similar, only one (in room Gamma) names the dying woman as Meketaten, the daughter of Akhenaten and Nefertiti. The other scene, in room Alpha, does not identify either the mother or her infant. It could certainly be that two different women, each of whom died in childbirth, are separately mourned. In the scene with the unnamed mother in room Alpha, Akhenaten and Nefertiti lean over the mother who has just died, while behind them a woman (nurse?) holds a newborn infant. Most significant, the nurse and infant are shaded by a fan bearer, indicating a royal baby. Martin plausibly suggests that the scene in room Alpha shows the birth of Tutankhamen, and that the mother is probably Kiya, the second wife of Akhenaten.[8]

Put together, the case runs like this: Someone gave birth to a royal child (hence the royal fan bearer). Kiya, a secondary wife, received special honors, such as her own little chapel, which suggests she had done something to raise her above the role of a harem wife. As it turned out, this elevated status did not last (she died in childbirth); her chapel was rededicated to someone else. Presenting a daughter to Pharaoh would not excite a father who already had six others. The possibility of a son would, and it would earn a picture in the king's tomb if it came to pass, especially if he had none by his primary wife. Hence, in all probability, Kiya, Akhenaten's second wife, bore the king a son. We know that Tutankhamen was the son of some king (from the Hermopolis blocks), probably not Amenhotep III and his elderly wife. The conclusion is tenuous, but I believe it is correct. Tutankhamen was the son of Kiya and Akhenaten. This would explain why Tutankhamen was never shown with the other princesses. He was born of a minor, though honored, wife of the pharaoh.

Merely because Tutankhamen was not shown in the official family portraits, we should not think he was neglected or ignored. Unless and until someone else came along, Tutankhamen stood just one step behind the heir apparent, Smenkare. We can assume that Tutankhamen enjoyed all the benefits and attention befitting a member of the royal household, one who might be pharaoh someday.

We are now in a position to reconstruct what young Tutankhamen's life must have been like at Amarna. Born in the middle of the greatest religious revolution Egypt had ever seen, Tutankhamen started his life in a bustling, energetic family at its peak, full of the optimism and excitement of a new movement, but distant from the rest of Egypt and its traditional gods. As a young child he wouldn't have understood the ideas his father preached, but he would have sensed that his father, the king, was an important leader.

Tutankhamen grew up in the royal nursery, along with six princesses, his half-sisters, all but one older than he. The heir apparent, Smenkare, was probably an older brother, or half-brother, more than ten years his senior, and may have been on his own already. Tutankhamen began learning to read and write around the age of four. Learning to read hieroglyphs is more difficult than one might think. It's not just picture writing. When you see an owl or a foot hieroglyph, the inscription isn't talking about birds and feet. The owl represents the sound of *M* and the foot the sound of *B;* many hieroglyphs are phonetic just like our alphabet. Tutankhamen learned twenty-five letters of the Egyptian alphabet, and then he started on the hundreds of other hieroglyphs that are ideographic—pictures of the words or idea they represent.

Hours upon hours would be devoted to writing hieroglyphs correctly with a reed brush the student chewed on until the end splayed and was soft, like a paintbrush. The scribal palette was a rectangular block of wood or stone with pits for blocks of red and black ink and a hollowed slit to hold the reed brushes. Tutankhamen's palette, later found in his tomb, was carved from ivory and inscribed with his name. When he was ready to write, he dipped his brush in a little bowl of water, touched it to the solid ink, and drew his hieroglyphs on broken bits of pottery for practice, later on papyrus. The hieroglyphs for writing show the implements Tutankhamen learned with: 𓏞 the palette, the little bowl, and the reed brush. Tutankhamen practiced by copying texts of the wisdom of earlier generations. Traditionally, maxims that would improve the mind as well as penmanship were favorites. "*Let your name go forth, while your mouth is silent.*" "*Report a thing observed, not heard.*" I suspect that as Tutankhamen grew older, he was given prayers to the Aten to copy.

Life was not all study for Tutankhamen. He must have gone swimming off the banks of the Nile with his sisters and children of the courtiers, along with an entourage of royal guards and nurses to watch for crocodiles. A favorite love poem from Tutankhamen's time laments, "My love is on one bank of the river, I on the other, and there's a crocodile on the sandbank." Tutankhamen learned to hunt ducks with a small bow, especially made for a boy's short arms, and probably delighted in hiding in the reeds waiting for his target, often assisted by one of his sisters. It was a sport that he enjoyed all his life. The young prince had few cares. His older brother was going to be king, so Tutankhamen did not bear the responsibility or need the training to officiate at state and religious functions.

When he was about eight years old, Tutankhamen probably learned to drive a chariot. An experienced charioteer must have accompanied him to control its two prancing steeds, until Tutankhamen was strong enough to handle the reins alone. His teacher would make the young prince practice for weeks to master the fine points of driving over rough and sandy terrain. Tutankhamen's chariot training was not to prepare him for battle someday—his father had no interest in military matters. It was so he could present a virile figure driving along the royal road in a family procession.

There were some things Tutankhamen missed out on. His father had pledged never to leave the city, so it is unlikely that Tutankhamen was permitted a trip to the delta, 250 miles north of Amarna, where the best duck and bird hunting was found in papyrus thickets so dense that two people ten feet apart couldn't see each other. There, fowlers caught twenty birds in their nets at one time. Tutankhamen would have heard conversations in the palace about such fabulous hunts, but he could not participate. He must also have heard stories about Thebes, the grand city with temples even larger than those at Amarna, where his grandfather had ruled and his father had grown up. But he couldn't visit there either. That was where the priests of Amun lived, and only recently his father had sent servants to carve out the name of Amun from all the temples, even from the top of Queen Hatshepsut's obelisk—although it was so high that the unenthusiastic workmen left it alone, figuring that no one would see it anyway.

By the time Tutankhamen was eight or nine he would have sensed troubles in his father's court. The foreign office was receiving letters from distant lands, far beyond the borders of Egypt, on little clay tablets hard as rocks. The tablets, ranging in size from two and a half to three and a half inches wide, and two and a half inches to nine inches long, were covered with small wedge-shaped writing, quite different from the hieroglyphs he was learning to write. They were written in Akkadian, the international language of the day. Many of the letters had been sent to Egypt from kings of other countries, Byblos (Lebanon), Ugarit (Syria), Assyria (Iraq), and Hatti (Turkey.) Others were sent by vassals requesting favors from the pharaoh. Many expressed puzzlement—why doesn't the king answer their requests?

For example, a succession of letters from a loyal prince of Byblos named Rib-Addi, Akhenaten's man in Lebanon, were filled with desperate pleas. He wrote no fewer than sixty-four letters. Rib-Addi is known from earlier letters to Akhenaten's father, during better times, that reveal a man of good business sense, able to conduct matters of state with dignity and pride. During Akhenaten's reign, Rib-Addi's position in Byblos had weakened; the faithful prince wrote repeatedly to Akhenaten telling of his plight, pleading with to Pharaoh to send troops.

> *What is Abdi-Assuta, the servant, the dog, that he should take the*
> *land of the king to himself?*
> *. . . So send me fifty pairs of horses and two hundred infantry, so that I*
> *may remain in Sigata . . .*[9]

When the troops were not sent, he wrote to the Egyptian General Amanappa:

> *To Amanappa, my father, thus (saith) Rib-Adda, thy son:*
> *At the feet of my father I fall down . . .*
> *Why hast thou held back and not spoken*
> *to the king, thy lord, in order that thou mayest march*
> *forth with archers . . .*
> *So speak this word to the king, thy lord . . .*
> *That he send help to me as quickly as possible.*[10]

When even this pitiful plea went unanswered, Rib-Addi wrote to Akhenaten again:

> *Rib-Addi spoke to (his)lord, the king of the lands,*
> *The great king, the king of battles . . .*
> *At the feet of my lord, my sun,*
> *seven times seven I fall down.*
> *Let the king, the lord know that all is well with Gubla,*
> *The faithful handmaiden of the king, from the time of his fathers.*
> *But behold, now Abdi-Asirti has taken Sigata to himself*

and said to the people of Amnia: "Kill your princes. Then you will be
as we are, and you will have rest."
And they did according to his words,
And have become as the Gaz-People.
And behold now,
Abdi-Asirti has written to the warriors:
"Assemble yourselves in the house of Nimit and we will fall upon
Gubla. . . ."
Thus have they formed a conspiracy with one another,
and thus I have great fear that there is no man to rescue me
out of their hand.
Like a bird that lies in a net, so am I.[11]

The plea remained unanswered. Rib-Addi was nearly killed.

A stranger stood with drawn dagger . . . against me;
but I killed him . . .
I cannot go [out of the gate] and I have written to the palace.
(But thou has not) sent an answer.
I have been wounded [nine] times
And have so feared [for] my life . . .[12]

One can only wonder what end befell poor Rib-Addi. Tutankhamen's father, an idealist and religious visionary, lacked all interest in dealing with the complex business of governing a major country.

And so Tutankhamen passed his childhood in privileged circumstances, with everything at his disposal a young boy could wish for. Except that he was confined to the boundaries of just one city. Since little was expected of him as long as Smenkare, his older brother, sat with his father on the throne, his life was otherwise carefree, perhaps dimly clouded by a sense that all was not right with Egypt. Then, one day, Smenkare died. On that day Tutankhamen's life took a very serious turn. He would one day be king. Within two years, his father, the pharaoh, died as well.

This death left the affairs of Egypt in disarray. Predeceased by his wives and by his only adult son, Akhenaten's death extinguished the last royal adult. There must have been great confusion about what should be done, where to begin picking up the pieces, who should take control. Ankhesenpaaten and her half-brother Tutankh*aten* were the only surviving royals, but they were children. Yet the question of who would succeed Akhenaten on the throne of Egypt was settled almost by default. The ten-year-old Tutankhamen was simply the only male of the royal line and Ankhesenpaaten was the only royal female. Tutankhamen alone could be pharaoh, although his half-royal blood would have to be supplemented by the full royal blood of his sister. Ankhesenpaaten and Tutankhamen married; Tutankhamen's skinny ten-year-old frame was placed upon the very large throne of the pharaoh of Egypt.

With a power vacuum created by Akhenaten's death and the fate of Egypt at stake, there must have been furious jockeying for position among the officials of the Amarna court. A pair of ten-year-olds could not take charge, whatever their titles. Each member of the inner circle must have had a strong and varied reaction to what should be done now that their eccentric leader was gone. Several men must each have thought he was the right man to successfully steer the nation through this precarious time.

The ones with the most to lose must have been distraught when they found their positions suddenly at risk. Meri-Re, the high priest of the Aten, owed his elevated position, great wealth, and high social status to the dreamer he followed to Amarna. Examination of his tomb, one of the grandest in the necropolis, fleshes out the picture. Meri-Re held the prestigious title "Fan bearer on the right hand of the king," but also listed "High Priest of the Aten," "Royal Chancellor," "Hereditary Prince," and "One Known to the King," as evidence of his crucial role in the management of the nation.[13] His tomb walls display Akhenaten installing Meri-Re as High Priest of the Aten, and lavishing collars and necklaces of gold upon him. Meri-Re was a key player in the new religion, and close to Akhenaten. He was almost certainly alive when Akhenaten died in the seventeenth year of his reign.[14] So he would be there to make decisions for the boy-king and push him to continue the support and practice of the new religion.

Another nobleman, Panhesy, would have seconded this counsel. He was "Second Priest of the Lord of the Two Lands," "Superintendent of the Granary of the Aten," "Superintendent of the Oxen of the Aten," "Northern Chancellor of the King," and "Intimate of the King."[15] Although second to Meri-Re in religious matters, Panhesy administrated and controlled the wealth associated with the Aten and the priesthood. He, too, is shown on his tomb walls laden with gold necklaces, while servants carry the collars, bracelets, and other ornaments given to him by the king.[16]

Also glued to the king's side was the grand courtier Aye, a contemporary of Tutankhamen's grandfather, Amenhotep III. Aye may have served the royal family through two generations already. He was perhaps the oldest member of the previous regime to follow the odd-looking Akhenaten on his quest for enlightenment and seems positioned above all other officials in the court. Aye's declarations and some of his actions show him protective of the pharaoh and his family; other actions, however, suggest scheming ambition, as we will see. At this stage in our investigation, the only thing we can say with certainty is that Aye was one of the few people surrounding the new pharaoh who had direct knowledge of a different regime than Akhenaten's.

Aye was the highest-placed official in the government. His tomb, the largest and most elaborate of all the nobles, displayed his titles: Fanbearer on the Right Hand of the King, Overseer of all the Horses of His Majesty, the Royal Scribe, and, most important of all, the God's Father. "The God's Father" was a title given only to those very close to the pharaoh (the living god), and could even indicate a royal tutor, who stands in for the father. "Overseer of all the Horses of His Majesty" suggests a military connection, though in Akhenaten's time it may have been honorary because the military was neglected.

Aye's wife, Tey, also held a high position in the Amarna court—Nurse to Nefertiti. Politically, they were the best connected couple at Amarna. Tey had easy access to the queen, so knew intimate details about palace life. Her husband, Aye, had the pharaoh's ear. Together they formed the eyes and ears of the palace. Their prestige at court is confirmed on the wall of Aye's tomb, where Akhenaten is shown awarding gold collars to both Aye and Tey in recognition of their services, making Tey the only woman placed in the ranks of "People of Gold," suggesting that she was a power in her own right. An inscription on Aye's tomb wall boasts:

> I was one favored by his lord every day, great in favor from year to year, because of the exceeding greatness of my excellence in his opinion. He doubled for me my favors like the number of sand; I was the first of the officials at the head of the people . . . My name has penetrated into the palace, because of my usefulness to the king, because of my hearing his teaching.[17]

These do not sound like the words of a selfless family retainer. They convey a self-aggrandizing view of someone who relishes all the trappings of power earned because of his outstanding abilities.

Twice on the walls of his tomb, Aye shows himself and his wife receiving honors and gold from the pharaoh. In one scene a man seated on a stool asks a young boy leaving the ceremony, "For whom do they rejoice, boy?" The boy replies, "They rejoice for Aye, the God's Father, together with Tey. They have been made people of gold" (fig. 4).

But work seems to have ceased on Aye's tomb long before Akhenaten died, which is peculiar, even ominous. A number of signs tell us so. There are several ways to tell when work stopped on a tomb. Sometimes an inscription gives the date of its carving—for example, "Year 12 of Akhenaten." Another clue is to note the way the Aten's name is written. Before year 9, his name was: "Re-Horakhty lives, rejoicing in the Horizon in his name Shu, which is Aten." After year 9 of Akhenaten's reign the Aten's name was changed to "Re, the father who has returned as Aten." Still another way of dating a tomb is by the number of Akhenaten's daughters shown. The fourth princess appears around year 9, the fifth around year 11, etc. The walls of Aye's tomb are inscribed with only the early form of the Aten's name, and just three princesses are shown in scenes of the royal family. It seems that work stopped on Aye's tomb around year 8 of Akhenaten's seventeen-year rule. Why? The answer may be that by year 8 of the new order, Aye, from his privileged position as an insider, saw that things were not going well at Amarna. He may have realized that Camelot was doomed. This is only speculation; what seems clear is that Aye had no intention of staying long enough in Amarna to be buried. The question is, what plans did Aye have for his future?

Someone had to rule the country in Tutankhamen's place, at least until the child approached adulthood. Meri-Re, Panhesy, and Aye are the three officials most likely to have imposed their wills on the immature king. Probably all three advised him, but there were crucial issues that divided the triumvirate. Who had the final say? Who was the real power behind the throne? Meri-Re, the high priest of the Aten, had the most to lose if the young king abandoned the Aten. Panhesy's wealth and position were also tied to the Aten's estates; he, too, would have advised Tutankhamen to continue his father's religion. Both would have urged, for their own sake if not the country's, that Amarna remain the religious and civil capital. But of the three possible regents, Aye held the highest rank—the only one titled "God's Father." Aye was not committed to either the new religion or the capital.

Almost immediately the real ruler of Egypt revealed himself. The decision was made to return to Thebes and resurrect the old religion. Only Aye, of the three Amarna leaders, makes the transition to the new regime. Meri-Re and Panehesy disappear from history; we can only imagine what happened to them. Although no inscription explicitly states that Aye became the vizier of Egypt, the equivalent of prime minister, most Egyptologists agree that he assumed that role.[18]

Now that he had control, Aye faced powerful interest blocks, such as the army and priesthood, grumbling loudly about the state of the country. Aye's power consisted of two very young royal children. His first step was to announce the restoration of the old regime by holding the coronation of the new pharaoh in Thebes, the traditional religious capital of Egypt. As soon as he could, Aye would have Tutankh*aten* and Ankhesen*paaten* change their names to show their association with the old god Amun, becoming Tutankhamen and Ankhesenamen (the "amen" part of their names is an English transliteration of Amun). Both acts would earn the support of the priests. The army would watch to see what lay ahead for them, but could take heart in the fact that the new pharaoh had at least ended the isolation in Amarna.

Sailing to Thebes for the coronation would have been the first time Tutankhamen and Ankhesenamen ever traveled outside of Amarna, distracting them from the death of their father and the turmoil of Amarna. As the boat sailed up the Nile they saw villagers lining the banks of the river hoping to catch a glimpse of their new king and queen. When they landed at Thebes, these children, raised in an isolated city with only one god, must have been overwhelmed by the bustling city, its multitude of temples and panoply of different gods. They were orphans separated from the only home they had known, about to denounce their religion. It must all have been quite terrifying.

Aye and his wife Tey would have identified the sights, but it would have been a dozen years since they had seen Thebes. No longer did the city glow with self-importance, beckoning with prosperity. It had become a darker, more dangerous place. Here the children would have been confronted with suspicious, even hostile looks, a frightening change from the pure adoring faces of simple farmers along the way. Tutankhamen and his bride must have clung to each other, perhaps holding hands, wondering what lay ahead for them in this frightening, large world. We know from portraits and inscriptions that a genuine love developed between them, perhaps nurtured by such shared, difficult early experiences (fig. 6).

They were installed in the once-grand palace of their grandfather, Amenhotep III. A king had not been in residence for almost two decades, so workmen and painters must have frantically prepared for the royal arrival. Built of mud brick, covered with plaster, beautifully painted with elaborate motifs, this palace was a sprawling affair, with gardens and lakes and spacious quarters for Pharaoh's queen, wives, concubines, and children. Tutankhamen's father had grown up here as Amenhotep IV. Aye may have been a visitor. No doubt old retainers would tell Tutankhamen and Ankhesenamen stories about their grandmother, Queen Tiye, and her fabulous pleasure lake, and about their grandfather, Amenhotep III, who had built as no one before him. They would tell them about tribute from foreign lands, paraded before the palace, exotic things like ostriches and giraffes, which the children had never seen. Compared to this busy palace in the center of a larger world, Amarna was an isolated ivory tower. Tutankhamen and Ankhesenamen would have to absorb a great deal, and quickly, in order to survive.

Then came the coronation. Tutankhamen stood before the gateway to Karnak Temple, the largest building he had even seen, looking onto a courtyard filled with thousands of priests who served the god his father had banished. For the crowd of Thebans thronging outside, this was their first glimpse of the new king who they prayed would return Egypt to the good old days.

Tutankhamen was purified with ritual waters poured from four gold vases. Now he could enter the house of the gods. The procession moved slowly past the obelisks of Tutankhamen's ancestors, Tuthmosis I and Hatshepsut, past the shrine erected by Tuthmosis III, stopping at various places for rituals and prayers. He was presented with the crowns of kingship—the tall white crown representing upper Egypt, then the red crown of lower Egypt—successively placed on his head. He became the "Lord of the Two Lands, " King of Upper and Lower Egypt." Then the blue "kepresh" crown (sometimes called the "War Crown") was conferred and he became the commander of the army (fig. 5).

The crowns of Egypt were revered as possessors of magical properties bestowing invincibility on those who wore them. Probably only one of each type existed at any time, passed from pharaoh to pharaoh on the day of his coronation. No such crown has ever been found in an excavation—these were the only royal objects the kings of Egypt were not allowed to take to their graves.

As the procession moved along the passageways between the temples, Tutankhamen neared his child-sized throne covered in gold. There he was presented with the royal symbols of his authority, the crook and the flail—Pharaoh was both the shepherd of his flock and its dominating master. Two sets of crook and flail were found in Tutankhamen's tomb, one child-sized set, used at Tutankhamen's coronation, the other was that of a full-sized pharaoh. The small set bore the name of the Aten, a last reminder of the life he was about to leave behind.

As Tutankhamen sat for the first time upon the throne, the high priest of Amun recited his five royal names:

1. The Horus name, associating the king with Horus, the Falcon god:
   "*Horus, Strong Bull, whose Images are Born.*"
2. The Two Ladies Name, associating the pharaoh with the cobra goddess and the vulture goddess:
   "*Whose Laws are Good, who Pacifies All the Gods.*"
3. The Golden Horus Name, a second association with Horus:
   "*Who Brings Together Divine Order, who Pleases the Gods.*"
4. The Prenomen, the first of the king's two names written in a cartouche, the oval signifying royalty, preceded by the hieroglyphs of a bee and a sedge plant, symbols of Upper and Lower Egypt:
   "*Re Manifests himself as Lord.*" "*Lord of Re's Being*"
   (Neb-Keperu-Re).
5. The nomen, the second name in a cartouche, preceded by hieroglyphs for "Son of Re," asserting the king's descent from the sun god Re:
   "Tutankh*aten, living image of the Aten.*" (At this stage his name had not yet been changed.)

After the five royal names had been bestowed on Tutankhamen, he was officially the Pharaoh of Egypt. The procession retraced its steps through the temple back to the entrance pylon; the ceremony was over. On his way to the palace for his own celebration with more lavish entertainment, the new king passed crowds feasting and rejoicing in the streets, thanks to liberally distributed gifts of bread and beer. There were dancers with weights in their long hair, so it swayed as they moved, musicians, hand clappers, and singers, all for the enjoyment of the new king. One can imagine the excitement that Tutankhamen and Ankhesenamen felt as they talked about the coronation and the fantastic gods and rituals. They must have been amazed to see the temple walls with images of strange gods who had human bodies and animal heads—lionesses, falcons, and rams. Why did the pharaohs shown on the walls offer incense and beer to them? Their father would never have done that. As grand as Thebes was, they must still have thought wistfully about the more familiar, quieter surroundings of Amarna. Thebes was too big and complicated.

After a short time, the young king and queen did, indeed, return to Amarna, but stayed only a year or so. With their father dead, the city had lost its soul. The decision had been made not to reconcile two estranged religious camps; one or the other must be abandoned if Egypt were to be unified. By now the children had grieved long enough, had learned that Amarna was not the world. The royal couple changed their names to reflect the return to Amun, the god of Thebes, becoming Tutankhamen and Ankhesenamen.

Within two years the royal court and government all moved to Thebes. The old religion and traditions of the past were fully reinstated. With no support or reason for existence, Akhenaten's holy city was virtually abandoned and his god declined into obscurity. But there were a few who could return to Thebes. Priests of the Aten may have had to remain in Amarna, unless they converted. Akhenaten's courtiers would face hostility in any other city for their participation in Akhenaten's hated policies. None of their names are found in any Theban records.

Of Akhenaten's high officials, only Aye seemed able to transcend the heresy and resume his career. He was guiding the policies of Tutankhamen in the right direction. Some would have viewed him with suspicion, but the priesthood enthusiastically greeted the restoration of Amun and the temples. Any criticism of Aye would have waned as skeptics observed a trend back to the old traditions. Under Aye's guidance,

Tutankhamen seemed to be doing everything right. It was a delicate balance, but Aye was a master of the high wire. He had earned the confidence of his young boss *and* the admiration of his priests. Aye must truly have been proud of his "excellent" work.

The Amarna dream had turned rancid. Ordinary citizens abandoned Amarna, moving en masse to Thebes, creating an overnight ghost town walked through only by priests of a religion that no one wanted, and courtiers without a court. One indication of how the Amarnans felt about their time in the city they abandoned is shown by what they left behind. In 1912 the German expedition to Amarna, led by Ludwig Borchardt, made a dramatic discovery while clearing debris from the house and studio of a master sculptor called Tuthmosis. When they entered a locked storeroom in the sculptor's house, the excavators found exquisite busts and heads of statues that Tuthmosis had not completed when the exodus from the city began. Among these pieces was the famous bust of Nefertiti. That such a work of art should be left behind can only mean that people did not want to remember the era they had helped create.

Akhenaten was branded a heretic. Less than fifteen years after his death, gangs of workmen were sent to Amarna to dismantle the temples and to reuse their blocks in building projects elsewhere. Amarna was razed to the ground. What had once been an oasis of beauty on a barren landscape became a lost city in a desert. Egypt's brief encounter with the Aten was over, monotheism would not return to the Nile Valley for 1,500 years. Egypt had shown it would not tolerate any change in its religion or the role of its pharaoh, not for another thousand years and not until it had lost its special place of dominance in the world.

The Amarna heresy was a unique departure from Egypt's tradition-bound history, what physicists today call a "singularity," an unparalleled event. The seeds of social revolution often take root in poverty and discontent; this movement sprang from prosperity. Most revolutions that shake political foundations are fraught with violence; Akhenaten's was peaceful. His dream was realized for a while because the person with vision carried the awesome power of a pharaoh, almost enough to pull it off. But he died too soon, ending what could have been a turning point in the history of the world. Today, we are so comfortable with monotheism that it is difficult to imagine just how revolutionary an idea this was for the inhabitants of the Nile Valley. For two thousand years Egyptians had worshipped numerous gods, their deities rising and falling in importance and evolving into aspects of each other, but they were never discarded. Often foreign gods, seen as aspects of Egyptian gods, were welcomed into the pantheon. When you already have a number of gods, a few more are no problem. Rather, why take any chance by excluding one who may be powerful? There was no reason to choose only one deity when many gods suited them so well. Monotheism forced people into a mode of thinking that seemed, if not unnatural, at least unreasonable. Even Akhenaten didn't comprehend the great danger of monotheism—that it is divisive. If there is only one god, then those who don't accept that god are wrong. Monotheism draws a line between "us" and "them," divides people and nations into believers and nonbelievers. No war was ever fought between polytheistic countries over whose gods were the true one. Compare this with the number of wars fought on behalf of the Jewish, Christian, and Islamic religions. Akhenaten had not realized that.

If a modern parallel would help us understand the Amarna revolution, consider the changes now taking place in Germany. Two halves of that nation had long been ideologically divided. One was led by a leader whose vision was out of touch with reality, who could support his ideal only through intolerance. In the end, he lost. The interesting part of the parallel is to observe what happened to his former followers and to all he had created after the movement failed. Today, almost no one in East Germany acknowledges support for the former regime. They rush to help pull down the old statues and buildings they themselves had erected. In ancient Egypt, too, there was a general denial of ever having been a part of Akhenaten's movement. Even names were changed to make assimilation possible—I can't imagine a citizen of Amarna named Aten-Em-Heb—"The Aten is in Festival"—returning to Thebes with his name intact. This is why there are so many unanswered questions about what happened at Amarna, as there are about the inner workings of communist Germany. Just as most communists did not keep souvenirs of their membership, the inhabitants of Amarna did not preserve artifacts of the revolution. The bust of Nefertiti was left behind because no one wanted it.

The man who caused it all assuredly did not rest peacefully deep in the confines of his Amarna tomb. Soon after the city was abandoned, all its tombs were robbed for the treasures they contained. The bodies of Nefertiti, Kiya, and the five princesses who died at Amarna have never been found. Like Akhenaten's, they were probably torn to shreds.

6

The Return to Thebes

Take a wife while you're young
That she make a wife for you
She should bear for you while you are young,
It is right to make people.

—*The scribe Ani*
circa 1400 B.C.

Tutankhamen had mounted a throne that wobbled uneasily from the neglect and divisions of the previous reign. Aware of the internal problems that beset Egypt, her foreign neighbors had grown defiant. The confederated tribes of Nubia, for example, brazenly joined forces in an effort to rid themselves of Egypt's domination. They halted shipments of gold and attacked the southern military outposts, sacking and burning. To the west of Egypt the countries of "Asia," as the Egyptians called them, claimed one excuse after another for reneging on their agreed tribute, cutting off necessary goods for Egypt. The revitalization of Egypt's economy depended on regaining control of "Asia" and Nubia for their irreplaceable resources. This would be the new administration's first priority—securing the wherewithal, that could then be used to resurrect the temples that had suffered so greatly from both neglect and religious fanaticism. The motto for Tutankhamen's reign would be: Restoration.

First, something had to be done about the army which had languished for years without direction, serving primarily as Akhenaten's personal bodyguard at Amarna. The troops had not marched north to Syria, west to Libya, or south to Nubia to gain territory and tribute, nor had they fought a war in years. The army had to be retrained and enlarged. Infantry had to be provisioned with the best weapons—spears, bows and arrows, and leather shields. The charioteers, the elite of the Egyptian army, had to be provided with horses, chariots, harnesses, and ornaments. A side effect of this renewal would be hundreds of jobs for the craftsmen who would provision the new army. Prosperity would begin.

To rebuild, Egypt would need timber from Lebanon, but the flourishing trade had practically ended. Choice cedar logs were going to other, more persuasive neighbors. Shrewd negotiators would have to be found so that this lucrative trade could be restored. Fear of a revitalized Egyptian army would aid immeasurably in the negotiators' ability to make favorable terms. The army was the key to all the problems, but rearmament cost money.

Administrative offices at Memphis were reopened, the languishing bureaucracy dusted off, revamped, and set into motion. While Akhenaten was lost in his own world at Amarna, the great bureaucracy of Egypt had deteriorated. Taxes were still collected, but inscriptions suggest that corruption was rampant throughout the system, as officials extorted grain from the farmers. An entirely new group of ministers and officials would be appointed to assure the smooth running of an improved bureaucracy.

Throughout Egypt's history, two constants remained—the river and the land. These elemental sources of Egypt's wealth had never failed before and would not fail this time. Crops would grow and be harvested just as they always had been, and the new tax collectors would be, it was hoped, honest. With careful supervision local governors could again be held accountable for their actions and the tax structures fairly revised.

Once trade goods and tribute again flowed into the country, the temples and shrines Akhenaten had closed would be reopened, sanctuaries of the gods would be rebuilt, and their gold cult statues restored. Craftsmen would again cast and carve statues by the thousands. Thebes would be reinstated as the religious capital of the great god Amun. Everything would return to normal. All this would require years of effort and a great deal of wealth.

The complex interdependence of funds and a stronger army leading to capital for rebuilding, all of which depended on more efficient collection of taxes, was more than an eleven-year-old pharaoh could comprehend. He would need the help of some very capable people. Nature would provide the natural resources, his new cabinet the guidance that would determine the direction of the country during the next decade, as Tutankhamen and Ankhesenamen literally grew up. To be sure, the young king and queen were visible—dedicating temples, officiating at festivals, commissioning works and restorations in the temples, no doubt greeting foreign dignitaries and appearing at banquets—but they were children who needed to learn.

While Tutankhamen grew and matured, so did his understanding of what it meant to be the king of Egypt. There is no reason to believe that he did not welcome this task and willingly assume more responsibility as time passed. He would have requested meetings with his officials, the viziers of Upper and Lower Egypt, the Overseer of the Treasury, Overseer of the Royal Works, and the Overseer of the Army, asking questions about every area of his vast domain. The country was vast, and the young pharaoh could not keep his eyes on everything, so his officials retained tremendous power. It was crucial that they be trustworthy and fair. The ancient proverb was: "Gracious king, lawful vizier."

Public-relations efforts showed the people that their new pharaoh understood what they had endured. An eight-foot-high stela was carved and prominently dedicated in front of Karnak Temple. Given that this is the earliest campaign speech in history, Tutankhamen's writer was truly inspired. At the very top of the stela, carved in relief, is a scene of Tutankhamen making offerings to Amun. Even if you couldn't read the hieroglyphs, the message was clear. Here was the pharaoh presenting incense to Amun. How things had changed from the past regime! In the text below, Tutankhamen laments the deplorable state in which he found the temples of Egypt, and describes all his efforts to restore them to their former glory.

> Now when this majesty arose as king, the temple of the gods and goddesses beginning from Elephantine to the marshes of the Delta . . . had fallen into neglect.
>
> Their shrines had fallen into desolation and became land overrun with the *Rata*-plants.
>
> Their sanctuaries were as if they had never been, their halls were a trodden path.
>
> The land was in confusion, the gods forsook this land . . .
>
> His majesty was administering this land, and making daily governance of the two river-banks.
>
> Then his majesty took counsel with his heart, searching out every excellent occasion, seeking what was beneficial to his father Amun, for fashioning his august image of real fine-gold . . .
>
> All the (offerings) of the temple are doubled, trebled, and quadrupled with silver, gold, lapis-lazuli, turquoise, all rare costly stones, royal linen, white cloth, fine linen, olive oil, gum . . . incense and myrrh, without limit of all good things . . .
>
> The gods and goddesses who are in this land, their hearts are joyful.
>
> The possessors of shrines are glad,
>
> Lands are in a state of jubilation and merry making,
>
> Celebration is throughout [the whole land] and good [conditions] have come to pass.[1]

There is a clear acknowledgment that, under his father's rule, the "Land was in confusion," the temples from north to south had "fallen into neglect." The text goes beyond citing religious problems and strikes at the

FIG.1: Colossal statue of Akhenaten, Tutankhamen's father. *Egyptian Museum, Cairo.*

FIG.2: Akhenaten's second wife, Kiya, Tutankhamen's mother, carved relief from Hermopolis. *Ny Carlsberg Glyptotek, Copenhagen. Photograph by Pat Remler.*

FIG.3: Lid from a canopic jar found in Tomb 55. Possibly Kiya, Tutankhamen's mother. *Metropolitan Museum of Art, New York. Photograph by Pat Remler.*

FIG.4: Aye and his wife Tey worshipping the Aten. *Tomb of Aye at Amarna. Photograph by Pat Remler.*

FIG.5: Head of young Tutankhamen, from a statue possibly made for his coronation. *Metropolitan Museum of Art, New York. Photograph by Pat Remler.*

FIG.6: Ankhesenamen offering lotus blossoms to Tutankhamen, detail of an ivory and wood chest found in Tutankhamen's tomb. *The Metropolitan Museum of Art, previously on loan from the Cairo Museum. Photograph by Lee Boltin.*

FIG.7: Small golden shrine decorated with scenes of Tutankhamen and Ankhesenamen. *The Metropolitan Museum of Art, previously on loan from the Cairo Museum. Photograph by Lee Boltin.*

FIG.8: Tutankhamen pouring perfume into Ankhesenamen's hands. Detail from small golden shrine. *The Egyptian Museum, Cairo.*

FIG.9: Ivory and wood game boards used by Tutankhamen and Ankhesenamen. *The Egyptian Museum, Cairo.*

FIG.10: The head of Aye, Tutankhamen's vizier. *Agyptisches Museum, Berlin. Photograph by Pat Remler.*

FIG.11: Statue of General Horemheb as a scribe. The inscription on the base boasts that he suppressed crime and lawlessness during Tutankhamen's reign. *The Metropolitan Museum of Art, New York. Photograph by Pat Remler.*

FIG.12: Huy, Tutankhamen's viceroy to Nubia. *Bode Museum, Berlin. Photograph by Pat Remler.*

FIG. 13A: Interior of gilded coffin for the larger fetus found in Tutankhamen's tomb with the wrapped mummy inside. *Photograph by the Egyptian Expedition, The Metropolitan Museum of Art, New York.*

FIG. 13B: Larger fetus partially unwrapped. *Photograph by the Egyptian Expedition, The Metropolitan Museum of Art, New York.*

FIG. 13C: The larger fetus. Note the damage at the top of the skull where Derry opened it to remove the linen inserted by the embalmers. Had the little girl lived, she would probably have been deformed. *Photograph by the Egyptian Expedition, The Metropolitan Museum of Art, New York.*

FIG.14A: External coffin (with lid removed) for the smaller of the two fetuses found in Tutankhamen's tomb. *Photograph by the Egyptian Expedition, The Metropolitan Museum of Art, New York.*

FIG.16: Floral collar worn by one of the mourners at the ritual meal during the burial of Tutankhamen. *The Metropolitan Museum of Art, gift of Theodore Davis, 1909.*

FIG.14B: The smaller fetus. *Photograph by the Egyptian Expedition, The Metropolitan Museum of Art, New York.*

FIG.15: The author with Dr. Fawzi Gaballah examining one of the fetuses from Tutankhamen's tomb. *Kasr El Einy Hospital, Cairo. Photograph by Pat Remler.*

My dear Carter,

It will interest you to know that I have just seen a finger-ring at Blanchard's which has on it the cartouche of Ankhesenamon alongside the praenomen of King Aÿ. This can only be interpreted as meaning that King Aÿ had married Ankhesenamon, the widow of Tutankhamen. The ring is of blue glaze and was found somewhere in the Eastern Delta.

Is there any chance of your going out to the Southern Valley to see the tomb of Aÿ. If you do go out there, there is a point that must be extremely interesting to settle. On one of the walls of the sarcophagus chamber there was figures

of King Aÿ with the Queen Tiy behind him with the following inscription over them:

Is there any trace at all of a figure behind Queen Tiy? and is the cartouche Aÿ simple for the name of . My notes on the tomb made some years ago do not help me on this point & it would be very interesting to settle it. If you have time do go out there: it would

take long to do it. Had I the time to run up to Luxor myself I would do so but I shall not be free till the end of may. When are you coming down to Cairo? With our love to you. Hall good luck

Yours ever

Percy E. Newberry

FIG. 18: Letter written by Percy Newberry, telling Howard Carter of the ring indicating that Aye married Ankhesenamen. *Courtesy Griffith Institute, Oxford.*

FIG. 17: Aye performing the opening of the mouth ceremony on Tutankhamen's mummy. Wall painting in Tutankhamen's tomb in the Valley of the Kings. *Photograph by Pat Remler.*

FIG.19: One of the hundreds of servant statues (*ushabtis*) placed in the tomb to accompany Tutankhamen to the next world. *The Metropolitan Museum of Art, on loan from the Cairo Museum. Photograph by Lee Boltin.*

FIG.20: Colossal statue of Tutankhamen from his mortuary temple. His name has been erased and the statue now bears the cartouche of Horemheb. *The Egyptian Museum, Cairo. Photograph by Pat Remler.*

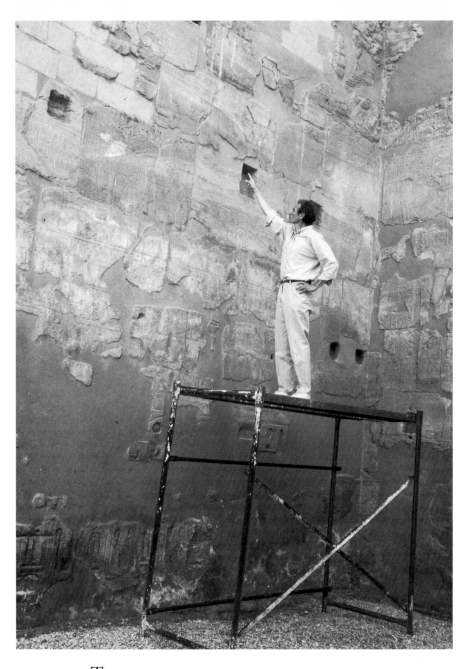

FIG.21: The only place in Luxor Temple where Tutankhamen's name has not been erased is high on the east wall of the Colonnade Hall. *Luxor Temple.* *Photograph by Pat Remler.*

FIG.22: Skull of Tutankhamen, showing the elongated head typical of the royal family in the Amarna Period.   *Photograph by the Egyptian Expedition, The Metropolitan Museum of Art, New York.*

FIG.23: The mummy of Tutankhamen reassembled on a sand tray after the autopsy by Dr. Derry. His mummy still rests in his tomb in the Valley of the Kings. *Photograph by the Egyptian Expedition, The Metropolitan Museum of Art, New York.*

FIG.24A: One of four miniature canopic coffins that contained Tutankhamen's internal organs. *Photograph by the Egyptian Expedition, The Metropolitan Museum of Art, New York.*

FIG.24C: The unwrapped contents of the canopic coffin: Tutankhamen's liver. *Photograph by the Egyptian Expedition, The Metropolitan Museum of Art, New York.*

FIG.24B: One of Tutankhamen's miniature canopic coffins with its lid removed and the wrapped organ still inside.
Photograph by the Egyptian Expedition, The Metropolitan Museum of Art, New York.

FIG.25: X ray of Tutankhamen's skull. The bone fragment visible in the upper left corner is the result of postmortem damage to the skull. Arrow points to the location of the possible blow to the back of the head. *Courtesy Department of Human Anatomy and Cell Biology, University of Liverpool.*

FIG.26: Author with Dr. Gerald Irwin, medical director of the Radiologic Technology Program at the C.W. Post Campus of Long Island University. Irwin was the first to suggest Tutankhamen may have lingered before dying from a blow to the back of the head. *Photograph by Gina Mosti.*

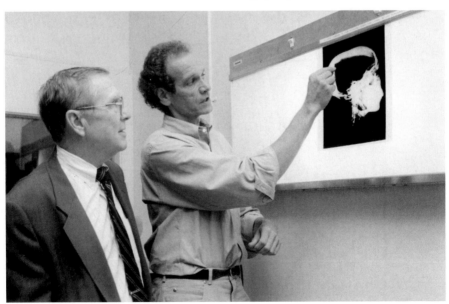

heart of Egypt's malaise. The army had been unsupported for years. The text carved on the stela states that during this time if Egypt's army were sent to Syria, "It met with no success at all." This isn't just a politician's campaign speech, it's a plan of action: build up the military, restore Egypt's wealth, and reopen the temples.

There is even a subtle, but unmistakable, declaration that the isolationism of Akhenaten's Amarna days was over. The stela refers to Tutankhamen on his throne in the palace in Memphis, where the stela was probably written, but the stela was erected in Thebes. This shows how far the country had already come. Egypt had a true king of both Upper and Lower Egypt, a pharaoh for all of the country.

Tutankhamen was about eleven years old when the Restoration Stela, as it is known, was carved. Someone was putting words into his very young mouth, but they were words the Egyptian public and the Amun priesthood wanted to hear. Their temples would be restored and the gods' offerings reinstated. But promises were not deeds—every proclamation issued by Tutankhamen must have been viewed with some doubt. Deeds required effective, intelligent administration. Who was going to implement all these wonderful plans?

The officials in charge were new players, men untainted by the Amarna days. Aye must have been instrumental in their recruitment, and he chose well. Maya, Tutankhamen's new treasurer, was central to the restoration plan. We know a great deal about the internal workings of the government during Tutankhamen's reign because Maya inscribed his autobiography on his tomb wall. He was in charge of collecting the taxes, overseeing their registry in the royal treasury, then allocating their distribution. He even supervised the casting of gold statues for the temples. From his office in Memphis, Maya dispatched an army of scribes to all the nomes (provinces) of Egypt to record how much grain was collected from each farmer.

Peasants were taxed not on how much they harvested, but on how much they *should have* harvested, as estimated by reading the Nilometer. Boulders along the banks of the Nile, "Nilometers," were inscribed with high water marks from centuries of Nile floods. During inundation each year, the Nilometers recorded how high the river rose in every part of Egypt. Once it was known how bountiful the Nile had been that year, officials calculated how much grain could be grown per acre. The farmers were taxed one portion of their predicted harvest. This system prevented tax collectors from having to search for hidden caches of grain. If a farmer's fields didn't produce what was expected, he still had to pay his full share. If, however, he was diligent and his land yielded more than the Nilometer estimate, the excess was his alone.

Maya's job was all the more difficult because money had not yet been invented. Grain was collected, transported to the royal warehouses, tallied, and stored. Once an order for disbursement came to Maya's office, the grain was weighed, counted, delivered and recounted again. Armies of scribes worked under Maya's direction up and down the Nile. Maya's brother, Nahuher, was a "Royal Scribe," indicating not that he took dictation from the pharaoh, but that he worked in the royal treasury, much as the "royal mail" in England consists of more than letters to the Queen. Eventually, there were so many "Royal Scribes" that a scribe who actually worked in the palace was given the designation "*True* Royal Scribe."

Maya's tomb lies just a few miles from Memphis at the ancient cemetery at Saqqara, the site of the first pyramid built more than a thousand years earlier. In Maya's day the necropolis had become a tourist attraction. Egyptians visited the ancient tombs in much the same way people visit famous cemeteries today. In times of difficulty, Egyptians could stroll through Saqqara to be reminded of Egypt's better days. So when Maya carved his autobiography on his tomb wall, he addressed it to "the people who come and want to divert themselves in the west and to have a walk in the district of eternity."[2] Maya was proud of the role he played in putting Egypt back together. He summarized his career: "In the beginning I was good, in the end I was brilliant."

But all these good deeds, reopening temples, recasting gold statues of the gods, and supporting the military, had to be paid for. In the eighth year of Tutankhamen's reign Maya was instructed "to tax the entire land and to institute divine offerings [for] all [the gods] of the land of Egypt."[3] When the new tax was levied Tutankhamen was nearly eighteen. He may well have engaged in long discussions with Maya revolving around the mark on the Nilometer that year and how much revenue could consequently be expected. Aye would have been party to their meeting, no doubt subtly guiding its direction. Although no one likes a tax increase, at least the farmers knew their payments were going toward reopening their temples and fashioning new statues of their gods. No longer did their grain flow to a city they had never seen, to support a god they did not worship and a pharaoh they did not understand.

Just a short walk from Maya's tomb is the tomb of a contemporary who was as important as Maya in the revitalization of Egypt, though in a very different way. Like most accountants, Maya would spend most of his life counting other people's "money." General Horemheb made sure there was something to count.

Horemheb, who had been elevated to the position of overseer of Tutankhamen's army, was a self-made man from the northern town of Hierakonpolis, home of the ram-headed god Herishef. He would have begun his military career as a young infantryman, either at the end of Amenhotep III's reign or at the beginning of Akhenaten's. As a young soldier working his way through the ranks, he must have found it disheartening to serve at a time when there were no wars providing the opportunity to distinguish himself, but Horemheb persevered. He must have been a man of determination, with the confidence and strength to command. Now a man in his prime, he held a crucial appointment in Tutankhamen's administration. As Overseer of the Army, Horemheb was the one who would reassert Egypt's control over western Asia and Nubia. With funds supplied by Maya, Horemheb recruited, equipped, and trained an Egyptian army that finally "marched out," to subdue Nubia. Once again, the supply of gold necessary for trade flowed into Egypt's treasury. There remained Syria–Palestine to conquer, which was also crucial to Egypt's well-being. Egypt had no forests, so it desperately needed cedar logs from Lebanon to build ships and the great doors and flagpoles of its temples. The hieroglyph for the word "god" is a banner on a staff ⸢, a staff of cedar.

Of course, we cannot know when meetings took place, or whether they occurred in Thebes or Memphis, but we can imagine the young pharaoh growing into manhood, eager to take the responsibility to lead his country, consulting with his treasurer, Maya, his general, Horemheb, and his faithful adviser, Aye. Should Horemheb's forces strike Libya first because they were the weakest, thereby seasoning the young troops for the big campaign into Syria? Or was it advisable to strike first at Nubia for more gold? At meetings like this the details for Egypt's recovery were hammered out. I imagine "the big three"—Maya, Aye, and Horemheb—each working in different ways. Maya ensconced in his office, surrounded by papyrus scrolls with scribes rushing to and fro reporting on revenues and losses. He was the accountant, conservative, orderly but always in the middle of things, the one who understood the finances of Egypt.

Aye worked in a very different way. He was the politician, working quietly from behind the scenes, orchestrating the moves of the other players. Perhaps, as at Amarna, he continued to be the eyes and the ears of the palace, remaining close to Tutankhamen, diverting contact with anyone else who sought the king's ear. An old Egyptian maxim says: "Do not reveal your heart to a stranger, he may use your words against you." That was Aye. We can begin to understand what a remarkably ambitious man he was. A small piece of inscribed gold foil discovered in the Valley of the Kings[4] adds a particularly interesting insight into his personality. Embossed on this foil is a scene in which Tutankhamen assumes the traditional conquering-hero posture, grasping a Libyan captive by the hair, ready to smite him with a curved sword. Behind Tutankhamen stands Ankhesenamen, his support. Traditionally, in front of the king would be the god to whom the enemy is being offered as a kind of sacrifice. But on this bit of gold, probably from a piece of furniture in Aye's tomb, Aye stands before the king in the position reserved for the god. Aye has not so subtly elevated himself to a divine position. Here was a man with truly grandiose dreams.

Horemheb was different. Although he, too, was an essential player in Tutankhamen's plan for recovery, he stood neither in the middle of things, nor behind the scenes pulling strings. Horemheb, like Aye, was an ambitious man, but he was more straightforward in his dealings. Approve a campaign and he would begin the march. As soon as his quartermaster submitted a list of the supplies needed—bronze battle axes, bows, arrows, shields, sandals, water skins, etc.—and they were received, he would be gone. Before long he would return with captives and tribute. Horemheb, campaigning for months at time, was not privy to the inner workings and politics of the palace He was the outsider, but an outsider holding a great deal of power.

In just a few years Horemheb's military expeditions regained all the territories that had slipped away from Akhenaten. Upon returning from a northern campaign, Horemheb paraded Asiatic prisoners before Tutankhamen; when he went south he returned with Nubian captives for his king. No one was safe from Horemheb's military raids, even Libyans—with their characteristic goatees and side locks—were captured and brought to work on the temples of Egypt.

Horemheb's successes were rewarded by a grateful Tutankhamen. As Egypt grew in strength, Horemheb grew in power. No longer was he only the commander in chief of the army; he was promoted to "Overseer of all Works of the King" and "Deputy of the King in the Entire Land." One of the titles that pleased him most had nothing to do with his military career, it was more like an honorary academic degree— "Royal Scribe." The general was so delighted that he commissioned a life-sized granite statue of himself seated in the scribal position with a papyrus scroll across his lap (fig. 11). The inscription on the base of the statue confirms his attention to regulations and their enforcement:

> *I am the recorder of the law,*
> *Who gives direction to courtiers*
> *Wise in speech, there's nothing I ignore.*[5]

Horemheb constructed a tomb at Memphis, the most beautiful and elaborate in the entire cemetery. As Overseer of the Royal Works he commanded the best craftsmen in the land. The sculptures and wall carvings are among the finest ever produced in ancient Egypt, master-pieces by any standard. Although they are traditional in their style, a flu-idity of line and an attention to detail shows the hands of craftsmen trained in Amarna who survived that era. Horemheb's tomb was topped by a small temple above the ground, complete with a courtyard and columned hall. His descendants could come, sit in the shade of the columns, and have a meal in honor of their ancestor. As they ate, they would be surrounded by carvings of Horemheb's great battles against the "wretched Asiatics," the inhabitants of "Vile Nubia," the "barbarians of Libya." They would see Horemheb receiving collars of gold from the pharaoh he served, Tutankhamen. It was a military man's version of par-adise regained.

While Horemheb, Aye, and Maya worked to resuscitate Egypt's economy and dominions, Tutankhamen's task was to reassure the priests that he embraced the old gods of Egypt. His first major building project in Thebes—the completion of the Colonnade Hall in Luxor Temple—was a stroke of genius. His grandfather, the great King Amenhotep III, had built the 150-foot-long hall, but died before it was decorated. When Akhenaten banished the gods of Thebes and moved to Amarna, the columns stood bare, and remained so for more than a decade. Tut-ankhamen was advised by Aye, no doubt, to decorate the hall with scenes from Egypt's most important religious festival.

This was a project that Tutankhamen and Ankhesenamen could be-come fully involved in. They no doubt visited the temple often and asked questions while the priests, scribes, and artists discussed how to best illustrate the story of the Festival of Opet. These meetings also pro-vided classes for Tutankhamen on the nature of a religion that was com-pletely new to him. It must have been something like Bible school or catechism through pictures.

This shrewd decision to complete the colonnade identified Tut-ankhamen with his grandfather whom the priests of Amun respected for his works. In this way he emphasized his continuity with the royal line, and could be recognized by the priests as the legitimate heir to the throne, yet distanced him from his father's aberrations. This worked elegantly to extinguish priestly fears that he might be too much his father's son.

We can only wonder what Tutankhamen's private reactions were to the new religion. Was he willing and receptive, or did he secretly still pray to the Aten? What was he thinking as he played his prominent part in religious festivals?

The Colonnade Hall was decorated with scenes of the most glorious of all the festivals in Thebes—the Opet Festival. It celebrated the annual visit of Amun and his family to Luxor Temple. Opet was the ancient name of Karnak, the temple where the festival originated, and home to the Theban trinity: Amun (the father), Mut (his wife) and Khonsu (their son). At the opening of the Opet festival the statues of Amun, Mut and Khonsu were taken from their shrines in Karnak temple, placed in divine barques, and sailed one and a half miles along the Nile to Luxor Temple (southern Opet). Tutankhamen's decorations show precious details of the joyous procession as it traveled south to Luxor Temple, and the return of the procession to Karnak at the end of the festival. Tutankhamen himself is prominently featured in the reliefs on the west wall of the colonnade. He makes offerings to the gods Amun, Mut and Khonsu, accompanies the barques to the edge of the Nile, sails with the gods on their journey up the Nile, follows the barques from the banks of the Nile to the facade of Luxor Temple, and makes an offering to the gods in their sanctuaries in Luxor Temple.[6] Could anyone demonstrate greater devotion?

When the festival of Opet was reinstated, the people of Thebes must have been overjoyed, lining the east bank of the Nile to see the boats of the gods and to catch a glimpse of this Tutankhamen who had restored the old religion. When the procession moved inside Luxor Temple, thousands crowded into the open courtyard to view the shrines as they were carried to their temporary homes deep inside the temple, where the common people could not go. Knowing, at least from the scenes on the temple walls, that Tutankhamen presented offerings of incense, meat, vegetables, beer, and wine to the gods, the common people must have been filled with joy. It was the first time in years that their pharaoh had honored their gods. I am sure that many wept.

Despite the excitement of the people and their own busy days, Tutankhamen and Ankhesenamen must have missed their father, and their former life at Amarna, where their days were more free. Gradually, however, the pleasures of living in Thebes and Memphis, with all the variety that Egypt offered, must have seemed the better course.

From their palace in Memphis it was a short trip to the Delta for the finest bird hunting in the land. Skimming the marshes in flat-bottomed skiffs made of papyrus stalks, fowlers set nets and waited to snare passing flocks. Tutankhamen especially loved hunting with a bow and arrow. Lightweight wood shafts with tiny sharpened wood arrow-heads—bird points—were best, which traveled faster than a bird could fly. (Tutankhamen's bows and arrows were found in his tomb.) Along with Ankhesenamen, the two spent some of their happiest hours together in the marshes, he shooting at passing ducks and she readying the next arrow for him. When they tired of the bow and arrow, there was the throw stick, far more difficult to master—shaped something like a boomerang. It took a strong arm to throw it hard enough to down a bird in flight.

From their southern palace in Thebes they went ostrich hunting in the desert, which was always an adventure. While his charioteer chased the birds, Tutankhamen, beside him, shot his arrows from the bouncing chariot. The diversions of the young king and his queen were many, and it seems likely that his advisers were happy to have them occupied with hunting and sports.

Another endeavor that occupied Tutankhamen's time was building his tomb. The young king chose a site next to his grandfather's tomb in the West Valley. Amenhotep III had dug the first tomb in the area, and not far from it stood an unfinished tomb (WV25) that most Egyptologists agree was begun by Amenhotep IV, before he changed his name to Akhenaten and moved to Amarna.[7] If the identification of this tomb is correct, Tutankhamen's tomb was sited next to his grandfather's and near a tomb once intended for his father. Work began on Tutankhamen's tomb when he was just entering his teens. Construction would have proceeded at a leisurely pace, for the overseer of the works surely believed he had years and years before the finished tomb would be needed.

A royal architect drew the floor plan, then presented it to the Overseer of the Royal Necropolis. A draftsman marked the cliff wall with the outline of the doorway; then, starting at the top, carvers began to chip away the rock with bronze chisels hammered by wooden mallets. Tombs always began at the top so that the carvers swinging their mallets were assisted by gravity, rather than having to constantly raise their mallets higher and higher. As the chips mounted, young boys scooped them into straw baskets and carried the rubble away from the tomb. In a few weeks a descending passageway became evident that daily went deeper and deeper into the bedrock until assistants with bronze mirrors were called to reflect sunlight down the shaft so the workmen could see. After the passage reached the depth prescribed by the architect, a large room was carved from the living rock, but leaving square pillars to support the ceiling. As soon as the rough work was completed, more experienced carvers smoothed the walls to prepare them for decoration. The tomb was now large enough for a left-hand gang and a right-hand gang to work simultaneously. As chisels dulled, boys would carry them to the surface for sharpening. It was a team effort. All the workmen and their families lived together in a small village near the Valley of the Kings, a village that was walled so that it could be sealed shut at night. These people included draftsmen, carvers, painters, sculptors, artisans who carved hieroglyphs, and overseers—all necessary to prepare a tomb for eternity.

As Tutankhamen grew up, he could more actively participate in the discussions with Aye and Maya about finances, meet with foreign envoys when trade agreements were discussed, select his own servants and tutors, and decide whom to reward for faithful service. He was, after all, the grandson of Amenhotep III, the great diplomat and shrewd administrator. Governing was in his blood. Fortunately, the tomb of Huy, one of Tutankhamen's most trusted ambassadors, has been preserved. It provides a clear sense of the role Tutankhamen played. At this point, he was a teenager. Horemheb had just subdued Nubia; so a viceroy was needed to administer the territory. Nubia was counted on for tons of gold annually, along with luxury items such as ebony for furniture, ivory for jewelry, giraffe and leopard skins—all symbols of Egypt's opulence. The viceroyage was a critical position (fig. 12).

Huy records on his tomb walls that he was summoned to the palace to receive the seal of the viceroy for stamping the gold that would be shipped back to Thebes. Since the bygone days of the Old Kingdom, small cylinder seals had been signs of authority. In fact, the hieroglyphic word for treasurer included a seal on a cord, worn as a badge of office around the neck. So when Huy was called to the palace at Thebes, it was a great day in his life. Huy's entire family was permitted to watch the great event. He was led before his pharaoh, where he bowed and was greeted by a member of Tutankhamen's cabinet who said: "The Land from Nekhen to Nesut-Towey has been given to thee." Huy answered: "May Amun of Nesut-Towey grant all that you have commanded, oh sovereign, my lord." Tutankhamen then commanded that he depart and return with gold, ivory, ebony, giraffes, all good things found in Nubia. Note that it was not Tutankhamen but a member of the cabinet who gave the commission to his agent. Tutankhamen merely seconded that order.

With his seal of office firmly in hand, Huy left the palace to prepare for his expedition to Nubia. One of his sons bore the title "Master of the Horse." On the walls of Huy's tomb we see horses peeking out of their stalls as his ship heads for Nubia. There are no records of the voyage to Nubia or his stay there, but we can imagine that Horemheb's recent campaign had removed any obstacles that could have prevented Huy from performing his duties. Not surprisingly, the expedition was a complete success. Huy returned north to Egypt with a fleet loaded with treasure so extensive that its presentation to Tutankhamen had to take place outside in the courtyard of the palace. There were endless piles of gold, cast into rings the size of bracelets, heaps of ivory and ebony, a live giraffe, and more. Slaves in manacles were paraded before the young king so he could select those that pleased him. There was a herd of especially fat Nubian cattle, highly prized as offerings to the god Amun. During the feast of Opet, a cow's horns were topped with carved hands; between them was a tiny Nubian head. When the animal lowered its head, Nubia symbolically paid homage to Egypt.

Pleased with the procession—he must have loved the giraffe—Tutankhamen rewarded Huy with gold necklaces. I wonder if he thought of the times at Amarna when his father had distributed gold necklaces from the Window of Appearances. But, in the case of Huy, these were not bribes for following the faith, but rewards for a job well done. Many of the gold objects placed in Tutankhamen's tomb were due to Huy's labors. The famous solid gold coffin may have been fashioned from massive gold shipments from Nubia, thanks to Huy.

As the years passed, Tutankhamen and Ankhesenamen grew into young adults and fell in love. She had been at his side since they were both ten years old and was now portrayed, either standing or kneeling, beside her pharaoh in almost every depiction. The royal workshops produced statues of the handsome couple, seated side by side, wearing the crowns, respectively, of the god Amun and his wife Mut. One pair of these statues of the young king and queen, in Luxor Temple, still smiles down on passing tourists.

Unlike all his predecessors with harems, Tutankhamen never married additional wives, another indication that he and Ankhesenamen were very close. But, since they were the last survivors of the Eighteenth Dynasty, they would have to produce children if the royal line was to continue. Otherwise, when the time came to choose the next pharaoh, Divine Order could be disrupted and Egypt could be thrown into turmoil.

The couple did their best to fulfill this obligation. Ankhesenamen became pregnant. While the court prepared for the birth of the next king or queen of Egypt, she was tended by the Royal Physician, a man renowned for his skills and healing abilities.

Ancient Egyptians called medicine "the necessary art" and regulated the profession carefully, with specialists in various areas. The highest ranking physicians were priests. Since Sekhmet was the most important god associated with the medical arts, it was the priests of Sekhmet who produced the best doctors. This is somewhat surprising since their lioness-headed goddess was feared throughout Egyptian history for her temper, and at one time she almost destroyed mankind. Priests of Sekhmet often had several titles, one medical, another magical. Nedjemou, for example, was "Chief of the Priests of Sekhmet" and "Chief of the Physicians," while Heryshefnakht was "Chief of Magicians," "High Priest of Sekhmet," and physician to the pharaoh. In addition to priest-physicians, the *wabu*, there were the *sunu*, who were the lay physicians. Since the medical profession was carefully regulated with severe penalties for improper practice, the *sunu* were almost certainly trained in medicine, although they were not associated with any particular temple nor devoted to a particular god. Thus their practice was probably more eclectic than the priest-physicians, as they could draw from all available sources.

While both the priest-physicians and the lay physicians used a combination of sound clinical medicine and magic, there was a third kind of physician who was not trained in medicine, but used only incantations, amulets, and magic to cure his patients. Most of the medical papyri that have survived come from this third class of medical men, for they list spells and potions with little evidence of scientific knowledge or careful observation.

Ankhesenamen's personal physician would have specialized in gynecology, "diseases of women." This was her first child, "the opener of the womb," and as she neared the end of her term a birthing stool was prepared. Egyptian mothers sat on a mud-brick stool so that gravity would assist the birth process. (The slang for giving birth was "sitting on bricks.") This was such a basic part of Egyptian life that the hieroglyph for "born" shows a seated woman with the baby's head emerging.

But before Ankhesenamen used the birthing stool, misfortune struck. As she entered her eighth month, she miscarried and lost her child, a little girl. Had the child lived, she would have been deformed, with a curved spine and one shoulder higher than the other. There were probably whisperings in the palace of a curse on the child or the mother.

The Royal Magician would have been summoned. Because medicine in ancient Egypt was practiced by both clinical physicians and magical healers, the specific kind of illness determined the method of treatment. If the cause was known, as with broken bones or crocodile bites, then the treatment would be nonmagical. For a crocodile bite, the wound was sewn closed and raw meat placed on it. If, however, the illness was something such as a fever, where the cause would be unknown to Egyptians, it might be attributed to demons or malicious magic, consequently the treatment would be magical. There was even a specialist trained in "unknown diseases," who probably dealt with illnesses of no known cause. Reproduction was not fully understood in ancient Egypt, so the cause of the miscarriage may well have been attributed to a curse. Ankhesenamen's miscarriage, combined with the fetus's deformity, would require a magician healer to assure it would not happen again. In such cases a wax image of Toth, the god of writing and magic, was fashioned and placed on burning coals under the birthing stool. Ankhesenamen may have sat on the birthing stool so that the smoke could enter her womb and purge it of whatever malicious forces were at work. The miscarriage was more than just a tragedy of state. Egyptians loved children, had large families typical of agrarian societies—lots of children to help in the fields. Tutankhamen and Ankesenamen suffered personally. A popular maxim was: "Marry young and have many children." At the age when they should be starting their family, Tutankhamen and Ankhesenamen were off to a shaky beginning.

Because the fetus was stillborn and had never breathed life, it was unnamed. Had the baby lived to take its first breath she would have had a soul—a Ba and a Ka, the two most important aspects of the soul. The Ba of the deceased was always shown on tomb walls as a bird with a human head that could fly in and out of the tomb while waiting for the resurrection of the body in the west. The Ba was the personality, essential for resurrection. In one ancient Egyptian literary work,[8] a man contemplating suicide is scolded by his Ba who tells him that if he kills himself, the Ba will desert him and ruin any chance for immortality. Another part of the soul was the Ka, a kind of spiritual double that resided within the mummy. Without a Ba and a Ka the fetus had no chance for resurrection. This was the Egyptian religion but it meant little to a pair of young parents who had experienced all the hopes and dreams of parents in every age and seen them crushed. Going against all tradition, they had the little girl mummified.

The fetus was only twelve inches long, so small that special tools had to be crafted for the mummification. A tiny wire was inserted through the nasal passage into the cranial vault to remove the brain. Small strips of linen soaked in resin were next inserted into the skull to dry and preserve the tissue to prevent putrefaction. Then an incision, less than an inch long, was made in the left side of the abdomen to remove the internal organs. But here, even the considerable skills of the royal embalmers failed them. The fetus was too small. No tool could be devised to enter the cavity and remove the stomach, liver, kidney, and intestines without terribly damaging the body. The embalmers left the organs where they were, injecting resin into the abdominal cavity, sealing it for eternity. Bandagers carefully wrapped the baby in pure linen strips while priests recited the ancient prayers. A miniature coffin was carved for the fetus and coated with black resin. Thin gold leaf bands, imitating mummy bandages, placed on the outside of the coffin, were inscribed with the phrases "The venerated one" and "The Osiris"—for the child had no name. A second, smaller coffin rested inside the first with a prayer to Osiris inscribed on the front, in the hope that the god of the dead would intervene and assist the child in the next world. The priest laid the fetus inside the smaller coffin and recited spells from the Book of the Dead, continuing the recitation as the coffin was placed inside the larger one and the whole package wrapped with pure linen bandages. When the bandages were in place, the clay seal of the royal necropolis—a jackal above nine bound captives (symbols of Egypt's traditional enemies)—was attached. The little mummy was ready for burial with her parents one day. The tragedy of the miscarriage, yet another sad misfortune in their young lives, must have drawn Ankhesenamen and Tutankhamen even closer.

As Tutankhamen entered his eighteenth year, the three threads of Egyptian society—the priesthood, the military, and kingship—finally had become woven into a whole fabric. The temples of Amun thrived. Thebes was again dominated by the activities of Luxor and Karnak Temples, the centers around which much of Tutankhamen's restoration revolved.

Constant activity hummed in the temples. The decoration on the colonnade was nearing completion; its dazzling bright colors made the temple live. Other walls were repaired, new plaster added where the old had fallen away, so skillfully repainted that the repairs couldn't be seen. Shining bronze decorations were affixed to the great temple doors and shrines. All was attended to by the growing ranks of priests. Now, each morning the priests opened the doors to the inner sanctuaries to let the first rays of the sun enter the chamber, as they anointed the gold statues of the gods with perfume and sacred oils, painted their eyelids with eye shadow, and placed bread, onions, beer and fruits before each god for its morning meal. Then the priests chanted the prayer to Amun:

Pilot who knows the water,
Helmsman of [the weak],
Who gives bread to him who has none,
Who nourishes the servant of his house.
I take not a noble as protector,
I associate not with a man of wealth,
I place not my share in another's care,
My wealth is in the house of my [lord].
My lord is my protector,
I know his might, to wit:
A helper strong of arm,
None but he is strong,
Amun who knows compassion,
Who hearkens to him who calls him,
Amun-Re, the King of Gods,
The Bull great of strength, who loves strength.

Workshops had reopened next to each temple, producing the sacred oils and white linen required by the priesthood. Bakeries and breweries flourished. Storehouses began to fill with goods, animals were gathered for sacrifice, petitioners left offerings. Dreams were interpreted from the dream book in the temple library. For example, "if a man sees himself in a dream with a dwarf—bad. Half his life is gone." The old religion was running at full steam again.

The military was also strong—Horemheb had forged Egypt's army into a force to be feared. The tradition of Egypt's kingship had been restored, Tutankhamen made offerings at the altars of Amun and participated in the Opet festival. Under Maya's watchful eye, the storehouses of Egypt had filled. As all could see for themselves: the promises of the Restoration Stela were being kept.

Tutankhamen began construction of his mortuary temple on the west bank of the Nile. He chose a site a few miles from his tomb. It was a handsome rectangular building, with several colossal statues of the king standing at the entrance, intended as a memorial where Tutankhamen could be worshipped for centuries after his death. When Maya allotted funds for the temple, he also donated land, as a kind of annuity, to the Ka priests who would be the caretakers of the temple, making offerings for the soul of Tutankhamen. The produce of the land would pay for generations of caretaker priests and the eternal upkeep of the temple. Tutankhamen decorated the temple with scenes of himself in his chariot, leading the army into battle. Probably he had not yet ridden out with Horemheb on a campaign, but he expected to someday; he was young. The scenes on the temple walls reassured the people that their king was strong enough to lead the army, just as the great Tuthmosis III had.

So far Tutankhamen's reign had returned Egypt to the good old days, an era of prosperity, expansion, and tolerance. But, just as Divine Order seemed to have been restored in Egypt, two more tragedies struck the ill-fated teenagers. Ankhesenamen, five months into her second pregnancy, miscarried—another little girl. It must have been devastating. Surely they were cursed. Well aware that they were the last survivors of the great Eighteenth Dynasty, Tutankhamen and Ankhesenamen had to produce an heir; Ankhesenamen must bear a son. The second tiny fetus was wrapped and placed in a small coffin similar to her sister's, in the hope that Osiris, god of the dead, would at least grant her life in the next world.

Despite the revitalized economy and religion, if Tutankhamen were to die without an heir, Egypt would again be thrown into turmoil. Those wielding power would be pitted against each other in a wrestling match to win the throne. Egypt could be torn apart again. No one worried much about such a slight possibility; Tutankhamen was young, there was abundant time to produce an heir. Then the unthinkable happened.

In January of 1323 B.C., Tutankhamen, the eleventh ruler of the Eighteenth Dynasty, died under mysterious circumstances. He was nineteen years old. Shortly thereafter, his name was erased from history, lost for 3,000 years. To understand why, we must turn now to the Valley of the Kings.

The Most Famous Tomb in History

Furnish your station in the Valley,
The grave that shall conceal your corpse;
Set it before you as your concern . . .
Emulate the great departed,
Who are at rest within their tombs.

—*The scribe Ani*
circa 1400 B.C.

Normally, Egyptologists excavate tombs that have been plundered practically bare, with only the walls to study. As we have seen, tomb wall scenes do supply a great deal of information, but imagine what could be learned if a tomb still contained everything that was buried with the deceased, including his most intimate objects, and imagine if the occupant were the pharaoh. Only one tomb in the history of Egyptology has been able to deliver that information. It was found across the Nile from Luxor in an area archeologists call "The Valley of the Kings."

The Valley of the Kings has a mystique all its own. It's the Boardwalk and Park Place of archaeology—the site where every excavator would like to land. It's not just what might be discovered that draws Egyptologists to the site; it's the overpowering sense of the history of the place, big history. This is where Ramses the Great, the pharaoh of the Exodus, was laid to rest, and where Hatshepsut, the Queen who would be King, was buried. All these tombs are in an area even a tired tourist can walk in fifteen minutes. A visitor with no knowledge of the area's history still feels something special here. Gazing across the barren landscape at the white limestone cliffs shimmering in the heat somehow evokes a sense of eternity, the sense that thousands of years have changed nothing. Three-thousand-year-old graffiti on cliff walls, where pious priests paused to inscribe their names, are still as bright as the day they were drawn.

Today, a visitor to the Valley first flies to Luxor and then takes the tourist ferry across the Nile to the west bank, before boarding a bus for the ten-minute ride to the site. Quickly, the occasional village disappears and fields of sugar cane give way to desert. Passing through a cleft in the hills—the entrance to the Valley of the Kings—nothing appears for a long minute except limestone cliffs on either side of the road. The tourist rest house suddenly appears, and then a quarter of a mile later, the bus stops in the middle of an arcade of peddlers' stalls heaped with souvenirs. Once past the entrance gate a visitor can leave the gauntlet of vendors behind and follow neatly painted signs to the tombs of Tuthmosis III, Ramses VI, and, straight ahead, Tutankhamen. Of the more than sixty known tombs in the Valley of the Kings, only a dozen or so are open to tourists.

When the Greek traveler Diodorus Siculus visited the Valley in the middle of the first century B.C., the priests of Thebes told him their lists recorded forty-seven tombs, but only fifteen remained, the others having been destroyed by treasure hunters.[1] Fifteen centuries later the English clergyman Richard Pococke sailed up the Nile to visit the Valley in 1739, but could find only nine tombs that could be entered.[2] When Bonaparte[3] invaded Egypt in 1798 he brought along a group of scientists who explored the Valley, and charted sixteen tombs, eleven of which were open. Their "quick and dirty" survey was a remarkable achievement, considering that Napoleon's soldiers were fighting the Mameluke warlords who controlled Egypt at the time, and bullets were flying as the savants risked their lives to measure and record the tombs.

The first systematic excavations in the valley were conducted in the nineteenth century by Giovanni Battista Belzoni, the Italian giant turned adventurer. Trained as a hydraulic engineer, the six-foot-seven-inch Belzoni made his living as a circus strongman before traveling to Egypt in search of treasure. From 1815 to 1819, Belzoni excavated sites up and down the Nile. He was the first person in modern times to enter the pyramid of Khephren, the second largest at Giza, and also the first to enter the great temple of Abu Simbel, built by Ramses the Great, in Nubia. But Belzoni concentrated much of his efforts in the Valley of the Kings, where he believed the greatest treasure would be found. He wasn't so much interested in increasing knowledge as in finding ancient artifacts he could remove from Egypt to sell.

When tombs were cut into the valley walls, vast quantities of stone chips had to be removed and dumped outside, where they remained untouched for thousands of years. Belzoni used the mounds of chips to guide him to a tomb's location. Entrances to many of the tombs had been covered and lost. Sometimes an overhanging cliff collapsed and fell over the entrance, but more often an occasional torrential rainstorm passing through the valley washed mud, sand, and even boulders into the entrances. As centuries passed, the tombs gradually filled with rubble, hiding their entrances for centuries, sometimes forever.

Employing about twenty local workmen at a time, Belzoni excavated the most likely spots, and, although he uncovered several tombs, all had been plundered in antiquity. The most beautiful of these was the tomb of Seti I. Magical spells carved on the walls of Seti's tomb ensured his safe journey to the next world. "The Book of Gates," "The Book of Praising Re in the West," and "The Book of What Is in the Netherworld" were illustrated with paintings of the gods who would assist Seti in defeating his enemies. Above his burial chamber, an astronomical ceiling showed the Egyptian constellations against a dark blue sky. Belzoni, bedazzled by the tomb's brilliant colors, as bright as the day Seti was laid to rest, spent a full year making wax impressions so he could build replicas for an exhibition in London. The show was a sensation, creating one of the first waves of Egyptomania in Europe. Belzoni never knew that just a hundred yards away from Seti's tomb lay the greatest archaeological treasure ever, the tomb of Tutankhamen.

Following in Belzoni's footsteps, Jean-François Champollion, the decipherer of hieroglyphs, made his pilgrimage to the Valley of the Kings soon after Belzoni, but he wasn't interested in excavating. Thrilled with his newly acquired ability to translate hieroglyphs, Champollion was content to copy inscriptions on tomb walls.

Although known as the Valley of the Kings for centuries, no pharaoh's mummy had ever been found until a dramatic discovery in 1881. During the 1870s, antiquities of great beauty, bearing names of the kings and queens of Egypt, began to appear in the antique shops of Luxor. These rare pieces began arriving on the market at a time when bankrupt Egypt was being administered by a triumvirate of England, France, and Italy, to all of whom she was in debt. Each European country controlled a different segment of the Egyptian government; France was in charge of antiquities.

The Egyptian Antiquities Service had been founded by Auguste Mariette, who came to Egyptology in a rather circuitous way. When the papers of a relative who had made extensive drawings of the monuments of Egypt were sent to his family, Mariette studied them intensely, became so enthused about Egypt that he taught himself the hieroglyphic alphabet, and eventually landed a position at the Louvre Museum in Paris. Dispatched to Egypt to purchase manuscripts in 1850, he used the money instead to excavate the Serapeum, the burial place of the sacred Apis bulls. He returned to France with huge crates packed with antiquities—antiquities that are still on display at the Louvre. His greatest achievement was the founding of the Egyptian Antiquities Service, an attempt to stop the kind of looting that had initiated his own career.

The high quality of the royal objects being sold by Luxor dealers attracted collectors and museum curators from all over the world. Mariette himself purchased a *Book of the Dead* (a collection of magic spells buried with a mummy to assure resurrection in the next world) that had been prepared for Queen Henettowey, who lived some 300 years after Tutankhamen. Often incorporated in these papyrus scrolls were beautifully painted pictures of the gods and scenes of the next world. Egypt's dry climate allowed these papyrus rolls to retain much of their original color and vibrancy even after thousands of years. Henettowey's was nearly one hundred feet long and a remarkable work of art.

The next few years saw additional versions of the *Book of the Dead* appear on the market, all belonging to kings, queens, princes, and princesses of the family of Queen Henettowey. When, in addition to these papyri, beautiful jewelry also surfaced, it grew clear to Mariette that an intact royal tomb had been discovered and its contents were being sold piecemeal. He was determined to find the tomb before everything was dispersed or destroyed, but died in 1881 before he could complete his search. His successor, Gaston Maspero, made the search his top priority.

Evidence eventually pointed to the Abd er Rassouls, a family living close to the Valley. After intense questioning, one of the Rassouls revealed the location of the tomb. Two days later, the Rassoul brothers led Emile Brugsch, Maspero's assistant, to an elevated, winding path overlooking the Valley of the Kings that wound through the area known as Deir el Bahri—"the place of the northern monastery," the former site of an old Coptic monastery. Chimneylike outcroppings of rock lined the way through an uninhabited area, about a mile from the ruined temple of Queen Hatshepsut. Near the base of one rocky outcrop, a rectangular eight-by-ten-foot shaft descended forty feet straight down. After placing a palm log across the top of the pit to anchor a rope, first one of the Rassouls, then Brugsch descended. When the young assistant squeezed through the entrance at the bottom, the first thing he saw was a huge coffin, behind which were three more coffins, and past those, on the right, a corridor that ran more than seventy feet into the cliff. Littering the length of it were hundreds of small bright blue mummy-shaped statues, or *ushabtis,* buried with the deceased to serve him in the next world.

The corridor opened onto a room seventeen feet square, the floor of which was almost entirely covered with splendid coffins containing kings of the New Kingdom. Here lay Amenhotep I, Tuthmosis I, Tuthmosis II, and Tuthmosis III of the Eighteenth Dynasty—Tutankhamen's ancestors. Along with them were the Nineteenth Dynasty pharaohs Ramses I, his son, Seti I and *his* son, Ramses the Great. Further back in the tomb, the last room, higher than the others and twenty feet long, was strewn with the coffins and mummies of the Twenty-first Dynasty royal family whose *Books of the Dead* had initiated the quest. Here were the mummies of Pinedjem II, Queen Henettowey, and other members of that august family. The Rassouls had discovered the remains of kings and queens whose reigns spanned four centuries, from the Eighteenth Dynasty through the Twenty-first.

Brugsch, merely an assistant at the museum, was not a great scholar but had attended Egyptology classes in Cairo conducted by his more learned elder brother, Heinrich, so he was able to read the cartouches on many of the coffins. He realized that he was in the presence of the greatest pharaohs in history and that this was the most important find ever made in Egypt. But how had kings of so many different dynasties come to be together in one tomb?

By the Twentieth Dynasty, two centuries after Tutankhamen's death, most of the tombs in the Valley of the Kings had been robbed. An inspection of the Valley of the Kings during the Twenty-first Dynasty revealed this wholesale violation. Rather than continue futile attempts to protect isolated tombs, the violated bodies of the pharaohs were repaired, rewrapped, labeled with wooden tags, placed in new coffins when necessary, and removed to the communal tomb the Rassouls were later to discover. Hastily written accounts on the walls of the original tombs and inscriptions on the pharaohs' coffins and bandages detailed the dates and places of transit. Combining these records made it possible to reconstruct the steps priests of the Twenty-first Dynasty took to preserve the mummies of their ancestors.

The Deir el Bahri cache was considered secure enough that the priest-king Pinedjem II chose it for his own resting place. The inscriptions recording the last movements are written in black ink on the wall at the bottom of the shaft of the Deir el Bahri tomb. On Pinedjem's burial day, the bodies of Seti I and Ramses II were interred with him, and there they remained, undisturbed, for 3,000 years.

As important and unique as the Deir el Bahri discovery was, the findings were poorly documented. After two hours in the tomb, Brugsch realized that the crew's candles might set fire to the dry wooden coffins, so he quickly left the tomb. He then decided that the mummies and the funerary equipment had to be moved to Cairo as soon as possible. The inhabitants of nearby Gourna had for years made their living by robbing tombs. When they learned how much they were soon to lose, there was no telling what they would do. No time was taken to record where each coffin was found in the tomb, and not a single photograph was snapped nor a drawing made of the items *in situ*. Within two days all the coffins, canopic chests, and funerary equipment were hoisted to the surface. Three hundred men carried these treasures to the west bank of the Nile where the coffins, mummies, and statues were ferried to the east bank and loaded onto the museum's steamer for their journey to Cairo. When word of the boat's royal cargo became public, fellaheen women lined the banks of the Nile and wailed mourning cries, just as their ancient ancestors must have done in marking the passing of their kings.[4]

The Deir el Bahri cache had an important effect on excavations in the Valley of the Kings. The find showed how extensive tomb robbery had been in ancient Egypt and how unprotected the tombs were. As a result of the Deir el Bahri discovery, the mummies of Tuthmosis I and II were now in the Cairo Museum, and, although their tombs had not yet been discovered, it was certain they had been plundered, emptied of anything of value. There was good news as well: even with all the royal mummies contained in the cache, there were still plenty of important pharaohs unaccounted for—Tuthmosis IV, Amenhotep III, Merneptah, as well as other lesser known kings. Perhaps their tombs had escaped destruction and plunder.

In 1898, when Victor Loret discovered a second royal cache containing the mummies of Amenhotep III and other kings, attention began to focus on Tutankhamen, until then a practically unknown pharaoh. If Cleopatra, who ruled Egypt a thousand years after Tutankhamen, had been asked about him, she would have responded with a blank look.

Petrie's excavations at Amarna had shown that Tutankhamen was part of a religious revolution, making Amarna a hot subject among Egyptologists. At the same time, various royal tombs—all robbed—had been found in the Valley of the Kings, but not Tutankhamen's. Nor was his mummy among those saved by pious priests from the plundered tombs. It was not unreasonable to think that somewhere in the Valley of the Kings the mummy of Tutankhamen might still rest undisturbed in his tomb. The search for Tutankhamen began in earnest.

To excavate in Egypt, an archaeologist needed the permission of the Antiquities Service, which was not difficult to obtain at the beginning of the century. The "concession," as it was called, usually stipulated the area in which the excavator could dig and the length of time, during which everyone else was excluded from that area. Objects found would be divided between the Antiquities Service and the excavator. It was a good deal for both parties. The Antiquities Service with its limited funds got free labor and new objects for its museum; the excavator got what he wanted—knowledge, objects, or both. Some, like Petrie, came for knowledge. When Petrie received his share of the division of funds at the end of a season, he kept the most interesting pieces to form a study collection that evolved into the Petrie Museum at University College in London. The rest he divided among the patrons who had funded his excavations.

Other excavators came primarily for objects to enhance their own collections, or simply for the thrill of the hunt. Theodore Davis, a wealthy American lawyer and businessman, came for the hunt. Davis wintered in Egypt on his houseboat, *The Bedouin,* a rather elaborate affair complete with piano and crystal chandelier. Looking for a diversion, he decided to excavate but needed an experienced hand working with him to garner the permission. Enter Howard Carter, who began his career under Flinders Petrie.

Carter's introduction to Egyptology came via his natural talent as an artist. His father made a living painting animal portraits for wealthy patrons. His children—Howard was the youngest of eleven—inherited their father's talent. Howard's father had for years been the family portrait painter for Lord Amherst's family, so as a young boy Howard had accompanied his father to Didlington Hall, the family seat that housed Lord Amherst's collection of Egyptian antiquities. Amherst was involved with the Egypt Exploration Fund, a British society recently formed to excavate and record the monuments of Egypt. One of its excavators, in need of an artist to help draw the tomb walls at Beni Hassan, not far from Amarna, suggested that the artist be a "non-gentleman," as such a person would require less than a person of high breeding and thus some expenses could be saved. Young Howard Carter, since he had almost no formal schooling, fit the bill perfectly. Lady Amherst recommended the boy and he boarded a steamer bound for Alexandria. Carter quickly proved to be both competent and hardworking, able to live happily in the simple surroundings of an expedition camp. Soon he was sent to learn the rudiments of excavation techniques from Petrie at Amarna, skills that would later serve him well.

Petrie, who didn't know the young excavator well enough to trust his work, commented:

> . . . Howard Carter came as a lad of seventeen to join me in order to do some excavating for Mr. Tyson Amherst. His interest then was entirely in painting and natural history, and I little thought how much he would be enabled to do. To keep his work distant, I left him to the clearing of a temple site. There he found the broken statues of the queen, torsos and masses of chips from them.[5]

This was one of those curious quirks of history where the paths of two great men cross and neither realizes the significance. Petrie, though still a young man, was by now the most skilled excavator in Egypt, and had begun uncovering early clues to the life of Tutankhamen. Neither

Petrie nor Carter could have had any idea that a quarter of a century later, Carter would discover the tomb of Tutankhamen and become the most famous Egyptologist of all time. Indeed, as Carter worked on the site, he probably handled objects inscribed with Tutankhamen's name but had no idea who Tutankhamen was.

Carter went on to work on other excavations, learning the techniques of archaeology so well that in 1899, at the age of twenty-six, Carter was appointed by Maspero as Chief Inspector of southern Egypt for the Antiquities Service. Carter was energetic, hard working, and concerned about preserving Egypt's monuments. His duties included constructing iron doors on tomb entrances to prevent vandalism and theft, installing electric lights so tourists could see the wall paintings, restoring temples, and preventing thefts. Carter seems to have taken a special interest in the latter duty. He recorded one incident that verges on a Sherlock Holmes story.

Carter had prepared the tomb of Amenhotep II for tourism. He placed the king's mummy in its sarcophagus, displayed many of the objects that Loret had found, and installed an iron gate so the tomb could be locked at night. In spite of these precautions, on November 20, 1901, the tomb was broken into, the mummy of Amenhotep II damaged, and some objects stolen. Carter's report shows just how determined he was in tracking the criminals.

Nov. 28th 1901.—The following day I again went to the tomb of Amenophis II . . . It had been reported to me formerly by the parquet that the padlock of the tomb had been stuck together and made to look all right by means of little pieces of lead paper. . . . I found more small pieces of lead paper beneath the door and a little round piece of resin, probably from a sont-tree. This piece was the exact size of the socket for the tongue in the padlock and gave me a small clue; for on 11th Nov., it had been broken into, the lock being forced by a lever and made to look all right by the means of resin that stuck it together, the material and method in both cases being exactly the same.

I must add before going on further that I had grave suspicions against Mohamed Abd el Rasoul in the case of the Yi-ma-dua tomb, and I watched this man whenever possible, he being a well-known tomb plunderer and his house being quite near the tomb.

. . . I carefully compared the footprints in both tombs and found them to have a strong resemblance. In both cases, *the footprints, being prints of bare feet, are of one person only* . . . I then took photographs, to scale as near as possible, of the foot marks of bare feet, and measured them up very carefully.

During the meantime the spoor-man tracked footprints from Biban El Moluk to the village of Goorneh and to the house of Soleman and Ahmed Abd El Rasoul. These men were arrested . . .

30th Nov. 1901—I went to the parquet and . . . requested to leave to inspect the footprints of Mohamed Abd El Rasoul. This I did at Markaz, and found them to agree totally with my photographs and with the measurements which I had taken in the tomb of Amenophis II and Yi-ma-dua. The measurements agree to a millimeter.[6]

When Carter heard that Davis was interested in excavating, he suggested that he could arrange a concession in the Valley of the Kings for him, and, when Carter's duties as chief inspector permitted, he would supervise the work. In their first year of excavation they found the plundered tomb of Tuthmosis IV. Many of the funerary objects had been left by the ancient robbers including beautiful blue ushabti figures, and part of the pharaoh's chariot that was decorated with battle scenes. Davis was elated, and although the partnership was favorable to both men, it was not to last. In 1904, Carter was transferred north to oversee the monuments of Saqqara, fourteen miles south of Cairo. There he was involved in an altercation that ended his career with the Antiquities Service.

An unruly group of French tourists had tried to enter a tomb without tickets, forced their way past the guard, and refused to leave the tomb. Carter was called. When the French attacked the local guardians, Carter told them to defend themselves and a melee ensued. The French were outraged that an Egyptian workman had hit them, but Carter defended the guards' actions and wanted to prosecute the French. In colonial Egypt, it was unheard-of for an Egyptian to strike a European. The matter reached the highest European diplomatic levels in Egypt and Carter was asked to apologize. He refused. Maspero sympathized with Carter, but was forced to reprimand him and the outraged Carter resigned, never to return to the Antiquities Service. He was a free agent.

In the meantime, Davis, now without the services of Carter, employed twenty-two-year-old Edward Ayrton to continue the excavations in the Valley. The son of a diplomat, Ayrton was born in China, and at nineteen traveled to Egypt to excavate with Petrie. Like most of Petrie's disciples, he was well trained and served Davis well, discovering the plundered tomb of the pharaoh Horemheb, one of Tutankhamen's generals who later became king. He also found the first clue to Tutankhamen's tomb—lodged under a rock—a faience cup bearing the pharaoh's name. This provided the first solid link between Tutankhamen and the Valley of the Kings. Excited by this find, Ayrton and Davis continued the search, and, in 1907, came upon a small pit containing the remains of an ancient meal. Mixed with the food, cups, wine jars, and floral garlands were mummy wrappings that bore the name of Tutankhamen. Clearly, Tutankhamen had been buried in the Valley, but Davis didn't understand what he had found. He thought he had uncovered reburied plunder from Tutankhamen's robbed tomb. Actually these were the remains of the meal eaten by the family and close friends of Tutankhamen on the day of his burial, along with leftovers from the materials used at his mummification. When Davis found a small unfinished tomb in 1909 containing ushabti figures, and some gold foil with the name of Tutankhamen, he concluded that he had found the plundered tomb of Tutankhamen.

Each year, Davis published his finds in a series of sumptuous books. At the end of each book was a catalog of the objects found, written by a professional Egyptologist. Some of these books incorporated watercolor illustrations by Howard Carter, who was then unemployed and grateful for the work. In the preface Davis gave his opinions, unhindered by facts or advice from Egyptologists. In the preface to the volume on the Tutankhamen findings, Davis concluded, "I fear the Valley is now exhausted."[7] He would soon give up his concession to excavate in the Valley, opening the door for Carter.

During the period that Davis worked in the Valley of the Kings, George Edward Stanhope Molyneux Herbert, Fifth Earl of Carnarvon, began his own series of excavations just outside the Valley. Carnarvon, a wealthy aristocrat and collector, had a passion for breeding racehorses and racing automobiles, and had the unfortunate distinction of being in the world's first near-fatal automobile crash in 1903. Advised to travel to Egypt to recover from his injuries, he developed a keen interest in archaeology and, like Davis, thought he would enjoy the diversion of excavating. His accident had injured his lungs and left him frail, so he could never actively participate, but he wanted to have some role. One excavation artist noted Carnarvon's true love of Egyptology:

The unhealthy color of his complexion was made more conspicuous by the fact that his face was pitted from smallpox. But when he discussed Egyptology, his pale lusterless eyes lit up with enthusiasm."[8]

When Carnarvon applied to Maspero for permission to excavate, Maspero saw a chance to help the impoverished Carter. He suggested that Carnarvon employ Carter. In 1907 he and Carter formed a partnership: Carnarvon would finance a series of excavations and Carter would direct the work.

They were an odd couple. Lord Carnarvon had grown up with immense wealth, had great personal charm, and exhibited all the social graces; he was a man very much at ease with himself and, as was the fashion of the wealthy, he dabbled in the occult. He gave and attended parties where mediums gazed into crystal balls, held seances, and generally enjoyed himself.

Carter, on the other hand, came from a hardworking middle-class family where he developed a no-nonsense attitude toward life, viewing issues as either black or white—right or wrong. He was a sincere, hardworking man who had few social skills and little personal charm, a bachelor, and very much a loner. They were an unlikely team, but a lasting friendship developed. The relationship was always that of the lord and his servant, but they cared for and protected each other.

The year that Carter and Carnarvon formed their partnership, the Davis-Ayrton team found yet another tomb containing a royal coffin and a mummy. Before the excavation dust had settled, Davis would declare it was the mummy of Queen Tiye, Tutankhamen's grandmother. Arthur Weigall, the new Chief Inspector of Antiquities for Luxor, declared it Akhenaten, and George Daressy, the French Egyptologist working in the Egyptian Museum, announced that the mummy was Tutankhamen. In the end they were all proved wrong; Tutankhamen's brother, Smenkare, had been discovered.

TOMB 55

Of all the royal mummies discovered, none has caused more controversy than the one found in Tomb 55 in the Valley of the Kings. Situated near the tomb of Ramses IX, this tomb received the new number 55, and is known as KV55 (King's Valley 55). As Davis and Ayrton cleared the debris, a flight of steps appeared that had been cut into the bedrock. Clearing it revealed a doorway leading to a second set of steps that descended into a tomb, at the bottom of which stood a dry wall built of large limestone chips. Not traditional tomb architecture, the wall had obviously resealed a tomb that had been opened in ancient times. Removing the blocking wall revealed a descending corridor nearly filled to the ceiling with limestone chips to deter tomb robbers. An open space near the ceiling suggested that it hadn't worked; the tomb had been plundered.

The crowd present for the opening of the tomb included Gaston

Maspero; Arthur Weigall, the Inspector of Antiquities for Upper Egypt; Joseph Lindon Smith, an artist who had worked for several Egyptologists; and Smith's wife; Corinna. Nearly all of those present have left accounts of what happened on that clear January day in 1907. None of them agree with the others.

First to enter the tomb was Joseph Lindon Smith, whom Maspero selected because his slight build allowed him to squeeze through the narrow passage. As Smith inched forward on top of the chips, he encountered a large gilded wooden door. Quickly sketching the inscriptions, he returned to show them to Maspero, who read the name of Queen Tiye, wife of Amenhotep III and mother of Akhenaten. The door was so fragile that when, for the first time in 3,000 years, a gentle breeze entered the tomb, the gold leaf flaked off and floated to the ground. As the door was too fragile to be moved, Smith carefully crept alongside it and continued downward into the tomb.

The tomb was unfinished. What served as the burial chamber was an unpainted, roughly hewn room about eighteen square feet. More wooden panels lay on the floor and against a wall. In a niche cut into one wall, Smith could see four beautiful alabaster canopic jars with finely sculpted lids in the form of a woman's head (fig. 3). What drew Smith's attention among the jumble, however, was a badly damaged but beautiful coffin lying with its lid ajar near one wall. The coffin, like the rest of the contents of the room, had suffered water damage from rain dripping through a crack in the ceiling. The coffin had once rested on a wooden funerary bier that had collapsed, causing even more damage to the coffin. Still worse, at some time in antiquity, a rock had crashed onto it from the ceiling.

Thousands of inlays of paste and semiprecious stones formed the protective wings of a falcon encircling the coffin. More impressive than the coffin itself was the fact that inside lay a body—obviously undisturbed—for on its head remained a golden vulture, symbol of the pharaoh's power.

No one recorded how long Smith remained in the tomb, but it must have seemed like an eternity to the group waiting outside for his report. When he finally emerged, he described things as best he could. Maspero asked a few questions and sent him back to look for water damage and to sketch the objects. Smith sketched the coffin, then returned to make a second report. Everyone was impatient to enter the tomb, but they had to wait for workmen to clear a passage, and to put down boards to accommodate Maspero's ample weight.

Davis's butler was sent to bring a picnic hamper from his large houseboat on the Nile. Over lunch the group discussed the discovery. Davis was delighted, convinced that they had discovered the tomb and mummy of Queen Tiye. After lunch they were at last able to enter the tomb.

All but two of the wood panels have since disintegrated, but from what was observed in the tomb in 1907, it is clear that they were the remains of a gilded shrine that had once enclosed the coffin of Queen Tiye. Her shrine was apparently made for her by her son, Akhenaten, and shows him with his mother worshipping the Aten. Some time after the burial, someone had hacked out Akhenaten's image from the shrine, but the figure of Queen Tiye was untouched. And, nestling in a rectangular niche carved into the wall were the four canopic jars, meant to hold the mummy's internal organs, with lids in the shape of a woman's head.

Because of the fragile condition of the coffin lid they had to wait for a conservator to strengthen it so it could be removed. In the meantime, each object had to be photographed *in situ* before it could be moved from the tomb to the daylight. Several days passed before a conservator and a photographer arrived from Cairo. On the day they unwrapped the mummy everyone present had a sense of the event's historical importance. They would be the first people in more than 3,000 years to look upon the face of this famous queen of Egypt. Maspero, Weigall, Ayrton, Joseph Lindon Smith and his wife, Corinna, and Theodore Davis and his companion Mrs. Andrews all filed into the room. Also present was Harold Jones, an artist who worked for Davis; Arthur Quibell of the Antiquities Service arrived later. After the group gathered solemnly around the coffin, the lid of which had been removed by the conservator, Maspero asked Joseph Lindon Smith to do the unwrapping because he had ". . . the gentle hands of an artist."

Gold sheets the size of a piece of writing paper covered the mummy from neck to feet. Because gold does not tarnish, the ancient Egyptians associated it with eternity, encasing the mummy in gold, to ensure preservation. As Smith removed each sheet of gold, he handed it to Maspero for inspection, and Maspero pronounced each of the twelve "uninscribed." The mummy was now exposed, the left arm lay across the breast and the right arm along the side, a pose normally reserved for royal women. Three gold bracelets encircled each wrist. Davis now had even more evidence supporting his Queen Tiye theory. Maspero asked Smith to feel under the wrappings in the area of the neck and upper chest for the pectoral that should have been there. When Smith delicately began the procedure, they were confronted by a scene like something from a horror film.

> But no sooner had my hand touched the surface of the mummy than it crumbled into ashes and sifted down through the bones. So it was with the entire body until nothing remained except a pile of dust and disconnected bones with a few shreds of dried skin adhering to them. The water that had got into the tomb explained the cloth resembling the consistency of the ash of a cigar. In feeling around I found pieces of a broad necklace of gold pendants, inlaid plaques, lotus flowers of gold and numerous minute beads.[9]

It was a strange assortment of things in Tomb 55: objects belonging to Tiye, Akhenaten, Smenkare, and, many Egyptologists now believe, Kiya's canopic jars. How did all these objects of Tutankhamen's family come together there? The most likely explanation is that after the tombs of Amarna had been looted, some loyal servant gathered whatever remained, transported it to Thebes, and reburied the cache in Tomb 55. Today, most Egyptologists believe the body in Tomb 55 was Smenkare, Tutankhamen's brother. Tutankhamen was still missing.

As soon as Theodore Davis relinquished the Valley concession, Carter and Carnarvon took it over. They set out to conduct what they called "a systematic and exhaustive search" of the Valley, but work was delayed by the start of World War I until late in 1917.

Carter was convinced that the best bet for an undiscovered tomb was in a triangle formed by the tombs of Merneptah, Ramses II, and Ramses VI, the only area in the Valley that had not been fully excavated. Workmen cleared thousands of baskets of debris as Carter worked down to the base of the well-known tomb of Ramses VI. A group of ancient workmen's huts were uncovered, probably left behind from the construction of that tomb. The huts would have to be cleared to proceed further, but that would have closed access to the Ramses VI tomb, one of the most popular tourist sites. So Carter moved his work to another part of the Valley until tourism abated.

Five years went by with no success as Carter assiduously searched the Valley. Carnarvon came to agree that Davis was right, that the Valley was played out. Because of the bond that had developed between Carnarvon and Carter, it must have been difficult for Carnarvon when he invited Carter to Highclere Castle in 1922 to inform him that he had decided to end the excavation. After so many years with no results Carter could not have been surprised, but he was not ready to give up. He made a counterproposal. They would continue for one last season for which Carter would pay the expenses, though Carnarvon could keep anything they found. Carnarvon, touched by the bold gesture from the unmoneyed Carter, agreed to finance one last season.

It was not until November 1922 that Carter returned at last to the triangle he had left for later and began clearing the huts. On November 4, one of the workmen discovered a step cut into the valley floor. After another day of clearing, a stairway was exposed. At sunset on November 5, after the twelfth step, the upper part of a doorway with the royal necropolis seal still in place was uncovered. Carter knew they had discovered a king's tomb, but could not determine which king. Through a small hole near the top of the door, Carter could see that the passage behind the plastered door was filled with rubble to deter tomb robbers. The tomb might be intact. What bothered Carter was the narrow stairway, only six feet wide; the entrances to other royal tombs were considerably wider. Somehow able to keep his excitement in check, Carter filled in the stairway with sand and rubble and cabled his patron, Lord Carnarvon, in England:

> *"At last have made wonderful discovery in Valley; a magnificent tomb with seals intact, re-covered same for your arrival; congratulations."*

Carter waited almost a month for his friend, who arrived in Egypt the last week in November. Arrangements were finally made to open the tomb. The stairway was cleared again, and this time Tutankhamen's cartouche was revealed on the lower part of the sealed door. When the door was opened, however, the excavators could see an ancient narrow path through the rubble, almost certainly made by ancient robbers. The tomb had been entered before.

An entire day was devoted to clearing the thirty-foot-long, descending passage. Strewn amongst the limestone chips were alabaster jars, pottery and workmen's tools. Finally, a second sealed door was reached. This time there was clear evidence of the door's having been breached and resealed. Carter made an opening in the upper left corner of the doorway to insert a candle for testing the air inside. At first the flame fluttered in escaping hot air, then Carter saw, "wonderful things."

The room into which Carter and Carnarvon peered was packed with all the possessions Tutankhamen would need in the next world. Chariots, statues, game boards, linens, jewelry, beds, couches, chairs, even a throne, were all piled on top of each other. The ancient robbers had apparently been caught in the act or frightened away soon, because little had been disturbed. The tomb was virtually intact.

At last it seemed that the details of the unknown pharaoh Tutankhamen would be revealed. When Carter made his discovery, two popular references on the history of ancient Egypt existed, both written by Petrie's American counterpart, James Henry Breasted. Trained as a pharmacist, Breasted soon realized that Egyptology interested him more than dispensing drugs, so he left for Germany to study hieroglyphs. The Europeans were far ahead of America in offering formal courses in Egyptology, so Breasted studied with Adolph Erman, a great philologist, and was the first American awarded a doctorate in Egyptology. Petrie was an excavator, Breasted a philologist; each was interested in completing a picture of Egyptian history, but they took different approaches. Petrie wanted to discover new material; Breasted wanted to translate it.

At the turn of the century Breasted began an incredible one-man campaign to record all the historical records of ancient Egypt. For eleven years he roamed up and down the Nile, translating inscriptions on temple and tomb walls, often risking his health. His diary entry for November 14, 1906, reads,

> We are at work at 6:00 AM, and the sun is long down before we stop. I spent yesterday on a ladder, copying from a glaring wall upon which this fierce sun was beating in full force; and I rose this morning with one eye swollen shut. Even with dark glasses, I sometimes find work on a sunlit wall impossible.[10]

After this exhaustive research Breasted published his five-volume *Ancient Records of Egypt*.[11] He had found only one monument from the reign of Tutankhamen, the tomb of Huy, Tutankhamen's viceroy to Nubia. When Breasted later wrote his 600-page *History of Egypt*[12] he devoted less than a page to Tutankhamen. There simply wasn't more to say. Carter hoped to fill in the history.

As the excavation of Tutankhamen's tomb proceeded, the information Egyptologists had been waiting for did not come to light. Spectacular objects were found, but nothing mentioned who the king's parents were or provided details or insight into what had happened during his brief reign. There was a fleeting moment of excitement when a box of "papyri" was found in the antechamber, but when examined closely it turned out to be rolls of linen, turned yellow over the centuries. Tutankhamen had eluded his discoverers.

Carter and Carnarvon, delighted with their discovery, reacted in very different ways. Carnarvon, the collector, was thrilled by the beauty of the objects. Carter, with his artist's training, could of course appreciate their beauty, but, as an archaeologist, his interest lay in discovering the hidden history of Tutankhamen. In this he was disappointed.

Carter never knew that Tutankhamen may have suffered a blow to the back of the head, nor did he suspect foul play. But even now, seventy-five years later, we can still look to the tomb for clues about what happened during Tutankhamen's brief life, and most of all for clues about his death.

THE GOLD SHRINE

The jewelry was, of course, spectacular, but for me, the most touching object found in the tomb was a small wooden shrine covered with gold that once housed a statue of Tutankhamen. Only a foot and a half high, it is actually a model of a life-sized shrine (fig. 7). When Carter opened its tiny doors, he saw two little recessed sandal prints on the floor of the shrine, where the statue, stolen by thieves in ancient times, once stood.[13] The outside of the shrine is carved with eighteen scenes of Tutankhamen doing all the things he loved—hunting marsh fowl with his bow, receiving flowers, being perfumed—and always beside him is Ankhesenamen. She brings flowers to Tutankhamen and ties a necklace around his neck. When he hunts, Ankhesenamen sits at his knee holding his next arrow. The king pours perfume on his bride's hands (fig. 8). These are not standard scenes produced from workshop patterns. This is a portrayal of a young couple devoted to each other, engrossed in each other. Their marriage took place for political reasons when they were children, but clearly a great affection grew between them. The scenes on the shrine show them constantly touching, holding hands. They were teenagers in love.

The shrine's inscriptions never mention Tutankhamen as "True of Voice," deceased, so this is no hastily fashioned funerary object commissioned for his tomb. It was probably a gift from Ankhesenamen to her husband. It is her love letter written in gold. The shrine isn't the only sign of love between Tutankhamen and Ankhesenamen. Even the royal throne shows Ankhesenamen tenderly adjusting Tutankhamen's broad collar.

The royal couple spent a great deal of time together, whiling away the hours playing games. Tutankhamen took three different sets of board games with him to the next world. One of his favorites was "Senet," something like our modern game of Monopoly (fig. 9). The Senet board consists of three rows of ten squares. Some of the squares were labeled "very good" and some were labeled "water"—the equivalent of "go to jail." The pieces were shaped like chess pawns, but in some elaborate sets they were lions' heads. We do not know the rules for the game, but it seems to have involved a race between players to avoid the pitfalls, such as "water," to reach the end of the board first. Moves were determined by throwing sticks.[14] The game was so popular that kings and queens are shown playing Senet on their tomb walls. They also played "Twenty Squares." The squares were arranged in a T. We can only surmise that the players lined their game pieces on the outer rows of the board, and, using throwing sticks to determine their moves, attempted to make their way down the center aisle.[15]

Tutankhamen was buried with nearly three dozen jars of fine wine, each holding several gallons. Egyptians were so fond of wine that they often showed the process of wine-making on their tomb walls. One nobleman from Thebes, Senefer, had the roof of his tomb left uneven so that a grape arbor painted on the ceiling would appear realistic. Another Theban nobleman, Nakht, showed the pressing of grapes, with several men in large vats trampling the grapes to release their juice. The wine in Tutankhamen's tomb was quite a treasure. The jars are labeled as to the vintner, vineyard, and year of bottling. Many of the jars are labeled from the "Estate of Tutankhamen"; most are dated to year 5, probably a vintage year. One bottle was labeled "year 31" of the pharaoh's reign, so it must have been saved from his grandfather's wine cellar. It was more than thirty years old when placed in the tomb. Of all the wine in Tutankhamen's tomb, only four of the jars were labeled "sweet." Tutankh-amen liked his wine dry.[16]

Tutankhamen seems to have loved hunting above all other sports. Scenes decorating his linen chests and shrines show the king hunting and fowling. An ostrich feather fan depicts the young king hunting ostriches with a bow and arrow from his chariot. Behind the king, a striding ankh sign holds an ostrich-feather fan that is also decorated. If one could see the decoration on it, it would be another ostrich-feather fan, a picture of the picture in the picture. Tutankhamen also hunted ibexes and gazelles. Dozens of bows and hundreds of arrows were placed in his tomb so he could continue his hunts in the next world.[17]

Objects in the tomb tell us a good deal about *what* Tutankhamen liked, but they say precious little about *whom* he liked and his relationships with those around him. Was he fond of the members of his court? Did he trust them? Did he welcome Aye's guidance? Tutankhamen's tomb doesn't reveal much about his family either; there were few visible mementos of his parents, sisters, or brother, other than Ankhesenamen. Perhaps mention of his family was too painful a reference to Amarna. But Howard Carter did find a great heirloom from Tutankhamen's grandmother in the tomb. A miniature coffin that held an even smaller gilded anthropoid coffin was inscribed for the boy king, and contained a curious assortment of objects: a tiny painted wooden coffin, some scraps of cloth, and a linen parcel containing a solid gold statuette of a kneeling king, identified as Tutankhamen's grandfather, Amenhotep III. An even smaller coffin inscribed with the name and titles of Tutankhamen's grandmother, Queen Tiye, held a lock of her hair.

Heirlooms from previous rulers or family members were often found in royal tombs. Sometimes an unguent jar belonging to a relative, or a scarab inscribed with a loved-one's name, was placed in a tomb as a keepsake. The plait of Queen Tiye's hair was the memento of a revered grandmother and it helped Egyptologists establish Tutankhamen's lineage, but it also provided a clue that may have helped identify her mummy.

When Victor Loret discovered three unwrapped, unidentified mummies in a side chamber in Amenhotep II's tomb, no one believed they would ever be identified. The mummy that appeared on the left in contemporary photographs was dubbed "The Elder Lady." Photographs clearly show her right arm resting at her side and her left arm across her chest, a pose associated with royal women of the Eighteenth Dynasty. Edward Wente, a University of Chicago Egyptologist, suggested in the 1970s that the Elder Lady might be either Queen Hatshepsut or Queen Tiye.

Like fingerprints, hair is unique to each individual. If the hair found among Tutankhamen's heirlooms matched that of the Elder Lady, then she was Queen Tiye. The Egyptian Antiquities Organization is, however, extremely cautious in permitting samples from the royal mummies—even a few hairs—to be taken. They had to be convinced that the project held a good chance of identifying the Elder Lady as the venerable Queen Tiye.

As a first step toward gaining permission, Dr. James Harris, author of *X-raying the Pharaohs*, took a cephalogram of the Elder Lady in 1975, a technique that permits a precise plotting of cranial measurements. Computerized data from the Elder Lady were compared with those of the mummy of Tuya, Queen Tiye's mother, to determine if the two women were similar enough to imply a mother-daughter relationship. The test showed a remarkable similarity, increasing the chance that the elder lady was Queen Tiye. Permission was granted for hair samples to be taken from the head of the Elder Lady and the plait of Queen Tiye's hair.

Both samples were scanned by electron microprobes to chart their chemical composition. The hair found in Tutankhamen's tomb matched that from the head of the Elder Lady almost exactly. The authors of the study concluded they had found Queen Tiye.[18]

If the objects in the tomb's first room didn't reveal the king's unknown past, perhaps Tutankhamen himself would. Beyond the antechamber, in the sealed burial chamber, lay the long dead pharaoh. But Carter and Carnarvon couldn't get to him until the room was empty. Removing the objects from the antechamber took more than a year. The Metropolitan Museum of Art in New York had loaned Carter their master photographer, Harry Burton, to record the placement of each object in the tomb. This was essential because sometimes wooden objects are so fragile that they turn to dust when touched so the only record of their existence is the photograph. In a *New York Times* account, Burton told of just such an experience.

> I remember, when we were clearing a series of XVIIth Dynasty tombs, which had been infested with white ants, the preliminary photographs were literally the only record of most of the wooden objects found. The coffins appeared to be in perfect condition, but when touched they collapsed into dust.
>
> There was one very attractive small wooden statuette of a girl in one of these tombs, which appeared to be quite sound. It was standing quite alone, and after the general view of the chamber had been taken, the camera was turned on to it. I intended to expose a plate for two minutes, but after it had been exposed for one and three-quarter minutes the figure suddenly collapsed, and nothing remained but a small heap of dust. I immediately switched off the beam of light, put a cap on the camera, and went off to develop the plate. Fortunately the negative turned out to be quite good, and, although the statuette no longer existed, we had a complete record of it. This is only one of many similar cases.[19]

The Metropolitan Museum had no official connection with the Carter-Carnarvon excavation, but their team was excavating outside the Valley when the discovery was made. Realizing how many priceless objects were involved, they put their team at Carter's disposal. Even in Egypt, nothing of the magnitude of Tutankhamen's treasures had been found before; the entire archaeological community formed a support system.

Sometimes objects were so fragile that they had to be conserved in the tomb before they could be moved. Wood pieces had to be strengthened and wrapped, but Tutankhamen's clothes presented the greatest problems. Often the linen fell apart at the slightest touch, so the pattern of the thousands of beads and gold sequins had to be recorded first so that, in the event that a garment turned to dust, the decorations could later be applied to new cloth. Arthur Mace, the Metropolitan Museum's conservator, estimated that there were nearly 50,000 beads on one garment alone. He covered many of the smaller garments with wax so the beadwork would remain intact while the clothing was moved. It took Mace three weeks of intense work just to empty one chest of clothes. As Mace and Burton worked to clear the antechamber there were moments of wondering about the boy-king, who they hoped lay in the next room. Mace even pondered how he died.

> We have reason to believe that he was little more than a boy when he died, and that it was his successor, Eye, who supported his candidature to the throne and acted as his adviser during his brief reign. It was Eye, moreover, who arranged his funeral ceremonies, and it may even be that he arranged his death, judging that the time was now ripe for him to assume the reins of government himself.[20]

I know of no Egyptologist who ever commented on this suggestion, yet, as we will see, Mace was not far from the mark.

On February 16, 1923, the antechamber was finally cleared. When Carter broke through the wall into the burial chamber, he was faced with what seemed to be a wall of gold. Actually, he was looking at a gilded wood shrine that enclosed the body of Tutankhamen. The shrine was 16 feet 8 inches by 10 feet 9 inches, nearly filling the burial chamber, making it difficult for Carter to move in the narrow space between the shrine and the walls. The doors to the shrine were closed so Carter didn't know that inside were three more shrines, one inside the other, all surrounding Tutankhamen's sarcophagus. Each shrine had to be dismantled and removed from the chamber before the next could be examined, a difficult task because of the confined space. The job had been easier for the ancient workmen, who had assembled the shrines from fresh, strong timber. Carter had to deal with dry, brittle wood.

Still visible were the ancient instructions for assembling the shrines painted in black and white ink by the carpenters. On the front of the side panels was the hieroglyph ⟨glyph⟩ —meaning "front" and on the rear was ⟨glyph⟩ —meaning "rear." These hieroglyphs matched those on the roofs of the shrines that were to be aligned accordingly—the ancient equivalent of "insert tab A into slot A." The workmen had been directed to place the shrines so the doors would open to the west, and the king could emerge into the next world, but somehow they got it backwards. Tutankhamen would have walked into this world rather than the next.

Once the shrines were dismantled and removed, the sarcophagus was at last revealed. Carved from a single block of yellow quartzite, a beautiful winged goddess on each corner protected Tutankhamen with outstretched arms. The lid was of pink granite painted to look like the yellow quartzite of the base—a precursor of faux marble. In the rush to prepare Tutankhamen's burial, something must have gone wrong and the original lid broke, so a lid of pink granite was substituted. But here, too, the stone masons had a problem: the second lid developed a crack, which they repaired with plaster and paint.

This haste with which Tutankhamen's tomb was prepared made Carter's job more difficult, as he frequently encountered the workmen's mistakes. The crack in the lid of the sarcophagus, for example, made it difficult to lift in one piece, but eventually block and tackle were brought and ropes were placed beneath the lid so that it could be hoisted. One step closer to his goal, Carter wrote:

> Many strange scenes must have happened in the valley of the tombs of the kings since it became the royal burial ground of the Theban New Empire, but one may be pardoned for thinking that the present scene was not the least interesting or dramatic. For ourselves it was the one supreme and culminating moment—a moment looked forward to ever since it became

evident that the chambers discovered in November 1922 must be the tomb of Tut Ankh Amen and not a cache of his furniture as had been claimed. None of us but felt the solemnity of the occasion, none of us but was affected by the prospect of what we were about to see—the burial custom of a king of ancient Egypt thirty-three centuries ago. How would the king be found? Such were the anticipatory speculations running in our minds during the silence maintained. The tackle for raising the lid was in position. I gave the word. Amid intense silence the huge slab, broken in two, weighing over a ton and a quarter, rose from its bed.[21]

The group working in the tomb, together with the assembled dignitaries, peered into the sarcophagus, but as if through a mist. They could not make out any details. Only after gazing into the sarcophagus for a while did they realize that they were looking at gauze-like shrouds covering the coffin inside the sarcophagus. When the shrouds were rolled back, Carter and the group were confronted with more than they could ever have hoped for, a seven-foot anthropoid coffin of unsurpassed workmanship bearing the likeness of Tutankhamen. On the forehead perched the cobra and vulture, symbols of Upper and Lower Egypt— the pharaoh's dominion. And encircling these symbols of power was a miniature funeral wreath, still perfectly preserved, a sight that so moved Carter that he became quite sentimental:

> . . . But perhaps the most touching by its simplicity was the tiny wreath of flowers . . . around these symbols, as it pleased us to think, the last farewell offering of the widowed girl queen to her husband, the youthful representative of the "two kingdoms."
>
> . . . many and disturbing were our emotions awakened by that Osiride form. Most of them voiceless. But in that silence, to listen—you could almost hear the ghostly footsteps of the departing mourners.

Our lights were lowered, once more we mounted those sixteen steps, once more we beheld the blue vault of the heavens, where the sun is Lord, but our inner thought still lingered over the splendor of that vanished pharaoh, with his last appeal upon his coffin written upon our minds. "Oh Mother Nut! Spread thy wings over me as the Imperishable Stars."[22]

The wreath had been fashioned from olive leaves, blue water-lily petals, and cornflowers all fastened to a papyrus base. This touching memento will provide us with a clue to the murder of Tutankhamen.

Carter and his team of excavators now believed they were within a week or two of seeing the mummy. Inside the rectangular stone sarcophagus was the anthropoid coffin. Inside that would be two more, then, finally, the mummy of Tutankhamen. The removal and opening of the inner coffins would be difficult because they fit tightly inside each other. But once the problem was overcome, they would at last gaze upon the face of the lost king. But as Carter neared that long anticipated moment, Tutankhamen began to slip away.

Lord Carnarvon died unexpectedly in Cairo from a severely infected mosquito bite. His sudden and tragic death gave rise to rumors about a curse in the tomb. Carter and Carnarvon held thoroughly opposite views on the occult. Carter was a strong anti-spiritualist, while Carnarvon was attracted to the occult and often visited mediums and psychics. It was Carnarvon's personal psychic, Velma, who promoted the idea of a curse on the tomb. After Carnarvon's death, Velma published an account of her last sittings with Lord Carnarvon, saying that he was the victim of "powerful occult forces." Before he was to leave for Egypt to open the newly discovered tomb, Carnarvon asked Velma to read his palm. At that meeting she saw a thin spot in his lifeline and she warned Carnarvon, "I see great peril for you. Most probably—as the indications of occult interest are so strong in your hand—it will arise from such a source."[23]

Intrigued by what he had been told, Carnarvon returned for one more session before his departure. This time Velma looked deep into her crystal ball. Carnarvon also peered into the sphere, but it was cloudy and all he could make out was a temple. The skilled Velma could see far more. First, she gazed upon an ancient Egyptian funeral where an elderly official was placing a gold mask on a young man in a coffin. Then the image changed into a group of men, led by Carnarvon, working in the Valley of the Kings. Mysterious flashes emanated from the tomb. Then the old official appeared, surrounded by people who called for punishment of those who defiled the tomb. The last vision Velma saw was Carnarvon, standing alone in a storm of occult flashes.

Velma warned Carnarvon not to return to the tomb, to offer some excuse to the public for not proceeding with the excavation. But Carnarvon felt he had to go, saying, "A challenge to the psychic powers of the ages, Velma! What a challenge!" Soon after their meeting, he was dead. Velma, of course, wrote her account after Carnarvon's death, a great story that gave "the Curse of Tutankhamen" eternal life.[24]

Now Carter had to handle every crisis by himself, a job for which he was ill-suited. It was Carnarvon who possessed the social skills necessary to deal with people, whose personal charm put everyone at ease. Carter, although a fine Egyptologist, was socially ill at ease, had a rigid, quarrelsome personality, and completely lacked diplomatic skills. Carter continued the work on the tomb after the death of his friend and benefactor, but things did not go well thereafter. Almost from the day the tomb had been discovered, bad feelings existed between the Egyptian Antiquities Service and Carter and Carnarvon. One source of conflict had been how the publicity was handled. To avoid dealing with the hundreds of newspaper reporters requesting information about the tomb, Carnarvon sold the exclusive rights to the London *Times*. This allowed the busy excavators to deal with the inquiries of just one journalist. It also meant that Egyptian reporters were not permitted to interview Carter or Carnarvon. The Egyptians viewed this as British colonialism at its worst; tensions only increased as work on the tomb continued.

The sarcophagus lid was lifted on February 12, 1924. The next day

Carter invited his colleagues' wives to the opening of the outer coffin, but no wives of Egyptian officials were asked. The Egyptian Antiquities Service thereupon refused permission to the European wives. The message to Carter was clear: "This is our tomb, not yours."

They were right. Carter was a good man, but the stress of being responsible for the greatest archaeological treasure the world had ever seen was getting to him. He was behaving as if the tomb were his property. There were stories of his taking ancient objects back to the dig house to use as paperweights. He was constantly being badgered to show the tomb to important visitors but always refused, even when requests came from the Egyptian Antiquities Service. His view was that the Antiquities Service had no right to disturb him while he was working—and he was always working. The great iron door that Carter had placed at the entrance to the tomb and locked became a symbol of "Inglesi colonialism." So when the Egyptians insisted that Egyptian wives be present, Carter snapped.

He posted a notice at the Winter Palace Hotel in Luxor stating that he and his colleagues could not work under such restrictions, and that he was closing the tomb. The Egyptians responded in kind, sending police to lock Carter out of the tomb. There was little that Carter could do about this, so with the sarcophagus lid precariously suspended in midair, he departed for a lecture tour of America.

The Egyptian government knew that Carter was the only man for the job so an agreement was reached that returned Carter to work. But it was not until October of 1925 that the lid of the first of the three nesting coffins was finally set aside. Removing three coffins crammed one inside another proved a delicate task that consumed most of the 1925–1926 season. The lid of the first coffin had four silver handles, two on each side, that proved strong enough to raise it. The second, equally beautiful, six-foot-eight-inch anthropoid coffin, was now revealed, under its own shroud. It, too, bore floral wreaths. This coffin gave Carter his first inkling that the mummy might not be in the best of condition. Some of the inlays in the decoration had fallen out, indicating that there had been moisture in the coffin.

Because of the delicate condition of the second coffin, it was decided to remove the entire coffin, rather than just the lid. This was done, although no one could explain the enormous weight of the coffin they hoisted, then lowered onto planks of wood set across the stone sarcophagus.

The second coffin had no handles and fit inside the outer one with less than half an inch to spare on either side. Carter screwed strong eyelets into the outer coffin, removed the planks, and lowered it back into the sarcohapgus rather than raising its contents. This left the second coffin, still holding the innermost one, resting on the wooden platform. With room to maneuver now, the lid of the second coffin could be lifted, and the third, innermost coffin, revealed. This coffin was the reason for the unexpected weight. It was solid gold, weighing nearly 250 pounds.

The details on the gold coffin were obscured by a black coating, the remains of magical unguents that had been poured over it. The liquids had run into the bottom of the second coffin, gluing the two together, but the handles on the lid of the gold coffin allowed it to be lifted. At last the mummy of Tutankhamen was uncovered. Carter wrote:

> At such moments the emotions evade verbal expression, complex and stirring as they are. Three thousand years and more had elapsed since men's eyes had gazed into the golden coffin. Time, measured by the brevity of human life, seemed to lose its common perspectives before a spectacle so vividly recalling the solemn religious rites of vanished civilization. But it is useless to dwell on such sentiments, based as they are on feelings of awe and human piety. The emotional side is no part of archaeological research. Here at last lay all that was left of the youthful Pharaoh, hitherto little more that the shadow of a name.[25]

Like its gold coffin, the mummy had been liberally doused with unguents, which explained the evidence of moisture in the second coffin. Luckily, the famous gold mask protected the head of the pharaoh, but the rest of the body was in poor condition. An autopsy would prove difficult.

To soften the unguents, Carter took the coffins and the mummy outside into the sun, noting in his day book:

Nov. 1st. Removed the Royal Mummy to No. 15. It took ten men to bring it out of the tomb and carry it up. Placed in the sun for a few hours . . . Heat of the sun not sufficient today to make any real impression upon the pitchlike material which has stuck fast the mummy and coffins.

Nov. 2nd. Found that heat of the sun was of no avail in freeing the mummy from its coffin. In consequence, the examination of the Royal Mummy must necessarily take place as it lies.[26]

Dr. Douglas Derry, Professor of Anatomy at Cairo University, was given the responsibility of working with the body. Assisted by Dr. Saleh Bey Hamdi, Director of Sanitary Services in Alexandria, Derry began unwrapping it on November 11, 1925. Other attendees were Pierre Lacau, Director-General of the Antiquities Service, Harry Burton, the photographer loaned to Carter by the Metropolitan Museum of Art, in New York, and several Egyptian officials. No wives were present.

The unguents had caused a chemical reaction with the bandages, darkening them by a slow spontaneous combustion. Because the bandages could not be unrolled in such a state, heated wax was brushed over the outer layer so it could be cut away in a large piece. When the wax had cooled, Derry made a longitudinal incision and peeled back the first layer, to reveal amulets and jewelry incorporated within the wrappings. In all, 143 spectacular objects were removed with the bandages.

Finally, Tutankhamen was revealed, a young man with handsome, regular features (fig. 22). But when an attempt was made to remove the mummy from its coffin, it was discovered that the sacred oils had congealed, and Tutankhamen was glued to his coffin. First, Derry tried to chisel the mummy free, then he switched to heated knives, both operations causing considerable damage to the body. Finally, in desperation, he cut the mummy in half at the third lumbar vertebra so it could be removed in sections.

Derry's treatment of the mummy provides a good example of how carelessly the physical evidence that could reveal the cause of Tutankhamen's death was treated. Carter had little idea how much information could be gained by a careful investigation, so he abandoned the mummy to Derry's rough handling. If Tutankhamen's throne had been stuck in unguents, I doubt that Carter would have permitted it to be sawed in half. The unguents would have been chemically analyzed and a solvent devised to free the throne without damage. No so for poor Tutankhamen. The mummy was in poor shape when Derry started to work on it, but was in far worse condition when he finished.

The arms and legs had become disarticulated from their joints so Derry could clearly see the tops and bottoms of the long bones. This enabled him to calculate Tutankhamen's age at death. In young people, the ends of the long bones, the epiphyses, are loosely connected by cartilage that becomes bone as the person grows older. The average age at which the epiphyses join to the long bone is known, and the degree of this union is a reliable criterion of age. In the case of Tutankhamen, the kneecap could be easily lifted to examine the lower end of the femur, the longest bone in the leg. The epiphysis was separate from the shaft and movable. Tutankhamen was indeed a boy-king. Derry wrote:

> This part unites with the shaft about the age of twenty. At the upper end of the thigh bone that prominence known as the great trochanter was almost entirely soldered to the main bone, but on its inner side a definite gap showing the smooth cartilaginous surface where union was still incomplete, could be well seen. This epiphysis joins about the eighteenth year. The head of the femur was fixed to the neck of the bone, but the line of the union was clearly visible all round the articular margin. This epiphysis also unites about the eighteenth or nineteenth year. The upper end of the tibia was also united, but the lower end appeared to be quite fused. As this latter portion of the

tibia is generally found to fuse with the shaft at about age eighteen, Tut-Ankh-Amen, from the evidence of his lower limbs, would appear to have been over eighteen but below twenty years at the age of his death."[27]

Derry's estimate was accurate. Tutankhamen was about eighteen years old when he died, a handsome young man of slight build, about 5 feet 6 inches tall. Given Derry's techniques, there was little hope that he would determine the cause of death. That would have to await future generations and future technologies.

Because Tutankhamen was the only pharaoh ever found undisturbed in his tomb, the Antiquities Service decided that, rather than removing him to the Egyptian Museum in Cairo, this king should remain where he was found. The reassembled body of Tutankhamen was placed on a wooden litter filled with sand and put inside the largest outer coffin, then lowered into the sarcophagus where it remains today (fig. 23). Tourists peering into the open sarcophagus see the outer coffin, but few realize that the mummy still lies inside.

Once the burial chamber was emptied, Carter began to clear the small side room he called the "Treasury," the entrance of which had been boarded up so none of the objects would be damaged while work progressed in the burial chamber. The delicate condition of many of those objects and the precarious way they had been piled on top of each other made clearing the room extremely difficult, so it was not until 1927 that the task was completed. The Treasury was heaped with Tutankhamen's finely carved model boats with elaborate riggings, wooden statues of Anubis, the god of embalming, and a beautiful alabaster shrine holding the four miniature canopic coffins that contained Tutankhamen's internal organs.

Another simple wooden box held two miniature coffins. Inside rested the neatly wrapped mummies of Ankhesenamen's two miscarriages. One was slightly more than a foot long, the other approximately ten inches long with a tiny cartonnage (papier mâché) mask over the face. Carter removed the wrappings from the smaller of the two, revealing the five-month-old female fetus (figs. 14a and 14b). This was the first time the excavators knew of the tragedy. If either of these little girls had lived to maturity, the royal line would have continued, and Egyptian history would have been quite different.

The larger of the two fetuses was still wrapped when Dr. Derry received it for examination in 1932 at the Department of Anatomy at Kasr el Einy Hospital in Cairo (figs. 13a, 13b, and 13c). He unwrapped it, revealing the second female fetus, which he estimated to be seven months old. Four inches longer than her sister, who showed no signs of mummification, this child was developed enough to have been embalmed. Across the left side of the abdomen ran an embalmer's incision less than an inch long. The abdominal cavity was stuffed with linen, but Derry does not mention the internal organs, which are probably still inside—had they been removed, canopic jars would likely have been provided. Derry could see that despite the fetus's small size, the embalmers had removed the brain and forced linen into the cranium. Never one to worry about preserving a mummy, Derry broke through the cranium to remove the linen and there found the wire used to force the fabric into the skull. This is the only embalmer's tool ever to be found inside a mummy. Derry threw it away.

It is undeniable that Derry's handling of the three mummies in Tutankhamen's tomb was irresponsible, caused irreversible damage, and that a great deal of valuable information was irretrievably lost. But Derry was working in an era when the field of mummy studies was in its infancy and he shared the attitude of most of his predecessors who believed that mummies in themselves were of little value.[28] In the wake of Derry's destruction, could anything be learned today that would tell us how Tutankhamen died?

8

Dead Men Tell Tales:
Tutankhamen's Mummy

There is no man who does not die.

—*Sayings of Ankhsheshonq*
circa 300 B.C.

Today, non-destructive techniques are available for studying mummies. If Tutankhamen had just been discovered, his mummy could be examined using several high-tech processes, such as CAT scans, without the need to unwrap it. Derry focused his entire autopsy on the bones he had violently examined. He paid little attention, if any, to the body's soft tissues because no one then, least of all Derry, realized how much information is retained in the muscles and internal organs. There was no knowledge of DNA; electron microscopes and advanced chemical analysis did not exist. It was just becoming possible in Derry's day to examine tissue from mummies under a microscope, and this didn't seem to interest Derry.

Medical experts in our era employ several processes to look at both soft tissue and bone to determine the circumstances of a death. First, they autopsy the body to learn whether unusual substances were retained in organs and tissues, and what the subject had eaten and how recently. Second, they use X rays, or more advanced equivalents such as CAT scans, to view the bones. Bones can reveal not only the age of the deceased and what diseases he suffered, but also whether a trauma, such as a blow by some object, was the likely cause of death. Each of these processes contributes valuable information that the other does not.

However, ancient tissues provide a special problem for modern tests. They are so brittle that they crumble if sliced thinly enough to be put under a microscope. In a note in the *British Medical Journal* for 1909, Marc Armand Ruffer, a French physician working at the Cairo Medical School, discussed the difficulties he experienced in his first attempts to section tissue fragments of mummies.[1] Ruffer persevered and developed a technique to soften tissues by soaking them in a solution of alcohol and 5 percent carbonate of soda, a process that permitted sectioning and microscopic examination. Ruffer was a pathologist, trained to study diseases and causes of death, while Derry was an anatomist, unfamiliar with microscopes and chemical analysis. Had they joined forces, a great deal more would have been learned about Tutankhamen and the fetuses. Were the little girls healthy when aborted? Was Ankhesenamen suffering from a disease when she miscarried? Most important, was there any evidence of disease in Tutankhamen's body at the time of his death?

Anyone interested in answering these questions would have to reexamine all the evidence, but surprisingly some of it had disappeared. In 1971 F. Filce Leek, an English dentist, was given permission by the Egyptian Department of Antiquities to examine and X-ray Tutankhamen's fetuses, but when he opened their coffins in the Egyptian Museum, the mummies were not there.[2]

This, too, was Derry's fault. Throughout his long career, he had been given numerous mummies and fragments of mummies to take away for examination but he rarely returned them. They simply accumulated in a storage room at Kasr El Einy Hospital where he worked. After his death the mummies remained in storage, forgotten. Then, in

June 1992, newspapers reported the discovery of 528 mummies and parts of mummies in the hospital storeroom—Derry's cache had been found. There, along with King Zoser's foot, were the two fetuses. Prior to this announcement only a few people had known about the hoard, one of whom was R. G. Harrison who had X-rayed Tutankhamen in 1978.[3] He went to the storeroom and found and X-rayed the larger of the two fetuses, finding that there was an abnormally high right clavicle, and other indications of scoliosis and spina bifida.

Derry had said of the smaller fetus, "There is no abdominal incision and no indication as to how the body was preserved." I wondered about this. Why would one fetus be mummified but not the other? Both had similar wrappings, both were placed in coffins. Perhaps the smaller fetus was too tiny for the royal embalmers to work with. In the hope of examining the smaller fetus to settle this question, I contacted Dr. Fawzi Gabella, Head of the Anatomy Department of Kasr El Einy Hospital to see if he could locate the mummy. The hospital had recently received a grant from an American anthropologist to catalogue and properly store the mummies in their collection, so everything had been recently inventoried, boxed and labeled. Without hesitation, Dr. Gabella told me he had the mummy. I was invited to come to the hospital to examine it.

When I arrived at Kasr El Einy Hospital I found two Dr. Gabellas. His wife, also an anatomist teaching at the hospital, greeted me. Both she and her husband were eager to see what we could learn about the fetuses. They ushered me into a storage room piled high with small wooden boxes with intriguing labels—"Middle Kingdom princess?" "Old Kingdom, head only." I have worked with mummies for years, but had never seen anything like this. My fantasy was to be locked in that storage room for a few years so I could examine each box carefully, but I would be allowed to order in meals from the great chicken restaurant down the street.

Dr. Fawzi Gabella located two small wood boxes slightly larger than shoe boxes. When the lids were removed, I was face to face with Tutankhamen and Ankhesenamen's children. For more than a year, I had been trying to piece together Tutankhamen's fragmented life. To me, these fetuses were more than examples of mummification; they reflected a family's tragedy. Since Tutankhamen probably will remain sealed in his sarcophagus for quite some time, this was probably as close as I would ever get to him.

I had brought Harry Burton's photographs of the fetuses, taken when they were first discovered. In the seventy years since the photographs, the fetuses had deteriorated somewhat, but because of this deterioration I was able to answer my question. The cranial bones of the smaller fetus had disarticulated, allowing us to see that, just as with the larger fetus, linen had been packed in the skull, and the skin on the abdomen was cracked, revealing a bit of linen protruding from the abdominal cavity. The smaller fetus had, indeed, been embalmed. Remembering how much Derry had damaged the mummy of Tutankhamen, I didn't even want to touch the fetuses; I just looked (fig. 15).

Now, it was time for me to reexamine Derry's work with Tutankhamen. When he performed the autopsy on Tutankhamen's mummy in 1925, little except the boy-king's age at the time of death was determined. This opened the door to all kinds of speculation about the cause of his death. Because of his slender build, and because he died young, tuberculosis was suggested, but there was no way at the time to test for this. Additional direct investigation of the mummy had been prevented by the Antiquities Services' decision to leave Tutankhamen in his tomb. Had the body been moved to Cairo, it could have been X-rayed.[4]

To Derry it might have seemed pointless to X-ray the already-exposed bones of Tutankhamen, but X-rays reveal bone density that tells us a great deal about diet and illnesses during a person's life. For example, if there is a serious illness prior to maturity, the long bones stop growing, which shows on an X-ray as a white line across the bone. An X ray of Tutankhamen's mummy could have told him a great deal, but in 1925 there were no portable X-ray machines in Egypt that could have been brought into the Valley of the Kings. The most famous king in history had to wait forty years for his X rays.

It wasn't until the 1960s that science really woke up to the value of mummies. With new techniques for analyzing tissue samples, physicians and health scientists realized that mummies often held just the information they needed to understand modern diseases. The field of paleopathology was born. The term was first coined in 1892 by R.W. Schufeldt, a German physician, from two Greek roots (παλιος, "ancient," and παθος, "suffering"). It means the study of diseases, or pathological conditions, in ancient people.

To understand a modern infectious disease and predict its course, it is necessary to study its development through history. By analyzing Egyptian mummies and comparing the frequency of their pathological conditions with those of modern man, we glean insights into whether modern modes of living are the cause of specific diseases, or if the diseases have been around for centuries. For example, arterial disease is frequently attributed, along with our high-fat diets, to the stresses and strains of contemporary life. If ancient Egyptians also suffered from arterial disease, such theories would be placed in doubt.

By the 1960s, with scientific knowledge increasing at a fantastic rate, specialization had become essential. No one physician could read the literature in every field; the general practitioner became outmoded; teams of specialists became the rule. A similar trend overtook the study of mummies. No single physician commands all the skills required to autopsy a mummy and analyze the various tissue samples, or possesses the expert knowledge of botany, chemistry, and biology necessary to extract all the information the body offers. Paleopathologists now treat mummies like patients, doing as little harm as possible and bringing in specialists as needed to study specific problems—hematologists for blood, dentists for teeth, etc. Working virtually alone, Derry didn't have a chance to collect all the information that Tutankhamen's mummy offered.

The field of paleopathology had blossomed by the 1960s, leading R. G. Harrison, a University of Liverpool anatomist, to believe that studying the Egyptian royal mummies would shed new light on old questions. His first subject was the mystery mummy from Tomb 55, whom we now know was Smenkare, Tutankhamen's brother. Harrison examined, measured, and X-rayed the bones to determine its age at the time of death. The sternum or breastbone is a good indicator. As we grow older the costal notches, where the ribs attach, ossify, causing us to become less flexible. X rays showed that the fourth and fifth ribs of the Tomb 55 mummy had recently joined, although the facets of the fourth still showed a cleft. This indicated death at an age of nineteen or twenty, just like Tutankhamen's. A similar process of ossification occurs in the vertebrae, but is completed at about twenty-four years of age. The thorax and vertebrae were not completely ossified in the Tomb 55 mummy, indicating that Smenkare was certainly less than twenty-four years old when he died.

R.G. Harrison's X rays and measurements of the mummy revealed important information. He ended his report with the plea that "a reappraisal of the anatomical and radiological features of Tutankhamun is urgently necessary, and it is to be hoped that such an investigation may be made possible in the not-too-distant future."[5] In 1969 Harrison got his chance.

He was given permission by the Egyptian Antiquities Organization to bring a portable X-ray machine into the tomb of Tutankhamen. This would be the first time since Carter and Derry had replaced Tutankhamen in his coffin that anyone had seen the young king. Aware that a team approach was necessary, Harrison, the anatomist, brought radiologists, dentists, physicians, and Egyptologists. They were only permitted to work during daylight hours, and the tomb had not been closed to tourists, so surprised visitors looked on as they worked. There would be several surprises for Harrison as well.

For one thing, the mummy was in far worse condition than anyone had expected. Neither Carter nor Derry had published the fact that they had sawed Tutankhamen in half to free him from the inner coffin, so X-raying Tutankhamen was a piecemeal process. The head was carried to the machine and X-rayed, then the limbs, and so on, until a complete set of films was produced. The team had permission to work for only two days. On the first day they made a set of test exposures, which they developed that same evening in the bathroom of their hotel. Fortunately, they stayed at the Winter Palace, a grand old hotel in Luxor, with commodious bathrooms. They developed their X rays in one sink, fixed them in another, then washed them in the bathtub.[6] They came out fine.

The X ray of the torso provided the first surprise. Tutankhamen was missing his sternum and part of his ribs! Derry had not noticed this because of the black resin that covered the chest. Perhaps Tutankhamen was handled roughly in the embalmer's workshop and the damage was concealed by a coat of resin. Others suggested that the missing parts were the result of an accident or of intentional violence that caused Tutankhamen's death.[7] Part of Smenkare's sternum was also missing, but I have no explanation for this curious similarity other than perhaps embalmers used some special technique on both of these mummies. An argument against my view is that Smenkare died at Amarna and probably would have been embalmed there. Tutankhamen almost certainly was embalmed at a different embalmer's shop located in Thebes or Memphis. Harrison offered no hypothesis on the question. He moved on to other matters, such as determining Tutankhamen's age.

Using the same criteria he had applied to Smenkare's mummy, Harrison determined that Tutankhamen was about nineteen years old at the time of death, just as Derry had suggested almost half a century earlier. X rays of the spine dispelled any notion that Tutankhamen died of tuberculosis. Tuberculosis generally damages the epiphysial plates between the vertebrae; Tutankhamen's were perfect.

Then came the X ray of the skull, the X ray that first led me to suspect that Tutankhamen might have been murdered. On the later BBC documentary about his findings, Harrison simply pointed to a density on the X ray at the base of the skull and said,

> This is within the normal limits, but in fact, it could have been caused by a hemorrhage under the membranes overlaying the brain in this region. And this could have been caused by a blow to the back of the head and this in turn could have been responsible for death.

Harrison was cautious, never mentioning murder, merely a possible blow to the back of the head.

One reason the possibility of the murder of Tutankhamen has not received detailed attention is that Harrison never published a full scientific report of his X-raying of Tutankhamen, merely popular accounts.[8] His ominous words presented in the television documentary were never clarified by a complete written report and consequently the X ray was misunderstood by the experts.

We must remember we are not dealing with a normal X ray, but one of a mummified skull. Careful reading of the film is necessary, along with knowledge of the embalming process. The X ray clearly shows what appears to be an abnormal thickening of the interior of the skull in two places—at the top and at the back of the head (fig. 25). But what we are seeing is not bone, but resin introduced into the cranium during Tutankhamen's mummification. After Tutankhamen's brain was removed through the nasal passages, hot resin was poured into the skull to cauterize the interior, in case any of the brain remained. Once the resin was inside the skull, it hardened to become radiopaque, like bone. What Tutankhamen's skull shows is two fluid levels of the resin as it was poured in and then hardened. This means that resin must have been poured into the skull at two different times, with the mummy in a different position each time. Let's reconstruct what happened 3,300 years ago in the embalmer's shop.

Imagine the body of Tutankhamen flat on its back lying on the embalmer's table. A hook is inserted in his nose, breaking the ethmoid bone behind the nasal passages. The hook enters the cranium and is rotated to break down the brain so it becomes semi-liquid. Then Tutankhamen is turned on his stomach, with his head hanging over the table, so his brain, pulled by gravity, runs out the nose. The cranium is now ready for resin. Once again the body is placed on its back and a ceramic bowl with two small tubular spouts is filled with hot resin. The pipettes are placed in the nostrils and the bowl tilted so the resin runs through the nose and into the cranium. Gravity controls where it goes. Since Tutankhamen is lying on his back, the resin forms a pool at the back of the skull. When it cools it creates the first of two fluid levels. This resin burned out any bits of brain tissue that may have remained at the back of the skull. Next, the body of Tutankhamen is positioned on the table so the head hangs over the end, with his chin pointing to the sky. Once again resin is poured in to form a pool at the lowest point, this time the top of the head. This burns out bits of brain from the front of his skull and creates the second fluid level on the X ray. The X ray lets us understand a specific event that took place thirty-three centuries ago.

But the skull X ray shows something that seems far more relevant to the question of the cause of death. A bone fragment is clearly visible inside Tutankhamen's skull. Could this fragment have been the effect of a violent blow struck at the pharaoh's head with evil intent, a blow that killed Tutankhamen?

Actually, this little piece of bone is the red herring in the case. It has caused nothing but confusion and led researchers away from the trail of murder. Because Harrison never published his theory in a scientific journal, and most researchers had only heard that he mentioned a blow to the head, they assumed Harrison was talking about this fragment as having been violently dislodged by a blow. Harrison never said anything of the kind. As a matter of fact, he suggested that the fragment was a piece of the ethmoid bone broken off when the embalmers forced the hooked instrument into the cranium to remove the brain. But this explanation can't be right. Ethmoid means "sieve" in Greek. Because that bone is porous, it splinters when broken, and the bone fragment in the skull is substantial, not a splinter, so the fragment inside the skull cannot be a piece of the ethmoid. It must be a piece of another bone.

Which other bone almost doesn't matter. Harrison was still correct in his view that the bone was broken off *after* death. It could not have *caused* the death. For the sake of argument, let us assume that the fragment was dislodged by a blow to the head while Tutankhamen was alive, and he subsequently died. Now imagine the embalming process once again. The brain is removed but the fragment remains loose in the skull. Now comes the time to pour resin into the skull while Tutankhamen's body is lying on its back on the table. The bone fragment would now have fallen to the lowest point inside the skull—the back of the head. When the resin cools, the fragment would be embedded in the resin. If by some chance, the bone was adhering to another part of the skull, and the resin missed it, then the second application of resin to the top of the skull—when Tutankhamen's head hung over the embalmer's table—would almost certainly have enveloped the bone fragment within the resin. So, if the bone fragment had been dislodged when Tutankhamen was killed, it would have been embedded in radiopaque resin during the embalming process and would never appear on the X ray. This, of course, is not the case. The bone fragment is clearly visible on top of the resin. The only possible conclusion is that the bone was dislodged after death. In fact, the bone must have been loosened, not only after death, but after the introduction of the resin into the skull.

There were plenty of opportunities for the fragment to have been broken off after the resin was poured into the skull. The body remained in the embalmer's shop for more than a month while dehydrating in natron, plenty of time for damage to occur. Mummies were frequently damaged while they were in the embalmer's shops. Roy Moodie's pioneering X-ray studies in 1926 at Chicago's Field Museum of Natural History was one of the first to reveal such careless work. One X ray showed that in order to fit the mummy of a seven-year-old boy into a coffin that was much too small, the embalmer had removed the boy's arms, broken the legs at mid-thigh, and thrown away the lower halves of his legs.[9] My favorite example of embalmer skullduggery is that of the Lady Teshat in the Minneapolis Institute of Arts. Although the title "Lady" suggests that she was an adult, Teshat died as a teenager. A CAT scan of her mummy showed that her cadaver was roughly handled, resulting in several broken bones. It also revealed that between her legs lay a second adult skull! No one is sure why it is there, but it is quite possible that the head of another mummy became detached in the embalming house and was temporarily misplaced. Then, after that mummy was bandaged without its head and returned to its unknowing relatives, the head turned up. Not knowing what to do with an excess head, the embalmers bound it up with Lady Teshat.

While a mummy with two heads is unusual, mummies missing body parts are common. Sir Marc Armand Ruffer, the former president of the Sanitary Council of Egypt, unwrapped two mummies dating from the Persian period. After describing the wrappings (one bandage was more than eighteen feet long), he discusses the sorry state of the mummies.[10] When a body is mummified, it becomes so brittle that, with rough handing, it can break. In the case of one of Ruffer's mummies, the embalmers had broken her back and run a stick through the body to restore its rigidity. When this was insufficient, heated resin was poured inside and outside the mummy to obscure the defect. (This technique for hiding their mistakes under a coating of resin may be exactly what Tutankhamen's embalmers did to hide the damage to his rib cage.) The second mummy Ruffer examined showed just how bad embalmers could be. It looked like the first mummy, but the foot bones were found in the abdominal region and the arm bones were where the thighs should have been. The atlas vertebra (so named because it is on top of the spinal column supporting the head) had been pierced by a stick that went through the foramen magnum and into the skull. So while the wrappings indicated a whole body, inside lay a disarticulated pile of bones. With mummies receiving this kind of treatment from embalmers, it is not difficult to imagine a fragment of Tutankhamen's skull being dislodged in the embalmer's workshop. And we know this wasn't the only rough handling Tutankhamen's mummy received.

The violence done to the body by Derry and Carter in their attempt to free Tutankhamen from his coffin is documented. Although neither Carter nor Derry published details of what they did to Tutankhamen's mummy, their manuscript notes are revealing. Carter's diary for November 16, 1925, states:

> The whole of today's work was concentrated upon the head of the mummy. It was found like the body of the King. The back of the head was stuck (in the case) to the mask—so firmly that it would require a hammer and chisel to free it. Eventually we used hot knives for the purpose with success.[11]

Hammering and chiseling certainly could loosen a bone fragment. Thus it seems extremely likely that, one way or another, the piece of bone is post mortem, having nothing to do with Tutankhamen's death. This, I believe, is further confirmed by a second X ray taken ten years after Harrison's X ray of Tutankhamen's skull. Dr. James Harris, a professor of orthodontics at the University of Michigan, was given permission to X-ray the skull of Tutankhamen. Harris already had carried out pioneering work on X-raying the royal mummies in the Egyptian Museum in Cairo.[12]

He was using X rays to determine relationships between the mummies by noting similarities in facial features—family traits. Because he was a dentist, Harris was especially interested in dentition. When he saw Harrison's X ray of Tutankhamen's skull he was disappointed because the teeth were not as clear as he would have liked. After his work on the Egyptian Museum mummies, he was granted permission to open Tutankhamen's coffin and X-ray the skull. His X ray seems to confirm that the now famous bone is indeed loose and not embedded in the resin, because the bone appears in a different place on his X ray than on Harrison's. At least I think it does. Harris never published the details of how he took the X ray, nor does he even state *that* he took the X ray. In the index to his book *An X-Ray Atlas of the Royal Mummies*,[13] Harris refers to the X rays of Tutankhamen, but they are not on page 378 as stated. The only place the X ray appears is on a microfiche card in the back pocket of the book (second card, row A, Number 2). The card is difficult to read, and when I asked Dr. Harris for a copy of the X ray, he was unable to supply it, so my reading of the microfiche must remain tentative.

The reason experts have overlooked the possibility that Tutankhamen was murdered is that when Egyptologists and paleopathologists looked at the Tutankhamen X ray they saw the bone fragment in the skull and mistakenly thought that this was the supposed evidence for a blow to the back of the head. They correctly deduced that it had been dislodged postmortem. Then, they concluded the fragment provided no evidence for a blow to the back of the head. In all the excitement about the bone fragment, they neglected to look further for what Harrison had seen, the dark spot on the X ray at the base of the skull.

When I hosted a television documentary on the murder theory, I never mentioned the bone fragment, because it was not relevant to the real evidence for a blow to the back of the head. The *Los Angeles Times* wrote an article on the documentary and asked Dr. James Harris for his opinion. Here again, the bone fragment was confused with the evidence for a blow to the back of the head. The article states: "He [Harris] confirms that there is a bone sliver but notes that it could have been produced during mummification. . . ."[14] Again referring to the bone fragment, Dr. Nicholas Reeves, a leading Tutankhamen scholar commented, "Sadly Harrison (the anatomist) did not live to publish his thoughts on this feature, and it is not clear whether he believed the damage to have been sustained before death, accidentally, or intentionally."[15]

In addition to Harrison and Harris there was a third person who could have addressed the issue of the blow to the back of the head, but he too made a curious omission. F. Filce Leek, the dentist on Harrison's X-ray team, wrote an entire book titled *The Human Remains from the Tomb of Tutankhamen*, yet he only briefly mentions that he was a member of the team.[16] Incredibly, he never discusses the results of the X rays. For his analysis of the mummy of Tutankhamen, he relies almost entirely on Derry's autopsy from half a century before!

Because there has been no scientific publication of the two sets of X rays of Tutankhamen, there has been considerable misunderstanding about the evidence for a blow to the back of the head, especially among researchers outside the medical field who have no experience reading X rays. One surprising example comes from a leading British scholar of the Amarna period, Cyril Aldred. Aldred says, "the recent reexamination of (Tutankhamen's) mummy has shown that he sustained a wound. Probably by an arrow, which penetrated his skull in the region of the left ear."[17] It is not clear what Aldred's evidence for the arrow is, for this is one of the rare times he does not give his source.

Given the omissions and confusions surrounding Tutankhamen's X rays, it was clear that a careful reexamination of the material relating to Tutankhamen's death was necessary. My first step was to get a copy of Harrison's X ray, but he had died in 1979. His colleague R.C. Connolly was still at the University of Liverpool and he kindly sent me prints of the X ray along with a friendly note that was far from encouraging.

> I am afraid there is really nothing beyond our original publications on the subject which I can add about these radiographs . . . Apart from the obvious features referred to in previous publications they really do not contribute anything particularly significant either to the procedures for mummification in the Eighteenth Dynasty or more important, to the cause of death.[18]

Connolly is a senior lecturer in physical anthropology who knew anatomy far better than I, but I had to see it for myself. When the X ray arrived, I took it to my university's Radiological Technology Department to see what they would say. They were fascinated by the X ray but suggested that my only hope of getting any new information was to show the X ray to our medical advisor, Dr. Gerald Irwin, head of radiology at Winthrop University Hospital. Dr. Irwin has considerable experience in reading the X rays of head trauma patients. My hope was that his combined radiology and trauma expertise might allow him to see something new.

First, I showed him the BBC video of Harrison's explanation of the X ray. Then he studied the X-ray print of Tutankhamen's skull. He agreed with Harrison. There could indeed have been a blow to the back of the head; the X ray was evidence for a hematoma, an accumulation of blood beneath the skin. But then Dr. Irwin noticed something else. Inside the skull, near the location of the possible blood clot, an area of increased density showed. This is what would be expected from a calcified membrane formed over a blood clot. Physicians call it a chronic subdural hematoma—a phenomenon that takes considerable time to develop.

Dr. Irwin also observed that the area of the skull where the alleged blow occurred is unusual for trauma—at the back of the head, right at the point where the neck joins the skull. This is a well-protected spot. Tutankhamen would have had to have been struck from behind, perhaps while he was sleeping on his side or back, to cause a trauma there (fig. 26).

What does this all mean? First of all, let me make clear that Tutankhamen's X ray does not prove he was murdered. No X ray by itself can ever do so. An X ray can show that a patient received a blow to the head, even that the blow probably killed him, but not that the blow was stuck by someone with evil intent. There will always be other possibilities that the X ray by itself will not eliminate. Further, interpreting X rays is an art, which is why some are experts in reading these films and others are not. X rays show some clear white areas—bone—and other cloudy areas whose interpretation calls for special skill. Even among experts, some will see a cloudy area as a growth of a certain sort, others will see a mere blur in the film.

In Tutankhamen's case, two renowned experts saw evidence of a hematoma in his skull. Did Tutankhamen trip and hit his head? Given the location of this hematoma, that is unlikely. By itself, evidence of a fatal blow to the back of the skull in a place where an accident is unlikely would never convince a jury to convict. But it would certainly be enough to cause a thorough investigation by the police to see if they could turn up additional evidence. They would label the X ray "indication of suspicious circumstances."

That much is clear. What is less certain is whether calcification formed over the hematoma. Dr. Irwin was quick to point out that the X ray does not unambiguously establish that, because the cloudy area is simply too faint to know for sure. It raises the possibility, however, that Tutankhamen did not die suddenly which, in turn, raises some difficult questions. If Tutankhamen lingered for the minimum two months required for calcium formation, what was his state of consciousness? Remember, this is before IV feeding and there is no evidence the Egyptians used feeding tubes. An unconscious Tutankhamen could not have been kept alive for two months. If there was a thickening, then Tutankhamen must have remained conscious at least long enough to be fed, perhaps drifting in and out of consciousness. He would have lingered until the pressure on the brain built up by the hematoma became too great, and then lapsed into a coma and died from dehydration or pneumonia.[19]

The suggestion that Tutankhamen may have lingered is very tentative, but it in no way affects the murder thesis. I mention it merely because it is part of the puzzle that may become important at some later time. In fact, physical evidence by itself never proves murder. A bullet in the brain does not show intent to kill, motive, means, etc. The X ray of Tutankhamen's skull suggests a blow to the back of the head. That is all it can do. To support a case for murder an investigation of the circumstantial evidence is crucial. Can we show that someone had the opportunity and the motive? It is here that the case will be made or not.

9

A Widow's Plea

Do not concern yourself with him,
The Asiatic is a crocodile on its shore.
He snatches from a lonely road,
He cannot seize from a populous town.

—King Khety Nebkaure
circa 2150 B.C.

In most murders, events surrounding the death raise the first suspicion of a crime. The sinister events that followed Tutankhamen's death would prompt any modern detective to think of foul play. They begin with a letter Tutankhamen's widow addressed to the king of the Hittites, the ancient Hatti—a traditional enemy of Egypt who pressed hard against Egypt for possession of her territories.

We learn about this letter because the Hittites were great record keepers. Excavations in Turkey have yielded thousands of clay tablets from their archives, recording everything from land deeds to military exploits. At the beginning of this century a dig at the ancient capital of Bogazköy found archives dealing with a variety of matters. One group of these tablets chronicled the reign of King Suppiluliuma, written by the king's son, Mursilis II. The composition is known today by the uncatchy title "The Deeds of Suppiluliuma as told by his son Mursilis II." Of the dozens of fragments that constitute the texts, the one that recounts Ankhesenamen's frantic letter is the "Seventh Tablet."[1]

The letter is extraordinary. The queen of Egypt writes to Egypt's traditional enemy, the Hittites, and says that she is afraid and wants to marry a Hittite prince and make him king of Egypt. Nothing like this had ever happened in Egypt. We must examine this letter very carefully.

While my father was down in the country of Carchemish, he sent Lupakki and Tarhunta [?]—zalma forth into the country of Amka. So they went to attack Amka and brought deportees, cattle and sheep back before my father. But when the people of Egypt heard of the attack on Amka, they were afraid and since, in addition, their lord Nibhuruiya had died, therefore the queen of Egypt, who was Dahamunzu [?] sent a messenger to my father and wrote to him thus: "my husband died. A son I have not. But to thee, they say, the sons are many. If thou wouldst give me one son of thine, he would become my husband. Never shall I pick out a servant of mine and make him my husband! . . . I am afraid!"[2]

The queen of Egypt who wrote the letter is called Dahamunzu, and her husband ("their lord") is called Nibhuruiya. Who were these royals? Their names are transliterations of Egyptian names into the Hittite language; an attempt not to translate, but merely to convey the phonetic sounds. There can be little doubt that the king was Tutankhamen, whose prenomen (one of his two given names inscribed in a cartouche) is Neb-kheperu-re.[3] The Hittites transliterated these sounds into "Nibhuruiya." If the king is Tutankhamen, then the widowed queen must be Ankhesenamen, his only wife. Yet, the name Dahamunzu does not look or sound anything like Ankhesenamen. What was probably transliterated was the Egyptian phrase *Ta Hemet Nesewt*— "The King's Wife"— the way she signed her letter.[4]

Ominously, Ankhesenamen says she is afraid. What frightened the queen of Egypt? Her country was safe and stable at the time, thanks to Horemheb's strong army. The administrators Aye and Maya had returned Egypt to prosperity. After the death of her husband, Ankhesenamen's position should have been that of the most royal, most powerful person in the land. But was it? The Hittites imply that they caused her fright by attacking neighboring Amka, which, although far from Egypt's borders, made the queen fear for her safety. This explanation seems improbable given Egypt's strength. Rather than pointing to a real concern that would agitate Ankhesenamen, their explanation seems a conceit, a boast Hittites would like to believe.

The truth is that the death of Tutankhamen left Ankhesenamen alone. Her life before had been full of change and turmoil, but at least her husband had been there to share the burdens and decisions. Without him beside her, there was a more sinister reason for Ankhesenamen's fear. The sequence of facts that leads up to her expression of fear culminates in a most unusual statement: "Never shall I pick out a servant of mine and make him my husband!" Of course, it was inconceivable for an Egyptian queen to marry a servant. What could have pressured Ankhesenamen into marrying the wrong man, a force so strong that it frightened her?

Ankhesenamen must have written the letter soon after Tutankhamen's death, for Egypt could not remain without a king for long. But the line of succession was not clear: she and Tutankhamen had no children and Ankhesenamen was the last member of the royal family. In such circumstances, whoever married her would become Egypt's king. Ankhesenamen's letter indicates that she was being forced to marry someone, a commoner—"servant." What an extraordinary act of desperation to write to an enemy requesting marriage to one of its princes, yet it must have seemed the lesser of two great evils. Never in the history of Egypt had a queen requested marriage to a foreigner to make him king of Egypt.

The walls of the tomb of Horemheb, Tutankhamen's general of the army, show just how remarkable Ankhesenamen's plea was. Horemheb delighted in covering his tomb with scenes of the Hittite captives he had vanquished. Egypt's generals fought and herded manacled Hittite prisoners before Tutankhamen.[5] What circumstances could have caused Ankhesenamen to beg a husband from these people?

Imagine her anxiety as she composed her letter to the Hittite king. Scribes in the Egyptian court could write in Akkadian, the international language of the day, but a letter written by a court scribe would be placed in official archives and become general information in the palace. Ankhesenamen would not have wanted that. Surely Aye, who was Tutankhamen's counselor, would never condone a foreigner's rule over Egypt. If nothing else it would jeopardize his position in the court, for a Hittite king would appoint his own officials. General Horemheb, who had risked his life battling the Hitittes, certainly would not approve of such a letter—he would never serve under a mortal enemy. So Ankhesenamen's letter could not be an official communication between two powerful nations. It was a personal plea written to the only person, in her mind, powerful enough to help her—the Hittite king. Ankhesenamen probably wrote the letter herself in hieroglyphs on a papyrus scroll—it could be translated later by scribes in the Hititte palace—all she required was one person she could trust who could deliver her plea.

Her decision lends insight into Ankhesenamen's character—she was frightened and naive. Growing up in peaceful Amarna, she had never heard the horrors of battles with the Hittites nor listened to stories of their atrocities. She must have believed an army was the only force powerful enough to save her. She must have convinced herself that if she made their prince the King of Egypt, a Hititte force would ride to her rescue. Who in Egypt was so powerful that she believed only a mighty army could sway him from his course?

So incredible was Ankhesenamen's request that even the Hittite king didn't believe it.

When my father heard this, he called forth the Great Ones for council [saying]: "Such a thing has never happened to me in my whole life!" So it happened that my father sent forth to Egypt Hattusa-ziti, the chamberlain, [with this order]: "Go and bring thou the true word back to me! Maybe they deceive me! Maybe [in fact] they do have a son of their lord! Bring thou the true word back to me!"[6]

The chamberlain's journey was a lengthy one—through the Taurus Mountains, then eastward to the plain of Aleppo in Syria where he crossed the Orontes River near Kadesh, and continued south to the Egyptian border. He was undoubtedly met at the border, but by whom? There were obviously at least two opposing factions in the Egyptian court—Ankhesenamen who wanted to marry the prince, and those forcing her to marry the unnamed "servant." Unfortunately, the Hittites do not tell us what Hattusaziti, their chamberlain, learned in Egypt. We do know, however, that when he returned to his country, he was not alone.

But when it became spring, Hattusaziti [came back] from Egypt, and the messenger of Egypt, Lord Hani, came with him.[7]

The Hittites mention that it was spring when their ambassador returned from Egypt. Does this match what we know about Tutankhamen's death? Blossoms on his funerary wreaths tell us in which season Tutankhamen died. One wreath was woven from cornflowers that bloom in Egypt from mid-March to the end of April. One of Tutankhamen's floral pectorals included mandrake and woody nightshade, both of which ripen and bloom in March and April.[8] Thus, Tutankhamen was buried between the middle of March and the end of April, which, given seventy days for proper mummification before his burial, places his time of death in the preceding December or January.[9] If Ankhesenamen wrote her letter in January, it would have reached the Hittite capital in February. The chamberlain's (Hattusaziti) round trip would have taken a little under two months. Traveling quickly, for there must have been a sense of urgency, Hattusaziti would have returned by April, the spring, as the archive indicates. All the evidence is consistent, so this indeed is an ancient record of actual events.

While negotiations with the Hittites were proceeding, Tutankhamen's body was being mummified, his coffin finished, his tomb furnishings prepared for the day of the burial, which drew nearer and nearer. How long could Egypt go without a king? How long could Ankhesenamen hold out?

When word reached her that a Hittite had arrived in response to her letter, she must have believed he was the prince she had sought. How disappointing to discover it was only an aged chamberlain come to verify her strange request. We have no details about Hattusaziti's stay in the Egyptian court, but we can imagine a desperate queen aware that time was running out. Perhaps it was not too late. She sent a second letter.

> Why didst thou say "they deceive me," in that way? Had I a son, would I have written about my own and my country's shame to a foreign land? Thou didst not believe me and hast even spoken thus to me! He who was my husband has died. A son I have not! Never shall I take a servant of mine and make him my husband! I have written to no other country, only to thee have I written! They say thy sons are many: so give me one son of thine! To me he will be husband, but in Egypt he will be king." So, since my father was kindhearted, he complied with the word of the woman and concerned himself with the matter of a son.[10]

The Egyptian envoy, Hani, must have confirmed what Ankhesenamen's letters claimed. Suppiluliuma spoke to Hani, expressing his fear that if a prince were sent to Egypt he would be held hostage, rather than anointed king. We can imagine the desperation in Hani's voice as he pleaded with Suppiluliuma that all would be well if he sent a son to Ankhesenamen.

> Oh my lord! This [is . . .] our country's shame! If we had [a son of the king] at all, would we have come to a foreign country and kept asking for a lord for ourselves? Nib-hururiya, who was

our lord, died; a son he has not. Our lord's wife is solitary. We are seeking a son of our lord for the kingship in Egypt, and for the woman, our lady, we seek him as her husband! Furthermore, we went to no other country, only here did we come! Now, oh our Lord, give us a son of thine![11]

This is the Hittite account of Hani's speech on behalf of his patron. Suppiluliuma asked that an old peace treaty between Egypt and Hatti be brought from the archives and read aloud, then he declared:

Of old, Hattusa and Egypt were friendly with each other, and now this, too, on our behalf, has taken place between t[hem]! Thus Hatti and Egypt will continuously be friendly with each other![12]

Some ninety days after Ankhesenamen's first letter, Suppiluliuma sent a son to Egypt to become Ankhesenamen's husband and king. By now all seventy days of mummification and ritual prior to Tutankhamen's burial had passed and his body had been resting in the tomb with all its treasures for nearly a month. Only then did the Hittite prince begin his journey to Egypt to claim his bride. The archive tablets break off at this point, but the end of the drama is continued in another Hittite text, "The Plague Prayers of Mursilis."

But when my father gave them one of his sons, they killed him as they led him there. My father let his anger run away with him, he went to war against Egypt and attacked Egypt. He smote the foot soldiers and the charioteers of the country of Egypt. But when they brought back to the Hatti land the prisoners which they had taken, a plague broke out among the prisoners and they began to die. When they moved the prisoners to the Hatti land, the prisoners carried the plague into Hatti land. From that day on people have been dying in the Hatti land.[13]

The prince of the Hatti was murdered on the border of Egypt. By whom? Certainly the prince traveled with an entourage of guards, servants, and gifts. In addition, there should have been a delegation of Egyptian officials to greet and then escort the prince to Ankhesenamen. It is unlikely that so many people could have been massacred by a band of outlaws. The Hittites, who were about to forge a tie with Egypt, had nothing to gain by assassinating their own prince. Suspicion points to some Egyptian with the authority to order a troop of cavalry to murder a foreign emissary traveling under a flag of truce. The one who had the most to lose if the prince and Ankhesenamen married, was, of course, "the servant," the one whose chance for Egypt's throne would vanish. To find the murderer of the Hittite prince, and the suspect implicated in Tutankhamen's death, we must uncover who "the servant" was.

The first clue is found on the walls of Tutankhamen's tomb.

THE FIGURE ON THE WALL

As we know, nonroyal Egyptians decorated their tombs with paintings of daily life to show the gods how they wanted to live in the next world. Sometimes even their preparations for burial are shown, with carpenters and craftsmen preparing the coffin and shrine for canopic jars. Once in a while we even see the funeral itself. In the tomb of Ramose, the mayor of Thebes during Tutankhamen's father's time, the entire funerary procession is displayed, complete with all the objects brought to the tomb—Ramose's headrest, sandals, clothes—everything he needed for the next world. Professional mourners, all paid to wail Ramose's mummy into the tomb, cry and throw dirt on their heads. The tombs of royalty were quite different because they were covered with religious texts inscribed on the walls—*The Book of the Dead, The Book of Gates, The Book of What Was in the Next World*—instead of the charming daily life scenes of nobles' tombs. The walls of Tutankhamen's tomb do portray one realistic scene from life—the pharaoh's burial.

In modern times, the interest in Tutankhamen's tomb has focused on the treasures, furniture and the mummy, with the wall paintings receiving relatively little attention. Even now, despite their dissimilarity to all other royal tomb paintings, they have not been completely studied. Royal tombs are large, complex affairs, virtually every wall of which is beautifully decorated with religious scenes and texts intended to ensure the pharaoh's immortality. The same magical principle guides most of the texts—"the word is the deed." If you say it, write it, or depict it, it will happen. Thus, if you say, "The pharaoh is welcomed by the gods," it will happen. If you show the deceased king greeted in the next world by Osiris, the god of the dead, it will happen. Egyptians seem almost insatiable when it comes to magical spells. The more texts and scenes, the better.

This is where Tutankhamen's tomb is unusual. Only one room, the burial chamber, is painted—almost certainly because there was so little time to prepare the tomb after his unexpected death. In that one painted room, twelve baboons—the guardians of the twelve hours of the night—are depicted sitting patiently on one wall, waiting to assist Tutankhamen. They will ensure that Tutankhamen, like the sun, makes the successful journey through the night before rebirth in the next world. The partition wall that closed the burial chamber, after Tutankhamen was placed in his coffins and the shrines assembled around him, also conveys purely religious significance. That wall shows Tutankhamen given life by Hathor, goddess of the West. Behind him stands Anubis, the jackal-headed god of embalming, who has successfully completed his job and holds an ankh, the sign of life, in his hands. These two walls tell us little about Tutankhamen. It is the other two walls that present actual records of what took place and hold the clues to Tutankhamen's murderer.

On the east wall, a funeral procession is shown that brings Tutankhamen's mummy to the tomb. The mummy rests inside a shrine, mounted on a sled. Twelve pallbearers, wearing white linen headbands, pull their king's mummy to the tomb; two of them with shaven heads, wearing the robes of high officials, are Pentu and Usermont, the chief officials of Upper and Lower Egypt.[14]

Not much insight there. The last wall, the north wall, is seen by all tourists who visit Tutankhamen's tomb and has been widely reproduced in books. Little do most people realize that it contains a substantial clue to Tutankhamen's death.

The nobles of Thebes often included the opening-of-the-mouth ceremony on their tomb walls, but, until the discovery of Tutankhamen's tomb, a royal depiction of this ceremony had never been seen. It is strange that the king who returned Egypt to its traditional religion should so breach custom in his own tomb. Whoever was overseeing the decoration of Tutankhamen's tomb was moved by some reason to change the traditional iconography.

The north wall shows Tutankhamen standing upright in the form of the mummified Osiris. Hieroglyphs above his head make it clear that the figure is Tutankhamen, king of Upper and Lower Egypt, not Osiris. He stands in front of a low table on which a ceremonial feather has been placed along with an offering, the leg of a calf. On the other side of the table a man stands, a figure we can identify as the high priest because he wears the leopard skin of that office. The priest raises the opening-of-the-mouth instrument toward Tutankhamen's mouth, an act that will give him breath and life in the next world. If the priest were only wearing the leopard skin, it would look like the traditional ceremony, but one feature makes this scene unique in all the annals of Egyptian history. The high priest wears a pharaoh's crown. Tutankhamen's successor is performing the ritual. The inscription above his head reveals his identity. It is the old vizier, Aye (fig. 17).

If we reconstruct the events immediately following Tutankhamen's death, it seems obvious that Aye was responsible for including a picture of himself on Tutankhamen's tomb wall, and that he was "the servant" Ankhesenamen desperately tried to avoid marrying.

1. As soon as Tutankhamen died, preparations for his burial and the decoration of his tomb began, not before his death. Certainly Aye, the vizier, looked after these details. So Aye himself ordered that he be shown as pharaoh on the wall.

2. As the scene of Aye as pharaoh was being painted, Ankhesena-men was writing to the Hittite King requesting that he send a son to marry so she will not be forced to marry a "servant."

3. The prince, traveling to marry Ankhesenamen, is murdered on the border of Egypt, a deed probably initiated by someone who had much to lose if the prince married Ankhesenamen.

4. Aye becomes king of Egypt.

The tomb painting and chronology of events all point to Aye as a prime suspect in the murder of the Hittite prince, and, I believe, the murder of Tutankhamen as well. Aye controlled the government. Between the time of Tutankhamen's death and the crowning of his successor, Aye, as vizier, was the most powerful man in the country, above even the widow of the recently departed king. With his control of the palace guard, even of the army, he could indeed force Ankhesenamen to marry him. If, as the X rays suggest, foul play may have caused Tutankhamen's death, we have to ask who would gain from killing the king. The answer is clear. The death of Tutankhamen allowed Aye to seize the throne.

The tomb scene of Aye as king leaves two large questions dangling. How did Aye, a commoner, become king of Egypt, and what happened to Ankhesenamen?

THE NEWBERRY RING

The explanation of how Aye became pharaoh was found in a Cairo antiquity shop in the spring of 1931. It was common practice at that time for Egyptologists to visit antiquities dealers to learn what had turned up on the market and to look for interesting inscriptions and scenes of historical importance. Egyptologist Percy Newberry, who had written a catalogue describing the thousands of scarabs in the Egyptian Museum in Cairo early in his career,[15] often visited the dealers looking for new scarabs, the small amulets carved in the shape of a beetle.[16] In the spring of 1931, while examining a box of these amulets at Robert Blanchard's shop, Newberry found a blue faience finger ring among them, consisting of two cartouches—those of Aye and Ankhesenamen. Such a combination of cartouches on the same ring could only mean one thing. Aye had married the widowed Ankhesenamen. They were king and queen.

Newberry immediately wrote to Howard Carter:

> Maison Mitarchi
> Sharia Bayuni
> Zamalek
> Gezira
> Cairo

My Dear Carter,

   It will interest you to know that I have just seen a finger-ring at Blanchard's which has on it the cartouche of Ankhesena-men along side the prenomen of King Ay. This can only be interpreted as meaning that King Ay has married Ankhesena-men the widow of Tutankhamen. The ring is of blue glaze and was found somewhere in the Eastern Delta. . . .[17]

Newberry's publication of an article about the ring[18] answered the first question. Aye became pharaoh by marrying Ankhesenamen, but as in any good murder mystery, there was a problem—the ring disappeared. Newberry had seen and copied the ring in Blanchard's shop, but didn't buy it. Later, it probably was sold to a tourist unaware of its historical significance and so it disappeared. As the decades passed, some Egyptologists began to doubt that the "Newberry Ring" truly existed. Fortunately, in the early 1970s a ring almost identical to Newberry's was purchased by the Ägyptisches Museum in Berlin. The ring had never been placed on display so I wanted to confirm its significance with my own eyes. I called the museum and spoke with a curator who told me she had never heard of such a ring! After my initial shock, we both realized what had happened. Berlin's two Egyptian collections—East and

West Berlin—had recently been combined, and curators were not yet completely familiar with each other's collections. The ring was indeed located, and a month later I held the fragile bit of evidence in my hand.[19]

Its hieroglyphs were exactly as Newberry had copied them in 1931, although I don't think this was the ring he had seen. Newberry describes it as consisting of a "blue glaze," while the ring in my hand was white. I could see small traces of an original blue, but most of the color had faded away; it was, after all, commissioned to celebrate a wedding 3,000 years ago. Undoubtedly several copies of the ring were produced at that time, and this was a second one. Without doubt, Aye had married Ankhesenamen.

In the Ägyptisches Museum in Berlin I came face to face with the prime suspect. Staring out at me from a Plexiglas vitrine was a life-sized plaster mask of Aye, prepared as an intermediate step before sculpting some bust in stone. It is the face of a mature man with a strong jaw and muscular neck, identified as Ay because of a resemblance to the portraits in his tomb at Amarna[20] (fig. 10). As I looked at the decidedly sinister face of Aye in the vitrine, I noticed that there was a streak of red paint on his upper lip. I couldn't help but think of blood. Perhaps it was what I knew about him that gave this man such an ominous appearance, but I think the casual passerby would not invite someone who looked like this to dinner. If Ankhesenamen was indeed married to him, what was her fate?

In his letter to Howard Carter (fig. 18), Newberry also wondered about this and suggested a way to trace her:

> Is there any chance of your going out to the Western Valley to see the tomb of Ay? If you do go out there, there is a point that would be extremely interesting to settle. On one of the walls of the sarcophagus chamber there was a figure of King Ay with the Queen Tiy behind him. . . .
>
> Is there any trace at all of a figure behind Queen Tiy? And is the cartouche big enough for the name of Ankhesenamen? My notes on the tomb made some years ago do not help me on

this point and it would be very interesting to settle it. If you have time do go out there: it wouldn't take long to do it. Had I the time to run up to Luxor myself I would do so but I shall not be free till the end of May. When are you coming down to Cairo? With our love to you and all good wishes.

Yours sincerely,
Percy E. Newberry

We don't know if Carter ever went to the Western Valley to look at Aye's tomb as Newberry suggested. Few people do because of its out-of-the-way location. As soon as Aye became pharaoh, he appropriated the remote tomb originally begun by Tutankhamen. Aye was entitled, as pharaoh, to a tomb in the Valley of the Kings, but chose an unorthodox Western Valley site. Aye not only took Tutankhamen's throne and wife, he took his tomb.

Because the Western Valley was so isolated, it had been overlooked by early travelers to Egypt. The scientists who accompanied Napoleon's Egyptian expedition in 1798 explored the Western Valley, discovering the nearby tomb of Amenhotep III. Aye's tomb must have been covered by debris at that time, for it remained undiscovered until 1818 when Belzoni, searching for treasure, happened upon it.

It was in the western valley that one of the French savants discovered a large tomb, which he found open, but was quite unknown before his time. I went to visit the tomb, and found it very extensive and in pretty good preservation. My curiosity did not end here. I went farther on in the valley, and in one of the most remote spots saw a heap of stones, which appeared to me detached from the rubbish. I happened to have a stick with me, and on thrusting it into the holes among the stones, I found it penetrated very deep. I returned immediately to Gournou, and procured a few men to open the place. Unfortunately, both

Mrs. Belzoni and myself had been much afflicted for some time with the opthalmus, which was so severe upon me at this time, that I could scarcely see anything before me.

I took the men into the same valley the next morning; but in consequence of my eyes being so bad, it was some time before I could find the spot again. On removing a few stones, we perceived that the sand ran inwards; and in fact, we were so near the entrance, that in less than two hours all the stones were taken away. I had caused some candles to be brought, and I went in, followed by the Arabs. I cannot boast of having made a great discovery in the tomb, though it contained several curious and singular painted figures on the wall, and from its extent, and part of a sarcophagus remaining in the center of a large chamber, having reason to suppose that it was the burial-place of some person of distinction.[21]

Belzoni didn't know it, but he had uncovered the tomb of King Aye. Plundered in ancient times, there was little to interest Belzoni, but Newberry, with his knowledge of the aftermath of Tutankhamen's death, realized that its tomb paintings could provide part of the answer to Ankhesenamen's fate.

The traditional scenes of the pharaoh greeted by the gods of the next world are carefully reproduced in Aye's tomb, but one wall is a complete surprise. Aye included an exact copy of a scene from Tutankhamen's tomb—the twelve guardian baboons of the hours of the night. For reasons of his own, Aye associated himself with his dead predecessor. On another wall, Aye hunts in the marshes. Standing beside him is his wife, the queen.

Pharaohs often included portraits of their queens in their tombs so their spouses would accompany them through eternity. We would expect the same for Tutankhamen—especially since Ankhesenamen was both childhood friend and devoted wife. I have probably lectured inside Tutankhamen's tomb two dozen times to my students, explaining the significance of the wall paintings, but until I started to think about the murder theory, I never noticed who wasn't there—Ankhesenamen. Given their devotion to each other, and the fact that Ankhesenamen was alive when the walls were decorated, this was an egregious omission. Only when we remember that Aye was overseeing Tutankhamen's funerary preparations, including the painting of the walls, does the absence of Tutankhamen's wife from his tomb begin to make sense. Even so shortly after Tutankhamen's death, Aye had planned to marry Ankhesenamen. He did not want her to spend eternity with her first husband.

If Aye omitted Ankhesenamen from Tutankhamen's tomb, she should appear on the walls of his own sepulcher. Under normal circumstances she would be there. If Aye became king by virtue of marrying her, then she was the queen of Egypt, "the Great Wife."

We have no record of Carter or of anyone else looking for Ankhesenamen on the walls of her second husband's tomb. Like Newberry and others interested in the tangled affairs of the late Eighteenth Dynasty, I wondered about her fate. So I made the trek to Aye's tomb.

Walking up the desolate wadi that formed the Western Valley, I couldn't help but hope I would see some trace of the young queen. When I entered the tomb, I quickly found the scene where Aye is shown with his queen. She stands regally behind Aye, as hieroglyphs proclaim her "The King's Great Wife." But who is this queen? The name in the cartouche has been hacked out. There are only two reasonable possibilities for the identity of this queen: 1) Tey, Aye's first wife who was with him at Amarna, and 2) Ankhesenamen, who was already queen of Egypt when he married her. Which one is pictured is clear, despite the erasure. The cartouche is far too short to hold the long name "Ankhesenamen," but is just right for "Tey." No second queen stands behind Tey. Ankhesenamen has disappeared from history. Tey was a powerful woman in her own right, the only woman at Amarna ever awarded a gold collar by Akhenaten. She was the "nurse," or confidant, of Nefertiti, and she knew Ankhesenamen well, perhaps even serving the young queen in Thebes. Once Aye became king, Tey rose to even higher status, but she could never be "the King's Great Wife"—not while Ankhesenamen lived.

THE MISSING WITNESS

The last word from Ankhesenamen is her second desperate letter to the Hittite king, reaffirming that she is telling the truth, that she desperately wants a Hittite prince to marry. The Berlin Museum's ring indicates she lived after that—at least long enough to marry Aye—then she vanishes without a trace. It is not just 3,000 years that have obliterated Ankhesenamen. She should have been depicted on the walls of Tutankhamen's tomb, accompanying him throughout eternity, and, even if she died soon after her marriage to Aye, there should be some mention of her in his tomb. And where, after all, is her tomb?

No tomb for Ankhesenamen has been found. Even if it existed and was robbed clean in antiquity, there should be traces. If Ankhesenamen was buried as a queen of Egypt, her tomb would have contained furniture, clothing, jewelry, and a coffin. Tomb robbers in ancient Egypt took anything of value, breaking the furniture, stripping it of gold leaf, melting down the jewelry, leaving the tomb in a shambles, but what remained would still show there had once been a burial of Ankhesenamen. There would be broken canopic jars, fragments of wood boxes for clothing and toilet objects, objects worthless to any thief, but some would have carried the name of Ankhesenamen. Along with the queen's name, there would be an indication that she was dead, that these were objects from her tomb. Following her name would have been the hieroglyphs for "True of Voice."

Egyptians used many euphemisms for the dead, such as "he went west," and was "a westerner"—not unlike our "dearly departed." Another phrase they used was "true of voice." They believed that the deceased would appear in the Hall of the Double Truth in front of forty-two gods. Here he would present his case, telling why he should be admitted to the next world. Chapter 125 of the *Book of the Dead* told him what to say—that he had harmed no one, didn't divert the irrigation ditch from his neighbor's field, etc. At the end of his plea, his heart would be weighed on a balance scale against the feather of truth—the origins of our scales of justice. If the scale balanced, the deceased was declared "True of Voice" and admitted into the next world. If the scales did not, then the deceased's heart was eaten by the "Devourer of Hearts" and he went out of existence. "True of Voice" became a synonym for "deceased." The objects that should have been in Ankhesenamen's tomb would have had "true of voice" after her name.

Even a badly plundered tomb leaves traces of the occupant; objects appear on the antiquities market; excavators thoroughly mapping and clearing a robbed tomb find fragments; but of Ankhesenamen, married to two kings of Egypt, there is no clue. Either her tomb is yet to be discovered or she was never properly buried, and her name was erased from history. While I hope her tomb may be discovered some day, I fear that the latter might have been her end.

ROUND UP THE SUSPECTS

At this point, the clues include: X rays of Tutankhamen's skull indicating "a blow to the back of the head"; Ankhesenamen writing of her fear and refusing to marry a servant; the Hittite prince being murdered; and finally, Ankhesenamen marrying a commoner (servant), then immediately disappearing from history. All raise suspicions of foul play. We started with one death—Tutankhamen's. Then we found a murdered Hittite prince, followed by the suspicious disappearance of the royal heiress. The three deaths may be connected. If so, who are the principal suspects? As in any murder case, their subsequent actions have to be closely watched for missteps that reveal their guilt.

Aye
Immediately after Tutankhamen's death Aye had his image painted prominently on the tomb of the young king he served. While we might think that, if he was the murderer, he would do everything possible to distance himself from his victim, quite the opposite occurred. There is a

reason, however, why even as Tutankhamen's killer, Aye would want to show himself as a king administering the last rites to the previous monarch. This was a way to legitimize his own claim to the throne, his continuity in the succession. It is significant that, although he had himself portrayed on the tomb wall, he omitted Ankhesenamen, Tutankhamen's wife, as if he had other plans for her. Aye then appropriated the tomb in the Western Valley begun by Tutankhamen and copied decorations from Tutankhamen's tomb, again associating himself with the former pharaoh. To associate himself even more closely with Tutankhamen, Aye added his title of "the God's Father" as part of his new pharaonic name.

Aye ascended the throne in his sixties. He lived for less than four years after becoming king, leaving posterity even fewer traces of his reign than Tutankhamen did. Aye's tomb was badly damaged by tomb robbers, but not until after an official desecration—his name was erased wherever it appeared on his tomb walls.[22] This attempt at *Damnatio Memoriae* was not unusual in ancient Egypt. Names held such great magical significance that Egyptians often said, "To say the name of the dead is to make him live again." If a person's name was erased from his monuments, he no longer existed; with the last trace erased, he was damned forever. This attempt at ensuring that Aye would not enjoy the pleasures of the next world extended beyond erasing his name. Even his ushabtis, his servant statues, were destroyed. Being of no monetary value, ushabtis were usually left by tomb robbers, but, in Aye's tomb, the destruction was so thorough that not one of him as king has ever been found.[23] Someone was making very sure that Aye would not fare well in the netherworld.[24]

Horemheb

Since General Horemheb succeeded Aye as pharaoh, he was in the best position to order the desecration of Aye's tomb. To understand why Horemheb would want this, we have to study his career. Horemheb may have begun his military service during the reign of Tutankhamen's father, but he did not join the religious migration to Amarna.[25] Instead, he rose to prominence under the next pharaoh, Tutankhamen, becoming "Great Commander of the Army," "King's Deputy," and "Overseer of the King's Works," and earning a dozen other titles.[26] Apparently born of humble origins, Horemheb rose quickly in the service of the young pharaoh. One of his rewards, his monumental tomb at Saqqara, is the largest of any of Tutankhamen's officials. No private individual on his own could afford to send an expedition to quarry the stones and employ the hundreds of skilled craftsmen to carve and decorate the blocks of such a tomb, unless it were a gift from the pharaoh. Horemheb showed scenes of his military campaigns in Nubia, Libya, and Syria all over his tomb walls, for it was he who regained control over Egypt's foreign territories that had been lost by Akhenaten.

We can imagine the anger of a warrior toward Akhenaten, the pacifist pharaoh, but even stronger must have been his reaction to Ankhesenamen's letter to the Hittite King. Horemheb had risked his life fighting Hittites; now the queen wanted to marry one of them and make him lord of Egypt—Horemheb's king! It would, therefore, not be surprising if Horemheb had a hand in murdering the Hittite prince. The curator of the Egyptian Department of the Louvre, in Paris, Mme. Desroches-Noblecourt, has no compunction indicting Horemheb for the murder of the Hittite prince.

> Prince Zannanza of the Hittites duly set out with his escort, but Horemheb's police, "the men and the horses of Egypt," murdered him on the way.[27]

Could anyone have ordered a military intercession against a Hittite prince without at least the acquiescence of the commander of the armed forces?

Horemheb continued as commander in chief of the armed forces throughout the reign of Aye, but when the aged Aye died, Horemheb, with the force of the military behind him, proclaimed himself king. Now that he was the top dog, Horemheb's true character revealed itself.

Horemheb eradicated all traces of Tutankhamen, even though this pharaoh was responsible for his rise to prominence. The first target was the colonnade at Luxor Temple, the one Tutankhamen had completed for his grandfather, Amenhotep III. Scenes of the Opet festival were left intact, but Tutankhamen's name was hacked out wherever it appeared and replaced by Horemheb's name.[28] When the gods looked down upon the walls of Luxor Temple, Horemheb would receive the credit (fig. 21). Even Tutankhamen's mortuary temple, where pious priests made offerings for his soul, was desecrated. The colossal statues that once stood in front of that temple no longer bear the name of Tutankhamen. Close examination reveals that the cartouches are carved deeper than the other hieroglyphs, because the statues were first usurped by Aye, then his name was replaced by Horemheb's (fig. 20). Nothing remains of Tutankhamen except his youthful face.

The restoration stela erected by Tutankhamen in Karnak Temple, proclaiming a return to the traditional ways, no longer bears his name. The few visitors who stop to look at it in the Egyptian Museum in Cairo see the name of Horemheb, carved a bit deeper than the rest of the hieroglyphs. Horemheb did such a thorough job of erasing all traces of Tutankhamen that it has been difficult to piece together a picture of Tutankhamen's life. As is characteristic of military people, his attention to detail and ability to command others ensured a thorough job.

Does this wanton erasure betray an anger against Tutankhamen that could have erupted in murder? One fact seems to answer "no." Horemheb's assault on Tutankhamen's name doesn't seem to have been personal because he left the young king's tomb intact and may even have been the one who resealed it after it was partially robbed. The eradication of Tutankhamen's memory was part of a broader rewriting of history, erasing all traces of the Amarna period and those connected with it, which included Tutankhamen and Aye.

When Horemheb took office, Akhenaten's temples to the Aten at Karnak probably still stood. By the time his reign ended, the Aten's temples had vanished. Horemheb ordered the temples dismantled, and he reused the blocks for fill in a great gateway he built in his own honor at Karnak Temple. To complete the systematic destruction of all evidence that the Amarna period existed, he sent teams of workers to Akhenaten's city in the desert to demolish every structure in the town down to its foundation.

Intent on blotting out the memory of Akhenaten, Tutankhamen, and Aye, Horemheb began counting the years of his own reign from the death of Amenhotep III. Horemheb, as Aye's successor, should have begun his reign with year one, but instead began with year 30. It was as if Horemheb had been crowned king immediately after the death of Amenhotep III, so the twenty-nine years of Akhenaten, Smenkare, Tutankhamen, and Aye never existed. Then Horemheb sent stone carvers to his own tomb at Saqqara, where he was depicted as a commoner, a mere general of the army. The workmen carved the cobra, the sign of royalty, on Horemheb's forehead so he would be remembered only as a pharaoh.

All indications show that Horemheb's rewriting of history was no personal vendetta, it was government policy. The Amarna heresy and those connected with it had to be wiped away. To an amazing degree the fiction worked. On the official lists of kings, like the one at Abydos, Horemheb's name appears immediately after the name of Amenhotep III.

However, one exception to Horemheb's destruction of anything and anyone related to Amarna was allowed to remain. The tomb of Tutankhamen went unviolated. Not so with Aye's tomb and Akhenaten's. The reason may have been simple sentiment. Horemheb had risen to greatness under Tutankhamen and may have felt affection for the one who had awarded him power and wealth. Out of sight, the tomb was not an obvious reminder of the heresy, so the young pharaoh could slumber peacefully in his tomb even if he no longer existed officially above ground.

Today, we would call Horemheb a law-and-order pharaoh. He reorganized the courts, installing "men of good character," telling them not to accept bribes. "What will [people think] of men in your office . . . who violate justice?" he asked. As an ex-military man he exacted strict punishments for criminals. Those guilty of extortion had their noses cut off and were exiled. Anyone caught stealing received one hundred blows.[29] Throughout his twenty-seven-year reign, Horemheb strived to restore Egypt to its former position of greatness. He built temples and shrines to the gods, and sent military expeditions far and wide. When at last he lay in his tomb in the Valley of the Kings, Egypt was in far better shape than when he took over the kingship. Of course, that does not mean he was innocent of murder.

THE INDICTMENT

After Tutankhamen's suspicious death, one other murder certainly occurred (of the Hittite prince) and another may well have (of Ankhesenamen). Were all three deaths connected, was a single murderer at work? Given all the evidence, two likely suspects stand out—Aye and Horemheb. Let's consider each one.

The strongest evidence for a crime comes from the Hittite archives, which make a specific charge—the murder of their prince. Clearly, the Hittites viewed that event as an official Egyptian act of aggression, for they declared war on Egypt. They believed that officials at the highest level of Egyptian government were involved. Both Horemheb and Aye must be considered possible culprits in this death. Each had a strong motive. Horemheb, the career military man, had battled the Hittites all his life, and saw one of them about to become his king. Doing away with the Hittite prince would force the powers in charge to pick an Egyptian king. Aye's motive would have been more personal. He wanted to be king. At the moment Ankhesenamen was writing to the Hittites, he was having himself painted as pharaoh on the wall of Tutankhamen's tomb. It was clear to everyone in power but Ankhesenamen that Hittites were enemies, not to be trusted. The Hittite prince could never be allowed to reach Egypt.

Both Aye and Horemheb had the means. Aye as vizier of Egypt controlled the government. When he learned of Ankhesenamen's plans to marry a foreigner, it would have been a simple matter to alert the border patrol of a possible "Hittite invasion" under the cover of a flag of truce.

For Horemheb, too, it would have been easy to direct a chariot division to meet and destroy the prince and his entourage. Egyptian soldiers hearing that a Hittite was on his way to rule Egypt would have been willing to risk their lives to prevent this distasteful event.

Horemheb and Aye each had a motive, and each had the means. It could even be that they connived together. Wanting to ascend to the throne, Aye contacts Horemheb who abhors the idea of serving a Hittite king. The commander in chief of the army, for his own reasons, agrees to do Aye's dirty work—not an unlikely scenario.

If these events took place today, Horemheb and Aye would be questioned separately, and each offered a chance to plea-bargain in exchange for informing on the other. The most likely outcome would be an indictment of both for the murder of the Hittite prince.

What about the other two suspicious deaths, of Ankhesenamen and Tutankhamen? Today, we would look to see who had the motive and the means, then bring in an indictment against that person.

If Tutankhamen was murdered, the evidence points to Aye more than Horemheb. Although both had strong motives, Aye alone had the means. The situation is spelled out on the walls of the tomb of Rekmire, a vizier who held office more than a century before Aye. The tomb is decorated with two motifs—hieroglyphic texts and daily-life scenes—both proclaiming the power of the vizier in ancient Egypt. He had access to every luxury in the land, hosted elaborate banquets where the finest food was served. Musicians and dancers entertained, while a multitude of servants attended to the desires of his guests. Rekmire was so proud of his exalted status that he described his responsibilities as vizier. One line of hieroglyphs on the tomb wall tells it all, "Let no one enter or leave the royal residence without the vizier's knowledge"; he alone was responsible for who went in and came out of the palace. Aye could easily arrange for someone to dispatch Tutankhamen with a blow to the back of the head while the young king slept. He could orchestrate a perfect assassination in which no one would see a stranger enter, then leave Tutankhamen's room. Aye did not have to commit the crime with his own hands. He was an older man who, given his position of power, would have scores of fawning followers willing to do his bidding.

Did Aye have a motive that would drive him to such extreme measures? As Tutankhamen grew to manhood, he must have felt more and more capable of making his own decisions, becoming increasingly difficult to control. Aye would see his own power and influence slipping away. If Ankhesenamen were to have a son—and she was young enough to have every hope of doing so—it would end any hope that Aye would ever be pharaoh. He may have sensed his time was running out. Further, Aye was an intimate in the palace who had watched one pharaoh almost ruin a great country before another took the throne who was, in Aye's eyes, a child. How could Aye, who commanded all the machinery of the country, not feel that his abilities to rule overwhelmed their accidents of birth? He deserved to be pharaoh.

For Aye to become pharaoh, there had to be two deaths in a short period of time, and one of them was clearly murder. When we add the forced marriage of Ankhesenamen and her subsequent death, there is good reason to believe a string of murders occurred.

ANKHESENAMEN

Lacking any record of Ankhesenamen's death, and her tomb and body, the weakest case is the one for her murder. We know only that she was afraid, that she did not want to marry a servant, then she married Aye and disappeared from the historical record. Here, all we can cite are possible motives for murder. When Aye married Ankhesenamen, he became the king of Egypt, gaining the title and the power. Although he no longer needed her, why would he dispatch his new wife? Perhaps Ankhesenamen suspected her new husband of complicity in Tutankhamen's death and was making accusations. After all, she told even the Hittite king she was afraid.

Then, too, we must consider Aye's wife of forty years, Tey, who agreed on one matter with the twenty-year-old Ankhesenamen. Neither wanted Aye to replace his old wife with a young queen. Tey, as we noted earlier, was a woman of considerable social standing, so it is doubtful that she would happily take second place to another wife. Tey may have supported or even suggested the murder of Ankhesenamen. After all, Aye's tomb is decorated with paintings of his faithful wife Tey as the "great wife," the queen of Egypt, where not a trace of Ankhesenamen is seen.

General Horemheb also had a motive. Aye was an elderly pharaoh with no heirs. When he died, the throne of Egypt would again come up for grabs, and Horemheb, with the military at his back, would have a good chance at that prize. Ankhesenamen was a potential obstacle in his path to the throne. Horemheb would have known about her two miscarriages, which showed that she was capable of conceiving. If she had a child with Aye and it was a male, Horemheb's quest for the throne would end. It is even possible, although we have no evidence of it of course, that Ankhesenamen was carrying Tutankhamen's child at the time of his murder.

Where do these possible motives lead? My guess, speculative though it must be, is that Aye murdered not one but probably two and possibly even three people—Ankhesenamen, the Hittite prince, and Tutankhamen, though Horemheb was his accomplice in the death of the Hittite. I believe that Horemheb was not unhappy to see Tutankhamen dead, for his aged successor would be a commoner who opened the door for another commoner—himself—before long. That does not mean he killed him. He had not the ready means. Of course, a determined assassin, if willing to die in the attempt, can get to anyone. But if Horemheb had ordered the deed, he would have to deal afterward with the powerful Aye. His path to the throne could only be over that second, very powerful, body. Yet, Horemeheb had no reason to battle Aye; he was young enough to wait a few years for his turn. Nor did Horemheb have a compelling need to kill Ankhesenamen, not with Aye already at an age when the birth of a son was unlikely to even a young wife.

Aye had everything to gain from the death of Tutankhamen at an unnaturally early age. He had the means to pull off the murder of the pharaoh and not be caught. Aye had all the same reasons to prevent the Hittite prince from reaching Egypt. Poor Ankhesenamen, his obviously unwilling bride, was the one powerful person in Egypt who could accuse Aye of complicity in Tutankhamen's death. Aye, who had murdered two people to get his throne, would not find one more murder very difficult to ensure that he kept his throne.

NILEGATE

If Aye really murdered Tutankhamen, how did he get away with it? There are several answers, each one adequate in itself. During Tutankhamen's time the population did not rise up against their ruler when they were outraged by something he had done. There was no sense of accountability. Two parallel tracks—one for royalty and one for the common people—ran through the society which never intersected, allowing no mechanism by which the people interacted with their pharaoh. The people of ancient Egypt would never rise up against Aye.

At the time of his coronation a pharaoh became divine, a god on earth, the son of the sun god Re. He was so far removed from the people of Egypt they wouldn't dream of interacting with him. In our modern world, with television, radio, and newspapers, it is hard to imagine a country where most of the population lived and died without ever having seen their ruler. The people knew that Tutankhamen was dead, and little more. No news bulletins broadcast his illness or cause of death, nor would anyone wonder. One god had been replaced by another, it was their affair.

The second reason Aye could get away with murder is that no mechanism existed to accuse him, let alone bring him to justice. We are so accustomed to a system of checks and balances that it is difficult to imagine anyone being truly beyond the law, but, with the pharaoh dead, no one occupied a higher office than the vizier. The situation was like our Watergate. The President, our highest official, may have been guilty of crimes, but the highest law officer in the land, the attorney general, was also involved in his criminal conduct. How, under such circumstances, could the President be indicted, let alone convicted? In Watergate, the congress and senate made enough noise to ensure that something was done. Ancient Egypt had neither a congress nor a senate; there was absolutely no way Aye could have been subjected to legal process. Aye's immunity from prosecution is another reason marking him the more likely culprit than Horemheb.

Proof that Aye could get away with murder is found in a single sentence written in the vizier Romose's tomb: "Let no man punish the vizier in his office." The vizier was the highest law official in Egypt; he was the Supreme Court. With Tutankhamen dead, no one alive could punish Aye. He didn't even have to commit the perfect crime because he was beyond the reach of the law.

It was, indeed, possible to kill a king and get away with it. Afterward, this murder, if ever recorded, was methodically eradicated. When Horemheb became king, he erased every trace of anyone involved in the Amarna Heresy, including all the files on Akhenaten, Tutankhamen, and Aye. Everything was destroyed, including, I suspect, valuable information about Tutankhamen, his reign, relationships with his advisors, and even possible clues to his murder.

THE DEFENSE

When I began discussing the murder theory with colleagues, lively discussions ensued. Some agreed, some didn't, but the debates were always interesting and rational. Things changed, however, when The Learning Channel television documentary I had been working on presented the murder theory publicly.

A documentary has to tell a story in a simple and straightforward manner. The audience may be unfamiliar with ancient Egypt and they may be distracted, so it is important to make points clear and easy to understand. The show received good reviews and high ratings, but this has little to do with the probability of the theory being correct. Shows about alien encounters receive good ratings, too. Soon after the program aired, several close colleagues acted strangely distant. It was then that I discovered I wasn't the only one with strong feelings about Tutankhamen. One said to me, "Oh Bob, didn't you know it was Horemheb?" Another felt that I had slandered Aye, whom she viewed as a grandfather figure for Tutankhamen. Lengthy discussions and letters followed, until it became clear to me that the other side had never been presented. I had been acting as a prosecutor, presenting the case against Aye. What would Aye's attorney say? I am glad to have the chance here to present the other side's view.

The defense might begin by defending Aye's character, pointing out that he was a family man, devotedly married for forty years or more, a member of the royal court, loyal to both Tutankhamen and his father. A religious man following the Aten, he had inscribed the most complete version extant of the *Hymn to the Aten* on his tomb wall at Amarna. Further, he attended to the burial of Tutankhamen with loving care. Heirlooms, prized possessions, beautiful funerary equipment, a solid gold coffin, all were placed in the tomb. Clearly Aye loved Tutankhamen. He was a loyal servant of the royal family, not some traitor who would murder the king as he slept.

The burial of Tutankhamen's brother, Smenkare, in Tomb 55 is further evidence of Aye's loyalty to the royal family. The coffin, mummy, and the funerary equipment in the tomb all point to someone who realized that the burials at Amarna would be further desecrated, and had the coffin and mummy moved to Thebes so they would be preserved. This too was a loving act, which, given the times, was also a courageous one. Almost certainly Aye made these arrangements. What emerges is the profile of a devoted family confidant and guardian, not a serial killer.

If we examine how religious movements characteristically develop we will see Aye's actions as those of a sincere servant of the royal family. The vision of Akhenaten was fresh, exciting, positive when his ideas were first presented at Thebes. As always, the majority clung to the traditional religion, but some among the younger people became true ers. Liberated from centuries of dogma, they followed their charis-

araoh to build a new city in the desert. We can easily imagine

ong these first converts of Akhenaten, although he was no

you ter at the time. Aye rose to the highest position in Amarna, all the while devoutly practicing the new religion, but being more mature, Aye was the first to return to his senses. When he realized things were amiss, Aye led the way back to the old gods, guiding young Tutankhamen. He engineered the migration and return to traditional values. This was not a case of someone following the expedient path for his own gain; he was a cult member who had regained his senses.

With Aye's character and good intentions established, his defense might now show that Horemheb is a far more likely suspect in the murder of the Hittite prince. The ambush had to have the acquiescence if not the blessing of the General Horemheb. It was Horemheb, not Aye, who fought and hated the Hittites. If we must choose a prime suspect, surely it is Horemheb, a military leader trained to take quick and forceful action when needed.

With regard to the alleged murder of Ankhesenamen, it must be pointed out that there is no body. A young queen's husband died; would it be unusual for a woman at such a time to be distraught? Afraid? It is the most natural thing in the world. It would be natural, too, that Aye, who had guided the young couple and the country for a decade, continued ruling Egypt. There is nothing sinister in his *pro forma* marriage to Ankhesenamen. He remained her adviser, saved her from whoever the unnamed servant was, and assumed control of Egypt.

It is true that there were three deaths in just a few short months, but why view this as sinister when a far more reasonable explanation is provided by the Hittite archives? At the end of the Hittite tablet that describes the retaliatory strike against Egypt is the statement that the Egyptian prisoners taken to Hatti brought the plague. So there was a plague in Egypt. Would it be suspicious, given that circumstance, that two people in close contact die within a short period? The common cause for the deaths of Tutankhamen and Ankhesenamen was not Aye; it was the plague. The defense rests.

These are strong arguments, serious objections to the theory that Aye is a murderer. Let us examine each one.

THE PROSECUTION RESTS

Aye did, indeed, inscribe the long version of the Hymn to the Aten on the wall of his tomb at Amarna, but this was the most politically correct tomb decoration one could possibly have at that time. What better way to curry favor with Akhenaten? When Aye decorated his second tomb in the Valley of the Kings, he showed only the traditional gods, not a single reference to the Aten. Does this show religious devotion to the traditional gods? It seems rather to suggest that Aye believes in the god(s) expedient at the moment. Aye had no firm religious convictions, which is why he orchestrated the move of the royal court back to Thebes.

Aye indeed buried Tutankhamen with care, which is exactly what we would expect any murderer in his place to do—try to show that he loved and cared for the deceased. He even includes a picture of himself in Tutankhamen's tomb. Other signs also demonstrate Aye's close association with Tutankhamen. After the young king's death, Aye completed a small temple as a memorial to him.[30] All this attention to Tutankhamen was designed, I maintain, both to throw suspicion elsewhere and also to establish Aye's legitimacy as his successor. After all, Aye's sole claim to the throne was that he was married to Tutankhamen's widow. The possibility that a kindly old Aye saved Ankhesenamen from some other, unnamed, "servant" is a red herring. Aye was the power in Egypt; no one could frighten him. If he wanted to remove someone who frightened Ankhesenamen, he had only to say the word—unless it was him that she feared.

The discovery of Tomb 55 raised many questions, not the least of which is who was responsible for the reburial of Smenkare and objects from Amarna. Given Aye's position of power in Thebes, I think he had to be the one, but not necessarily as a loving family servant. Perhaps Tutankhamen, longing for his family, ordered whatever remained of his family's burial be brought to Thebes. It seems that once Tutankhamen died, Tomb 55 was opened, under Aye's orders, so Smenkare's miniature canopic coffins could be appropriated for Tutankhamen's burial—not exactly respecting the family burial vault.

I do agree that Horemheb was the one who killed the poor Hittite prince. Military force was necessary for that act and Horemheb would have provided it to avoid serving a Hittite king. Yes, Horemheb was responsible for the death of the Hittite prince, but does that release Aye from coresponsibility? Surely the vizier of Egypt would have had to authorize such an action. It is far easier to imagine Aye and Horemheb acting in concert than to think of either as a lone assassin in this event. Aye would not have the ability to attack without military agreement, and Horemheb would not have the authority without government approval.

As to the murder of Ankhesenamen, the defense makes a good case. There is no physical evidence for violence here, as there was with Tutankhamen, nor is there the report of a murder, as with the Hititte prince. All we have is circumstantial evidence. A young woman who is afraid disappears. True, she says she will never marry a servant and then marries Aye, a commoner, but even if she were forced into the marriage, it does not mean that she was subsequently murdered. In a modern court of law, we would never get an indictment against Aye for the murder of Ankhesenamen.

The claim that both Tutankhamen and Ankhesenamen were killed by a plague is interesting, but is not supported by the Egyptian records. We have no evidence of a plague in Egypt at this time, though records exist of plagues in other times. It is not surprising that the Hittites would attribute their suffering to their enemy, whether that was the cause or not, much as syphilis was called "the French Disease" by the Germans and "the German Disease" by the French.

However, we must remember that we are not in a court of law. We cannot call witnesses who have been dead for thirty-two centuries. What we must look for is not a conviction, but simply the most reasonable explanation for all the facts. The case against Aye rests on a combination of facts—an X ray suggesting a blow to the back of the head, a widow's letter expressing her fear of being forced to marry a servant, the murder of her Hittite fiancé, the ring showing she married Aye, the painting of Aye on Tutankhamen's tomb wall, and the complete disappearance of the widow afterward. Any single fact by itself does not prove the case, but taken together they indicate not one but two, and possibly three, murders. The dominant thread throughout is Aye. It is he who benefited most from Tutankhamen's death, and he who had the greatest opportunity. Given the evidence, the most reasonable explanation is that Aye is guilty of the murder of Tutankhamen, King of Upper and Lower Egypt, and Lord of the Two Lands.

Epilogue

Crime never lands its wares;
In the end it is justice that lasts.

—*Ptahotep*
circa 2275 B.C.

Soon after Tutankhamen was buried and the funeral party departed and his tomb was sealed, robbers broke into the tomb. They broke off the arrowheads from Tutankhamen's arrows (bronze was valuable), fine linens from chests and unguents from jars were taken, as were other valuable items that would not be traceable to the dead king's tomb. The robbers must have acted hastily, fearing detection. Working in near darkness, they grabbed gleaming golden furniture, only to discard it on the staircase when it became clear that it was gilded wood. The next day when the robbery was detected, officials, perhaps supervised by Maya who in addition to his role as treasurer was Overseer of the Works of the Royal Necropolis, resealed the tomb and blocked the entrance passage with tons of limestone chips in the hope of avoiding further robberies.

However, these efforts were not successful. The tomb was once again entered by robbers, who tunneled through the top of the stone chips and into the tomb. Estimates of the work involved suggest a period of seven or eight hours to tunnel through the mass of limestone chips.[1] So, starting under cover of darkness, the thieves would have finally entered the tomb near daybreak. Fearful of the light of day, they hurriedly searched small chests and grabbed whatever jewelry came to hand. It is possible the thieves were caught in the act, or nearly caught, since a twisted scarf containing eight solid gold rings was abandoned near the entrance. If any of the culprits were captured, their punishment would have been impalement on a sharp stick until death released them from their pain.

The tomb was resealed once again, until Howard Carter discovered it 3,000 years later. Two hundred years after the robberies, Ramses VI began construction on his tomb near the site of Tutankhamen's. His workmen dumped tons of limestone chips dug from the new tomb on top of the entrance to Tutankhamen's older one, obliterating all traces for more than thirty centuries. Tutankhamen finally rested well.

Aye did not survive long after the death of Tutankhamen. His reign of less than four years left little to remember, especially since his monuments were destroyed by Horemheb. Even at Aye's mortuary temple, his name was replaced with Horemheb's cartouches; his tomb in the west spur of the Valley of the Kings, once intended for Tutankhamen, suffered the erasure of his name. Aye appears on none of the Kings Lists of ancient Egypt. He is remembered today only because of his association with Tutankhamen.

When Horemheb succeeded Aye as pharaoh, he attempted to erase all traces of his three predecessors– the kings associated with the Amarna heresy. So it is Horemheb whose name appears on the Kings Lists as the successor to Amenhotep III, as if the kings in between had never existed. This fiction was not due to Horemheb alone. He did, indeed, date his reign from the death of Amenhotep III, but later kings were all too happy to leap over Akhenaten, Tutankhamen, and Aye to skip to Horemheb and count him as one of their own. The irony is that the obliterated Akhenaten and Tutankhamen were legitimate kings, blood descendants of the kings of the Eighteenth Dynasty. Horemheb had not a drop of royal blood, but he did have the army behind him, and in troubled times power resides with the army.

Horemheb ruled for twenty-seven prosperous years. He erected his own version of Tutankhamen's restoration stela at Karnak Temple, claiming that it was he who restored the temples, ended corruption, and reestablished divine order throughout the land. However exaggerated, Horemheb did in fact take firm administrative control of Egypt. Ruling from Memphis, he placed the army under the command of two generals, one for the south and one for the north. He replaced the high priests with men drawn from the army whom he could trust. Courts of law were established in all the major cities of Egypt, with judges reporting directly to Horemheb. Corruption was dealt with severely and justice was promised to all. Horemheb built extensively at Karnak and also constructed a large tomb for himself in the Valley of the Kings, far grander than Tutankhamen's little pit. When he died, in very old age, he left a well-administered, orderly country, but no children.

The country then faced a situation similar to the morass after Tutankhamen's death. There were no heirs at all, not even a female who could elevate someone to the throne by marrying him. But precedents had been set by the murders and machinations in the aftermath of Tutankhamen's death. Egypt had now experienced two pharaohs who were commoners, so a third became more possible than ever before. Like Aye before him, the vizier of Egypt took on the pharaohcy after Horemheb. This vizier had been an army comrade of Horemheb and served as commander in chief before Horemheb selected him to serve as vizier. He was as common as the commonest soldier; his father was a mere captain in the army. He was probably selected to succeed Horemheb because he had a son and grandson. When he died, there would be no doubt about succession. This man founded a great dynasty of long duration.

His name was Ramses, the first of many pharaohs of that name. I like to think that his dynasty, the nineteenth, was the consequence of the sad events discussed in this book. If so, the ending was not without its glory. Ramses I, a contemporary of the aged Horemheb, lasted less than two years as pharaoh, but his son, Seti I, was vigorously middle-aged and enjoyed a reign of fifteen solid years. He started the country in a new direction, away from the intense concentration of energies on Thebes and its god Amun. He called his reign the "Repetition of Birth," the Egyptian version of the Renaissance, and constructed one of the greatest temples in Egypt, not in Thebes but some distance north at Abydos, the birthplace of Osiris. It was to be a truly national temple with a chapel dedicated to Osiris, of course, but others for Isis, Horus, Ptah of Memphis, Re-Harakhti of Heliopolis as well as Amun of Thebes. And, beginning a practice that would become monomaniacal with his son, installed one chapel to himself. This was a man in the old mold, who saw his country's greatness as inseparable from its pharaoh's accomplishments. Appropriately, he had the largest, most magnificent tomb in the Valley of the Kings constructed for his eternal glory.

Seti's son bore a name no less familiar to us than Tutankhamen's—Ramses, known as "the Great." As a young pharaoh he led Egypt's armies as the great fighting pharaohs of the Eighteenth Dynasty had done before. As a mature pharaoh he built great monuments rivaling those of earlier kings. Ramses had more children than any other pharaoh, boastfully listing one hundred progeny. After a reign of sixty-seven years Ramses, old and wizened, met the fate that lies in store for us all. His legacy was a country as strong as ever before, a country covered through its length and breadth with temples and statues proudly bearing the name of Ramses. In a sense, he was Tutankhamen's legacy.

Whatever the impact of Tutankhamen's life on his country or its future course, his name resounds today throughout the world. The names of Aye and Horemheb are recognized only by specialists. If the ancient Egyptian adage, "To say the name of the dead is to make him live again," has any truth, Tutankhamen still lives, but not those who may have caused his death.

History is not just facts and cold stones. It consists of people motivated by fears, hopes, and desires just like ours. The objects they leave behind are not impersonal; they carry the marks of their owners' lives, accomplishments, and dreams. The artifacts discussed in this book still exist. It is still possible to stand in front of the floral collar worn by Ankhesenamen, Aye, or Horemheb at the funerary banquet held when Tutankhamen was laid to rest. It resides in New York's Metropolitan Museum of Art along with a statue of the young Tutankhamen, probably carved for his coronation at Thebes, and a magnificent statue of Horemheb with its law-and-order inscription. One can still visit Tutankhamen's tomb in the Valley of the Kings and see Aye, frozen in time, performing the Opening of the Mouth ceremony eternally on the boy-king he may have murdered. In the Egyptian Museum in Cairo, Tutankhamen's restoration stela stands in a quiet corner on the first floor. Look closely at the deep carving of the cartouches, where Horemheb replaced Tutankhamen's name with his own. This is real history.

Appendix
TESTABLE THEORIES

In chapter 8 we discussed the speculation that Tutankhamen may have lingered before dying. As we mentioned, this is far from certain, but it had to be stated because it is a real possibility and part of the overall picture. Although this is merely a theory, it is important to note that it is a *testable* theory that future research can either refute or confirm. There are methods of determining if Tutankhamen had been ill for a long time and whether he died of dehydration. The proof lies in the contents of four miniature gold coffins in the Egyptian Museum in Cairo.

When Tutankhamen was mummified, his internal organs were removed, dehydrated, wrapped in linen, and placed in four small gold coffins about twelve inches long that had originally been prepared for his brother, Smenkare. The lid of each coffin is inscribed with a prayer for Tutankhamen by one of the four sons of Horus—gods who were to protect the mummy's internal organs. Imseti guarded the liver; Hapi, the lungs; Duamutef, the stomach; and Qebhsenuf, the intestines. When Tutankhamen was buried, the coffins were placed in an alabaster shrine, described by Howard Carter as one of the most beautiful objects in the tomb.[1] They were then anointed with the same black unguents that had been poured on the mummy.

Carter commented that the miniature coffins were tiny replicas of the second of the three coffins in which Tutankhamen was buried, but he never discussed their contents. As far as I know, the organs haven't been seen since the 1920s when they were photographed by Harry Burton from the Metropolitan Museum of Art. The museum kindly sent me a set of Burton's photographs, and the photos show that the internal organs were not damaged by the oils, their linen wrapping had not turned black. A further series of Burton's photographs shows one of the organs unwrapped and in good condition. These organs, still in the Egyptian Museum in Cairo, could hold important clues to Tutankhamen's death.

If Tutankhamen died in a coma, then the intestines and stomach should be empty, and analysis of the liver could show what nutrients he absorbed during his last days. Carter never realized just how much information is contained in a mummy—or part of a mummy. With modern forensic technologies ancient murders can be solved. It is important to understand that the theories we are discussing about Tutankhamen's death are not mere speculation. They are empirically verifiable, and can be tested.

In an experiment performed in 1993, Ronald Wade, director of Maryland's State Anatomy Board, and I mummified a human cadaver in the ancient Egyptian style.[2] Using replicas of ancient tools and natron from the Wadi Natrun in Egypt, we hoped to answer questions about Egyptian mummification techniques. When the experiment was completed we had an Egyptian-style mummy. We sent small samples of tissue from the mummified organs to Dr. Michael Zimmerman, Head of Pathology at Maimonides Medical Center in Brooklyn. Zimmerman's passion is paleopathology. Besides having his M.D., he earned a Ph.D. in physical anthropology, so he is uniquely qualified to solve ancient medical mysteries. Wade and I had the full medical history of our modern mummy, but didn't reveal it to Zimmerman. After his analysis of the tissues, Zimmerman was able to give us a remarkable description of the last days of our subject's life right down to the amount of fluid in his lungs. The tissue samples sent to Zimmerman had been mummified, so it is quite possible that similar analyses could reveal how Tutankhamen spent his last days.

If Dr. Irwin's theory about Tutankhamen's lingering is correct and there was a significant hematoma that remained for some time after the injury, then there should be a buildup of hemosiderin (concentrated blood matter) and elemental iron on the bone in the area.[3] This might be detectable with a high-powered CAT scan. If and when the mummy of Tutankhamen is examined again, this should rank high on the list of procedures to be performed.

The organs of Tutankhamen raise interesting questions. There are four miniature coffins, but there are more than four internal organs. What happened to the other organs? Which ones were actually placed in the miniature coffins? If we wanted to reassemble poor Tutankhamen, it seems several parts would be missing. The lungs, liver, stomach, and intestines are the organs mentioned in connection with the four sons of Horus. What about the kidneys, spleen, pancreas, and gall bladder? In spite of all the mummifications performed, the ancient Egyptians had only a rudimentary knowledge of anatomy. There isn't even a hieroglyph for the pancreas,[4] but this is understandable if we look at how the embalmer worked.

The internal organs were removed through a small incision made on the left side of the abdomen. The embalmer inserted his hand into the incision, cut an organ free, and pulled it out through the incision. The embalmer was working blind, unable to see the relative positions of the organs, or even how many organs there were. Within the mass of intestines, the pancreas or other organs could easily be overlooked. The kidneys, located behind the peritoneum, were often left in place, for they are difficult to reach from the side. In truth, we really don't know which of Tutankhamen's organs were placed in the small coffins. What is certain is that they are not all there, and some may be partial, but still they are important clues.

When Wade and I performed the modern mummification, one of the most difficult procedures was removing the liver, the largest organ in the human body, through the small incision. We were using replicas of ancient ceramic jars to hold the organs, and even after dehydration in natron we were unable to fit the whole liver in our replica of an ancient Egyptian canopic jar. I had to section it. There is no way the liver from a nineteen-year-old male the size of Tutankhamen could have fit in one of the miniature canopic coffins. I suspect that the embalmers cut off as much as would fit in one of the miniature coffins, wrapped it, and placed it in the coffin. The rest must have been discarded along with any other organs not preserved.

Still, whatever organs or parts of organs remain from Tutankhamen, they have not yet been examined by anyone with experience in paleopathology. They will certainly provide invaluable information about Tutankhamen's last days.

Notes

INTRODUCTION

1. Christopher Frayling, *The Face of Tutankhamen* (London: BBC Television, 1992).

2. Karin L. Sandnass, "Dietary Analysis of Prehistoric Lower and Middle Osmore Drainage Populations of Southern Peru Using Stable Isotopes (Delta C-13 and Delta N-15)" (Paper presented at the Second World Congress on Mummy Studies, Cartagena, Colombia, February 6–10, 1995).

CHAPTER 1: THE KING MUST DIE

1. James Henry Breasted, *The Edwin Smith Surgical Papyrus* (Chicago: University of Chicago Press, 1930).

2. William J. Darby et al., *Food the Gift of Osiris* (London: Academic Press, 1977), vol. 1, p. 331.

3. Nicholas Reeves, *The Complete Tutankhamen* (London: Thames & Hudson, 1990), pp. 136–39.

4. Geoffrey Martin, *The Hidden Tombs of Memphis* (London: Thames & Hudson, 1991), pp. 148–49.

5. T. J. C. Baly, "Notes on the Ritual of Opening the Mouth," *Journal of Egyptian Archaeology* 16 (1930): 173–86.

6. E. A. Wallis Budge, *The Book of the Opening of the Mouth* (New York: B. Blom, 1972), vol. 1, pp. 184–86.

7. Thomas George Allen, *The Book of the Dead* (Chicago: University of Chicago Press, 1974), p. 34.

CHAPTER 2: EGYPT BEFORE TUTANKHAMEN

1. Trevor Watkins, "The Beginning of Warfare," in *Warfare in the Ancient World*, ed. Sir John Hackett (New York: Facts on File, 1989), pp. 15–19.

2. Yigel Yadin, *The Art of Warfare in Biblical Lands* (New York: Mcgraw-Hill, 1963), vol. 1, p. 53.

CHAPTER 3: TUTANKHAMEN'S ANCESTORS

1. James Henry Breasted, *Ancient Records of Egypt* (London: Histories & Mysteries of Man, 1988, reprint), vol. 2, pp. 43–44.

2. Arielle P. Kozloff and Betsy M. Bryan, *Egypt's Dazzling Sun* (Cleveland: Cleveland Museum of Art, 1992), p. 59.

3. Elizabeth Riefstahl, *Thebes in the Time of Amenhotep III* (Norman, OK: University of Oklahoma Press, 1964), p. 5.

4. John Romer, *Valley of the Kings* (New York: William Morrow, 1981), p. 161.

5. Ibid., pp. 161–62.

6. Loret prepared the mummies for shipment to Cairo—but, just before loading them on the boat, he received an order from the Ministry of Public Works to replace the mummies in the tomb and seal it. Many Egyptians viewed archaeologists as foreigners robbing their heritage. They believed their kings should lie undisturbed where they were found. Politics had superseded archaeology.

7. G. Elliot Smith, *The Royal Mummies* (Cairo: l'Institut Français, 1912), pp. 46–51.

8. Guido Majno, *The Healing Hand* (Cambridge, MA: Harvard University Press, 1977), p. 109.

9. Ray Winfield Smith, "Computer Helps Scholars Recreate an Egyptian Temple," *National Geographic* (November 1970): 634–55; Ray Winfield Smith and

Donald B. Redford, *The Akhenaten Temple Project* (Westminster: Aris & Phillips, 1978).

10. Donald Redford, the excavator of Akhenaten's temples at Karnak, shares my view of Akhenaten's sed-festival as extraordinary, but recently another scholar, Jocelyn Gohary, has suggested that Akhenaten was trying to stay as close to traditional ritual as possible. Jocelyn Gohary, *Akhenaten's Sed-Festival at Karnak* (London: Kegan Paul, 1992), p. 167.

11. Reed E. Pyeritz and Cheryll Gasner, *The Marfan Syndrome* (Port Washington, NY: National Marfan Foundation, 1994), pp. 8–9.

12. Victor A. McKusick, "The Defect in Marfan Syndrome," *Nature* 352 (July 25, 1991): pp. 279–80.

13. Many thanks to Dr. Jessica Davis, New York Hospital, for her most helpful discussions of Akhenaten as a Marfan's syndrome patient.

CHAPTER 4: AMARNA—THE HOLY CITY

1. Barry J. Kemp, "The Window of Appearances at El-Amarna, and the Basic Structure of the City," *Journal of Egyptian Archaeology* vol. 62 (1976): pp. 81–99.

2. Gardiner Wilkinson, *Modern Egypt and Thebes* (London: John Murray, 1843), vol. 2, p. 76.

3. Margaret S. Drawer, *Flinders Petrie: A Life in Archaeology* (Madison, WI: University of Wisconsin Press, 1995), p. 208.

4. William Flinders Petrie, *Tell el Amarna* (Westminster: Aris & Phillips, 1974, reprint), pp. 41–42.

5. Ibid., p. 6.

6. William J. Murnane and Charles C. Van Siclen III, *The Boundary Stelae of Akhenaten* (London: Kegan Paul, 1993), pp. 36–37 (based on their translation and transcription).

7. Ibid, pp. 36–37.

8. Cyril Aldred, *Akhenaten* (London: Thames & Hudson, 1988), p. 48.

9. Miriam Lichtheim, *Ancient Egyptian Literature* (Berkeley: University of California Press, 1976), vol. 2, pp. 96–99.

10. Cyril Aldred, *Akhenaten King of Egypt* (New York: Thames & Hudson, 1988), p. 48.

11. Donald B. Redford, *Akhenaten, The Heretic King* (Princeton: Princeton University Press, 1984), p. 234.

12. Barry J. Kemp, "The Window of Appearances at El-Amarna, and the Basic Structure of the City," *Journal of Egyptian Archaeology* 62 (1976): 81–99.

CHAPTER 5: TUTANKHAMEN'S PARENTS

1. Cyril Aldred, *Akhenaten and Nefertiti* (New York: Brooklyn Museum, 1973), p. 220.

2. Aidan Dodson, *The Canopic Equipment of the Kings of Egypt* (London: Kegan Paul, 1994), p. 55.

3. Williman C. Hayes, *The Scepter of Egypt* (New York: Metropolitan Museum of Art, 1959), vol. 2, p. 294.

4. H. W. Fairman, "Once Again the So-Called Coffin of Akhenaten," *Journal of Egyptian Archaeology* 47 (1961): 29–30.

5. This possible friction between the two wives is hinted at in the title of an article about Kiya. See Angela P. Thomas, "The Other Woman at Akhetaten," in *Amarna Letters III* (San Francisco: KMT, 1994), pp. 73–80.

6. Barry J. Kemp, "Outlying Temples of Amarna," in *Amarna Reports VI* (London: Egypt Exploration Society, 1995), pp. 411–62.

7. Urbaine Bouriant, *Monuments Pour Servir a l'Étude du Culte d'Atonou en Egypte* (Cairo: Mission Français d'Archaeologie Orientale du Caire, 1903).

8. Geoffrey Thorndike Martin, *The Royal Tomb of Amarna* (London: Egypt Exploration Society, 1989), p. 40.

9. Samuel A. B. Mercer, *The Tel Amarna Tablets* (Toronto: Macmillan, 1939), vol. 1, pp. 267–69.

10. Ibid., pp. 271–73.

11. Ibid., pp. 275–77.

12. Ibid., p. 291.

13. Norman de Garis Davies, *The Rock Tombs of Amarna—Part I: The Tomb of Meryra* (London: Egypt Exploration Fund, 1903), p. 15.

14. W. M. Flinders Petrie, *Tell El Amarna* (London: Methuen & Co., 1894), p. 33. In his excavations, Petrie found a pottery fragment with this inscription: *year 16 good wine . . . The great seer of the Aten Ra-Mery.* So Merire was alive at this time.

15. Norman de Garis Davis, *The Rock Cut Tombs of Amarna—Part II: The Tombs of Panehesy and Meryra II* (London: Egypt Exploration Fund, 1905), p. 29.

16. Ibid., plate 10.

17. Norman de Garis Davis, *The Rock Cut Tombs of Amarna—Part V: The Tomb of Ay* (London: Egypt Exploration Fund, 1912).

18. Donald Redford, *Akhenaten: The Heretic King* (Princeton: Princeton University Press, 1984), p. 216; Rosalie and Anthony E. David, *A Biographical Dictonary of Ancient Egypt* (London: Seaby, 1981), p. 26.

CHAPTER 6: THE RETURN TO THEBES

1. John Bennett, "The Restoration Inscription of Tutankhamen," *Journal of Egyptian Archaeology* 25 (1939): 8–15.

2. Geoffrey T. Martin, *The Hidden Tombs of Memphis* (London: Thames & Hudson, 1991), pp. 171–72.

3. Ibid., p. 147.

4. Theodore M. Davis, *The Tombs of Harmhabi and Touatankhamanou* (London: Constable, 1912), p. 128.

5. Miriam Lichtheim, *Ancient Egyptian Literature* (Berkeley: University of California Press, 1976), vol. 2, p. 101.

6. The Epigraphic Survey, *The Festival Procession of Opet in the Colonnade Hall* (Chicago: The University of Chicago Oriental Institute Publications, 1994), 1:xix.

7. Nicholas Reeves and Richard H. Wilkinson, *The Complete Valley of the Kings* (London: Thames and Hudson, 1996), pp. 116–17.

8. Hans Goericke, *The Report About the Dispute of a Man with His Ba* (Baltimore: Johns Hopkins Press, 1970).

CHAPTER 7: THE MOST FAMOUS TOMB IN HISTORY

1. Diodorus Siculus, *Library of History,* book 1, vol. 46 (Cambridge: Harvard University Press, 1968), p. 165.

2. Richard Pococke, *A Description of the East* (London: W. Boyer, 1843), vol. 1, p. 98.

3. *Description de l'Egypte* (Paris: L'Imprimerie Impériale, 1812), vol. 2, plate 77.

4. The mummies and coffins arrived safely at the Egyptian Museum in Boulaq. Brugsch unwrapped only one of the mummies, that of Tuthmosis III, the greatest of the warrior pharaohs. The mummy had been buried in the Valley of the Kings, plundered, rewrapped by the Twenty-first Dynasty embalmers, and reburied in the Deir el Bahri tomb.

   When Brugsch unwrapped the Egyptian king, he and his colleagues became the first in modern times to see the mummy of one of the greatest pharaohs of ancient Egypt. What they saw was shocking. The king's body was in a horrible state, the head separated from the body, the legs and arms disarticulated, and the feet broken at the ankles. Brugsch performed a crude, quick autopsy that yielded little information. He did not continue with the other mummies, perhaps fearful that he would find them in a similar condition.

5. W. M. Flinders Petrie, *Seventy Years of Archaeology* (New York: Holt, 1932), p. 152.

6. Howard Carter, *Annales du Service des Antiquitiés de l'Egypte* (1902) 3: 115–21.

7. Theodore M. Davis, *The Tombs of Harmhabi and Touatankhamanou* (London: Constable, 1912), p. 3.

8. Joseph Lindon Smith, quoted in *The Complete Valley of the Kings,* by Nicholas Reeves and Richard H. Wilkinson (London: Thames & Hudson, 1996), p. 6.

9. Ibid, p. 64.

10. Charles Breasted, *Pioneer to the Past: The Story of James H. Breasted* (New York: Scribner's, 1943), p. 181.

11. James Henry Breasted, *Records of Ancient Egypt* (Chicago: University of Chicago Press, 1906–1907).

12. James Henry Breasted, *History of Egypt* (New York: Scribner's, 1924), pp. 133–34.

13. There is also a theory that the shrine never had a statue. See M. Eaton-Krauss and E. Graefe, *The Small Golden Shrine from the Tomb of Tutankhamen* (Oxford: Griffith Institute, 1985), pp. 5–6.

14. Edward Falkener, *Games Ancient and Oriental and How to Play Them* (New York: Dover, 1961).

15. Grahme Davis, "Reconstructing Rules for the Ancient Egyptian Game of Twenty Squares," *KMT* (summer 1993): 83–85.

16. Leonard H. Lesko, *King Tut's Wine Cellar* (Berkeley: B. C. Scribe Publications, 1977).

17. W. M. McLeod, *Composition Bows from the Tomb of Tut'ankhamun* (Oxford: Griffith Institute, 1970); W. M. McLeod, *Self Bows and other Archery Tackle from the Tomb of Tut'ankhamun* (Oxford: Griffith Institute, 1982).

18. J. E. Harris et al., "The Mummy of the 'Elder Lady' in the Tomb of Amenhotep II: Egyptian Museum Catalogue Number 61070," *Science,* June 9, 1978, p. 1199; recent research, however, has suggested that in spite of the close match of hair samples, the mummy of the Elder Lady is not Queen Tiye. Dr. Renate Germer compared the dried blood of the mummy of the Elder Lady with that of Tiye's parents, Yuya and Tuya, and found it highly unlikely that the Elder Lady could be their daughter. Tutankhamen's grandmother may still be missing.

19. Harry Burton, *New York Times,* February 15, 1923.

20. Arthur C. Mace, *Bulletin of the Metropolitan Museum of Art,* The Egyptian Expedition, 1922–1923, p. 6.

21. Howard Carter, *The Tomb of Tutankhamen* (New York: Cooper Square, 1963), vol. 2, p. 51.

22. Ibid., pp. 52–53.

23. Velma, "The Fatal Curse from the Tomb," in Christopher Frayling, *The Face of Tutankhamen* (London: Faber and Faber, 1992), p. 244.

24. Velma wasn't the only one talking about a curse. Two weeks before Lord Carnarvon's death, the novelist Marie Corelli had predicted disaster for those at the site. In more recent times the curse flames have been fanned by Philip Vandenberg in his book *The Curse of the Pharaohs.* He says, "however, the scholars especially were less euphoric. In fact, they became increasingly nervous. The reason for their concern was an ordinary clay tablet Carter had found in the antechamber. He had it catalogued, as he did the other objects. Then, a few days later, Alan Gardiner decoded the hieroglyphics on it. The inscription read: *Death will slay with his wings whoever disturbs the peace of the pharaoh.* Neither Carter nor Gardiner nor any of the other scholars present feared the curse then or took it seriously. But they worried that the Egyptians laborers would, and since they were dependent on native helpers, mention of the clay tablet was

wiped from the written record of the tomb's discovery. Even the tablet itself disappeared from the artifact collection—but not from the memory of those who read it. (The tablet and the curse on it are cited everywhere, but it was never photographed and is considered lost.)" (p. 20)

The tablet never existed, there are no reliable references to such a curse, and it is certainly un-Egyptian to speak of death as being with wings. Over the next few decades, whenever anyone who worked on the excavation died, the curse was invoked. In his book (p. 103), Vandenberg says: "Tutankhamen's autopsy at the Anatomical Institute of Cairo University on November 11, 1925, had tragic consequences: Alfred Lucand died soon after from a heart attack, and a little later Professor Derry died of circulatory collapse." This is nonsense. There was never an autopsy of Tutankhamen in Cairo. The mummy is still in the tomb where it was found. Lucas died of a heart attack in 1945, twenty years later, not soon after the autopsy. Professor Derry did not die "a little later," but in 1969 at the age of 87, more than forty years after he autopsied the boy-king in his tomb. Although the evidence is slim, the idea of the "curse of Tutankhamen" continues to intrigue people.

It was Velma's account of the curse that established a precedent for psychics of her day to claim that they also had warned Carnarvon of a curse on the tomb. Chiero, the famous palm reader, published his account of the curse on the tomb. By far the most elaborate of the curse stories, it involves a mummy's hand, a long-dead Egyptian princess, and a curse on those who would remove objects from Tutankhamen's tomb.

Chiero published his account more than a decade after Carnarvon had died, but claimed he had sworn affidavits from those who witnessed the incredible events that he describes. Chiero's tale begins with a trip he made to Egypt prior to World War I to prepare wax casts of the ancient carvings. One evening his guide asked him to come to the hypostyle hall at Karnak temple. When they reached the hall, his guide produced, from beneath a broken sphinx, a mummy's hand complete with a gold finger ring. The trusty guide explained that this was the hand of Akhenaten's daughter, Meketaten. He related the tale that only she had remained true to her father's religion when everyone else had abandoned the Aten, and she had formed an army and marched on

Thebes. Meketaten was killed in the subsequent battle and her hand severed and mummified as a grim reminder to those who might stray from the true faith of Egypt. Chiero had been singled out to become the custodian of the hand to see that the prophecy associated with it was fulfilled.

The hand was to travel the world, but after a great war was fought, and the tomb of her brother-in-law Tutankhamen was discovered, the hand would be reunited with the rest of the mummy of Meketaten. Chiero says that he accepted this great responsibility and carried the hand with him wherever he went, but after World War I, strange things began to happen. The hand had been as hard as ebony, but now the skin began to soften, and then to ooze blood. For more than thirty years Chiero had carried the hand around the world, but this was too much, so he and his wife decided to cremate the hand on Halloween Eve in 1922. As the hand was consumed by flames, a beautiful and elegant princess, Meketaten, appeared, complete with both her hands. The next day Tutankhamen's tomb was discovered. (Chiero had his dates wrong, but it didn't seem to hurt his story.) The princess appeared once more to Chiero, this time with a warning for Lord Carnarvon. None of the treasures from Tutankhamen's tomb were to be removed or death would claim him while he was still in Egypt.

Chiero published this account of the curse in *Real Life Stories* in 1934. Because he was one of the most famous clairvoyants of his era, his embellishment of the curse helped to keep the myth alive.

25. Howard Carter, *The Tomb of Tutankhamen* (New York: Cooper Square, 1963, reprint), vol. 2, p. 82.

26. F. Filce Leek, *The Human Remains from the Tomb of Tut'ankhamun* (Oxford: Griffith Institute, 1972), p. 5.

27. Douglas E. Derry, "Report on the Examination of Tutankhamen's Mummy," in Howard Carter, *The Tomb of Tutankhamen,* vol. 2, pp. 158–59.

28. The Deir el Bahri cache of royal mummies found in 1881 had the potential of providing considerable data on royal mummification techniques, yet the mummies were ravaged by notable Egyptologists who did not know what to look for, nor did they take the time to make careful notes when they performed an unwrapping. Maspero was in France when the mummies were transported

from Thebes to Cairo, so it was Emile Brugsch, his assistant, who began their unwrapping. Chastising him in the official report, Maspero says, "Within the first few weeks of their arrival at Boulaq, Mr. Emile Brugsch could not resist the desire to see for the first time one of their faces, and opened, without permission, and during my absence, the mummy of Tuthmoses III" (M. Maspero, *Les momies royales de Deir el-Bahri*, Paris: Mission Archéologique Française, 1889, p. 525). Occupied with translating the coffins' inscriptions and the labels on the mummies, Maspero waited several years before unwrapping the mummies. But when he began he was in a frenzy, tearing through one mummy after another.

By order of the Khedive of Egypt, on June 1, 1886, the mummy of Ramses II was unwrapped. Attending were the Khedive, his entire council of ministers, various doctors, archaeologists, artists and others. In his report Maspero attempts to create the impression that everything was done scientifically and with caution. He explains that every measurement was taken by two of those present, then verified by two other attendants (Maspero, pp. 525–26). In truth, the proceedings were shoddy. Maspero unwrapped *three* mummies that day, two kings and a queen—the start of a good poker hand, but bad Egyptology. The next week, in a single day Maspero unwrapped the mummies of Seti I, Seqenenre Tao II, and Ahmose I. In less than one month, from June 9 to July 1, twenty-one mummies of the Deir el Bahri cache were stripped of their wrappings. One can only wonder what Maspero's hurry was. This was how mummies were treated, so Tutankhamen's rough handling should not be surprising.

Most of the royal mummies that escaped Maspero's hands were later unwrapped by Grafton Elliot Smith, a physician who had the necessary training, but who also worked too quickly. During 1905, Smith unwrapped nine mummies, including those of Tuthmosis IV, Ramses IV, Ramses V, Ramses VI, Siptah, and Seti II. Smith's account of these unrollings is almost obsessively brief, allotting each pharaoh a mere page or two (G. Elliot Smith, *The Royal Mummies*, Cairo: Institut Français d'Archéologie Orientale, 1912). His descriptions provide a few insights into royal mummification, such as position of the abdominal incision, but at times he is clearly more interested in the features of the royal visage than how the pharaohs were mummified.

CHAPTER 8: DEAD MEN TELL TALES

1. Marc Armand Ruffer, "Notes on the Histology of Egyptian Mummies," *British Medical Journal* (1909): 11.

2. F. Filce Leek, *The Human Remains from the Tomb of Tut'ankhamun* (Oxford, Griffith Institute, 1972), p. 23.

3. R. G. Harrison et al., "A Mummy Foetus from the Tomb of Tutankhamen," *Antiquity* 53 (1979): 19–21.

4. The first X ray of a wrapped mummy was published by Flinders Petrie in 1898 as the final illustration in his excavation report of Dashasheh, a site eighty miles south of Cairo. The developed film showed the leg bones of a mummy through the wrappings. Petrie realized that X rays permitted the Egyptologist to know what was beneath the mummy bandages without unwrapping, but his example was not widely imitated. When Tutankhamen's tomb was discovered in 1922, the only royal mummy to have been X-rayed was Tuthmosis IV, who was transported in a taxi from the museum by Elliot Smith and Howard Carter to a hospital in Cairo that owned an X-ray machine.

5. R. G. Harrison, "An Anatomical Examination of the Pharaonic Remains Purported to Be Akhenaten," *Journal of Egyptian Archaeology* 52 (1966): 116.

6. R. G. Harrison and A. B. Abdalla, "The Remains of Tutankhamen," *Antiquity* 46 (1972): 10.

7. Dennis Forbes, "Abusing Pharaoh," in Christopher Frayling, *The Face of Tutankhamen* (London: Faber and Faber, 1992), pp. 291–92.

8. R. G. Harrison, "Post Mortem on Two Pharaohs: Was Tutankhamen's Skull Fractured?" *Buried History* (1972): 18–24; R. G. Harrison, "Tutankhamen's Postmortem," *The Lancet* (1973): 259; R. G. Harrison, "The Remains of Tutankhamen," *Antiquity* 46 1972): 8–14.

9. Roy L. Moodie, *Roentgenologic Studies of Egyptian and Peruvian Mummies* (Chicago: Field Museum of Natural History, 1931), p. 23, plate 14.

10. Marc Armand Ruffer, "Notes on Two Egyptian Mummies Dating from the Persian Occupation of Egypt," in *Studies in the Paleopathology of Egypt* (Chicago: University of Chicago Press, 1921), pp. 127–38.

11. Quoted in F. Filce Leek, *The Human Remains from the Tomb of Tut'ankhamun* (Oxford: Griffith Institute, 1972), p. 7.

12. James E. Harris and Kent R. Weeks, *X-raying the Pharaohs* (New York: Scribner's, 1973).

13. James E. Harris and Edward F. Wente, *An X-ray Atlas of the Royal Mummies* (Chicago: University of Chicago Press, 1980), p. 378.

14. *Los Angeles Times,* January 17, 1997.

15. Nicholas Reeves, *The Complete Tutankhamen* (London: Thames & Hudson, 1990), p. 118.

16. F. Filce Leek, *op. cit.,* p. 17.

17. Cyril Aldred, *Akhenaten, King of Egypt* (London: Thames & Hudson, 1988), p. 297.

18. Letter to the author, dated April 1, 1996.

19. Thanks are due to Dr. Michael R. Zimmerman, Director of Clinical Laboratories, Maimonides Medical Center, Brooklyn, New York, for his helpful discussion on this question.

CHAPTER 9: A WIDOW'S PLEA

1. Hans Gustav Guterbock, "The Deeds of Suppiluliuma as Told by His Son Mursilis II," *Journal of Cuneiform Studies* 10 (1965): 47.

2. Ibid., p. 94.

3. Donald Redford has argued that there is a scribal error and the king named is Akhenaten, but it is not a convincing argument. For a discussion of this issue see Alan R. Schulman, "Ankhesenamen, Nofretity, and the Amka Affair," *Journal of the American Research Center in Egypt* 15 (1977): 43–48.

4. Walter Federn, "Dahamunzu (KBo V 6 iii 8)," *Journal of Cuneiform Studies* 14 (1960): 33.

5. Geoffrey Thorndike Martin, *The Hidden Tombs of Memphis* (London: Thames and Hudson, 1991), plate 41; Cyril Aldred, *The Development of Ancient Egyptian Art* (London: Tiranti, 1961), plate 144.

6. Guterbock, *op. cit.,* pp. 94–95.

7. Ibid., p. 96.

8. Nigel F. Hepper, *Pharaoh's Flowers* (London: HMSO, 1990), pp. 9–10.

9. There is an alternative theory about the time of Tutankhamen's death. Because the Hittite text says "But when the people of Egypt heard of the attack on

Amka, they were afraid. And in addition, their Lord Nephururiya had died. Therefore the Queen of Egypt . . . sent a messenger to my father . . ." Trevor R. Bryce believes that the Amka campaign and the death of Tutankhamen occurred at about the same time. This would change the season of Tutankhamen's death, because from the Hittite accounts we know the siege was in early autumn. Bryce's scenario involves Tutankhamen dying toward the end of August, the siege in October, and Ankhesenamen's first letter being sent in November. Bryce admits that the burial took place in Spring, but wants to assume that it was delayed for six months while Ankhesenamen waited for the Hittite prince. But this is based on the assumption that the Amka campaign and the death occurred at the same time. It is quite possible that the queen only learned of the Amka affair months later, or perhaps not at all. As we have said before, her fear seems to have come from the "servant." She never mentions the Amka campaign. Also there is no need to assume the burial of Tutankhamen would have been delayed. Egyptian religion demanded the body be buried seventy days after death. It seems far more likely that the funerary bouquets are the best indicator of the time of death. See Trevor R. Bryce, "The Death of Niphururiya and Its Aftermath," *The Journal of Egyptian Archaeology* 76 (1990): 99–105.

10. Ibid., pp. 96–97.

11. Ibid., pp. 97–98.

12. Ibid., p. 98.

13. Albrecht Goetze, "Palace Prayers of Mursilis," in *Ancient Near Eastern Texts,* ed. James B. Prichard (Princeton: Princeton University Press, 1955), p. 395.

14. Nicholas Reeves, *The Complete Tutankhamen* (London: Thames & Hudson, 1990), p. 72.

15. Percy E. Newberry, *Scarab-shaped Seals* (London: Constable, 1907).

16. The Egyptians were especially fond of puns, and the hieroglyphs for beetle 𓆣 (pronounced *kheper*) also meant "to exist." So if you wore a scarab amulet, your continued existence was ensured. Another reason the scarab was held in special regard is that the ancient Egyptians believed the beetle bore its young without the union of male and female. This false belief arose simply because the beetles were never seen mating. Actually, after fertilization the female deposits her eggs in a piece of dung and rolls it into a ball, so that when they hatch, the newborn will be provided with food. Since this was the only part of the reproductive

cycle the Egyptians saw, they assumed the beetle was somewhat like the god Atum who begot children without a female partner.

Scarab amulets were made from a variety of materials, faience and stone being the most common. Like other amulets, holes were incorporated in their design so they could be suspended on a chain and worn. While the top was carved to resemble the beetle, the bottom was usually flat, with an inscription. Often the inscription was merely the owner's name, so that the amulet would bring him continued existence. Scarabs could also be used as seals. If the owner wanted to seal a jar of wine and be sure none of the servants sampled it, he could plaster the top of the jar and press the bottom of his scarab into the moist plaster. Then if the seal were broken, it could not be repaired undetected.

17. My thanks to Diana Magee of the Griffith Institute, Ashmolean Museum, Oxford, for supplying a photocopy of Newberry's letter.

18. Percy E. Newberry, "King Ay, the Successor to Tutankhamen," *Journal of Egyptian Archaeology* 18 (1932): 50–53.

19. My thanks to Drs. Dietrich Wildung and Hannelore Kischkewitz of the Ägyptisches Museum, Berlin, for their help in locating the ring and making it available.

20. Cyril Aldred, *Akhenaten and Nefertiti* (New York: Brooklyn Museum, 1973), p. 181.

21. Giovanni Battista Belzoni, *Narrative of the Operations and Recent Discoveries in Egypt and Nubia* (London: Murray, 1820), pp. 123–24.

22. Otto J. Schaden, "The God's Father Aye," in *Amarna Letters II* (San Francisco: KMT, 1992), p. 108.

23. An ushbati of Aye as a commoner, made during the period he served Tutankhamen, was auctioned at Sotheby's in New York on December 17, 1997. It is one of the most beautiful ushbatis ever made.

24. Otto J. Schaden, "Clearing the Tomb of King Aye," *Journal of the American Research Center in Egypt* 21 (1984): 39–64.

25. There is an Amarna tomb for the military commander Paatenemheb, and because of the similarity in the two names, some have suggested that this is Horemheb's tomb. See Christiane Desroches-Noblecourt, *Tutankhamen* (New York: New York Graphic Society, 1963), p. 284.

26. Geoffrey T. Martin, *The Hidden Tombs of Memphis* (London: Thames & Hudson, 1991), p. 52.

27. Christiane Desroches-Noblecourt, *Tutankhamen* (New York: New York Graphic Society, 1963), p. 276.

28. Epigraphic Survey, *The Festival Procession of Opet in the Colonnade Hall* (Chicago: University of Chicago Press, 1994).

29. Ronald J. Leprohon, "A Vision Collapsed, Akhenaten's Reforms Viewed Through Decrees of Later Reigns," in *Amarna Letters* (San Francisco: KMT, 1991), pp. 66–73.

30. The blocks from this temple are now scattered, but they seem to show Tutankhamen in battle scenes fighting Asiatics—the earliest known royal chariot battle scenes. See William Raymond Johnson, "An Asiatic Battle Scene of Tutankhamen from Thebes," Doctoral dissertation, University of Chicago, 1992.

EPILOGUE

1. Nicholas Reeves, *The Complete Tutankhamen* (London: Thames & Hudson, 1990), p. 96.

APPENDIX: TESTABLE THEORIES

1. Howard Carter, *The Tomb of Tut-Ankh-Amen* (New York: Cooper Square Press, 1965, reprint), vol. 3, p. 48.

2. Bob Brier and Ronald S. Wade, "The Use of Natron in Human Mummification—A Modern Experiment," *Zeitschrift für Ägyptische Sprache und Altertumskunde* 124, no. 2 (1997): pp. 89–100.

3. Dr. Michael Perry, Chief of Trauma Radiology, University of Maryland school of medicine, suggested this to me.

4. Kent Weeks, *The Anatomical Knowledge of the Ancient Egyptians and the Representation of the Human Figure in Egyptian Art* (Ann Arbor: UMI Dissertation Information Service, 1970), pp. 74–5.

Bibliography

Albright, William F. "The Egyptian Correspondence of Abimilki Prince of Tyre." *Journal of Egyptian Archaeology* 23 (1937): 190–203. Discussion of one section of the Amarna Letters and the difficulties in translating them.

Aldred, Cyril. *Akhenaten and Nefertiti*. New York: Brooklyn Museum, 1973. Catalog to accompany the exhibition at the Brooklyn Museum. Many unusual illustrations with excellent descriptions.

———. *Akhenaten, King of Egypt*. London: Thames & Hudson, 1988. Although somewhat dated, this book was written by the foremost Akhenaten scholar and is still a basic work on Tutankhamen's father.

———. "The Beginning of the El-Amarna Period." *Journal of Egyptian Archaeology* 45 (1959): 19–33. A great Akhenaten scholar describes Akhenaten's early years.

———. *The Development of Ancient Egyptian Art*. London: Tiranti, 1961. Discussion of the how Egyptian art developed.

————. "The End of the El-Amarna Period." *Journal of Egyptian Archaeology* 43, (1957): 30–41. A discussion of the relationship between members of the court during the last years at Amarna.

————. "The Tomb of Akhenaten at Thebes." *Journal of Egyptian Archaeology* 47 (1961): 41–65. An attempt at reconstructing the events that led to the mummy and funerary objects being placed in Tomb 55. The conclusion that the body was Akhenaten's was reached before the later autopsy of the mummy showed this to be unlikely.

————. *Tutankhamen's Egypt.* New York: Scribner's, 1972. Excellent popular account of Tutankhamen's reign.

Allen, Thomas George. *The Book of the Dead.* Chicago: University of Chicago Press, 1974. A translation of the spells necessary for immortality in ancient Egypt.

Anthes, Rudolf. *Tutankhamen Treasures.* Washington, D.C.: Smithsonian Institution, 1961. Catalog of the first exhibition of Tutankhamen objects in the United States.

A Short Description of the Objects from the Tomb of Tutankhamen. Cairo: Institut Français, 1927. One of the early catalogs of the objects from Tutankhamen's tomb displayed in the Egyptian Museum in Cairo.

Arnold, Dorothea. *The Royal Women of Amarna.* New York: Metropolitan Museum of Art, 1996. Far more than just the catalog of the Metropolitan's exhibition held in 1996–1997. The book includes important essays on various aspects of life at Amarna and makes many suggestions about the women of Amarna. Extraordinary photographs of Amarna art.

Baikie, James. *The Amarna Age.* New York: Macmillan, 1926. A good account for its time but now dated.

Baines, John. *Stone Vessels, Pottery and Sealings from the Tomb of Tut'Ankhamen.* Oxford: Griffith Institute, 1993. A valuable work that contains an especially interesting article on the seal of the necropolis used to reseal the tomb after the robberies.

Baly, T. J. C. "Notes on the Ritual of Opening of the Mouth." *Journal of Egyptian Archaeology* 16 (1930): 173–86. Details of the ritual as it was probably performed on Tutankhamen on the day of his burial.

Beinlich, Horst, and Mohamed Saleh. *Corpus der Hieroglyphischen Inscripten aus dem Grab des Tutankhamuns.* Oxford: Griffith Institute, 1989. Copies of all the hieroglyphic inscriptions in the tomb. No translations—for Egyptologists.

Bell, Martha R. "An Armchair Excavation of KV 55." *Journal of the American Research Center in Egypt* 28 (1990): 97–137. A fascinating attempt to reconstruct the order in which the objects were placed in the tomb. Careful detective work.

Bennett, John. "The Restoration Inscription of Tut'Ankhamen." *Journal of Egyptian Archaeology* 25 (1939): 8–15. Complete translation of Tutankhamen's promise to restore order to Egypt.

Bille-de Mot, Eleanore. *The Age of Akhenaten.* New York: McGraw-Hill, 1906. Clear presentation of the Amarna Revolution with some unusual illustrations.

Bosse-Griffiths, Kate. "Finds from 'The tomb of Queen Tiye' in the Swansea Museum." *Journal of Egyptian Archaeology* 47 (1961): 66–70. Shows just how careless the excavators of Tomb 55 were.

Brackman, Arnold C. *The Search for the Gold of Tutankhamen.* New York: Mason/Charter, 1976. Popular account with some unusual bits of information.

Bratton, F. Gladstone. *The Heretic Pharaoh.* London: Hale, 1962. Popular account with a biblical slant.

Breasted, James Henry. *Ancient Records of Egypt.* Vol. 2. 1905. Reprint. London: Histories and Mysteries of Man, 1988. Breasted's translations of hieroglyphic inscriptions on the monuments of Egypt show just how little was known about Tutankhamen before the discovery of his tomb.

———. *The Edwin Smith Surgical Papyrus.* Chicago: University of Chicago Press, 1930. Translation of the only medical papyrus from ancient Egypt dealing with trauma, especially to the head.

———. *A History of Egypt.* New York: Charles Scribner's Sons, 1919. Shows just how little was known about Tutankhamen before the discovery of his tomb.

Brier, Bob. *Egyptian Mummies.* New York: Morrow, 1994.

Brier, Bob, and Ronald S. Wade. "The Use of Natron in Human Mummification—A Modern Experiment." *Zeitschrift für ägyptische Sprache* 124, no. 2 (1997). Re-creation of ancient embalming techniques.

Bibliography

Bristone, E. S. G. *Naphuria: The History of the True Akhenaten.* London: Jenkins, 1936. Based on the *Amarna Letters,* this eccentric theory claims that Akhenaten's grandfather was the pharaoh of the Exodus.

Brothwell, Don, and A. T. Sandison. *Diseases in Antiquity.* Springfield: Charles C. Thomas, 1967. Important survey of diseases and injuries in the ancient world. A bit dated but still useful.

Bryce, Trevor R. "The Death of Niphururiya and Its Aftermath." *Journal of Egyptian Archaeology* 76 (1990): 97–105. Discussion of Ankhesenamen's letter to the Hittite king.

Budge. E. A. Wallis. *The Book of the Opening of the Mouth.* 1909. Reprint. New York: B. Blom, 1972. Detailed description of the ritual that must have been performed on Tutankhamen on the day of his burial. Somewhat dated translations.

———. *Tutankhamen, Atenism, and Egyptian Monotheism.* New York: Brill, n.d. Reprint of a work by the eccentric former Keeper of the British Museum's Egyptian and Assyrian antiquities. Dated, but the discussion of the Aten cult is still interesting.

Burridge, Alwyn L. "Akhenaten: A New Perspective." *The Society for the Study of Egyptian Antiquities Journal* 23 (1993): 63–74. The first suggestion in print that Akhenaten suffered from Marfan's syndrome. Some of the symptoms described are not quite accurate.

Carter, Howard. "Report on the Robbery of the Tomb of Amenothes II." *Annales du Service des Antiquités de l'Egypte* 3 (1902): 115–21. Carter displays his detective abilities in tracking down the modern robbers of the tomb of Amenhotep II.

Carter, Howard. *The Tomb of Tutankhamen: Statement.* Brockton, MA: John William Pye, 1997. Reprint of the 1924 document Carter privately circulated just before the Egyptian Government locked him out of Tutankhamen's tomb. A fascinating look into the archaeological politics of the times.

Carter, Howard, and A. C. Mace. *The Tomb of Tutankhamen.* 3 vols. 1923–1933. Reprint. New York: Cooper Square, 1963. Reprint of the three volumes by Carter describing his excavation of the tomb. Fascinating reading.

Carter, Michael. *Tutankhamen the Golden Monarch.* New York: McKay, 1972. Popular and slightly sensationalizing account.

Bibliography

Cerny, Jaroslav. *Hieratic Inscriptions from the Tomb of Tut'Ankhamun.* Oxford: Griffith Institute, 1965. Translations of the inscriptions in the cursive form of Egyptian writing. Includes the lists of objects in the various boxes in the tomb.

Christie, Agatha. *Akhenaton.* New York: Dodd, Mead, 1973. A three-act play about Akhenaten and Nefertiti.

Chubb, Mary. *Nefertiti Lived Here.* London: Bles, 1954. Delightful account of excavation life at Amarna.

Clayton, Peter A. *Chronicles of the Pharaohs.* London: Thames & Hudson, 1995. A useful reference work briefly describing each pharaoh's reign.

Collier, Joy. *The Heretic Pharaoh.* New York: John Day, 1970. A popular account focusing on the possibility of a connection between Akhenaten and Moses.

Connolly, R. C. "Microdetermination of Blood Group Substances in Ancient Human Tissue." *Nature* 224 (1869): 325. The technique used to establish the close family relationship between Tutankhamen and the mummy in Tomb 55.

Cottrell, Leonardo. *The Secrets of Tutankhamen's Tomb.* Greenwich, CT: New York Graphic Society, 1964. Young adult book.

Darby, William J., et al. *Food the Gift of Osiris.* London: Academic Press, 1977. Detailed account of food and eating habits in ancient Egypt.

David, A. Rosalie and Anthony E. *A Biographical Dictionary of Ancient Egypt.* London: Seaby, 1992. Brief biographies of some of the important figures in Tutankhamen's era.

Davies, Norman de Garis. *The Rock Tombs of Amarna.* Part 1. London: Egypt Exploration Fund, 1903. The first volume in Norman de Garis Davies's series on the tombs of Amarna. This volume records the tomb of the high priest Meri-Re.

———. *The Rock Cut Tombs of Amarna.* Part 2. London: Egypt Exploration Fund, 1905. The tombs of Pa-Nehsey and Meri-Re II are described.

———. *The Rock Cut Tombs of Amarna.* Part 3. London: Egypt Exploration Fund, 1905. The tombs of Huya, overseer of the house of Queen Tiye, and of Ahmes, another highly placed court official.

———. *The Rock Cut Tombs of Amarna.* Part 4. London: Egypt Exploration Fund, 1906. The tombs of several court officials are described.

———. *The Rock Cut Tombs of Amarna.* Part 5. London: Egypt Exploration Fund, 1907. The tomb of Aye with the great hymn to the Aten is described in detail.

———. *The Rock Cut Tombs of Amarna.* Part 6. London: Egypt Exploration Fund, 1908. The last in the series on the tombs of Amarna.

Davies, Norman de Garis, and A. H. Gardiner. *The Tomb of Huy, Viceroy of Nubia in the Reign of Tutankhamen.* London: Egypt Exploration Society, 1926. One of the few monuments from the reign of Tutankhamen is described.

Davis, Theodore M. *The Tomb of Queen Tiye.* 1910. Reprint. San Francisco: KMT, 1990. Reprint of Theodore Davis's account of the famous Tomb 55. In spite of contrary evidence, Davis published the tomb as that of Queen Tiye. The report has an excellent introduction by Nicholas Reeves, the Tutankhamen scholar.

———. *The Tombs of Harmhabi and Touatankhamanou.* London: Constable, 1912. Davis's erroneous conclusion that he had discovered Tutankhamen's tomb, which led to his statement that "the Valley of the Kings is now exhausted."

De Gans, Raymonde. *Tutankhamen.* Geneva: Fermi, 1978. General popular work on the life and times of Tutankhamen.

Description de L'Egypte. Vol. 1. Paris: L'Imprimerie Impériale, 1812. Drawing and maps by the artists who accompanied Napoleon when he invaded Egypt in 1798.

Desroches-Noblescourt, Christiane. *Tutankhamen.* New York: New York Graphic Society, 1963. Probably the most popular book ever on Tutankhamen. The author is a senior Egyptologist with the wonderful ability to make the period come alive. The book contains quite a few speculations.

Devi, Savitri. *A Son of God.* London: Philosophical Publishing, 1946. An interesting discussion of Akhenaten's religion by a modern admirer, including letters from Aldous Huxley on the Amarna religion.

———. *Son of the Sun.* San Jose, CA: Rosicrucian Library, 1956. Expanded version of the title above.

Diodorus Siculus. *Library of History.* Book I, 46. Cambridge: Harvard University Press, 1968. Accounts of an ancient traveler to Egypt.

Dobson, Jessie. "A Curator's Curiosity." *Annals of the Royal College of Surgeons of England* (1959): 331–37. Discussion of an elongated skull found in Egypt that looks similar to the shape of the heads of Akhenaten's family.

Dodson, Aidan. *The Canopic Equipment of the Kings of Egypt.* London: Kegan Paul, 1994. Includes a detailed description of the broken sarcophagus and canopic chest of Akhenaten.

Bibliography

Drower, Margaret S. *Flinders Petrie, A Life In Archaeology.* London: Victor Gollancz Ltd., 1985. A colorful description of one of the pioneers of Egyptology.

Drury, Allen. *A God Against the Gods.* New York: Doubleday, 1976. Historically based novel about Akhenaten and Nefertiti.

———. *Return to Thebes.* New York: Doubleday, 1977. Sequel to the title above, this volume covers Tutankhamen's reign.

Eaton-Krauss, M. *The Sarcophagus in the Tomb of Tutankamen.* Oxford: Griffith Institute, 1993. Detailed and important study by a major Tutankhamen scholar. Shows the sarcophagus was altered at least once before Tutankhamen's burial.

———. *The Small Golden Shrine from the Tomb of Tutankhamen.* Oxford: Griffith Institute, 1985. Wonderfully detailed analyses of the scenes of Ankhesenamen and Tutankhamen on the miniature shrine.

Edwards, I. E. S. *The Treasures of Tutankhamen.* New York: Viking, 1972. Catalog that accompanied the traveling exhibition of treasures from Tutankhamen's tomb.

Edwards, I. E. S., et al., eds. *The Cambridge Ancient History.* Vol. 2. Parts 1–2. Cambridge: Cambridge University Press, 1973–1975. A monumental reference work, these volumes deal with the Amarna age.

Edwards, Margaret Dulles. *Child of the Son.* Boston: Beacon, 1939. A book for young adults with the monotheism of Akhenaten clearly explained.

Elerick, Daniel V., and Rose A. Tyson. *Human Paleopathology and Related Subjects.* San Diego: Museum of Man, 1997. Bibliography of thousands of books and articles on disease and trauma in the ancient world.

El-Khouly, Aly, and Geoffrey Thorndike Martin. *Excavations in the Royal Necropolis at El'Amarna 1984.* Cairo: Institut Français, 1987. Examination of two tombs in the side valley near Akhenaten's tomb. One may have been prepared for Tutankhamen when he first became king at Amarna.

El-Najjar, Mahmoud, and K. Richard McWilliams. *Anthropology.* Springfield: Charles C. Thomas, 1978. What bones can tell about a long-dead person.

Epigraphic Survey. *The Festival Procession of Opet in the Colonnade Hall.* Chicago: Oriental Institute of the University of Chicago, 1994. Complete publication of the hall decorated by Tutankhamen but later usurped by Horemheb.

Fairman, H. W. "Once Again the So-Called Coffin of Akhenaten." *Journal of Egyptian Archaeology* 47 (1961): 25–40. An attempt to determine the identity of the mummy in Tomb 55 by analyzing the inscriptions on the coffin.

Fazzini, Richard. *Tutankhamen and the African Heritage.* New York: Metropolitan Museum of Art, 1978. Booklet discussing Egypt's relationship to Nubia during the Eighteenth Dynasty.

Federn, Walter. "Dahamunzu (KBo V 6 iii 8)." *Journal of Cuneiform Studies* 14 (1960): 33. Explains the phrase used to refer to Ankhesenamen by the Hittites.

Forbes, Dennis. "A New Take on Tut's Parents." *KMT* 8, no. 3 (1997): 85–87. Raises possibility that Smenkare and Meritaten were Tutankhamen's parents.

Ford, John. *Tutankhamen's Treasures.* Secaucus, NJ: Chartwell, 1978. Mostly pictures.

Fox, Penelope. *Tutankhamen's Treasure.* London: Oxford University Press, 1951. Good discussion of objects found in tomb.

Frankfort, H. "Preliminary Report on the Excavations at El-'Amarnah, 1918–19." *Journal of Egyptian Archaeology* 15 (1929): 143–49. Early excavation of the northern suburbs of Amarna, with diagrams of the houses.

———. "Preliminary Report on the Excavations at Tel el Amarnah, 1926–1927." *Journal of Egyptian Archaeology* 13 (1927): 209–18. Some spectacular photographs of finds at the residence of Panhesy and the Aten temple.

Frankfort. H., ed. *The Mural Painting of El-'Amarnah.* London: The Egypt Exploration Society, 1929. Beautiful reproductions of the Amarna paintings.

Frankfort, H, and J. D. S. Pendlebury. *The City of Akhenaten.* Part 2. London: Egypt Exploration Society, 1933. This reports the excavation of the city's northern suburb and includes maps and diagrams of the houses, as well as photographs of the objects found.

Frayling, Christopher. *The Face of Tutankhamen.* London: Faber & Faber, 1992. Based on the BBC's five-part television series and includes interesting material on Tutmania.

Freud, Sigmund. *Moses and Monotheism.* New York: Vintage, 1955. Freud's theory that Moses got monotheism from Akhenaten. Highly speculative—Freud knew very little about Egyptology.

Gardiner, Alan. "The So-Called Tomb of Queen Tiye." *Journal of Egyptian Archaeology* 43 (1957): 10–25. The leading translator of his era analyzes the inscriptions on the coffin in Tomb 55 and concludes that the mummy is Smenkare.

Goetze, Albrecht. "Palace Prayers of Mursilis." In *Ancient Near Eastern Texts.* Edited by James B. Prichard. Princeton: Princeton University Press, 1955. Translations of ancient texts from all over the Near East, including some relating to the aftermath of Tutankhamen's death.

Green, L. "A 'Lost Queen' of Ancient Egypt . . ." *KMT,* winter 1990–1991, pp. 23–67. Informative article on Ankhesenamen by an expert on women of the Amarna period.

———. "The Origins of the Giant Lyre and Asiatic Influences of the Cult of the Aten." *The Society for the Study of Egyptian Antiquities Journal* 23 (1993): 56–62. Two musicians playing a giant lyre, depicted in the Amarna tomb carvings, were Asiatic musicians in Akhenaten's court.

Guterbock, Hans Gustav. "The Deeds of Suppiluliuma as Told to His Son, Mursili II." *Journal of Cuneiform Studies* 10 (1965): 75–98. The definitive study of Ankhesenamen's letter to the Hittite king.

Harris, James E., and Edward F. Wente, eds. *An X-ray Atlas of the Royal Mummies.* Chicago: University of Chicago Press, 1980. An attempt at answering questions about family relationships among the royal mummies by X rays. Contains two X rays of Tutankhamen's skull.

Harris, James E., and Kent R. Weeks. *X-raying the Pharaohs.* New York: Scribner's, 1973. Pioneering study of what can be learned from X-raying mummies.

Harrison, R. G. "An Anatomical Examination of the Pharaonic Remains Purported to Be Akhenaten." *Journal of Egyptian Archaeology* 224 (1969): 325–26. Demonstrates that the blood groups of Tutankhamen and Smenkare are so close that they may have been brothers.

———. "Post Mortem on Two Pharaohs." *Buried History* (1972): 18–25. This is where Harrison says in print that Tutankhamen may have died from a blow to the back of the head by a blunt instrument.

———. "Tutankhamen's Postmortem." *The Lancet,* February 3, 1972, p. 259. The only expert to perform a modern examination of Tutankhamen's mummy explains that there is no evidence for pathological conditions such as Klinefelter's syndrome or Wilson's disease, as had been suggested by some physicians.

Harrison, R. G., et al. "A Mummified Foetus from the Tomb of Tutankhamen." *Antiquity* 53 (1979): 19–21. X ray of one of the two fetuses found in the tomb revealed the little girl would have been deformed if she had lived.

Harrison, R. G., and A. B. Abdalla. "The Remains of Tutankhamen." *Antiquity* 46 (1972): 8–14. The most detailed publication of the examination of Tutankhamen's mummy, but it is merely a preliminary report.

Hayes, William C. *The Scepter of Egypt*. Vol. 2. New York: Metropolitan Museum of Art, 1959. Catalog of the Metropolitan Museum of Art's collection. Includes detailed descriptions of the objects used at the last meal eaten outside of Tutankhamen's tomb on the day of burial.

Hepper, Nigel F. *Pharaoh's Flowers*. London: HMSO, 1990. Detailed and fascinating analysis of the botanical specimens found in the tomb of Tutankhamen. Crucial work in determining the time of year in which Tutankhamen died.

Iscan, Mehmet Yasar. *Age Markers in the Human Skeleton*. Springfield: Charles C. Thomas, 1989. How physical anthropologists determine age at time of death from bones.

James, T. G. H. *Howard Carter, The Path to Tutankhamun*. London: Kegan Paul, 1992. The definitive biography of Carter.

Janssens, Paul A. *Paleopathology*. London: John Baker, 1970. An older but still useful work on diseases and injuries in the ancient world.

Johnson, William Raymond. *An Asiatic Battle Scene of Tutankhamen from Thebes*. Ann Arbor: UMI Dissertation Services, 1992. Doctoral dissertation by an expert on carved temple blocks. Blocks from Tutankhamen's mortuary temple show Tutankhamen in battle.

Jones, Dilwyn. *Model Boats from the Tomb of Tutankhamen*. Oxford: Griffith Institute, 1990. Brief discussion of model boats and sailing in ancient Egypt.

Kemp, Barry J. "The Window of Appearances At El-Amarna, and the Basic Structure of This City." *Journal of Egyptian Archaeology* 62 (1976): 81–99. The excavator gives an overview of the city of Amarna and discusses one detail—the balcony where the royal family appeared before the people.

Kemp, Barry J., et al. *Amarna Reports*. Vol. 1. London: Egypt Exploration Society, 1984. The author is the excavator of the site, and this work begins an important series of publications of his finds at Amarna.

———. *Amarna Reports*. Vol. 2. London: Egypt Exploration Society, 1985. Reports on the workmen's village at Amarna, with detailed scientific analyses of the textiles and botanical material found.

————. *Amarna Reports.* Vol. 3. London: Egypt Exploration Society, 1986. Reports on the workmen's village, pottery finds, and the alabaster quarries.

————. *Amarna Reports.* Vol. 4. London: Egypt Exploration Society, 1987. Excavations of the workmen's village and a discussion of pottery found at the main city.

————. *Amarna Reports.* Vol. 5. London: Egypt Exploration Society, 1989. Excavation of the main city, discussion of the pottery found, and an interesting discussion of grain and bread baking.

————. *Amarna Reports.* Vol. 6. London: Egypt Exploration Society, 1995. Reports on the excavation of a private house at Amarna and also the smaller temple of the Aten called "Mansion of the Aten."

Kemp, Barry J., and Salvatore Garfi. *A Survey of the Ancient City of El-'Amarna.* London: Egypt Exploration Society, 1993. Detailed maps and plans of the city where Tutankhamen was born.

KMT: Amarna Letters. Vols. 1–3. San Francisco: KMT, 1991–1994. Written by scholars for a popular audience, these three volumes provide a wealth of readable material on all aspects of the Amarna period.

KMT: A Modern Journal of Ancient Egypt, summer 1991. This special issue of the popular magazine on Egyptology is devoted to discussions of Akhenaten.

Kolos, Daniel, and Hany Assad. *The Name of the Dead.* Ontario: Benben, 1979. Hieroglyphic inscriptions and their translations from some of the objects in Tutankhamen's tomb. Intended for the beginning student in hieroglyphs, this book contains some errors, but still it is a good way to start.

Kozloff, Arielle, and Betsy M. Bryan. *Egypt's Dazzling Sun.* Cleveland: Cleveland Museum of Art, 1992. Exhibition catalog for major show on Amenhotep III, Tutankhamen's grandfather.

Leek, F. Filce. "How Old Was Tutankhamen?" *Journal of Egyptian Archaeology* 63 (1977): 112–15. Suggests that Tutankhamen may have been as young as sixteen at the time of death.

————. *The Human Remains from the Tomb of Tut'Ankhamen.* Oxford: Griffith Institute, 1972. Description of Tutankhamen's mummy and the two fetuses found in the tomb. Much good information, especially quotes from Carter's diary. Leek, however, was unable to locate the two fetuses and relies on an earlier examination. He relies primarily on Derry's examination of Tutankhamen's mummy in 1925 and hardly mentions later important work.

Leprohon, Ronald J. "A Vision Collapsed, Akhenaten's Reforms Viewed Through Decrees of Later Reigns." *Amarna Letters.* San Francisco: KMT, 1991. A textual analysis of the aftermath of Akhenaten's revolution.

Lesko, Leonard H. *King Tut's Wine Cellar.* Berkeley: BC Scribe, 1977. A delightful discussion by a distinguished Egyptologist who has made his own version of the wine found in Tutankhamen's tomb.

Lichtheim, Miriam. *Ancient Egyptian Literature.* Vol. 2. Berkeley: University of California Press, 1976. Translations of Egyptian literature that give insights into the ancient Egypt mind.

Littauer, M. B. and J. H. Crouwell. *Chariots and Related Equipment from the Tomb of Tutankhamen.* Oxford: Griffith Institute, 1985. This discussion of the six chariots found in Tutankhamen's tomb is so detailed that you could construct one from the diagrams.

Mace, Arthur C. "The Egyptian Expedition." *Bulletin of the Metropolitan Museum of Art,* 1922–1923.

MacQuitty, William. *Tutankhamen's Last Journey.* New York: Crown, 1978. Photographs used to discuss the death and burial of Tutankhamen.

McKusick, Victor A. "The Defect in Marfan Syndrome." *Nature* 352, July 25, 1991. Scientific discussion of Marfan's syndrome.

McLeod, W. *Composite Bows from the Tomb of Tut'Ankhamun.* Oxford: Griffith Institute, 1970. The archery equipment, including arrows, quivers, etc., found in the tomb.

———. *Self Bows and Other Archery Tackle from the Tomb of Tut'Ankhamen.* Oxford: Griffith Institute, 1982. The archery equipment, including arrows, quivers, etc., found in the tomb.

Majno, Guido. *The Healing Hand.* Cambridge: Harvard University Press, 1977. Fascinating discussion of ancient medicine.

Manniche, Lise. *Musical Instruments from the Tomb of Tut'Ankhamen.* Oxford: Griffith Institute, 1976. Brief description of clappers, sistra, and trumpets from the tomb.

Bibliography

Martin, Geoffrey Thorndike. *A Bibliography of the Amarna Period and Its Aftermath.* London: Kegan Paul, 1991. An indispensable reference listing most articles and books on the subject.

———. "Excavations at the Memphite Tomb of Horemheb." *Journal of Egyptian Archaeology* 62–65 (1975–1979). This series of excavation reports presents each year's findings at the tomb of Tutankhamen's general.

———. *The Hidden Tombs of Memphis.* London: Thames & Hudson, 1991. Contains description of General Horemheb's tomb at Memphis and that of Maya, Tutankhamen's treasurer. Important information on the men surrounding the boy-king.

———. *The Royal Tomb at El Amarna.* Vol. 1. London: Egypt Exploration Society, 1974. Description of the objects and fragments found in Akhenaten's tomb in the remote valley outside Amarna.

———. *The Royal Tomb at El Amarna.* Vol. 2. London: Egypt Exploration Society, 1989. Detailed description of Akhenaten's tomb, including architecture and wall carvings. Martin suggests that one scene shows the birth of Tutankhamen.

———. "The Tomb of Horemheb, Commander in Chief of Tutankhamen." *Archaeology* 31 (1978): 14–23. Popular account of the tomb.

Meltzer, Edmund S. "The Parentage of Tut'Ankhamen and Smenkhkare." *Journal of Egyptian Archaeology* 64 (1978): 174–75. Explains why Akhenaten could be the father of Tutankhamen.

Mercer, Samuel A. B. *The Tell El-Amarna Tablets.* Toronto: Macmillan, 1939. Compilation, translation, and brief discussion of the *Amarna Letters.*

Merezhkovsky, Dmitri. *Akhenaton.* New York: E. P. Dutton, 1927. Early novel translated from the Russian. *Very* dated.

Montague, Jeremy. "One of Tutankhamen's Trumpets." *Journal of Egyptian Archaeology* 64 (1978): 133–34. Describes construction and use of the bronze trumpet from Tutankhamen's tomb. The silver trumpet shattered when it was played on a BBC radio broadcast in 1939.

Moodie, Roy L. *Roentgenologic Studies of Egyptian and Peruvian Mummies.* Chicago: Field Museum of Natural History, 1931. The pioneering study on the use of X rays to study mummies.

Bibliography

Moran, William L. *The Amarna Letters*. Baltimore: Johns Hopkins, 1982. The most recent and authoritative translation of the *Amarna Letters*.

Muller, Hans Wolfgang, et al. *Nofretete. Echnaton.* Berlin: Ägyptisches Museum, 1976. Exhibition catalog of objects from the Amarna period. Photographs of many objects not usually seen.

Murnane, William J., and Charles C. Van Siclen III. *The Boundary Stelae of Akhenaten.* London: Kegan Paul, 1993. The definitive work on the subject.

Murray, Helen, and Mary Nuttall. *A Handlist to Howard Carter's Catalogue of Objects in Tut'Ankhamen's Tomb.* Oxford: Griffith Institute, 1963. A key reference work. Carter described each item in the tomb on index cards. The cards were left to the Griffith Institute, and this work is the index for these notes.

Nahas, Bishara. *The Life and Times of Tut-Ankh-Amen.* New York: American Library Service, 1923. One of the first popular books written after the tomb's discovery. Dated and containing much from the author's imagination rather than from history.

Newberry, Percy E. "Akhenaten's Eldest Son-in-Law, 'Ankhkheprure." *Journal of Egyptian Archaeology* 14 (1928): 3–9. An early discussion of Smenkare.

———. "King Ay, The Successor of Tut'Ankhamen." *Journal of Egyptian Archaeology* 18 (1932): 50–52. First publication of the ring that indicates Aye married Tutankhamen's widow.

———. *Scarab-shaped Seals.* London: Constable, 1907. A basic study on Egyptian scarab amulets.

Paulshock, Bernadine Z. "Tutankhamen and His Brothers." *Journal of the American Medical Association* 244, no. 2 (1980): 160–64. A physician suggests that the statues of Tutankhamen with breasts indicate that he and members of his family may have had gynecomastia—feminizing of the male body.

Peet, T. Eric, and C. Leonard Wooley. *The City of Akhenaten.* Part 1. London: Egypt Exploration Society, 1923. Important detailed excavation report of the city of Amarna. Many photographs of walls now gone and of objects found at Amarna.

Pendlebury, J. D. S. *The City of Akhenaten.* Part 3. London: Egypt Exploration Society, 1951. This volume describes the central city of Amarna, including the palace, police barracks, and records office.

Bibliography

Petrie, William Flinders. *Seventy Years of Archaeology.* New York: Holt, 1932. Fascinating memoirs of the founder of modern Egyptology, including much on his excavations at Amarna.

———. *Tel el Amarna.* 1894. Reprint. London: Aris & Phillips, 1974. Account of Petrie's excavations at Amarna.

Phillips the Egyptian. *Tutankhamen's Victims in America.* Los Angeles: Egyptian Antiques, 1977. Wild and inaccurate, this book ends with several pages of reproductions for sale.

Piankoff, Alexandre. *The Shrines of Tut-Ankh-Amon.* New York: Harper, 1962. A discussion of the shrines that enclosed the sarcophagus, coffins, and mummy of Tutankhamen. A thorough and important analysis of their religious texts.

Pococke, Richard. *A Description of the East.* Vol. 1. London: W. Boyer, 1843. One of the early travel accounts, this book includes the first map of the Valley of the Kings.

Pyeritz, Reed E., and Cheryll Gasner. *The Marfan Syndrome.* Port Washington, NY: National Marfan Foundation, 1994. Publication explaining the genetic defect called Marfan's syndrome.

Reeves, C. N. *After Tut'Ankhamen.* London: Kegan Paul, 1992. Collection of research papers on the Valley of the Kings after the discovery of Tutankhamen's tomb.

———. *The Complete Tutankhamen.* London: Thames & Hudson, 1990. An indispensable reference work on all aspects of Tutankhamen, including his life, excavators, and objects in the tomb. Many photos and diagrams.

———. "A Reappraisal of Tomb 55 in the Valley of the Kings." *Journal of Egyptian Archaeology* 67 (1981): 48–55. An attempt to determine the identity of the mummy in Tomb 55. Suggests mummy may have been switched after it was sent to Cairo.

Reeves, C. N., and John H. Taylor. *Howard Carter Before Tutankhamen.* London: British Museum, 1992. Catalog of an exhibition about the life of Howard Carter before he discovered Tutankhamen's tomb. Wonderful illustrations.

Redford, Donald. *The Akhenaten Temple Project.* Vol. 3. Toronto: University of Toronto, 1994. Description of the pottery fragments found during excavations of Akhenaten's temples at east Karnak.

————. *Akhenaten, The Heretic King.* Princeton: Princeton University Press, 1984. Important work by the excavator of Akhenaten's temples at Karnak. As Redford's excavations continued, he grew to dislike Akhenaten more and more.

————. "Some Observations on 'Amarna Chronology.'" *Journal of Egyptian Archaeology* 45 (1959): 34–37. The excavator of Akhenaten's temples at Karnak discusses the confusing evidence regarding Akhenaten's reign.

Redford, Donald, et al. *The Akhenaten Temple Project.* Vol. 2. Toronto: University of Toronto, 1988. An important work by the excavator of Akhenaten's temples at Karnak; focuses on inscriptions and scenes relating to foreigners.

Redford, Susan and Donald. *The Akhenaten Temple Project.* Vol. 4. Toronto: University of Toronto, 1994. The tomb of a royal herald just before Akhenaten became king.

Riefstahl, Elizabeth. *Thebes in the Time of Amenhotep III.* Norman, OK: University of Oklahoma Press, 1964. Overview of the city of Thebes and all its glory during Amenhotep III's reign.

Robbins, G. "The Representation of Sexual Characteristics in Amarna Art." *The Society for Study of Egyptian Antiquities Journal* 23 (1993): 29–41. A discussion of the nude colossal statue of Akhenaten with no genitalia, suggesting that the feminizing of the statue indicates fecundity.

Romer, John. *Valley of the Kings.* New York: William Morrow, 1981. A lively account of the travelers and scholars who visited and worked in the Valley of the Kings, and their discoveries.

Romer, John and Elizabeth. *The Rape of Tutankhamen.* London: O'Mara, 1993. A somewhat slanted discussion of the condition of Tutankhamen's tomb and others in the Valley of the Kings.

Ruffer, Marc Armand. "Note on the Histology of Egyptian Mummies." *British Medical Journal* 1 (1909): 1005–6. An early work on soft tissues of mummies.

————. "Note on Two Egyptian Mummies Dating from the Persian Occupation of Egypt." In *Studies in the Paleopathology of Egypt.* Chicago: University of Chicago Press, 1921. pp. 127–38. A study showing just how careless ancient embalmers could be.

Saad, Ramadan, and Lise Manniche. "A Unique Offering List of Amenophis IV Recently Found at Karnak." *Journal of Egyptian Archaeology* 57 (1971): 70–72. A discussion of a block from one of Akhenaten's temples listing offerings he gave to the temple. A good example of the small clues that help Egyptologists piece together the big picture.

Sampson, Julia. "Amarna Crowns and Wigs." *Journal of Egyptian Archaeology* 59 (1973): 47–59. An example of how art historians examine stylistic details to identify and date Egyptian art.

Sandford, Mary K. *Investigations of Ancient Human Tissue.* Langhorne, PA: Gordon and Breach, 1993. Technical articles on chemical analyses of bone and tissue.

Sandnass, Karin L. "Dietary Analysis of Prehistoric Lower and Middle Osmore Drainage Populations of Southern Peru Using Stable Isotopes [Delta C-13 and Delta N-15]." Paper presented at the Second World Congress on Mummy Studies, February 6–10, 1995, Cartagena, Colombia. Discussion of state-of-the-art technology used to gain information from examination of mummies.

Sayce, A. H. "The Hittite Correspondence with Tut-Ankh-Amon's Widow." *Ancient Egypt,* part 2 (1927): 33–35. Translations of the Hittite response to Ankhesenamen's letter to the Hittite king.

———. "Texts from the Hittite Capital Relating to Egypt." *Ancient Egypt,* part 3 (1922): 65–70. Early publication of Ankhesenamen's letter to the Hittite king.

———. "What Happened After the Death of Tut'Ankhamen." *Journal of Egyptian Archaeology* 12 (1926): 168–70. Supplies a previously missing part of the Hittite response to Ankhesenamen's request to the Hittite king.

Schaden, Otto John. "Clearance of the Tomb of King Aye." *Journal of the American Research Center in Egypt* 21 (1984). The only excavation report on King Aye's tomb in the Valley of the Kings.

———. *The God's Father Ay.* Ann Arbor: UMI Dissertation Services, 1977. Doctoral dissertation on Ay, with much good material on his two tombs.

Severence, Catherine Needham. *The Last Day of Ikhnaton.* New York: Exposition Press, 1953. A romantic novel.

Shulman, Alan R. "Ankhesenamen, Nofretity, and the Amka Affair." *Journal of the American Research Center in Egypt* 15 (1978): 43–48. Discussion of Ankhesenamen's plea to the Hittite king, and the response.

Silverberg, Robert. *Akhenaten the Rebel Pharaoh.* New York: Chilton, 1964. A popular work on the life of Akhenaten.

Bibliography

Smith, G. Elliot. *The Royal Mummies.* Cairo: Institut Français, 1912. Catalog of the royal mummies in the Egyptian museum in Cairo. Contains an early description of the mummy from Tomb 55 that suggests it is Akhenaten.

————. *Tutankhamen.* London: Rutledge, 1923. One of the first books on the discovery of Tutankhamen's tomb. Mainly a historical curio.

Smith, Ray Winfield. "Computers Help Scholars Re-create an Egyptian Temple." *National Geographic* 139, no. 5, November 1970. Early use of a computer to reconstruct on paper Akhenaten's temples at Karnak.

Smith, Ray Winfield, and Donald Redford. *The Akhenaten Temple Project.* Warminster, England: Aris & Phillips, 1976. Detailed description of the project to reassemble on paper Akhenaten's temples at Karnak. Many important details.

Smith, Sir Sidney. *Mostly Murder.* New York: McKay, 1959. Fascinating autobiography of a famous professor of forensic medicine who applied his skills in Egypt to solve murders.

Strunsky, Simon. *King Akhenaten.* New York: Longmans, Green & Co., 1928. Early fiction stimulated by the discovery of Tutankhamen's tomb. *Very* dated.

Swales, J. D. "Tutankhamen's Breasts." *The Lancet,* January 27, 1973, p. 201. Physician's response to the suggestion that Tutankhamen's statues with breasts indicated a pathological condition.

Tabouis, G. R. *The Private Life of Tutankhamen.* New York: McBride, 1929. Description of daily life during the reign of Tutankhamen. Dated.

Tait, W. J. *Game Boxes and Accessories from the Tomb of Tut'Ankhamen.* Oxford: Griffith Institute, 1982. Excellent descriptions and discussion of the board games that Tutankhamen and Ankhesenamen played.

Taitz, L. S. "Tutankhamen's Breasts." *The Lancet,* January 20, 1973, p. 149. A physician suggests Tutankhamen's depiction with breasts is an artistic holdover from Akhenaten's reign.

Thomas, Elizabeth. "The Plan of Tomb 55 in the Valley of the Kings." *Journal of Egyptian Archaeology* 47 (1961): 24. Fifty years after the discovery of Tomb 55, there still was no published plan of the tomb. This one-page diagram is the first.

Tobin, V. A. "Akhenaten as a Tragedy of History: A Critique of the Amarna Period." *The Society for the Study of Egyptian Antiquities Journal* 23 (1993): 5–28. Discussion of the legacy of Akhenaten, with somewhat negative conclusions.

Ubelaker, Douglas, and Henry Scammell. *Bones: A Forensic Detective's Casebook.* New York: HarperCollins, 1992. A readable account of how physical anthropologists determine the cause of death from bones.

Vandenberg, Philip. *The Curse of the Pharaohs.* Philadelphia: Lippincott, 1975. Pure nonsense.

Van Den Bourn, G. P. F. *The Duties of the Vizier.* London: Kegan Paul, 1988. Gives an idea of the power held by Aye, Tutankhamen's vizier.

Velikovsky, Immanuel. *Oedipus and Akhenaten.* New York: Doubleday, 1960. A highly eccentric work that draws parallels between Akhenaten and the Greek king Oedipus. Fascinating reading, to be taken with a grain of salt.

Vergote, J. *Toutankhamon dans les Archives Hittites.* Istanbul: Nederlands Historisch-Archaeologisch Instituut, 1961. Discussion of Ankhesenamen's request for a Hittite prince to marry.

Walker, James H. *Studies in Ancient Egyptian Anatomical Terminology.* Warminster: Aris and Phillips, 1996. The latest word on the subject by a physician-Egyptologist.

Walshe, J. M. "Tutankhamen: Klinefelter's or Wilson's?" *The Lancet,* January 13, 1973, pp. 109–10. Physician's theory on why Tutankhamen's statues show him with breasts and sagging abdomen.

Watkins, Trevor. "The Beginning of Warfare in the Ancient World." In *Warfare in the Ancient World.* Edited by Sir John Hackett. New York: Facts on File, 1989, pp. 15–19. Discussion of warfare in ancient Egypt.

Weeks, Kent Ried. *The Anatomical Knowledge of the Ancient Egyptians and the Representation of the Human Figure in Egyptian Art.* Ann Arbor: UMI Dissertation Information Service, 1970.

Weigall, Arthur. "The Mummy of Akhenaten." *Journal of Egyptian Archaeology* 8 (1922): 193–200. Weigall's claim that the mummy in Tomb 55 was that of Tutankhamen's father.

———. *Tutankhamen and Other Essays.* New York: Doran, 1924. Weigall was Inspector-General of Antiquities when Tutankhamen's tomb was discovered, and his writings are full of interesting perspectives, but his imagination sometimes leads him astray.

Weller, Malcolm. "Tutankhamen: An Adrenal Tumor?" *The Lancet,* December 16, 1972, p. 1312. A physician suggests an adrenal tumor may have caused breast development in Tutankhamen.

Wells, Calvin. *Bones, Bodies and Disease.* New York: Praeger, 1964. Dated, but still a classic in the history of paleopathology by a master.

Wells, Evelyn. *Nefertiti.* London: Hale, 1964. A romanticizing and often inaccurate account of the Amarna period and Nefertiti.

Welsh, Frances. *Tutankhamen's Egypt.* Princes Risborough, England: Shire, 1993. A brief and useful discussion of the life and times of Tutankhamen and the objects found in his tomb.

Wente, Edward, et al. *Treasures of Tutankhamen.* New York: Metropolitan Museum of Art, 1976. Catalog to accompany the exhibition of Tutankhamen's treasures that toured the world.

Wilkinson, Gardiner. *Modern Egypt and Thebes.* Vol. 2. London: John Murray, 1843. One of the first guidebooks to Egypt; gives early impression of Amarna.

Winlock, H. E. *Materials Used at the Embalming of King Tut-'Ankh-Amun.* New York: Metropolitan Museum of Art, 1941. Not only embalming materials, but also remains of the ritual meal eaten outside the tomb on the day of burial.

Winstone, H. V. F. *Howard Carter and the Discovery of Tutankhamun.* London: Constable, 1991. Solid biography of Carter.

Wise, William. *The Two Reigns of Tutankhamen.* New York: Putnam, 1964. In addition to discussing Tutankhamen's reign at Amarna and Thebes, it includes a brief history of Egypt up to the time of Tutankhamen.

Wynne, Barry. *Behold the Mask of Tutankhamen.* New York: Taplinger, 1972. Not just another popular account, this book has interesting material not found elsewhere, especially on the possibility that Carter and Carnarvon entered the burial chamber before the official opening.

Yadin, Yigal. *The Art of Warfare in Biblical Lands.* Vol. 1. New York: McGraw-Hill, 1963. Overview of warfare in the ancient Middle East.

Index

Index

Index

Index

The "Old" Speak Out

The "Old" Speak Out

BONNIE BLUH

HORIZON PRESS NEW YORK

THANK YOU

In my three year search for older people I spoke with well over 500 women and men. Some wish to remain anonymous, others feel differently. I am grateful to all.

For their support and help I particularly want to thank my mother Mary Bluh, Hyman Bogan, Foster Parents for Adults, NYC, for his time and the wonderful story about the beginning of Foster Parents; Rita Galvin and Li Nutter of the same agency; Commissioner Alice M. Brophy, Department of Aging, NYC; Frances Brown, California Legislative Council, San Francisco, Calif.; The Dorian Group, Seattle, Wash.; Richard Driscoll and the wonderful players of Free Street Theatre Too, Chicago, Ill,; William Feinberg of Local 802 and all the members of the Senior Concert Orchestra, NYC; Rebella Graves, American Indian Community; NYC; Catherine and Tom Guzik, Little Brothers of the Poor, Chicago, Ill.; Mother Margerite Healy, Little Sisters of the Poor, Phoenix, Arizona; (JASA) Jewish Association for Services for the Aged, NYC; Ginarn Lao, Self-Help for the Elderly, San Francisco, Calif.; Gertrude Leyendecker, (RSVP) Retired Seniors Volunteer Program, NYC; Patrick Magee, Commission of Aging, San Francisco, Calif.; Marian Miller, Office of Aging, Chicago, Ill. for her help and the use of an office; Eleanor Morris, Director of the Office of Aging, NYC; Sheila McDiarmid, Vancouver Resources Board Co-ordinator, Sister Margaret Perry, Seattle, Wash.; Katherine Pring, Department of Aging, Denver, Colo.; Laverne Rector and the Senior Aides of the Harlem branch of the Department of Aging for their wisdom and openness; Councilman Hughie Schoff, Winnemucca, Nevada who personally drove me to meet the older people there; Reverend Michael Stark, New Orleans, La.; Jennie Steinback, Winnemucca, Nevada.

I also wish to thank members of the Senior Centers from coast to coast and in Vancouver who welcomed me and helped me enormously with this book. I particularly want to thank Morrie Berman and the very verbal and dynamic members of the 92nd Street YM-YWHA Senior Adult Center, NYC.

And a very special thank you to Morton Cohen, Laimute Druskis and Craig Lowy for their advice, encouragement and unfailing support.

For my grandparents

Annie Ziegler Bluh
whose life compelled me to write this book

Charles Kalman Bluh
who made me realize the spirit is ageless

CONTENTS

INTRODUCTION

The message I got through my years was to live for today, take each day as it comes. Don't worry about tomorrow. And like most people I lived for the day, not worrying about the future.

In 1971, living in Spain, writing a book, my future hit me like a slap in my face. I was at a disco with a younger friend, having a marvellous time when I suddenly noticed a few people watching me. I ignored it. But the eyes on me grew until I felt uncomfortable. I mentioned it to the man I was with. "Don't let them bother you," he said.

"What do you mean?"

"Well face it, Bonnie, you're not a kid. They don't expect to see a woman your age in a disco."

I looked around at the dancers. They were all young, in their teens and twenties. For the first time, I felt ill at ease dancing and for the first time I felt a door close in my face because I was older. That night I stared at my mirror. But I'm not old. I'm 44. That's not old.

The following year while I was applying for a job, the interviewer told me he couldn't consider anybody over 40. I did some fast calculations in my head and came up with a new birthyear, 1933, which made me 39. I was hired.

The experiences accelerated until I became aware that it wasn't how I viewed myself that mattered; it was the way others saw me. And if I felt this way at my age how do old people feel, or to put it selfishly, how am I going to feel twenty years from now?

I began to question any older person who would talk with me, my mother, her friends, people I knew, strangers on the street. A 74-year-old woman tells me, "The only good thing about getting old is the discount tickets for theatres and the half-fare on the subway. Aside from that you can keep it. I can't get a job because I'm too old. I can't go out at night because I'm afraid. I'd like to grow old gracefully if somebody'd tell me how."

A recently retired man: "You're a zero, a cipher. In this world you're supposed to contribute something, but how can you contribute if nobody wants you. When you're 64 and 364 days you're an active person. One day later they give you a party and a gold watch. Well, who in hell needs a watch when time means nothing anymore? It's ridiculous. The system is a farce."

But Sari Dienes, a sculptor, has a different view. "You have to accept change and go with it. You can't resist it. I think one of my successes in aging is I'm not resisting. I go along with it, you see."

But Sari Dienes is an artist and her work always has been the center of her life.

This is also true of Max McCarthy, a painter, who says, "Age kind of scares most people. Nothing in particular scares me. I think when you get older you begin to progress. Most people are hampered by fear, fear of change, fear of too many things. If they could get rid of fear, then they could go ahead must faster. They could progress, no matter what age."

Joe Smith, 93, of the famous vaudeville team, Smith and Dale, talks about how fast the time goes. "I think all performers and people in the acting business, when they're old, could look back and probably say, where did the years go for heaven's sake? I don't know how fast the time is going. You don't feel it."

Time has a way of accelerating for all of us, whether we work in the arts or not. The big difference is that most of us go from continuous activity, working, working, working, with maybe a two-week or four-week vacation, to a sudden stop. From an active life in which we wish for just an extra hour, an extra day, an extra week, that we can call our own, we're suddenly thrown into an entire lifetime that is our own.

But how does it feel to grow old?, I ask Lorna, 90, in Louisiana. "I don't know," she answers, "because everybody don't get old alike. Some folks are born old and some never get old. I never thought about getting older when I was young, but then I never thought I'd live this long." She bursts out laughing, then turns serious. "Of course you're never too old to have feelings. Don't get me wrong. I wouldn't let any man touch me but I still have the feelings. I'll tell you what I believe. The Lord has everything numbered, even the hair on your head. When the time comes, it doesn't matter if you're poor or rich. Your time is your time."

The ambivalence, according to Isabelle Van Frank, is that everybody wants to live but nobody wants to grow old, and you cannot do one without the other.

My experience at the disco, my experience in applying for a job has its younger counterparts. When I was younger I wasn't allowed in certain places because I was too young, so I lied about my age and couldn't wait until I was old enough to tell the truth. I've finally lived long enough to be able to go anywhere but find at times that I'm no longer welcome. I upped my age when applying for jobs as a teen-ager and now am working my way in the other direction.

But what is old?

My mother, Mary Bluh: A few years ago she suffered from a headache that wouldn't leave. Concerned, I took her to a doctor. After the examination he questioned her, "What were you doing before the headache began?"

"Dancing."

"Oh! For how long?"

"Seven hours."

He stared at her. "Do you think that's appropriate for a woman your age?"

She stares back. "It's appropriate for me."

Outside the office we look at one another and burst into laughter. My mother suddenly becomes the doctor. She looks down her nose at me. "Do you think that's appropriate for a woman your age?" And then, "Did you see the expression on his face? I thought he was going to pass out when I said seven hours.''

Three years later I sit with her in her lawyer's office. They are discussing a settlement due to her having broken a leg the year before. The lawyer turns to her and tells her the jurors will base their decision not only on the serious injury but the fact that she is over seventy. ''After all, Ms. Bluh, how many more good years do you think you have?''

I feel like kissing her when she answers, ''How many years do you think you have? You don't know any more about the years left to you than I do.''

The discussion went round and round but it became painfully obvious that the quality of life was not important but the amount of years she had lived would work against her. ''After all,'' he went on, ''whom would you award more money to, a 19-year-old or a woman your age?''

''That's agist,'' I said.

''Those are the facts of life,'' he stated. Firmly.

His argument applies to the mass consciousness that says, youth is good, youth is productive, youth is beginning. Old is through, at the end. Finished.

But what is old?

The arbitrary figure for old would be 62. I say 62 because that's the figure for social security in the United States even though most people are forced to retire when they're 65.

What is old age? I keep learning that it depends on where you are in your own age cycle.

I walk into the Clearview Nursing Home. It isn't just a nursing home. I've entertained here, danced the waltz with a 93-year-old man while I sang to this aging audience. I've spoken with women and men who are bright, articulate. Others who are confused. Angry. Reticent. Soft echoes from another time.

Clearview is where my 95-year-old grandmother lives. I feel my life surround me when I am with her. I want to tell her about my writing, the books now being published, but I can't. She is hard of hearing. She is blind. And she is mostly senile. She knows the me that lives somewhere inside of her, a place I try to reach but rarely can.

Yet James Charles Mattison at the age of 96 flew from Vancouver to London for the first time in his life and talks of the glorious adventure he had.

In October of 1975 against the advice of my then editor who thought I should be finishing my novel, I decided to travel the United States in search of older people. What I had seen in the previous three months of research led me to believe that the stereotype of older people is unfair and untrue. What's worse, they are defined by so-called experts, gerontologists and geriatric specialists, who rarely work with older people themselves but hide behind facts, figures and perhaps their own fear of aging. I thought it high time that somebody spoke to the older people themselves, because the only experts on any subject are the people living the experience.

I purposely chose people from all walks of life, not the famous who are pointed out to us and whom I greatly admire but are not, in my opinion, representative of the 23 million Americans who are over 65.

In the past three years I've spoken to over 500 people. In trying to find the largest sampling possible I traveled over 15,000 miles, spoke to people of all religions and races. Some are poverty stricken, others lower middle class, some middle class.

I wish to thank all the people who sat with me for hours and hours, sometimes days, explaining what it is to be old.

Those of you who are their age will certainly relate to the lifestyles and the experiences of the people in these pages. Those of you who have relatives and friends that age will recognize them. And those of you who walk around with unwrinkled faces and bodies, hang in there. This is your story too, your future, if you're planning to live.

WORKING OR RETIREMENT

I retired for the first time when I had my first kid. I remember thinking, how great, now I can have a second cup of coffee in the morning. The novelty of two cups of coffee didn't last long. Worse was when I met people and they asked what do you do and my answer was, "I'm a mother. I stay home." Those who were mothers clung to me like mad. Non-mothers, women and men avoided me with a yawn. After all, what can mothers discuss? Dirty diapers, formulas, how many burps came out of the darling child's mouth. Actually I had a lot more to say but I rarely got the opportunity. I was no longer part of the mainstream, which made me uninteresting. As a woman who no longer worked *out there* I became part of the sub-culture.

My dictionary defines work as the means by which one earns one's livelihood, the physical or mental effort or activity directed toward the production or accomplishment of something. But whether you're a professor or executive, a laborer or office worker, one thing is almost certain. When you reach the age of 65, your services are no longer wanted. Like it or not, you are thrust out of the vast society that works and produces. Although mandatory retirement is now in question, the statistics show that only 3% of the labor force are over 65 and the rest of the older people join the inner world of retirees. The inner world could be great but it is viewed as non-productive so it doesn't count. And the *theys* who say it doesn't count are generally those who are *out*

15

there working. But each day that goes by the inner world gets closer to all of us.

Shirley P., 65, came back from a holiday in California, returned to work and was told she would have to retire. She says she was totally unprepared since nothing had been said about her leaving. "I worked for that concern 26 years. It wasn't even the money. I had somewhere to go, a destination. Now I have to learn to do new things."

Her sudden retirement brought up a number of questions—what she would do with the rest of her life, where she would live, how to fill her days. Age is something she had never thought about.

"When you're geared to the business world as I was you don't consider yourself aged. You see me. I'm dressed but I'm not going anywhere. You just can't take 26 years out of your life and put yourself back into the kitchen. I had such wonderful rapport with the customers. You won't find that today, because the entire retail business has changed."

She talks about her life, how she was always busy working, how little time she had for simple things. She turns to me bewildered. "It's only been a week and I'm still in shock. You're an intelligent woman. What can I do with my time now?"

Marta Torrens, who plans to work one more year, is the owner of a commercial art firm. Retirement to her means leaving this country and going back to Cuba, a country she hasn't seen since 1951. I ask how she knows she'll like it after all this time and all the political changes. She's certain she will like it and even if it doesn't work as she expects she will not come back.

"People in this country age faster because they put a stop on their activities. In Cuba nobody stops dancing or singing at any age. But I wouldn't want to live with only people my age. That would be death. Here everything is run, run, make money. What's your security? What's your stocks? Then retire, sit down and die."

"Do you plan to retire, Marta?"

"No. I plan to start all over again. I want to go to the mountains to live. I plan to teach a good ten years."

An English teacher for twenty years, she is going to teach in the mountains, not in an institution. My question: is there compulsory retirement makes her laugh. "Who's going to retire me? If I want to teach I'm going to teach, even if I have to teach a mule."

Her life has been difficult. Her marriage was not a happy one. Her only child died. Forced to work all her life because of inadequate finances, she says, "I'm 68 and I don't know myself. I didn't do anything I wanted with my life. I always compromised. Having married and having a sick child and not being alone, but having to work and then being so dedicated to my work when my son died . . . Still I did not find myself. I want to part with everything that has been formed around me and just be completely alone with strangers. What do I know of what's attracted to me and what I'm attracted to? I want to find out in a strange place if I like the people I attract."

The mountains that Marta Torrens speaks of have much to do with her grandmother who dreamed of the Cuba of today. "I think of the peacefulness that my grandmother used to have, where she would go out into the field and look at the sky. She would call and say Marta, Marta, look, Venus is coming out, and she would talk to me of the stars and it was such a good feeling for me to sit next to my grandmother and I would love to be out there and talk to kids just as she did. When I was young it seemed the whole day would go in pleasure."

Retirement is out of the question for her. "Maybe it's like wanting to be part of the air. Let me tell you, it's only like each thing, each person or place is a situation that was, that ended. It has a certain duration, so if that ended it had its limit. You have to fit in someplace. I want to be remembered as part of a situation, a part of a thing, not me. Because that's the way you live. You're part of something. Isn't that so?"

In the RSVP (Retired Senior Volunteer Services Program) in

North Platte, Nebraska, I meet with Clark S., a retired principal who complains that in this land of plenty there are people with wants. He focuses on people his age, saying they are often cast aside. "It's unfortunate that people don't make plans for retirement until they're ready for it and then they don't know what they're going to do."

He feels there should be a definite course in pre-retirement. "I myself think retirement is beautiful. You can do as you wish and it's nobody's damn business. You don't have to answer to the clock. A person can sit and twiddle their thumbs but pretty soon they've got that real estate that's 8 feet long, 4 feet wide and 6 feet deep."

Art Smith says retirement originated with Mark Twain. "Mark Twain was supposedly giving a talk one day and he said, well, people ought to quit at 65. And that story was picked up, I'm told, by many organizations and the government and so we now have a 65 retirement age which is strictly fictional."

Mr. Smith co-hosts a radio show in Denver for seniors. A former radio broadcaster, he's been involved for the past five years in the Pre-Retiring Institute, and believes pre-retiring planning should begin in high school. "People think of it as, well, today I'm 65, and today I'm retired and I'll fish for the rest of my life, and it just doesn't work that way."

Dorothy Berry, a former social worker who co-hosts with Mr. Smith, never worked in radio before. She hopes the program will give older people the feeling that age doesn't limit them, that life goes on if you're involved in different experiences. "I think retirement is an individual thing. When I worked we had a woman in our office who was 50, who was down completely and they should have gotten rid of her. And then there was a woman who worked until she was 70 something or other and she could have gone on for another five years."

Charles Raymond, who heads the El Rinconcito in Tucson, a day care center for seniors, believes the problem starts long before the accepted retirement age. "My belief is, when we're talking of old age we're not talking 65 anymore. We're talking 45 and I'm convinced this is where the problem starts. With the economic situation the way it is many lose jobs of a permanent nature in their forties. I think if they don't get after industry about getting rid of these people they'd better lower the age of social security. Realistically if a person's out of work and can't get any and they're, say, 55 they'd better give them social security because that's all they're going to get.''

My conversation with Charles Raymond brought up another question. Suppose they do give people social security at 55. Can they live on it?

In New York, I walk into the Office on Aging, where Enid Allen, 77, is a senior aide assisting older people. A woman who's worked all her life, she lives in one room in a hotel. When I mention retirement she looks at me. ''What for? To sit in the lobby and get into trouble?''

She spends a great deal of time extolling the virtues of work, activity and then turns to me. ''I'll be honest with you. I like working and getting out among people but I couldn't stay home even if I wanted to. You need money to live when you get older and I don't know how they expect me to live on $241 a month. And while I'm at it I think social security is unfair. I should be getting more because I've been paying since the beginning. Why should somebody who earned more get more? If you earned a lot of money you probably saved it but people like me, well we were lucky to just pay our bills.'' She sighs, then smiles. ''I guess I'm doing Ok. There are lots of people who can't even get jobs at my age.''

Marshall LaRue, 73, spends his days with his wife in a senior center in New Orleans. He began working as a grocery clerk in the French Quarter when he was 15. He talks of pickled tongues in barrels, cocoa in barrels, large tubs filled with butter, the days before packaging. At 65, as manager of a large supermarket he was forced to retire. Retirement to him is wonderful. ''I fly around. I go wherever I want, do what I want.''

His life is great. He has a million things to do, time to spend with his grandchildren. "When I'm with them I become a different person. I can tell the way my heart feels when they're around, when we talk. They give me more pleasure than anything else because when I'm playing with them my heart feels different. I feel relaxed. I feel I'm accomplishing something. I feel satisfied."

He'd managed to save some money and, according to him, is more fortunate than most of the older people who come to this center. My first day there he points at the people leaving to be transported home. "Did you see that group taking the bus? They're going to go home and stick themselves in a bitty poor apartment up there in the project. Those poor people get stuck in an apartment and that's it. They can't do anything. They can't get a little dirt to put in a flower pot to have a flower. They're mostly the ones who come here, and it's pitiful."

The following day I sit next to him. This time his story changes. He's angry that the senior center offers nothing but a meal and an occasional trip. "They give us that old slop. If it wasn't for the company here I wouldn't come."

And again I question what it's like being retired. "Well I figure when you retire you're older and the older you get the more you're slipping down, the more you're slipping out of the business world, away from the people, away from friends. You're just like a leaf on a tree. As you get older you get dried up and burst into fall. And that's it. Unless you get mixed up in some kind of business."

Recently he discovered that the small neighborhood grocery store where he and his wife shop was up for sale. He discussed buying it with his wife who didn't like the idea, certain the work would be too hard. "She said you're too old and you'll get sick. And I said so what. When you get old and have nothing to do you get sick anyhow. It's sad but younger people just pass you by. Why, you're just left behind like an old car when you're on a highway and a brand new car is passing. The old car stays behind. The hell with you. Nobody worries about you. They just leave you behind.

"When I was in the grocery business I had thousands of friends. They used to look for me, to help out cashing a check, or ask for a box or whatever and the salesmen used to come to see me. All those people. I'd say hundreds of them used to call on me, used to make a living off me. Well, anyway all those people that I used to cater to and help and work with and all that kind of stuff—after I got out of the grocery business, boom! It was just like pulling a plug out of a bathtub. They don't know you no more. It's all over. It's finished."

I've always been accused of rushing my life away but it seems that life rushed by with very little help from me. It was only yesterday when I sat on a stoop dreaming, entered school for the first time, wrote my first story, bought my first lipstick, which was purple, to my mother's horror, had my first date, sang with a band. Married, had my own place, then one child and another and another. And now within a short time my children will be leaving me for their own lives. The rushing accelerates at a speed that's dizzying.

Standing in the middle of Bourbon Street I remember the New Orleans of 1951. All the jazz joints, no girlie shows, the enormous crowds of people at all hours. Now at two in the morning I find myself walking practically empty streets.

I rush from dialogue to dialogue, looking up at the iron grill verandahs, the narrows streets, the old stucco buildings that remain from so many years ago. I am rushing to see Livia Beauregarde, when a young woman stops me. She looks at me, her eyes shining. "God loves you," she says and begins talking of God and love and church.

When I ask what position women play in her church she is at first bewildered, then says she is talking about God and love. I ask again.

"I don't think you understand. I'm talking about how God loves you. I'm not interested in women."

"O.K. Fine. Then I'm not interested in talking about your church."

The streets are crowded with people. I move with them. A half block away I hear running feet on the pavement and turn. The young woman has caught up with me. She is breathless, her face has lost its smile. She grabs my shoulder. "Old woman, old woman," she screams. "You listen to me. I'm talking to you, old woman. Do you hear?"

The peoplefilled street seems to stop in movement. I stare into her blood-red face. "I can really feel all the love you've been talking about. It shines on your face."

Her hand drops from my shoulder. I continue walking, feeling numb. The word *old* resounds in my ear over and over again. But it isn't only the word that bothers me. It's the way she said it, with such hatred, such anger.

When I tell Livia about the incident she speaks of one she had in a restaurant when a waiter asked her husband if she was his mother. "That experience really made me wonder, because you know something, Bonnie, when you look at yourself you do not see yourself as others see you. And I look at myself and say, hey old girl you're looking pretty good today and somebody says would you like to have a seat on the bus and I immediately feel 90 years old."

"But Livia, I'm not talking about that. It was the ugly way she said *old*, as if it were a contagious disease."

She laughs. "In a way it is. You know, Bonnie, I had a facelift three years ago. That was a gruesome experience, a horrible process to go through. It must be one of the bloodiest operations. I was terribly bruised and I went into a depression for three weeks and was the bitch of the world. Don't let anybody tell you it's like going away for a rest cure. I'm still numb here." She points to one side of her face.

Livia Beauregard is a buyer for a department store. She can't conceive of the day she'll retire. Her doctor doesn't want her to, nor her husband, nor her husband's psychiatrist, who says, don't let Livia retire or she'll die. A grimace clouds her face.

"We are the forgotten people. Do you know I was taken off the insurance policy because as far as the insurance company is concerned I'm not there. I'm a zero. I can stay as long as I produce but you see there, Bonnie, is the trouble. You find yourself working twice as hard as you might have to because you are afraid they're going to say, she's slowing down because she's getting older.''

Livia, 69, is not forced to retire. However, a recent incident disturbs her. The head of the store suggested finding a replacement for her and asked if there was anybody she would like to train. Livia mentioned some woman and let the subject drop. A few days later he said to her, ''you're worried, aren't you?'' ''And I said, well, yes I'm worried when you say we have to think about a replacement. He said that we all have to think of replacements because we could be run over tomorrow and he had no intention of replacing me. Still, I feel uneasy.''

But not everybody wants to work forever. Some even leave before they're asked to. Eileen Glasford who lives in a tiny village called Gibsons Landing in British Columbia quit teaching when she was 62. She observed teachers who stuck it out until they hated their students and didn't want this to happen to her. She also wanted freedom from regulation, scheduled times. ''Those blinking school bells started to send me off the roof.''

She enjoys her retirement, spending her days walking around the village, going to the cafe. She calls herself a ''people person'' saying, ''I get all the gossip of the village and philosophize a great deal.'' She also works in the local bookstore, a cooperative venture.

Then there's Rose Schlesinger who worked as the assistant to the president of a large corporation. She decided to retire and enjoy life four years ago. She's never regretted her decision and spends her days at the YW-YMHA, taking yoga, physical fitness, dancing, playing bridge. She goes to the theatre, dance, museums and now has time to travel, all the luxuries which were impossible when she worked.

Folmar Blangsted, film editor who has worked on some of the

major pictures of our time, says he quit because he felt the movie industry had changed. "When you do anything theatrically, as you well know, since you worked in the theatre, you should have fun. Without fun and enthusiasm you get nothing but dead stuff. I said to myself, I have no mortgage payments, I have no children to send through college. What the hell am I doing working on this kind of junk and eating my heart out? So in my seventy-first year I quit. But I haven't retired, because retired means a rocking chair. I've taken a permanent vacation, because when you take a vacation you do what you want and you don't do what you don't want."

But these people quit because they wanted to.

There are also older people who cannot quit because of money.

Gertrude and Lilly are both employed by the same hotel in Winnemucca, Nevada. They are worn-looking. I don't know whether it's the desert sun or their lives that give their faces the deeply carved lines. But I do know their lives have been difficult. They've both worked as maids most of their married lives, supporting their children.

Gertrude. Although she can barely live on her $2.30 an hour salary she refuses to ask her five children for anything. She stares at me. "If I were starving I wouldn't ask them. No way. I wouldn't ask them for nothing. And I wouldn't move in with them either."

Widowed, forced to work because her social security wouldn't be enough, she is furious that she is only allowed to earn $3000 a year while collecting her social security checks. She had a confrontation with a man from the SS office. "I said mister you can keep it. You can go back to Carson City or wherever you came from and shove it."

She is equally furious that at her age she has to work, saying at 65 she doesn't think she should have to kill herself. "And don't ask me if it's a hard life. I'll tell you this, with the tips I get I couldn't get a cup of coffee and if I get any tips it's not from the rich. They're the cheapest people alive. People only tip when it makes them look big. Nobody sees them leaving a maid a tip, so they leave nothing. A porter carries a bag and they hand him a dollar bill but we scrub the same room for days and they give nothing.''

I aks her what she'll do when she's too old to work and she answers, ''If you're talking about asking for help from my children, that's their business. It's up to them to give me something if they want to. It's not up to me to say.''

She stands at the door defensively. ''Look, I don't know what you want but I've got to work. I can't stand here all day and gab with you. Just put in that book of yours I'm happy.''

Then there's Lilly. In two years she lost three people. Her husband in death, her daughter in death, her son by desertion. She looks bewildered, on the verge of tears. ''I work 37 years as a maid. When I work I'm happy. I don't have anything to live for now. When my daughter died my son didn't come to the funeral. We call him in Brazil. We wait for two days but he never came. My daughter-in-law was there with the three grandchildren. My grandson took me aside and he explained that for two and a half years his parents were divorced. I was very shocked, not the shock of divorce, but they never tell me. They tell me nothing.''

The tears that glisten in her eyes spill out. ''I call my son five times in Brazil. I write him letters. The last time he says to me I don't want your letters. I don't want you to call me anymore. You have your life and I have mine. I say to him God bless you and I hope you're happy.''

We stand together, Lilly and I, both of us crying. Her body is bony, ancient. ''I put my son through college. Even afterward I help pay for their home. I work for 35 years as a maid in one hotel. Why did my son say that to me? He's a professor and I'm nothing. When he had that fellowship at Stanford, he said mother I need help. Even if you don't leave me a penny when you die I need help now. Now he don't need help anymore.''

She sits on the hotel bed trying to compose herself. She talks about her life. Born in the Pyrenees Mountains of Spain 72 years ago, she went to Cuba when she was 15, then to the United States. "How I make my life I don't know. What you going to do? You have to work."

And then touching my face, tracing the wetness. "You cry for me. Don't cry for me. Today its 100% different. I wouldn't marry if I were young. I would never have children. I would work and save my money, be good to myself." But in the next breath she tells me she's paying her grandson's last year of tuition in college.

"Sometimes I say to myself why we're here and then I say because God put us here and that's the only thing that keep me alive."

I sit next to her. Our arms automatically go around each other. I cannot continue with the dialogue. Her eyes look up at me. "You're too soft. Look how soft you are. You got to be hard. Promise me. When you're old you got to learn to be hard."

I go to senior centers from coast to coast, speaking to people who are no longer working, people who have devoted their lives to one job or another. Not one believes in mandatory retirement, even those who find this time of their life happier.

On a bus heading for Denver, I speak with a man who retired ten years ago. He's annoyed that his retirement wasn't his choice, but the decision of his company. "I have a friend who says he's having the time of his life, but me, I'm just at loose ends. In the beginning I'd get up the same time and rush around like a nut and my wife would say what're you rushing for. And it would hit me like a ton of bricks, you've got no place to go. I'd be embarrassed to leave my home, to admit I was old enough to be retired. I thought this is it, this is the finish line."

And now. "Well you can see I'm travelling around with my wife but travelling is fun, not an occupation."

Aside from the 3% who work in the labor force, there are the artists, the professionals who have their own business, and the self-employed.

Emile Kahn had to retire from Montclair College when he was 66, only because he turned 65 during the school year. His retirement was only from teaching. He immediately began writing books, continued composing, did sixty recordings for Music Minus One. He has been the conductor of the Senior Concert Orchestra since 1971. Based in New York, it is the only orchestra of its kind.

Sari Dienes, 79, is the sculptor whom I met when I began writing this book and has since become a friend. She continues having art shows, working with a vigor that would tire anybody 30 years younger. Retirement is not a word in her vocabulary. The phrase she uses that stands out in my mind is "The spirit has no age."

Gladys Moon Jones was once a lawyer, became a journalist, and is a well known clairvoyant. At age 60 she began sculpting. When she was 68 she received her Masters in Fine Art. From 73 to 76 she went to Dijon University in France. She now sculpts daily, helps people through her psychic powers, is writing a book. Work to her is part of living. "I must tell you I am never afraid to try something new. I say thank you for everything and when you feel this way you are relaxed, you feel free and you're not sick and you don't get old."

Martha McClean who owns a cafe and service station in a small western town eyes me suspiciously. "What do you want to know? My age? I'm 77. What else do you want to know?"

"How many hours do you work?"

She laughs. "Oh, lets not talk about that. The alarm rings at four-thirty in the morning and it takes me a half hour to get out of bed. Then I work till eight at night."

Does she plan to retire ever?

"What would I do if I stayed home? I have fun here. I get to talk to people, find out what they do. As long as these old feet keep me up I'm going to work. Why should I quit? I see the people who stay home. They got this pain and that pain. Not that I aint got 'em too. I've got my share of pains but I just don't have time to think of 'em. Look, I can't talk no more. I've got to take care of my customers."

She moves to a nearby booth. "Charlie, good to see you. Where you been hiding yourself lately?"

Wendy whose age is questionable but is over 65, runs a house of prostitution which she lovingly calls a Cat House. My views on Wendy have little to do with age, but with the kind of person that peddles women's flesh. Wendy, a former prostitute, doesn't let morals enter into her consciousness. "I'll retire the day I die. As long as men want what we have to offer we'll be around."

On aging. "I love getting older. Why, your best years are yet to come." She may like aging but she doesn't like what age has done to her physically and has recently had a facelift. Her face is still swollen but she loves the way she looks.

More on age: "My oldest customer is 85 and he tells me every night, Don't ever leave. It's what I have to look forward to."

Although she admits her *girls* must retire at a certain age, the age being the late twenties, she herself as a Madame can go on forever. "Why I have more fun in the Cat House than most people do playing. So much of our business is friends and when you see them coming there you're glad. They are the only family I have. I'm a very fortunate woman. What person retires when they're needed and respected? Only a fool would do that. I have everything I want in that Cat House. Everything. And I wouldn't trade my last ten years for the rest of my life. I work seven days a week and love every minute of it. I made the right choice. How many people can say that?"

Dr. Madelaine Massenoir is a psychiatrist in Boston. I ask her age. At first she hedges, then says as long as I'm not using her name its alright. Her reason. "I would freely tell my age but some of my patients might be prejudiced. People might not come to a 74-year-old psychiatrist."

She doesn't like the way older people are treated by those people in their thirties who are in power. "They view them as oldies, the antiques, their ideas are outdated, their manners, their clothing, everything, even the way they talk to each other. Everything is passé. They don't see that these people count. Then of course we don't use old people so much. We do retire them and send them off and so the old people think of themselves that way. They take on the younger people's image of themselves very often. But I'm sure I thought the same thing.''

How does she view older people now that she's older herself? She admits that theoretically she thinks about them as not counting anymore but on a personal level she feels differently. ''Some of my friends are old. I have a friend of 80 and still working. I also have a friend who retired and used to be very interesting. When I meet her now the things she talks about are too narrow. She's very bright and she reads but she's not in life anymore. She's just stepped out.''

Dr. Massenoir does not plan to retire. ''Why should I? I think of myself as a first class analyst. I think as I grow older I'll reduce my hours but I can't imagine how one lives without one's work. I'll continue with my life until I can't anymore.''

In Vancouver, B.C. the voice on the other end of the phone asks, ''How old are you?'' and then when I tell him, ''Oh, are you the authority on aging?''

''No I'm not. The people I speak with are the authorities.'' ''Alright. Then that's fine. I'm sick of younger people as authorities on aging.''

The voice belongs to Dr. Alfred Bayne who has worked with older people for years and is now in the process of starting a large senior center in West Vancouver.

At the arranged bus stop where I meet him, he greets me warmly, walks briskly with me to his car, then stops and studies me. ''You're not a social worker, are you?''

I shake my head. ''Good,'' he says. ''They bore me. I go into geriatric meetings and they're telling the old people what's good for them. They come in starry-eyed and all they know is what they've read in books. They can't know anymore. I'm, if it's any interest to you at all, 88 years old. I worked until I was 80 which should prove you don't have to leave work.''

When Alf Bayne was 79 he suffered a massive stroke. Although his doctor insisted he was lucky to be alive, that he might still get another stroke, possibly a worse one, Dr. Bayne was adamant that he would be back at work. "My doctor was a good medical doctor but a poor psychologist. That was an awful thing to say to anybody. Of course I was sick, but I think my determination to go back to work caused a quick recovery. I think that was a great deal of it."

One year later he did retire. I ask why. He says he loved the personal contact with his patients but feels dentistry had gotten to the point where it was nothing but dollars and cents. The personal contact he loved was no longer there. "My doctor told me I was stupid to stop working and I would have been stupid had I not found something else to take up my time."

The something else is his total devotion to older people like himself, not only in the proposed center, but in working actively to see older people get a fair deal. He claims youth is a spoiled group of humanity. "Everything is spent on them, it's all theirs for the taking. The world went wild over youth. Now, take middle age. They're mostly able to take care of themselves. They can choose their life, their own amusement, their work, and they're in the most exciting time of their life. Now this same adult who goes along and could become anything, when they're 65, they call them into the office and give them a watch. Their usefulness to society is finished. Now, until senior citizens, who have been brain-washed for centuries and discarded by the young, until they realize they're people, the same people they always were, with the same attributes, with many of their qualities refined, until they become more militant and assert themselves, they won't be able to enjoy the great things that are here and one of them is work."

In New Orleans, my car's generator breaks down. Waiting for it to be fixed, I speak with Earl Guillot, in his late sixties, the owner of this auto repair shop. His feelings about retirement. "Retirement? I don't believe in it. What would I do? It's all wrong, this retiring business. You go to a college. You establish yourself. You learn. You get your Bachelor's, your Master's, your Ph.D. and then when you graduate you're too old to do anything. You work and then one day, plop, you're out of it. I don't think older people should retire. They should be in consultant work for younger people so they can learn." He pauses, then says, "I guess I'm luckier than most. It's my business, so nobody can retire me."

In the Office of Continuing Education I meet Mary Herrick, 82, who has worked all her life as an educator. "Somebody said old people should disassociate themselves and retreat to serene meditation in the world. That was a beautiful theory for everybody but the old people. If they would just disappear and vanish from sight, not bother anybody. One of the real reasons for senility is that old people stop doing things. They accept others' estimates of what they can do."

A woman who's never accepted what others think, she talks of lying in a hospital with a broken hip just seven years ago when she was 75, how people felt sorry for her, "wondering what this poor little old lady was going to do, so I decided to find out myself."

She got out of the hospital and found a full-time position as consultant at City Wide College, City College of Chicago.

She grins at me. "At my age, I'm useful as a token. The token old. Now, there's nothing different about me than when I was 22. The age of 65 for retirement is a completely artificial age invented by Bismarck when he started social security and people just accept it."

Statistics tell her that she'll live to be 95. Her projection is that she will need more sleep, probably limp a little more and work less hours but beyond that she expects to be doing the same work.

Does she ever reflect on her past? She looks at me unbelieving. "I reflect on how I'm ever going to get through the day, how I'm going to do this for my classes and when I'll have time to go to the cleaners."

Professor Giovanni Costigan, renowned historian, lecturer, author, was forced to retire two years ago when he was 70. I sit in his tiny office at the University of Washington. Although retired people don't have the right to an office on campus, Professor

Costigan was given what they call an office but what I call a walk-in closet. He protests, says he's glad to have anything. Then admits it's totally inadequate, that he cannot fit his books in the room, books that he needs for his work.

Retired people are also not supposed to teach but there was such an uproar about the retirement of Professor Costigan that evening courses were set up for the first time to accommodate students.

How does he feel about being forced to retire?

"I knew all my life that it was coming so I was perfectly prepared for it. It was no shock. I knew there was no alternative but I think it really is a problem. In some cases people should retire when they get older. I mean we do age, as you know, at different rates. Some people are perhaps old at 50! Others are young at 75. I don't think it's fair to say there should be no way of retiring people who have outlived their usefulness. The question is how to determine when they've done so. Mere age is not a proper criterion. I have known cases, and I'm sure you've known them too, of people who are kept on their jobs out of kindness when they're not really capable of continuing."

"From what I've seen, I know many people who are not only capable but when they're retired they haven't the vaguest idea of what to do."

"Indeed. Absolutely. That's another aspect of the problem. People are retired by law and usually provided with no alternative means of work unless they happen to be artists or intellectuals who write. I mean they have their self-made careers. Others are often in a very bad condition and our society, I think, often disregards them and treats them rather callously. In fact I have the impression that our whole culture is much more intolerant of old age than the older cultures of the Orient where old age is respected and where the person is in a sense more honored than ever. Aside from our lack of respect for age, we emphasize our love for youth. Each has its merits. I can't think of any solution but I think society must find one. In our case it's the injustice to the old."

"Professor Costigan, do you ever discuss your age?"

"It's a matter of public record. I'm 72 but you're about the first person who's ever asked me. I haven't the least hesitation about telling you but I don't usually have the need to discuss it. I think for any person who is interested in ideas or is a creative artist, for such a person life continues as abundantly as ever. If you read or think, you don't stop at 70 or any other age. So this minority, we may call them intellectuals or artists, are fortunate, but professionals and other people put all their energy into a certain occupation and are suddenly cut off and have no resources often to fill the gap. It's a very terrible position and I've known a few, and you probably have too, who've gone to pieces mentally."

The vast majority are people like Richard Hunter, a native American, who's 72. He hasn't gone to pieces but he's tremendously disturbed because he can't find work and feels inactivity makes people old. "If they'd give me a job I'd take it. A porter. I'd mop the floors. Anything. When people get old and do nothing they flop down. They get old quickly."

Ed Lowry is a member of the Hollywood Comedy Club, which was formed right after vaudeville died and actors came to Hollywood in droves looking for work. Today they give shows, raise money, help members who are in need. Ed writes a bulletin for the club, and the letters he receives from all parts of the country are to him his payment. "Without those things you can't survive and stay young."

A former entertainer who has travelled throughout the United States and Europe, he speaks of life, aging and retirement.

"You know what burns me?" he says. "When some kid says, 'you don't understand!' This is the most horrifying and degrading statement, because the kid saying it has never lived. They haven't been any place. First kids go to school for free until they're 18. After that they're permitted to work. Now, go back to our day when kids worked legally at 14. During the summer they worked when they were 10 as errand boys. There was no unemployment insurance, no welfare, no one to look after your mother if she was widowed so she either went to the poorhouse or was taken care of by her children.

"Now if you succeed when you're 65, they say that's enough. You're done. It's unfair. Then if you decide to work, or they let you work, the social security which you paid for 45 years has to be given back to the government unless you're over 72. So that person is out as far as the society goes and then those kids say you don't know nothing. All of a sudden you become a nonentity. You're nothing. They put us all in the same barrel. The social system eliminates us no matter how capable we are.

"Look at Jack Benny, Fred Astaire, Maurice Chevalier. It saddens me that this is a past time. You're seeing an extinct people. You'll never see that again."

In March 1978, Congress passed a law changing the age of mandatory retirement from 65 to 70. Although this certainly could be considered a breakthrough, it again puts a stop to human potential at a designated age. If this is the case, I think all the people in Congress over 65 or whatever age they set should be forced to retire as well.

I agree with Professor Costigan that there should be some way to solve the problem of retirement, but setting an age is the easy way out.

Shortly after I left Seattle, a bill was passed to outlaw mandatory retirement. Unfortunately it was not retroactive so Professor Giovanni Costigan's position was not subject to change.

FEELINGS

In the past few years I've been invited to speak at the Woman's Center in Queens College. The last time I was there, I decided to do improvisations. I asked the students to pretend they were sixty.

One had varicose veins and could hardly walk. Another was miserable because her husband died and her children were long gone. A glum-faced woman talked about sitting home all day waiting for her children to call. The improvisations went on and on and without exception every young woman saw herself finished at 60.

But in this group there was a 75-year-old woman. I asked her to play her own age. Then I asked a 23-year-old woman to play her 30-year-old daughter. The situation was that her two brothers had just left home.

The younger woman began, "Mom, I'm worried about you. What are you going to do now that we're all gone?" To which the older woman answered, "What do you mean? I'm going to have fun."

"How about my children? Aren't you going to babysit?"

"Listen," she said. "I did plenty between you and your brothers. Enough is enough. I'm studying, I'm dancing, I'm going places. I got my own life to live."

"How come you're dancing now? You never danced when Dad was alive."

"Naturally I didn't. Your father didn't like to dance so I became a wallflower."

As the improvisation progressed, I noticed the amazed expression on the student's faces. A woman that age saying she was entitled to her own life! A woman that age studying, dancing, having fun! Gradually they began smiling, actually cheering her. When the scene was over the students applauded. Most of them were around 20. We discussed their attitudes toward 60-year-olds and they readily admitted that it was literally impossible to visualize themselves at 60. Yet they viewed older people as decrepit, inactive, waiting for the phone to ring or a visit. And none, without exception, had given much thought to older people.

At the Department on Aging in New York, I speak with Commissioner Alice M. Brophy who tells me of a similar experience. She was invited by the New York Psychiatric Institute to confront attitudes toward aging with twenty other participants, most of them in their mid-thirties. They were asked to pretend they were 60.

"The women saw themselves as completely white-haired and on the border of senility. One man saw himself just getting over a stroke. Their concept of age was fantastic. When it came to me I was supposed to be 86. I said, 'I'm 86 and I've just been employed by the Department on Aging. I'm working on nutrition. I'm a guidance person and I cover the five boroughs. I go from place to place.'

"Most of the people at the session were falling apart because of their ideas on the old. Our fears of aging are tremendous. The feeling of aging, when you play-act, and you know this is not for real, shows the trauma of what it feels like to get old. I was really quite shocked that there was so much feeling there."

Since writing this book I have been so busy talking with older people that I never stop to question my own attitude. I find myself taking peeks in the mirror to see if I look old. What happened to my jaw line that seems to be growing by leaps and bounds? Each day it gets lower. I wish I could grow a mustache to hide the lines under my mouth. I am suddenly blurting out my age to everybody and looking for a reaction. When I'm told I look young for my age I'm insulted. When I get no reaction, which means I look my age, I'm equally insulted. Whatever they say, they can't win but neither can I.

Still I don't question my attitude about older people so it comes as a blow to me when Dr. Madelaine Massenoir confronts me. She has just mentioned that she was hard of hearing and I quickly tell her I knew younger people who were also hard of hearing. "There," she says. "Often when I talk about age you dismiss it."

I remember the last time I spoke with her. She said she had less stamina, that she had to force herself to be more careful about the way she dressed, she now takes a nap which she didn't do when she was younger. And each time she spoke I dismissed it, citing examples of younger people who had the same problem.

She looks hurt. "Whenever I discuss what happens when you're older and you don't want to hear it, you dismiss it."

"I'm sorry, Madelaine."

"Bonnie, you don't have to be afraid of old age. You say to me—sometimes when I say this happens when you get old—oh go on. You don't want to hear it because you're just as frightened as I am about old age and the woman downstairs and everybody. You must realize how much all people are afraid of old age. There's some secret displeasure and discomfort when one looks at older people. You can be quite easy if you know what's going on between us but if you don't realize it you'll have difficulty. I try to present myself as an old person and you must accept that. You can't minimize it or say it isn't necessary, because it *is* necessary. One doesn't accept old age but one has to learn to accept it and look at it in the face and live with it and that isn't any more difficult than facing one of the things we had to face in life—like being a woman, being a worker. It isn't a tragedy. We have to learn to look at it."

"Madelaine, I'm not afraid of old age."

"Then what is it?"

"I'm afraid of dying."

"You're not afraid of dying but how one will die. That is the fear. What is going to happen to make you die, how one might suffer. *How* is the important thing."

"I also realize I could die before you do."

"That's what my husband always said. I thought more of age when he died. I thought, I will die too. If he did of course I will too. Another thing is, you're not writing about death but about old age and old age is not a tragedy. It's a part of life."

"Madelaine, do you resent being called older?"

"Why should I resent it? I am older. You see the point is the whole society suffers when they say how awful it is to be old. It's all over the place and you know that. So you can't help being tainted by this a little. You can't help absorbing some of that. I had to overcome a great deal before I could accept the whole thing. It's a process you have to work at with yourself. You don't like to think about adolescence. It wasn't easy. Old age is different but you accept it."

We walk towards her home. "You know I have a theory that people who are young don't want to look at older people because they know that's where they're heading."

"Of course. This is absolutely true. People do avoid the elderly, which is why they are so lonely. It's very interesting about old age. I started making wills and living wills. Do you know about that?"

"Yes. You're talking about euthanasia."

We sit down in her living room, sipping tea. Dr. Massenoir admits that she herself hasn't actually thought much about age, that my visit has forced her to think of it. "My doctor said to me, don't run to buses and don't go on mountains over 7,000 feet. I can't tell you how that hurt me. I love to do that. I don't mean hanging by a rope. But walking. I wanted to take my little grandson to Colorado and I thought we could do a little mountain climbing. The fact that I can't do it, I mustn't . . . It's the first thing I have had to give up and that is terribly sad."

She talks of her years of mothering and marriage, which she enjoyed thoroughly, of how she's enjoying the freedom she has now that her children are all on their own. "That's one of the pleasant things of getting older, being able to do the things you always wanted but then many people live their whole lifetimes doing the things they like."

"Really! I don't know many people like that."

She laughs. "I don't either."

Possessions, once important to Dr. Massenoir, are less important as she gets older. She has a tendency to give them away to people who will enjoy them rather than waiting and willing it to them. But there is always the dichotomy, the not caring and yet wanting to be surrounded by possessions she enjoys. She laughs at this. "I'd like to die among the things I love. I should miss them if I didn't see them anymore. I feel sorry for people in nursing homes having to leave all their possessions behind."

Still she is not as fussy anymore. She points to a worn cushion saying this would have bothered her terribly years ago.

Never a conformer, she enjoys being a rebel and tells me she gets a certain amount of pleasure when people are aghast. But again she's vulnerable when it comes to her friends. "I care for the people I love so much that I'm very sensitive. They can hurt me, it's easy to hurt me. I will never learn." She looks at me with the childlike expression that is so much a part of her. "Isn't it easy to hurt you, Bonnie?"

"Yes. Very."

"People do think that emotions are kind of bad things. On the one hand we say we must be sensitive and on the other hand we don't want to be criticized and hurt so much but you can't have both at the same time."

I ask if she would call herself an optimist and she answers, "Yes. In spite of often having no reason to be I am optimistic and then of course I get a tremendous setback if something is the matter with me, like when I'm ill. I take it much more seriously than I used to. I was ill this winter for about a month and I was much more depressed about it than I've ever been and I think that has to do with old age but you see I'm better again. It surprises me, on looking back at that period, how very low I was. Although many people were terribly nice and I was so pleased to see how many friends I have I didn't care too much for my friends to come in and be good to me and that was really a bad feeling. And I think that has to do with old age because when you feel your body breaking down you are faced with, yes, the end is going to come now. Another thing I always find interesting is that things can't get better anymore. I practice the piano and the quickness in my hands, the strength in my fingers, that can't become more, that must become less. I can't go for a whole day's hike anymore. I have to limit myself. There are other physical things. They don't become better, they become worse. Your face falls, you can't cure it. I'm certainly not going to have a facelift or anything like that. So it's getting worse, it can't get better. That was a sentence I had to say to myself at a certain moment in my life."

I sip more tea, indulge myself in one of the petit fours she puts out. Madelaine drinks milk and admits she doesn't like sweets. She catches my look and smiles. "You can't tell that from what I'm serving but it's true. In the evening I have milk and fruit. I think it very important to set yourself at the table, light candles and make it pleasant for yourself and if you don't like eating by yourself bring a good book of poetry."

As I leave Dr. Madelaine Massenoir asks, "Did I help you at all? I hope you don't think I was too critical of you."

"No. I'm glad you spoke."

"Old age is something you just have to accept. You learn not to be so unhappy."

I'd heard about Helen Lindgren before I got to Denver, about her activities with the Grey Panthers, NOW, and other organizations. I'd heard about her extemporaneous speeches criticizing wars, racism, sexism, the B Bomber, the poverty of old age, charity, apathy.

At a recent utilities hearing where hundreds of older people

came she said, "We didn't come here to listen to your explanation. It's for you to hear us. Then the lawyer for the utility
company said, 'I just want to explain so you'll understand about
the raised prices' and I said 'We older people know more than you
think we know'."

The first day I met her we started with breakfast and ended late
at night long after dinner.

Helen, who's 83, has been fighting all her life. It's the principle
she's interested in, the fight for a better society. "Now since I'm
older, old I should say, I'm more outstanding because when
I was younger there were many other young people fighting but
not many of the older people today are speaking out. They
say,'Oh, Helen, that was good what you said', but they don't
stand up and support me. This is what my nature is but now that
I'm old, people expect me to pack up and retire. Well I'm not
going to and that's that."

Her battles have antagonized many people, including her
family. One year she decided that cards for holidays and birthdays
were ridiculous so she told everybody not to send them. She
asked them to send her a card when they had time to write
something, saying she wanted a special day when they were
thinking of her. Her stance had repercussions. Some stopped
writing altogether; others argued with her; her daughter was
annoyed. "Bonnie, she can't see me doing these things. She can't
appreciate my being an individual. I cause an awful lot of dissent
among my family and friends. They're always asking why I have
to be so difficult and different. They say to me, 'Helen why can't
you please people' and I say, 'Because it doesn't please me'."

She serves lunch, answers one of the countless calls she gets,
for this group and that group, and would she speak here or there.
She laughs. "I'm not really a speaker at all. Once they asked if I
would speak at a Woman's Day rally, and I said I will if I feel like
it. Well I got up and said something like this. 'I'm not a speaker.
I'm not an entertainer. I'm just a wrinkle-faced woman. I'm a
worker and an activist. I was marching in 1920 for women's rights,

for the vote but I thought and the garment workers thought it was not just for the vote but for equal rights and we haven't accomplished that yet'."

On Mother's Day she made a speech to a large audience. She told them Mother's Day was made for glorifying mothers and covering up the real issues that mothers were fighting for before the vote, to be recognized as equal citizens in every sense of the word.

Again the phone rings and again she agrees to speak somewhere. I ask if her husband was as much of a fighter. She says they were different but the same politically, then laughs. "Well, actually I wasn't married. I didn't believe in it. I used to call it a dog's license. I used to be proud that I had the courage not to marry. Although my husband was as principled as I he used to say, 'You don't have to go to the rooftops and yell it out'. He would say, 'Why do you tell the people these things when they don't ask' and I'd say I'm sure they want to know. Anyway in my day people didn't talk so much about sleeping together or abortions. They just did it."

"Why do you call him your husband?"

"I suppose I do it out of habit. I started saying husband when my daughter was born."

She speaks of her great admiration for Maggie Kuhn, who formed the Grey Panthers, her fight against stereotyping of any kind. "I feel the members don't talk enough about this. Very few people have the power of their convictions. They move around or they change groups, going from one to another but I have convictions that I'm strict about. I don't like, for instance, that in the Grey Panthers as in most organizations a few people take over and they run the organization their own way and exclude other people because they don't agree. If I don't agree I speak out."

She believes people become too complacent in groups and need to be activated. "Even so-called progressive women your age and younger will accept things rather than speak up and be defeated. They would rather be quiet and accepted. I tell the women if you speak up you might lose your job. I lost jobs myself. But older people aren't going to lose their jobs, they have nothing to lose. Yet most of them refuse to do anything and it's discouraging. Some of them say there's no use speaking up, there's no use fighting and I do sympathize with them. But I always use the argument that if none of us complained and none of us fought the quality of life would be much worse.''

What bothers Helen Lindgren about the way the old are treated? Well, for one thing she is angry that the government spends enormous amounts of money on nursing homes, claiming they're more interested in supporting profitmakers than in taking care of people. ''They give them pills to keep them nice and quiet. And another thing, I don't believe in charity. Charity wouldn't be necessary if the government was responsible, if we had jobs for people, if we had adequate income and housing and health care. Charity is like throwing a dog a bone. So I always fight for a better society, rather then patching it up.

''I have written to the newspapers and the President and one of the things I emphasize again and again is, how can people accept the fact that most old people when they retire are poor? They don't have investments and they don't have money to rely on. I make this statement all the time when I speak for the Grey Panthers. When people retire they have to give up their incomes. Often they go hungry and need food stamps. They are treated like third-class citizens who don't count after contributing all their lives to this society. We have so many programs that benefit the aging but they don't go out to reach these people. I tell them I don't have a car but if somebody will take me we'll go to the homes of these people. After all we know where they are.''

At dinner I marvel at her enormous energy, the power of her convictions and wonder if I'll have that fight. She stops eating, reaches over and spontaneously hugs me. ''Don't worry, Bonnie. You'll be fine. Look, I made it to 83. You will too.'' She laughs.

''When I think now of all the things I went through I'm surprised I lived through it. You know when I was an organizer for the garment workers union I was so outspoken I was arrested a few times. Like you, I always fought for what I believed in and now when I talk to you about it I'm aware, but the funny thing is I wasn't aware of it then. I just did it.''

How does Helen Lindgren spend her days when she isn't working for the aged or for other causes? "Oh, sometimes I look at the house and see how dirty it is. Who has time? I go through my papers. I relax and read. I go for a walk, to the library or to the museum and I feel so good knowing I have nothing to do. But if it happens for a few days I feel lost.''

Although she is very much against routine or ritual, last year she decided to make herself a party, inviting friends, many of them young, many from her organizations because she felt she didn't see them often enough. She told everybody not to bring her anything because she had too many things. "This time they brought me useful things like flowers and cheese and wine and writing paper. So I'm glad I'm living at 83 and healthy.''

I left Helen Lindgren knowing I'd found a friend. Her letters are full of her enormous zest for life, her constant fight for a better life for all older people. Her beautiful painting which she did when she was 80 sits in this room where I write, giving me much joy.

Every day, sitting at my desk, typing on my typewriter, I have a guarantee that, coming through my window, gliding on the air, is a voice and a guitar that sings *O Solo Mio* and *Sorrento* and other Italian songs. Sometimes the voice is joined with other voices. The first time I heard this off-key voice I called to my kids, "Listen, isn't it marvellous!" But after living in this apartment for ten months and knowing that unless it rains or snows I will have to write to the accompaniment of *O Solo Mio,* believe me, the thrill is gone.

Today I decided to see who was singing. I took the elevator down the twelve stories and walked where my ears led me. The old man stopped singing for a second, grinned at me. "Where are you going? Stay. Sing with us.''

An old man, playing a harmonica, nods at me and continues playing. A man in his late sixties, sitting in a chair, gets up for me. A woman who is drinking and singing welcomes me.

So we all sing and laugh and they ask me if I know Italian songs and I read their lips and sing along. During a pause I tell the guitarist I am writing a book on people over 65.

The woman says, "65! He's over 80."

He touches my hand. "Sure I talk to you. Why not? Tell me what you want to know. Anytime. I tell you."

He explains that he has been working in Park Slope as a caretaker-handyman for a neighborhood doctor the past 35 years; that on December 12, 1974 the doctor retired, which left him jobless. Now he comes from Manhattan to Park Slope every day, unless the weather is bad, to see his friends. And play his guitar. And sing.

"We used to pay 5¢ carfare and everything moved like silk. What's become of the money today? They get 50¢. Punks we got. You call them politicians? They're crooks."

Suddenly the man who offered me the seat stares at me. "What are you doing, writing a report on us? Where you come from, the CIA? Listen, sweetheart, I'm here 51 years and I know everybody but I don't know you."

"I just moved here last November."

The guitar player studies me, his eyes squinting.

"I'm gonna tell you something. If I had to do it all over again I'd do it over again. I meet all these wonderful people. Let me tell you something. I come here from Italy in 1904. I drove a team of horses and the weather was so cold. I had my compari . . . you know what compari is? My compari, he said, Anthony you come to work for us and I give you $12 a week. 20 hours a day I work for 20¢ an hour. I was a packer in the wholesale fruit market. On the 30th of March I got married. My compari, he bought a building for $43,000 so everything went along and I got to earn $50 a week. But on April 23, 1939, you know, the depression, we got kicked out. My compari he lost the building, everything."

Anthony Marola came to work in Brooklyn shortly afterward. His apartment in Manhattan is one he's had for 45 years, the apartment he shared with his wife and two sons. When I ask about his wife, he tells me she died 14 years ago, that he doesn't want to remarry. "I like to come here and be with my friends."

He eats once a day when he feels hungry. "Maybe tonight I feel hungry again so I eat ice cream, maybe a banana and that's all. I pay one dollar a day to come here because those crooks, sure they say I pay less because I'm old but I got to go on the subway the time they tell me."

When I ask him how he is so agile, so active, he explains, "I got to be active. Did I tell you I used to be a six-day bicycle racer on 26th street and Madison Avenue? That's the first Madison Square Garden, you know, and it was in 1911."

The entire time we talk I hear the man who gave me the seat mumble to the woman, to the other man, that he won't speak to me, he doesn't know me, I could be anybody. "How do I know you're a writer? I want proof."

I go back to my apartment and get *Woman to Woman*. He sees it, looks at my photo on the back, says, "That's her alright." Still he is dissatisfied. He turns to the woman and warns her about me.

She tries to appease him. "Don't be that way. Maybe God sent her to show the world we're alive, we have spirit, we have feelings. Young people don't understand us. Maybe they'll read her book and understand more. If you're not open to everything, you learn nothing. You have to listen to everything." She turns to me. "My husband, he was a giant. Men like him come once in a lifetime. But he loved me and you know why? Because I am simple. I listened to him."

The man nudges her. "Don't talk to her. You don't know her."

And the harmonica player is watching, saying nothing. I show them my book again, tell the man I feel hurt by his remarks. The woman begins to cry.

"Don't listen to him and his suspicions. He doesn't mean anything. All men are suspicious. They are babies. You see how they're little boys. My husband, he always looked for a younger version of me. All men look and in the end when he couldn't find one he said till death do us part. That was something for him to say, till death do us part. Towards the end he saw my potential and it made him feel bad. He started to see what I was like."

She began sobbing, grabbed me, held me while tears flowed from her eyes. "Don't be insulted because of what he said. He don't mean nothing."

I could only blurt out a "don't cry."

"All my life was like life and death to me. From the time I was a little girl it was life and death. My parents were disappointed in me and you know something, I was disappointed in them. I feel cheated and disappointed in myself."

"Why didn't you do more?"

"Because of the time, don't you understand? I couldn't make anything of my life so I made something of my husband's life. Don't you do it, you hear. The times are different now."

The harmonica player snickered. "Oh, all you women are alike. You got everything so why do you complain?"

"You see how they're little boys. They can't even communicate."

"I'm married to my wife for 45 years and we communicate all the time."

The suspicious man hasn't taken his eyes off me. "Listen, I didn't mean to offend you before. I'm sorry you were so insulted but how do I know you? I'm here 51 years and I don't know you."

"I told you I'm here less than a year."

"I got my job to think of. How do I know you won't get me in trouble?"

The guitarist excused himself, told us he was going back to New York. The married man challenged me. "Do you know the book telling men how to get along with women? It's written by some doctor."

"No."

"He says all women are born she-devils."

I stare at him. "Is that how you communicate with your wife, with that kind of feeling?"

He sneers. "What are you, a Ms.?"

"That's right. I am a Ms."

"That's what this doctor said in the book. He said all women are she-devils, they're all the same."

The woman stopped crying, turned to him. "Oh no, all women are different and we're all beautiful. It's men who are all the same. Everyone of you."

"You believe what she says?" he asks me. "You believe it?"

I'm too disgusted to respond.

The woman is laughing now. "She's a Ms. and has three sons. That's good. I like that. Listen, don't go away. At 3:30 they leave."

To show we're alive. To show we have spirit. These words resound like a symphony, said by so many of the people I spoke with, angrily, happily, triumphant. Then there are the other voices, people my own age confronting me, asking me why I stopped writing a novel to write about old people.

"I wouldn't want to read it."

"It's depressing. Why should I think about that now?"

My first answer to why I was writing the book was, I owe it to my grandparents and my mother and my father Morris Bluh who died in 1969 and would be cheering me on if he were alive.

But that's too pat even if it's true. I tend to agree with Madelaine Massenoir. Younger people, and that includes me, are afraid of their own eventual old age so I'm not exactly being altruistic. I'm also agreeing with Charles Raymond when he says anything we do now will help us later on. I also want to be able to look at my mirror image and not long for a mustache to hide the lines.

In Tucson, I am invited to a party where everybody but older people (older being 45 and up) is dancing. I join my age group and then get up, deciding even at my advanced age of 49 I have a right to dance too. A woman stops dancing, looks at me and says, "Hey, Bonnie can really dance."

I get on my high horse and say, "Of course I can dance. I taught at Arthur Murray and had my own studio."

Then I see her expression which is one of pleasure and I join her smile and dance on.

Lois Palmer is a woman who has enjoyed all the ages of her lifetime but like Livia Beauregarde she is disturbed that she's so changed physically. She groans, "I look horrible, old and ugly."

"You do not. I don't know why you say that." And she doesn't.

"So many people tell me that but I can't believe it. I wish I could. I know it's ridiculous at my age to wear make-up but I dislike myself less with make-up on than if I didn't have it on. And I can't quite get myself to stop touching up my hair even though it doesn't make sense. You can put down in your book that the years I enjoyed the most was when I was a sex object and I told my brother that when I was no longer attractive to men I knew my life would be over."

When Lois Palmer was 69 she moved to the French Quarter of New Orleans, leaving all her good friends in New York and Philadelphia where she lived and worked as a feature writer for magazines. Although she misses her friends she was attracted to the lifestyle here, the friendliness of the people. And the weather. "My prediction is 60 degrees cold. 70 cool. 80 comfortable and 90 grand. I like candle-bending weather."

She is presently writing her life story. Sex, she tells me, is what her book is all about. "Of course nobody would expect that from an 86-year-old woman but then people know so little about people in general, especially oldies. They put us in their neat little boxes." Her mind dances around the room. "My book. I want it to spring like Venus, full blown from the forehead of Zeus."

How does she herself feel about getting older? She says, "What does it matter? People look at you and see whatever age they choose anyhow, so let them decide. I was born free of all worry about age unlike most people who are age-conscious and devote energy to how old they are and how old you are. I really don't care. Of course, people do look down on me now because I'm old but I'm glad that I never looked down on anybody just because they were old. And I think if I've made any progress it's due more to older people than young ones.

"You can say this for me. I think the word 'golden-ager' is horrible. I would rather be called an oldie than anything I can think of, since I am older than anybody. And I do feel alienated but I'm terribly glad that I know people who are a great deal younger than I am."

She springs from the sofa, offers me tea, then is sorry she did, complaining the tea she orders hasn't arrived yet and all she has is supermarket tea which she dislikes drinking, much less offering.

I follow her into the kitchen while she puts the kettle on and continues talking. "I think you have to learn to accept being an oldie as you have to learn to accept what you are, even if you don't like that too much. The little old man who reads the gas meter said, how old are you and I said I'm much too old to talk about it. And he said, I've been watching you. You don't move like an old person."

She looks amused. "I may have the wrinkles but I don't walk like an old person. Before, I used to fly when I walked."

She takes me out into the garden in back of her house. The apartment she rents has just been reduced by her young landlord who is aware that her finances are limited. Ms. Palmer discusses money, saying it never meant much to her but now that she's forced to live solely on social security it is a problem. Still, she will not give up concerts or theatre which she loves. "Most of my friends ask if I regret throwing money away. I answer I enjoy every cent I wasted, wasted according to them."

When we finish tea, she shows me the garden, calling every bush and flower by name. She reminisces about the trip she took to Japan when she was 77. Suddenly she stops and gasps, "Oh my."

Lois Palmer spots a rather strange looking black and white

creature. "Bonnie, what do you think it is? Isn't it fascinating! I must show it to my landlord. Don't take your eyes off it," she says as she runs back into her apartment. My eyes are glued to this creature. She is back within minutes with a small box with airholes. Gently she places it inside. "Do you think it's safe? Do you think it's comfortable? Oh I can't wait to hear what Carl [her landlord] thinks it is."

It is late. We sit in her apartment talking. As I go to leave I ask Ms. Palmer if she ever gets lonely. She gives me a warm hug which I happily return. "It was so lovely being with you and sharing. That's the only thing I miss now that I'm old, not being able to run to anyone when I see something unusual. I want to tell somebody about it at the time but there isn't anybody usually."

Lois Palmer calls herself an oldie but Mike Sweetman calls himself old stiff.

He pokes through the industrial trash, a cap on his head, long rubber gloves on his hands, then stops to talk with me, a toothless smile on his face. "I was born in the town of lost souls on the Purgertory River in Lasan, Colorado."

I don't know if there is such a place but I do know there is a person named Mike Sweetman. He has lived in Seattle since 1942 and remarks that after travelling all over he likes this city the best. His working days ended when he was 66. I ask what he's been doing since then.

"Puttering. That's the best thing I could call it. Nothing much of importance to do. I haven't the strength to work."

I make one of my dumb statements. "You look happy."

"I'm not happy or particularly unhappy."

When I ask if he considers himself an old person he answers, "I certainly do. I'm 72 years old."

"What do you like to be called, senior citizen, old person, elderly or what?"

It's then that I get the answer, "Old stiff would suit me better. I like it better anyhow."

"Have you liked your life?"

He grins. "Not particularly, but I've lived it. I've done most everything that was hard and heavy and dangerous. Sheet metal work. I worked in the Texas oil fields since 1927. Those companies put you at anything and you did it or you got fired. There were no unions, no safety laws, no nothing then. It was raw and wild and rough. Of course those were Prohibition days, everything was moonshine."

He claims he never gets lonely, doesn't miss his old friends who are all gone. "Funny thing about life. I don't understand it, can't make any sense of it."

"Could you make any sense of it when you were 20?"

"No, not really."

"What was important then?"

"Hanged if I know. Probably moonshine."

"When you were 30?"

"I suppose by then the important thing was money. Still is of course. At 50 no change to speak of, not even today. I don't know. I always had the uncanny ability to see how things would turn out and it always got me in trouble. I could see what was happening in Korea and Vietnam. Attacking eastern Asia is like punching holes in a pan of soft dough. The holes fill as fast as they're made. That's what happens, don't you see. Not even Ghengis Khan could conquer that country. He'd conquer the seacoast but not the land."

He tells me he thinks a lot about history although he never studied it formally. School to him is waste of time. "You see there's too much emphasis put on school and environment. Schooling and environment only bring out what's there. Most people, for instance, ignore the basic rules of creation. Like produces like. If the parents have nothing, the kids have nothing. You take a Shetland pony. You can raise it in a thoroughbred stable but you can't make it into a thoroughbred. You can't tell me a Shetland pony is going to win. If you can make it into a thoroughbred I might change my mind. You might get there in 5,000 years. Christ said somewhere in the Bible that figs don't grow on thistles. I can't tell you where it is but I read it. It's all so simple."

He purses his lips, looks out into the street, then says, "I take it back. School is not a waste of time. You can always learn something, even old stiffs like me. Trouble is most people don't learn anything and others don't use what they learn. If the average person learned first-grade arithmetic they'd be better off. It takes a baseball bat to prove to the average person they're paying a lot when they buy things on time. They can't figure it out and it's so simple."

"What advice would you give young people?"

"I don't give advice. I'll tell you. All the elderly people, the clergy and the teachers and all those kind of people gave me advice when I was a boy and I don't say they were a bunch of lying so-and-so's but they might as well have been because everything they told me turned out to be untrue. Not a thing turned out the way people said. So there's no reason to believe I could give any advice that would be better."

"Mike, before, when I asked about your life you said you didn't particularly like it but you lived it. Is there something you think you missed?"

He nods. "Years ago I wanted to sign up with one of the Venezuela oil fields and work but I couldn't because of the depression. And I never learned to play any music. I would have liked that. I learned to dance when I was over 40. Hardest thing I learned to do in my life. I had to march in the army but I could never keep time."

"Is sex important?"

"It is and it isn't. It's the reason we're here but it's exaggerated most of the time. You see it's very simple. Sex isn't necessary for reproduction but it is necessary for evolution. Without evolution there'd be no change. The dandelions have no sex but a dandelion can't change. There's a lot of things that have no sex. Don't ask me why. If you don't adapt you die. You just disappear. And that goes for old stiffs like me."

"Mike, can I use your name?"

"If it would help, sure."

"I think you were great. I loved listening to you."

"It's all just common sense. I wish you luck with your book."

It's strange how we have to label people; youth, young adult, middle-aged and then finally old. "Old" must be a dirty word because there are so many substitute words, golden-ager, senior citizen, elderly. Lois Palmer wants to be called an oldie. Mike Sweetman an old stiff. But how do others feel?

I start with my mother who tells me what happened the first time she went to a camp for older adults. The camp was brand new. They drove from New York to the country in Pennsylvania in a hired bus. The sign as they made the turn off to the country road said VACATION CAMP FOR THE AGED.

"Bonnie, when we saw that sign there was such an uproar on the bus. We all felt indignant. We felt like we were going to a nursing home, a place where they put old people who have no place to go."

The minute they arrived at the camp they told the director, and one of the bus passengers got a pan of paint and a ladder and he painted the words FOR THE AGED out. "We all watched. I want you to know this is before we even unpacked."

As a result of this incident and similar ones my mother is now on the Advisory board of VASCA, Vacations and Senior Centers Association. She also objected to the word "camp," claiming it's no good and that one immediately thinks of little kids and what they do in camp, which is untrue. Since that time the names have been changed to Vacation Center or Lodge for Senior Adults.

I ask her what she thinks of the term golden-ager. "I don't like it. Well what's golden age? Is there a silver age or an aluminum age? What makes it golden? Why can't your younger years be golden and your older years as well. And I don't like senior citizen either. Why does age have to be pinpointed? I never say my old friends. I just say friends. Why do they have to label us? Why do they have to put a stigma on a certain age? Oh Bonnie, when I think of that man standing up on that ladder painting the words out and all of us cheering, what a sight. Imagine, they spent millions on this vacation center and that's the only name they could come up with. It shows how people's minds work. They just don't think.''

How do others feel?

In Chicago I meet three women from the Free Street Theater Too, a theater group of people over 60. I ask what they like being called.

ANNE: Older people, because that's what we are. I don't like senior citizen. I always hated that.

HILDA: This is not unanimous. I think senior citizen is perfectly fine. It's a perfectly honorable name. Senior citizens in Greece and Rome were highly honored.

BERTHA: In any place age is revered more than here in America.

ANNE: It's an empty phrase in the United States, a completely empty phrase. It's phony. Because they call you a senior citizen but they treat you as though you didn't exist and I think that's why I'm so angry about it. It's a lovely word and they're living on that phrase. The other thing is, they put you into a category so that senior citizens are supposedly all alike and we're not.

Dr. Alfred Bayne writes a column for a senior paper called *Silver Power*. He says he's very militant and will continue fighting to have senior citizens recognized for the people they are. "They're like fine china. The older they get the more precious they get. They don't lose any of their qualities."

He likes the term senior citizen and says, "I wear it like a badge of honor, wear it with pride. It only comes to the fortunate few. I think the most pitiful thing in the world is to see an elderly person that hasn't matured. It's like an infant trying to smoke a cigar. You mention the word old to them and it's a dirty word. I think, how simple that person is."

Dr. Charles Still, a physician in Phoenix who is on the Governor's Advisory Council for the Aged says, "You know we talk about the golden years being tarnished years. They're only tarnished because we let them be and I think there's a lot of negative thinking amongst older people as well. They think we can't make the situation any better so we'll just sit here and take it."

What does he like to be called? A person.

Louise Markham, 86, who works in San Francisco with people over 65 says, "I think all the euphemisms used for older people are ridiculous, tommyrot. I have no objections to being called old. I am old."

The majority agreed with my mother, that labeling was unnecessary and that until older people are respected for the people they are, the labeling will just feed the negative image.

My dictionary gives the definition of senior citizen: a person of or over the age of retirement. Under the definition is Usage: Senior citizen is objected to by some as a euphemism associated with the worlds of politics and advertising. It is acceptable to 47% of the Usage Panel.

First I'd like to know who is on the usage panel and second, why didn't the larger percentage win out? I myself would prefer to be called a character when I reach 65.

Forty minutes from Tucson is a community for retired people called Green Valley. One of the countless complexes for seniors that have sprung up recently, it has about everything you could want, if you like that kind of living, including a glorious climate and a view of the mountains.

Helen and Owen Evans share a home there. Owen, an accountant, works part-time at home. He was forced to retire from industry because of his physical condition. He was then 49. His disability has him in a wheelchair. He is disturbed that agism begins around 40 and believes that much of the problem has to do with insurance companies who ban older people because it affects the companies' pension and health insurance plans.

Helen Owens is the owner of a woman's apparel shop in the

large shopping complex. She bought the shop because "I've got to have something to do and I've never had time to play so I don't have hobbies."

She complains that only small size mannequins with young faces are available, that older women resent this. "On Sunday we do a fashion show. One of my models is just lovely to look at. She's a size 18 or 20 and she looks beautiful. Most older women here are not going to buy unless they can identify with the model."

Owen has spent two years on the Governor's Advisory Board on Aging. A major problem he feels is the negative view of older people. People who are older don't particularly feel old unless they're not feeling good physically. They merely look at these younger kids and it's the kids who are getting younger.

HELEN: There are advantages. A woman doesn't feel the competition she did when she was younger, except for a few that feel they have to have their faces lifted and all that kind of stuff.

OWEN: A big problem we face are the geriatric workers themselves. They're mostly younger people who are professionally dedicated to helping older people but 99% of them don't know what the hell goes on in the older person's mind.

HELEN: They *think* they know. Owen, remember the meeting in Phoenix where the young man, the teacher in geriatrics, talked about the man in his eighties who was up in a tree, pruning or something and he fell out of it? Well, to this young man this was fantastic but to us it was just stupid because that's something you don't do when you're in your eighties. To me the mind is important. Any fool can climb a tree. The point I'm trying to make is, these young people completely forget about the mind, any thoughts you may have, any intelligence. But they get very excited about somebody climbing trees.

OWEN: That they're physically able to do so is in itself remarkable. That they would do it is asinine."

BONNIE: I was at one of the senior centers and one of the women who was running the group was 22 and of course she knew everything about old age. She walked around like one big authority.

OWEN: This is what I was trying to get to—the fact that so many of these geriatric workers get it in their minds that they have learned what to do. And this is typical, a 22-year-old telling these older people what the hell to do. Why don't they utilize the brains and the experiences of older people, do a little retraining and put them in these positions?

HELEN: And at this same meeting that young girl from Flagstaff said a young man had put together a system where older people would come in and do the work and she complained that they weren't interested. We said it was because the younger man laid out the plan and then said you've got to be interested in this. Older people don't want to be told. We resent younger people telling us what to do just as younger people resent older people telling them.

They discuss a woman commentator who came to Green Valley to do a program on Sex Over Sixty. Helen agreed to have a group of women at her home. She asked Owen to go into another room but when the woman commentator came she brought a young man with her so Owen refused to leave.

HELEN: It was interesting because so many people think sex is dirty. You reach a certain age and you're supposed to forget about sex and, let's be frank, you don't. Well, anyway there was quite a discussion. The women felt there wasn't any particular change in their sex lives. The young man started out: 'Well, of course when you get older, there are such things as touching and patting each other on the back.'

OWEN: Boy, did they put him down.

HELEN: Yes, they put him down because it doesn't end just because you've reached a certain age. Why should you stop living when you get older, whether it's your sex life or your business life or whatever? We're conditioned to think that when we reach a certain age we're supposed to change completely, become a little old man or a little old lady, tend to your knitting. You may not be able to have children anymore but why should you stop?

BONNIE: Is sex as enjoyable?

HELEN: Actually it's more enjoyable. You don't have to worry about having children anymore.

OWEN: I don't think you turn off at any age. The younger generation seems to think that the older generation does. This isn't the case, physically or psychologically. And the younger people can't seem to understand us. They can't realize they're going to be there one of these days.

HELEN: Think back to when you were young, Bonnie. It was something that was going to happen way off there. You were never going to be like your mother or your grandmother. You just don't think about age. I didn't. And all of a sudden I looked in the mirror and there it was. It's a shock sometimes. You look at your friends and they're getting older, but not you. Anyhow, this woman interviewed just like you are, but in her Sex Over Sixty program she did most of her interviews in nursing homes and this is not representative of older people. But the young man had ideas of what aging was and he became very excited because he felt he was communicating with us on the same level. But when the women left we took them on a tour of Green Valley and he said to the woman newscaster, 'You must remember that you're not going to find this type of person in many places' and tried to get her back on the idea that when you're older you're sort of senile and all that type of thing.

BONNIE: That's ridiculous.

OWEN: It's ridiculous because we're not all that different.

HELEN: There's one more thing, and it's corny I know, but there's a difference between getting old and growing old. I think it's fun to grow old really because you're growing. You're not stopping. But when you get old you quit.

SEX

At the age of 15 I absolutely convinced myself that my parents who were all of 35 and 40 did not have sex. My parents! Never. I discussed it with my friends. They agreed. Their parents didn't have sex either. First of all it wasn't nice and we had nice parents. Secondly they were too old.

At the age of 44 in Italy, the year that I dejectedly walked out of the disco, a woman friend in her twenties told me sadly that her mother was just widowed. "But I'm thankful," she added, "that she no longer desires sex."

"Oh, I said. How old is your mother?"

"Forty-five."

"I'm forty-four," I gulped.

"You are?" she said. And then, not knowing what to say, said nothing.

Which just goes to show that things don't change that much, in young people's minds anyhow.

I ask Marta Torrens what it was like for her when she was younger. "When I was young, if a woman didn't enjoy sex she was supposed to keep her mouth shut. It also wasn't ladylike to have any desire for sex. But of course we had desires. People are people. But we didn't discuss it."

In Denver, a man in his seventies talks about his feelings today. "I'll put it this way. It's the icing on the cake. You can live without it but who wants to? I've got feelings like everybody else but there isn't much I can do about it. Nobody wants an old man."

In Cheyenne, I asked Helen G about the clitoris. She looked

puzzled, asked me what it was. She was amazed when I told her. And then giggled.

A man, 78, didn't believe there was such a thing and insisted I made it up. He yelled, "Get a dictionary. Get a dictionary. I'll prove it to you." When he saw it with his own eyes, he said, "Well I'll be danged."

Was he married? Yes. For over 50 years.

This is not surprising when I think back to my day. I reached puberty before I was twelve which came as a shock to both my mother and me. I was built straight up and down without a curve or bulge in sight. When I saw I was bleeding, to say I was frightened would be an understatement. I was sure I was dying. As a mattter of fact, it shocked me so that I passed out on the bathroom floor, the only time I've ever fainted in my life. My mother felt she had to do something about my ignorance so she went out and bought me a book explaining the so-called *facts of life*. The book was so technical I couldn't figure out which side was up. As for discussions on sex, my mother and I never had any until I was much older when the subject of sex was accepted, at least to talk about. As far as I was concerned sex went along with marriage, like dirty dishes, cooking and cleaning the apartment.

Sex is now a major subject, a subject pummelled to death by the media, rap sessions, shrink sessions, consciousness raising sessions, group encounters and on and on and on. If you're not doing it and enjoying it, you feel completely left out.

But what of the generation that was brought up uninformed, ignorant of their own bodies and needs and pleasures, the sexually repressed generation?

Nona lives in Seattle. She is 78. Married at 19, with three children before she reached the age of 26, she says sex always made her feel uncomfortable. "I never saw my husband undressed and he never saw me naked either. I never enjoyed intercourse. I don't know. We were all so ignorant in those days. Of course today it's so much better for the kids."

And for Nona as well. She masturbates with a vibrator, a gift her daughter bought her. "Sometimes it's two, three times a week, sometimes more, sometimes less. It's ridiculous to admit but I was past seventy before I reached my first orgasm. It scared me so I didn't use that machine for weeks afterward and then with the greatest trepidation. Now I accept it as a healthy alternative."

And her husband.

"Oh, he's been impotent for years."

Ruth is 69. Divorced for five years she admits her husband was a terrible man, that she should have divorced him years before. She stayed because of her children. "It's so strange but, miserable as he was, he was very gentle and loving in bed."

I ask if she feels she had a good sex life. She blushes. "Oh yes, very, but of course I have no way of comparing. However, I did have orgasms so I know what that is. I have a very good friend who's my age and she says she never had an orgasm. I feel sorry for her. At least I know what that feels like."

A man in his late seventies agrees to discuss sex if I don't use his name or the city he resides in. Widowed at the age of 55 he married a woman 20 years younger the following year. "I was a very virile man and loved to have intercourse. It was an important part of my marriage with my first wife. Sex was spoiled for me by the second one. One time I just couldn't have an erection. I don't know what happened but she said to me, what can you expect when you marry an older man? I was so disturbed I went to a doctor and he said is this the first time? Why, that happens to men in their thirties when they're tired. But my wife's statement so disturbed me, it made me nervous every time I got near her. Of course it spoiled the marriage too. She divorced me after two years and married a man ten years younger than she."

I ask him if he still has a sex life. He sighs, "All the sex life I now have is in my head. I could lie to you but what's the use."

Ronald R, 71, Boston. "My wife and I have a very active life in every way. I think a lot depends on your attitude and whether you enjoyed sex when you were young. Of course it's different when you age. Your body isn't as flexible and it takes longer to get aroused and sometimes I don't have an orgasm at all but my wife and I aren't so hung up on those things anymore. We were both so ignorant when we first got married, but we learned.''

"Is it more enjoyable when you get older?"

"I think so. At least you learn to be less inhibited, less stubborn. Well, I don't know. It's more intense when you're young but your ego often ruins the enjoyment.''

Florrie and Ed Lowry know each other since 1918. Both were in show business and both were married to other people. Through a series of coincidences, after they were both widowed, they met again. And saw each other. Then Florrie went off to Hawaii with a woman friend. While there she missed Ed and decided to call. ''I said, Eddie, I didn't know it but I'm in love and Eddie answered, 'So am I. Come on home'.''

EDDIE: I was 72 and Florrie was 70. And at 70 she could do six good choruses of dance and she still can.

They married ten years ago. I ask them about sex when you're older.

EDDIE: It's just about the same as when you're 28 or 30.

FLORRIE: It's more of an affection for each other. Do you know what I mean?

EDDIE: Oh, you have sex. It's a love sex. You're really in love and maybe it isn't as physical as often or as satisfying as often but it's more satisfying within the cockles of your heart than when you were just trying to prove how masculine and feminine you could be and how clever you could be with one another.

FLORRIE: And our feeling. We are so close we don't want to be away from one another. I'll be 79 and my baby here [she grins] we don't call each other by our first names. It's honey, dear, sweetheart, darling [she growls]. Daarling [grinning at Eddie]. When we first wake up in the morning we cuddle for the first half hour.''

EDDIE: Now you asked about sex and this is it. You might think this means nothing. A lot of people think sex is only the act of having sexual intercourse but it isn't.

Lilly M in Montana has been widowed for a number of years but not without male company. This does not include sex. "Not after I had a husband. No." And then "Honey, I had a few busters calling on me. One of them brought me the prettiest diamond I ever laid my eyes on, fifteen diamonds in platinum. I told him no. I wanted the ring but I didn't want him. I tell you it was the prettiest ring I ever did see."

I ask her if she didn't miss sex. "No. I didn't miss it at all. And looka here, honey, I had a son and he would've had a fit because he was number one on my list and he wasn't about to let anybody push him out. Well, it might have been a different story if I didn't have a son but you know how that is."

Eileen Glassford who was widowed when she was 40 and is now 68 chides me. "As I said to the other lady who interviewed me two weeks ago, you people talk about it too much. I haven't been married for some years and I'm one of those loyal people that just couldn't consider it. I think sex is a very private thing and I think loyalty comes into it and if you've loved somebody as I loved my husband you just don't go searching."

Dr. Charles Still believes a lot of older people develop psychological barriers after a certain age. "Sex is physically healthy for older people but they may be living with their children and there's a taboo set up."

A married man, he feels if he were unmarried and interested in marrying somebody he would pay attention to his children's wishes "because you may end up with them looking after you the rest of your life."

This certainly was the case with Lois Palmer who had a good relationship with a man her age. Both were in their late sixties. When they decided to get married the man's children objected because they were of different faiths and since the man was financially dependent on his children they didn't marry and eventually parted.

I ask Dr. Madelaine Massenoir about these psychological barriers. She explains her sexual feelings haven't changed but, yes, age has made her more inhibited about her body. "We think youth and beauty must be good which of course isn't true at all. When you have sex with younger people it becomes more difficult, because in sex it is the other person who sees you. I think always it is what you wish to see and if you find the person beautiful that is what I believe you see. I had an experience two years ago."

She pauses, then says, "Lesbianism is a social stigma. I couldn't speak to you freely if I didn't say that. I wouldn't be the same person. It is difficult for a woman. Maybe it is the same for a man. I know men and they don't want to come out. They don't want people to know. At any rate, I had an experience two years ago. She was a much younger woman. I remember that it took me quite some time to feel comfortable and this is when I really learned that it doesn't matter. The libido is not only involved with sex but with all sorts of things one enjoys. When I enjoy things I enjoy so avidly that I think it is something. When the libido is strong it can take in all things."

I ask Dr. Massenoir if her patients know she is a lesbian. She shakes her head, claims it would only hurt her professionally.

"The basic reason for prejudice is that people are afraid of their own homosexual feelings. I work with groups and when the word homosexual comes up there's a shudder in the room. After a year they accept their feelings. They don't have to act it out but they have to accept it. If I were a writer or an artist I wouldn't have the least hesitation in saying it and I must say that most of the people I'm around are not narrowminded.

"People ask me, how can you help people to be normal? I think bisexuality is normal. We're born bisexual. We're born neuter. I can't honestly call myself a lesbian. I'm a bisexual. Why should you exclude one sex? If you're really a mature person and you accept the person what difference should their sex make?"

To emphasize her point she talks of a patient who's in her late fifties and constantly says she wants a man although she's been abused by them. "For God's sake, what she needs a man for I don't know. She whines about having the man. She looks down on women. Yet she has two terribly exciting women friends. One is a lesbian. The lesbian hasn't proposed to her. I wish she would and then she could break out.''

"Do you think people become more rigid as they get older?''

"No. They were always rigid but I think as they become older it's harder to change. Most of the older patients I see come because of depression and you have to teach them how to live with themselves. People do withdraw into their shells when they get older. They think, for instance, that it's inappropriate and unbecoming to have sex. An analyst I know said to me, when I was sixty years old and she was several years older, my God, this woman is having a love relationship with someone her age. How embarrassing! She herself had given up on sex entirely.''

Not so for Betty, 73, who's married for 25 years to her 80-year-old husband.

This is Betty's second marriage. She calls her first marriage a nightmare. Still she stayed with him twenty years because divorce in those days was just not acceptable. "Psychologically I was frightened of sex. I never had any climaxes with him and it seems strange now that I stayed so long.''

She lived with her second husband ten years before deciding to marry him. She describes this marriage. "These are the best years of my life. When I kiss him I say you're beautiful and he laughs and says to me you know I have a secret. I love you more than ever. I wouldn't know what to do without you. The older we get the more I love him. We're compatible, even as far as sex is concerned. It's delightful. I enjoy it better today because he has patience with me and I have patience with him. So don't let people think that when we get on in age we're not vulnerable. I still have climaxes. We have sex three times a week and believe me it keeps us young.''

Dr. Alfred Bayne believes most men have difficulty between the ages of 50 and 65, but that a few virile men carry on indefinitely. "I think and hope Vi agrees with me that there's something far deeper. I'm not saying our sex life is finished. Don't misunderstand but each day we live there's something deeper and more meaningful. It's an appreciation. I appreciate her more. I don't know just what it is. It's a spiritual thing."

"Affection does not die," Vi adds. "Demonstrations of affection never die. It is there regardless of how it's expressed or we wouldn't be together. The other night Alf heard me at 2:30 in the morning and he got up wanting to know what the trouble was. The concern for one another is what counts."

"There's a great concern, Bonnie. It isn't a desperate concern. It's a natural flow of affection and concern for one another."

Jean McCarthy tells me sex was important when she was young but later on "it doesn't mean a damn. If I were in my forties or fifties I could live beautifully without sex and now I don't miss it at all."

Her husband Max agrees with her.

I ask when sex became less important and am told by Jean, "I think it depends on your health."

Max says, "I think it gradually stops, probably at about 60."

Jean interjects, "And I think men become impotent much earlier than women but the affection remains. It becomes stronger. It's deeper, let's say, it becomes deeper and gentler."

Max smiles at her. "It's a little different than what it was, the intimacy without the sex. You might say if a bird comes and eats out of your hand that's an emotion you like. Well the same thing happens when you get older. You don't think of the sex as much as you think of the intimacies."

Dorothy Berry talks about her husband. "When I hear him unlock the door there's just something about the way that house takes on a different feeling. I love being there by myself, when nothing is required of me, but when he comes home, oh, it's not that I'm tingling all over but it's just a warmness that comes in, it's a kind of completion. We love to touch and feel."

"And when you were younger?"

"It was just total exhilaration and it was something that I had not prepared myself for, that it was going to be this exciting and fun and, I don't know, it was just perfect. I suppose it was because we had a kind of understanding, an unconscious agreement and trust that you were free to be totally yourself, you see. And we didn't have to hold back or think, is he or she going to think that I'm this or whatever, you know. Like I say on the radio show, I'm so firmly convinced that sex has nothing to do with age.''

In Chicago, Anne B, aged 78: "People are people. There are some people who are oversexed at 80 and some people are undersexed at 20. I mean, I don't see why we have to divide all this. The point is we're always analyzing this and it's always according to age. We fall into the trap and the trap is this, you're a young person, you're a certain kind of person with interests and ideas whether it's sex or whatever. You're the same person you always were.''

Richard Hunter, 72, does not agree. "When I was 40 I was alive. When you're older it's an older life. Everything quiets down. Sex is not important. Might as well forget it. What's the use of remembering? Some people remember and get sick.''

Sari Dienes has a totally different view. "You see lots of people can love you but men fall in love with me now and I don't have to do anything. They are just titillated. They take me as I am and I don't have to marry them or have their children. I don't have to go to bed with them and it is just lovely. I'll tell you something. If you are a painter or a sculptor all your sex can go into your work, you know. The first time I heard that, you know who told that to me . . . Mark Tobey who is even older than I am. He said all my sex life goes into my work. It was many years ago that he said that and I liked the idea that one day I can just put my sex into my work and I won't have to depend on another person.''

Charlotte, 84, thinks for a long time before speaking. "If you need the flesh and you need to touch somebody I don't know if it wouldn't be the same thing to have a woman as to have a man. I feel if there's companionship, a closeness, what difference would it make if it were a woman? I've never had that experience because circumstances were different. I could do without a man if I had a woman who was close and intimate, one I could depend on. But you do need somebody to be close to, and it doesn't have to be a man. Still that's me but most women claim they do. They feel that way because it's accepted and having a woman isn't, but I don't see the difference.''

Livia Beauregard who is married to her third husband, a bisexual twenty years younger than she, says, "Everybody was sort of horrified when we got married but he felt it was time to settle down and I enjoy him because of his mind. Our marriage is a good one because we're friends. I mean, you can maintain a lover relationship for just so long no matter whom you are married to and then that becomes very ordinary. But it's important to have a friend, somebody you can talk to and somebody who's considerate. I think to myself, with all the problems we have, I am so much better off than these gals who are living alone and picking up a date every now and then or maybe going off to a bar and sitting there just hoping to talk to somebody. That can be grim and gruesome.''

Aside from a few women friends, most of her leisure time is spent with the male homosexual crowd. I ask her about women. She answers.

"I have seen women I would like to explore. I admit that. I think that all of us have a certain bi-quality, I really do. But nobody ever made a pass at me and I never made a pass at anyone. There was a gal, not so terribly long ago, a beautiful model, that I probably would have enjoyed going to bed with because she appealed to me that way and there have been a few others. I'd love to have an affair now if I could find somebody. I really would. Because I do not believe that when you're in your sixties you lose your sexual drive.'' She shrugs. "But I'm passive with women. I was brought up that way.''

Not so for Marjorie, 65. She says she had opportunities to marry but that was out of the question because she always knew she was a lesbian, even when she was a small child. She talks about being brought up in a small town. "When I discovered boys and girls were different *I knew* I was different but I couldn't let anybody else know it. I'd heard the word 'queer' used a lot among elders. They used to call them dirty and I said I can't let them know I'm a queer. I realize now I was around more lesbians than I knew but I was afraid to make the first pass and they were too. As for other people, years ago they thought we had two heads and we attacked people. We're just people with different sex preferences. Anyhow, all your sex crimes are committed by straight men. You don't hear about lesbians taking other lesbians on the street."

She talks of her life saying she likes being a lesbian. "I never use any artificial means in sex. I don't find it necessary or appealing. Years ago they had this butch and femme role but today they're getting away from that. If I wanted a man I'd find a man, so I don't want a woman who tells me she's a man or acts like a man or is domineering."

"Marjorie, how different would your life be if you were starting out today?"

"There's so much more publicity and understanding and there are more places to go to meet lesbians. It's so much easier for the people coming out today. I met Anita at a rap session and I was immediately attracted to her vitality and her keen mind." Still she stayed away fearful it would be a short affair. "I could never go to bed for sex only. I have to like the person, the personality, their likes or dislikes."

Marjorie and Anita have been together for a number of years. I ask Marjorie if her sex drive has changed over the years.

Her answer. "I think I desire sex as much but sometimes I'm too tired to do anything about it. Sex is important and necessary but a person could live without it. If something happened and Anita couldn't have sex I'd love her anyhow but in a healthy normal relationship it's something you need and desire. A sex drive is as natural as eating and self-preservation."

In Chicago, Doris, 75, says, "It depends on how you define sexuality, if you think of sexuality as the sex act. With some people it's discontinued earlier, that goes for young people too, and there are those who are not as interested either, so when you speak of sexuality as feeling for one another and a tenderness toward each other and that sort of thing, that's what sexuality really is.''

Roscoe, an 80-year-old jazz musician from New Orleans, says, ''I'm sick of these people saying the old folks just touch and pat each other. That ain't the truth no way. You start touching and petting and the next thing you know you're all roused up. We're doing the sex thing just like the young folks. Maybe we ain't sweatin' as much or breathin' as hard but it's sex we're having just the same as we did when we were younger. The trouble with the young folks and even older ones is they're ready to put us in the box before we're ready. I said to my son the other day when he told me, don't do this, don't do that, I said look leave me be, just don't bury me 'til I die.''

William lives in San Francisco. A man in his seventies he claims he was selfish as a young man. ''I thought of myself and of my satisfaction. I regret that I was so insensitive. Actually it took my wife's death to make me realize how unaware I was. My second wife taught me that sex wasn't having intercourse but the feeling you have for one another. We don't have sex as often. After all I'm no longer a young man but when we do I'm as concerned for my wife's pleasure as I am for my own.''

A widow of 70 says, ''Sex! Who cares! I never enjoyed it.''

''Do you ever go out with men?''

''Men. I'm disgusted with them. I can't stand the way they are. If the greatest man came up to me I wouldn't see him because I know what they're like underneath.''

Etta, 70, in Virginia was married for 20 years to a man who abused her. She pleaded for a divorce but her husband refused, saying he wouldn't ever give up his two sons. Etta left. ''It took such an act of independence to walk out on my children. I know women do that today but try to visualize what it was like in 1930.''

At 40, after several unsuccessful attempts to get her children back, she entered college, making a new life for herself. The new life included a lover. A woman. "I would never have initiated the affair but we did stay together for a long time. It was so sexually satisfying, the first time I'd ever been satisfied."

The relationship lasted ten years. When Etta's lover left her for somebody else she was so disturbed she moved to another city. "For a while after that I didn't care about sex. I thought if this is what it does to people, tearing them up, I don't want any part of it."

A year later she began a relationship with another woman. This one was married. It lasted another ten years. "The woman I remained with until she died was a lovely person. We were good friends but that strong physical attraction I had with the first woman just wasn't there. I'm not proud of that but I'm not ashamed either. The first woman, and this may sound strange to you, even though it lasted so long, I didn't respect. My father would have said of her, she has the smiles of an alley cat. Yet I would have continued with her if she'd wanted to."

Martin, in Los Angeles, age 66. "I married quite young believing this was the only way to go. My wife passed away about five years ago after a long illness. I felt I wanted to take care of her as long as possible at whatever personal frustration might ensue. She was a very remarkable lady and even though I am a homosexual, things have somehow worked out. I have two sons and am delighted with the way things have turned out. But my life might have been different had I understood myself and had the temper of the times been more congenial."

Martin tells me that aside from a few close friends he is a closet homosexual. "I value kindness in others more than anything. My world is very rewarding and sex is only a part of it."

He now has a monogamous relationship with a man much younger than he.

"I think the greatest change in my life occurred when he put his coat about me on a cold night walk and without embarrassment put his arms about me. It was unexpected but the most natural encounter of my life. Sex as a heterosexual was alright but not what I feel today. At 66 sex is what I imagine young love is all about. Perhaps I care about what people think of me but now there is more concern for my inner fulfillment. After I retire next year I will move away and be more open."

Effie is close to 80. Her husband died two years ago and she feels the loss in every way, including sex. "He was a marvellous man, just marvellous. Oh he had his faults like everyone else. Nobody's perfect." She admits her husband had problems sexually when he was 60, which brought on bouts of depression and anger. She says it lasted two years.

"We fought constantly. He blamed it on me. He said I wasn't responsive anymore. But we were very lucky. We found a good therapist. I had to practically drag him there but he went. The therapist pointed out that erections had little to do with masculinity which was very clever of her because I'm certain that was the problem. She also told us that the sexual life changes as you grow older but it doesn't have to end. I really don't care to go into detail but whatever she said did the trick because from that point on everything changed. In a sense we were closer than before. It wasn't that great excitement but it was very satisfying and in truth better because we became more aware of one another's needs."

"Would you say this is typical as you get older?"

"Oh I couldn't say, but you see what really is important is the type of person my husband was. He was a gentle soul, stubborn in many ways but one who wanted a good relationship. He was a marvellous man. When I look around at my girlfriends and see what they got I realize how blessed I was."

"And now?"

"I live on my memories, my dear."

A man in Chicago. "Why should I discuss my sex life with you?"

A 70-year-old widower in Philadelphia. "It would be great if I could find somebody to do it with."

When I ask him to explain he says, "Women aren't interested in sex. They never were." Was your wife, I ask? "That's my business and nobody else's."

A 74-year-old woman in North Platte, Nebraska. "You people are all alike. All you can think of is sex. Why can't you realize what we seniors need is companionship. Our problem is loneliness, not sleeping with somebody. Sex is for youngsters."

At the Retired Seniors Volunteer Program (RSVP) in North Platte a 68-year-old man says, "Sex is to keep the species going. The Lord just created us that way, to have sex for children."

How about sex and friendship? I ask him. His answer. "They are two entirely different things. Sex is what you have with your wife. A friend is an acquaintance that you like and enjoy. A man and his wife are one. They're not individuals."

Marion interjects. "Sex was not the most important thing in my husband's and my life. We just enjoyed each other so much, whether it was going off to a football game or basketball game or having a good time, maybe going to play cards or dance or something like that."

A woman in Denver tells me her sex life is better than ever. Her 50-year-old lover is responsible. "I'm an oddball," she says. "I always was. My husband didn't know his ass from his elbow. This guy is just gorgeous. He appreciates a mature woman."

Are there problems because of age? "Sure there are. You think I go around telling the world I've got a young lover? I'm telling you because you're writing a book and I'm hoping other women my age will read this and realize we're not through. Kids think we're finished but you can tell them for me we're not finished by a damned sight."

In New York a woman in her seventies says she used to go to Roseland for dancing but the men had other ideas. "Listen to me Honey. All those old men want is to get you into bed and then when they get you there they can't do a damned thing. They're all talk, full of hot air. At my age if I expect sex from an old man I'd be nuts."

And what does she do for sex? Jog.

One 70-year-old man said his sex life was beautiful. He confides he's having an affair with a 45-year-old woman. When I ask about women his age, he says, "Who wants an old woman?"

An 80-year-old man in Vancouver. "With all the problems the aged have it's ludicrous to discuss sex. We don't have enough money or adequate housing. Most of us don't dare go out at night and when you're widowed like me, you're always battling loneliness. We're castaways and sex has to be the lowest topic on the totem pole."

In Seattle. "The reality is quite simple. I can't speak for women but men generally become impotent in their fifties, not all mind you but I would venture to say the vast majority do. I still have sexual intercourse with my wife and we both enjoy it but it's only on occasion. Of course with all the medical advances that might change in time. As for touching and fondling and foreplay that goes on forever."

A 68-year-old married man in Vancouver explains sex was important when he was younger but is no longer important. I ask him what happened and he says, "I don't know. It just stopped. But my wife and I are closer together than we've ever been. We're a pair, more than friends. To me she's the ultimate. We seem to have a better understanding of each other than we've ever had."

Many widowed women like Eileen Glassford said they couldn't have sex because they would be unfaithful to their husbands. A number of women said sex was unthinkable unless you were married.

One 77-year-old woman claimed her feelings never changed but her husband become impotent five years ago and she wouldn't dream of finding anyone else. "He's a lovely man and if I did that it would destroy him. He feels badly enough as it is." And then, "I'd love to know what other women my age think."

A number of interviews were stopped almost before they started when the men began propositioning me. One, "You're a very sexy woman, do you know that?" Another, "The minute you walked in I said to myself, now there's an attractive woman.''

One married man who gave me a glorious interview ruined it for me at the end when he said, ''To sit in the room with an attractive woman gives me the most pleasure. What would be better than holding you in my arms, touching every part of you. We're mature people, we're both intelligent people. How pleasurable it would be.'' As he moved closer, I moved toward the door and left.

Four men asked me out on dates. One wrote me letters. Another called me on the phone until I finally was so rude he stopped calling. The saddest was a man in his eighties who said with much difficulty, ''I can see you're a very sensitive woman. Would you consider spending the night with me, just so I can hold you? I wouldn't offend you in any way. It's been so long since I held a woman in my arms.''

The funniest response was from an 87-year-old man in Vancouver, who as soon as the word sex was mentioned burst out laughing. ''You're getting kind of personal.'' Then another laugh. ''What a question! Is sex important.''

''Well, was it ever?''

''It has its place but I had to give it up. It leads to destruction.''

''Why?''

''Put that in brackets. Lusty flesh leads to destruction.''

''Are you saying that because of mistakes you made?''

''Well, we all make mistakes. We've all come up short. You know what I love the most? Personal contact. Oh my, it's a wonderful life. I sort of don't want to leave the old earth.''

In Harlem I meet with Ruth and Edith.

ME: How important was sex in your life?

EDITH: It was unimportant.

RUTH: It was important and I still think it important.

EDITH: Well now, I tell you the men have changed. You don't find men like you used to years ago. They've changed a lot. If I had a boyfriend we'd sit and talk and everything like that but they don't do that anymore. The first thing on their mind is sex.

RUTH: Not all the time.

EDITH: Now I invite a man to come and spend an evening and I'm not thinking of sex and it'll come to sex.

RUTH: You know, Bonnie, for some reason I never wanted to get married again. I've met men I liked but I just didn't want to go through that business of someone joining us together. No, I join myself to a man I love and as far as this junk of going through the wedding it's for the society and that's all it is. As for this love and friendship you mentioned, I met a man and we're still friends and we're still in love and he's old just like me.

ME: Ruth, is sex important in the relationship?

RUTH: Is sex important? Well, let me see. It's just as important as that sun that's shining out there. Now he's not near me but I hear from him and I see him anytime he comes north or I go where he is and it's wonderful. Everything is beautiful, everything is a part of life if you know how to use it. There are some people who abuse everything, love, friendship, sex. I'm close to him for 40 years and if I need help I can get on the phone or write a letter or send a telegram and I got it, so what more do you want.

HABITAT

A habitat is a type of environment. In the United States almost half of the 23.5 million people over 65 dwell in seven states: Florida, Illinois, Ohio, Pennsylvaina, Texas, New York and California. The first five states each have more than one million over-65's. California and New York have over two million each.

The majority of these people live in a family setting of one kind or another. Only one-third live alone or with non-relatives. Although the media stresses nursing-home residents, the latest statistic shows that less than 4% live in any institution, nursing homes included.

The average person spends most of his or her life in one area. As people get older it becomes increasingly difficult to change their habitat. There are children to be considered, old friends, a neighborhood where you are known and comfortable. Then there's your doctor, your dentist, your pharmacist, the grocery store where you get a hello. Yet many move because neighborhoods deteriorate.

Bryna Singleton, in Tuscon, admits she never would have moved if she hadn't been forced into it. "I never had the courage to go by myself and there wasn't anybody I could buy a home with." Seven years ago when she was 70 she bought a mobile home.

"I was quite thrilled when I woke up the first morning. The sun was coming in all the windows and it was so bright. I just love the brightness and I thought, oh, this is my first home."

She says retirement housing never entered her mind because "in my old age I'm not looking for luxury. I never had it and I don't long for it."

But others feel differently. Forty minutes from Nogales, Mexico, 25 minutes from downtown Tucson, in the Santa Cruz valley, is Green Valley, a retirement community where the Evanses live. Although Green Valley prefers not to be called a retirement community, 65% of its residents are over 65. The rents are reasonable compared to the rents of major cities but if you depended soley on your social security and you earned the maximum of $437.70 and were married, which means your wife received half of the social security as well, you could make it. If you earn the minimum of $114.30, or even more, forget it.

Owen Evans feels that the inability of people to prepare for their retirement is a large problem. He explains that many people try a retirement village for a winter, like it, sell everything, invest in an apartment or home in the retirement village and find they cannot make it financially on their social security or whatever money they've managed to save.

"When Helen and I first moved down here we got a two-bedroom apartment for $55 a month. That was a gimmick. It was half rent for the first year. Then it went to $110. That was still cheap. Now two bedrooms are about $200 a month. This means they've eliminated the lower income groups."

Green Valley management considers retirement age 50, which gives me a very strange feeling. Next year I am eligible to live here. But would I?

There are swimming pools, a health room with sauna, tennis courts, arts and crafts, a lapidary shop, table tennis, golf, tours and dancing. There is a large shopping mall. Ten buses a day go through the area to Tucson or Nogales. But the transportation leaves much to be desired unless you have your own car.

In 1975, 7500 people lived in Green Valley during the summer, 10,000 in the winter. At the rental office I am told they expect the population to reach 30,000 in ten years. I take the brochure and drive to the shopping mall. It looks like any other suburban mall except here the shoppers are older people. I stop a woman, ask her about life here. She says she came in 1969 because her husband had a health problem. When he died in November 1971 she went back to Michigan but didn't like the climate so returned to Green Valley. "I hope you'll write something favorable. It's just lovely. The people are wonderful."

A younger woman explains she and her husband are not retirees. "We live here because we didn't want to remain in Tucson. I drive the kids to a nearby school. There are many people here my age." How old is she? 45.

A man in his seventies loves it. "A lot of people don't think it's that great but my wife and I do. We're integrated here. Of course I think a lot of people got in the back door but that's ok. It doesn't bother me none."

Another woman. "You ought to speak to others. Of course some gripe about living here. I hear them but you can't satisfy everyone. I like it here."

A woman in her late seventies. "You can see for yourself that the scenery is magnificent and the climate outstanding but frankly this place is boring for somebody who spent her life in a big city. If you go to a concert in Tucson you have to have a car and the truth is there just isn't enough here to interest me. I can't wait to get back to Philadelphia. Those who say Philly is dead never lived in these parts."

On the outskirts of Phoenix is a community called Desert Crest. There I visit with Winnonah Montgomery, a former teacher who is one of the founders. She explains that her own mother's old age and illness, her isolation, made her realize that there just had to be a better way to live when you get older.

In 1950 she sought out business people, bankers and teachers. In 1958 Desert Crest was built. 160 people reside here. Approximately two-thirds are women. The home Winnonah and her friend Isadora share was built especially for them. The living room and kitchen are the center of this home and on either side is the bedroom and bathroom of each woman, assuring them privacy.

The monthly payments cover maintenance, recreation, transportation bus, doctors, drugs, hospital, meals for those who take them in the dining room. There is a laundry service, a cleaning service once every two weeks, gardening and a night watchman. The intercom system connects with a nurse so if you become ill during the night or anytime you just press a button and within five minutes the nurse appears. Outside, the grounds are well maintained. Covered walkways allow for maneuverability whether it rains or not.

Ms. Montgomery, 78 at the time of this interview, is extremely active in programs for aging and has been given the Senior Citizen of the Year award. Yet she admits, "This place is not for everybody. Not everybody wants to live with old people, even the old themselves."

I found Desert Crest in an out of the way area, beautifully maintained, ghettoized because it's so removed from the mainstream and certainly not a place where anybody can go without a good income. But people who do needn't worry about places like nursing homes. When you can no longer maintain your apartment or home you move to the lodge where you have your own room and bath and your meals are prepared and served in the dining room. When you are too old to live alone you move to the hospital.

Still there is alienation, a community of just one age group.

What do I write about the Pawnee? The residents sit around the lobby or the TV room or go for a walk or play pool or cards or talk to one another. They tell me there are parties and dances but I didn't see any in the time I was there. People are open and friendly, those that will speak with me, but there is an air of lethargy. The residents are mainly low-income people and in this hotel I find the largest percentage of bachelors. Since the Pawnee serves only breakfast and dinner, many of these bachelors have their lunch at the Salvation Army. I sit in the lobby and meet with a number of residents, all bachelors.

Walter. "Things are in an awful shape now. I can tell you that. Here I pay $162 a month for my room and two meals and I get $200 social security. Now how you gonna buy clothes or anything else, with the price of shoes and everything? That money, that social security, was intended for older people and now they give it to young people too. And I think there should be some sort of control on food prices so old folks could afford it. Just look at the price of coffee."

Bud. "The worst thing is they put us out into pasture, like some old horse that ain't worth nothing. Now why'd they do that? I'm as good a mechanic as I ever was, maybe better. But somebody, don't ask me who, decides you get to a certain age and you're finished. Well, I'm not finished by a dang sight but who's going to hire me?"

His solution. "Retire all those people in Congress. Retire all them rich people who own everything and let them see what it feels like and then maybe we'll get some action."

Richard. "The poor people pay for everything and in the end they get nothing. Work, work all your life and in the end, nothing. Now you take the President. He says he's going to help us out. You believe him? I don't believe him. If you ask me they should have put Mizz Lillian up as president. She's got more sense than he ever had."

Edgar. "This ain't so bad a place to live but you still need money. Doctors, for example. They're a damned disgrace. The prices they charge for the old is plumb is out of reason. Some won't even examine you. They'll just write out a prescription without taking your pulse or anything. Another thing, you take these hospitals, the care they give you and what they charge. You could push that button an hour or longer and they just come when they're good and ready."

Walter. "There's a guy here just come out of the hospital. He had to pay $500 above what Medicare paid. Now you tell me how a man living on $200 a month or thereabouts could pay that. This world is going to pot. I went through the depression time and it looks to me like it's getting back to those days.''

All agree that the worst thing about getting old is lack of money, loneliness and unemployment. Where did they live before? Bud, when speaking of his past, could be speaking for all of them. "We lived in the country, 15 or 20 miles from the nearest town. There were a hundred people there. All we had was a post office, a cafe, a bank. It was a good place to raise a family. They would neighbor a friend. We'd go to town in a horse and buggy and get groceries to last quite a while. We'd hang our meat in the windmill where it was cool. I thought it was the greatest thing in the world when they froze meat. I wouldn't mind living in a warm climate. I've never been to those places, Arizona or California or Florida.''

It's lunchtime and the men leave for the Salvation Army, all except Richard. "Looka here, Bonnie, see if you can get the book on record will you? I can't see good and I'd love to hear that book once you get it finished.''

Then there's the Plains Hotel in Cheyenne, Wyoming. The Plains is both the retirement hotel and senior center. From Monday to Friday a hot lunch is served for 50¢. The rest of the time there is card-playing, music, dancing and the usual talking.

Flo Harrison, one of the residents, invites me to her apartment. Living at the Plains suits Flo. "What could be better? I have an apartment, meals, everything. If I get bored I invite some people in to play bridge. It's heaven on earth as far as I'm concerned. I think I'm good for two more years. That's all I want to live. I know this woman who lives in a nursing home. That's not for me. I hope God gives me a good heart attack and wham.''

She speaks from experience. 15 years ago Flo had a massive heart attack. Still she chain smokes, knowing she should quit. In her bedroom are trophies she won for baseball, golf, bowling. She complains, "It just kills me not to do everything now. I tell you to sit around and talk to a bunch of old people bores me to tears. They don't know anything but to gossip and complain about everything. They say it's cold out, it's hot out. They just look for something to crab about.''

She explains that living at the Plains is like living in any neighborhood. You stay with people you like and avoid others. "I don't care if people like me or not. I never cared."

She talks about one of the residents who wanted to take her out for dinner. "I said to him, look at me now. When I get home, I take off my wig and take out my teeth. This old man, he never asked me out again."

She speaks of the changes, how Cheyenne is no longer safe for old people, how they're afraid to go out at night, how the sexual mores have plummeted, blaming it all on Kinsey, who according to her, "put sex on the U.S. map. Oh God, the world has changed so. I'm not surprised at anything anymore. I'm too old for all this."

Flo Harrison is eighty-two.

It all started with the Legend of St. Dymphna, an Irish princess whose father, the widowed king, decided to marry Dymphna and make her his queen. Horrified by his proposal she fled Ireland. She was captured near the village of Geel in Belgium by her father who had her killed by decapitation. Her death in 600 A.D. made her a martyr to the Belgians, who built a church and shrine in her name. Mentally afflicted pilgrims soon came to Geel seeking miraculous cures. These people were boarded with the local families. The arrangement proved to be therapeutic as well as practical.

So began the first placing of unrelated dependent adults in the care of private homes. The practice spread to other European countries and finally in 1885 the U.S. adopted the Geel Plan with Massachusetts the first state to have a Family Care Program. Today in New York City, Foster Homes for Adults accepts all categories of residents, aged, disabled, mentally ill and retarded.

In February 1977 when I first heard of this program I called and made an appointment. Now in October, after meetings, phone calls, etc., I am on my way with Li Nutter, who is the caseworker, to meet Regina, 63 and Lillian, 72. Although both had spent approximately 35 years in Creedmore, a mental institution, neither woman knew the other. Seven years ago, Foster Homes for Adults were called when the staff at Creedmore decided both women were well enough to live in a family atmosphere.

Their first experience proved to be successful. Unfortunately the woman they stayed with moved to another city so Foster Homes had to find another dwelling.

They chose the Randolphs. We park in front of the home, are greeted by Jenny Randolph and Regina and Lillian. Lillian, an extremely shy woman, serves us coffee, and cake she baked especially for us. She then disappears into the kitchen where she cleans up the lunch dishes. Regina retires to her room with a book.

Ms. Randolph explains why she chose to take in Foster Adults. "My father lived to a very old age and when he died at 94, I thought, if I could do something to help somebody else who's older, I would, because mostly when people get old nobody cares. They get pushed aside and I wanted to make them feel somebody cared."

The arrangement has had its traumatic moments: the night Regina had a heart attack and Lillian woke up the Randolphs; the ambulance ride to the hospital; the extra caring that Jenny Randolph gave during convalescence. The following year Regina discovered a lump in her breast and had it removed. Again a period of convalescence followed.

Jenny Randolph, who's spent the major part of her life working with mental patients, is equipped to handle most situations. Even the time when the Randolphs' dog was run over. Lillian and Regina were just getting used to living in their new home and suddenly became distraught because they had been attached to the dog. The Randolphs took them in their car, went to a pet shop and told the women they could choose a dog. They did. One that cost $200.

Upstairs I spoke with Lillian and Regina. The dialogue was difficult because I knew they'd been in Creedmore but it was suggested I make no mention of it, and let them speak of it if they wanted to. When I asked what they did in their middle years my questions ended in silence. Questions about aging produced puzzlement at first, as if it didn't apply to them, then answers like, I feel good, I don't feel old and it's important to keep busy.

What is significant is that these two women, if it were not for Foster Homes for Adults, would have spent their remaining days in Creedmore or be moved to a nursing home. Now they spend their days going to the local senior center, are part of a home atmosphere where they join the Randolphs on picnics, shopping trips, etc. During the summer they go to a senior camp for two weeks.

There are few alternatives to nursing homes. Foster Care for Adults is one. Another alternative is the day care center. El Rinconcita, which means cozy little corner or safe place is a day care center for older adults. Sponsored by Catholic Charities, Inc., it caters to people who are semi-handicapped or semi-dependent, those who live alone or are not capable of taking care of themselves. Designed to help those people and allow their families to go out to work, most of the elderly who come here on a daily basis live with their children. If it were not for El Rinconcita, this part time home for them, they too would be living in a nursing home.

Where do the participants come from? Most are from low-income or poverty levels. Most are Mexican and black who live within a five-mile radius of the center. They are transported by the one station wagon the center owns and Red Cross and Leap 3, a community service vehicle. They arrive as early as 7:30 in the morning and leave as late as 6:30 at night. Breakfast, lunch, mid-day snacks are served. Activities are sewing, macramé, beadmaking, ceramics, card-playing, pool, woodwork. There are discussion groups, morning exercises, physical therapy for the handicapped.

Participants are screened. Charles Raymond, the director, says, "We screen-in rather than screen-out. We know there's a certain amount of depression and there's loneliness so we say, we'll bring you in and then we'll find out where we're at with you rather than say no she looks like she's senile. Then in a week or two we'll discern where you're at." He believes that many people who appear senile are starving for attention, for somebody who cares and when they realize that at El Rinconcita many people care they become alert, different people.

Today is the day before Thanksgiving, the day El Rinconcita is celebrating the holiday. Charles Raymond and staff bring out the turkey. There is a prayer blessing the food and the people. We all sit at long wooden tables while the food is served family style. Most of the people talk to each other animatedly but there are a few who mumble to themselves or smile out into space. Charles tells me the center is the intermediate step before the nursing homes. "We're proving you can motivate people, keep them alive. We don't want to add years to their lives. We want to put life into their years. If you go to a nursing home you'll see people who should not be there. Yet they can't be left alone and this is where we come in."

Charles Raymond admits he was not interested in the elderly until he began working with them and feels most people don't want to face up to the fact that they're going to be old. "Anything you and I do now is a selfish motivation if you want to talk about it this way. You help now and this will help you later and don't kid yourself, the need will arise because only a damned fool thinks the society or relatives or our children are going to take care of us. This is not being critical but this is the way the world is. So when you're helping people in the aging area you're indirectly helping yourself because you're going to need help whether you're rich or poor. No amount of money in the world is going to buy a person the type of service they need."

There is no doubt in my mind after visiting El Rinconcita and comparing it to nursing homes, even the best, that whenever possible day care centers are certainly more advisable than nursing homes, not only from a humanistic viewpoint, but also economically.

The old priest has lived here for four years. He has a room, sparsely furnished but it contains all he needs. A Franciscan, he wears the habit with pride, complaining times have changed and most priests don't, that at a recent conference he attended only eight out of twenty-two priests wore the habit.

Born of a religious family Father John was ordained in 1915 when he was 26 years old. For two years he was assigned to work with the Apaches, then joined the army. After the First World War, he went back to missionary work among the Apaches.

As he talks a man peeks in, "Hello Father."

Father John bursts out laughing. "There goes my watchman. He keeps an eye on me all the time. We're not making love Father James."

"Are you telling more lies John?"

Father John grins back. "No. You can do better than I can."

The priest waves and walks down the corridor. "You can see he doesn't wear the uniform. Oh, did I tell you about the time I was staying with the Apaches? It was December. I went over to Three Rivers to be with them, had to cross high mountains to get there. We all slept in the same tepee and to keep warm they had a pit dug in the center where they put a lot of oakwood. In those days we all slept on the ground. The Apaches probably thought the white man is an old baby, he can't stand suffering so they put me next to the fire. At midnight I was shaking and one of the men said, 'Father you're cold', and I said in Spanish, we were speaking Spanish, *no tengo frio* which means I'm not cold. So I lay down and about an hour later it was just terrific. I was shaking all over. The Indian got up and said, 'Go to sleep with one of the old ladies. She'll keep you warm', and I said, *no tengo frio, no tengo frio*." He can't stop laughing. "Oh, they're really funny. I enjoyed it there. The more I got to know the Apaches the better I liked them."

He tells me that in a way they saved his life during the Second World War when he was captured by the Japanese. The main problem for the prisoners was starvation and it was Father John who was in charge of a work detail of 35 men. "I took them down where there were bananas and coconuts and all that good stuff and I told them now listen I don't want a one of you to steal any of that 'cause if you do you'll all be punished. I'll do the stealing. That's how I kept my buddies alive. Some of my friends asked me later, how come you didn't starve and I said, listen I was with the Apaches 31 years and they taught me how to steal and not get caught. Oh I love the Apaches and they knew it too.''

When I first discuss changes in the Catholic church the old priest disapproves saying things were fine the way they were, that changes aren't necessarily good. A person who refuses to be serious for long, he quips, ''You know when we get old God takes our memory away. You want to know why?''

''Why?''

''So we don't worry too much about the sins of our youth.''

Having changed the subject he talks about his trip to Mexico during the time they executed priests, how he swam across the Rio Grande wearing shabby clothes, finally ending up at the Shrine of Our Lady Guadalupe. ''I was warned not to go there. It was very dangerous but I said, they're not gonna catch me. Well, when I got there I saw about a thousand people going up the hill on their knees to that shrine and I said, by golly if they've got the nerve to do that in the presence of those guards I'm going to say mass here. And I said it. The soldiers looked the other way.''

I ask Father John how he came to the Little Sisters of the Poor. The smile is still on his face as he explains he was accompanying another priest, that they were to look over the place. ''But when I got here he said I was going to stay. He sort of tricked me.''

The smile on the old priest's face is no longer merry.

''How did you feel about it?''

''Well, I guess they felt I was too old to be at the parish where I stayed and there was nothing I could do.''

''Don't you resent the way it was done? Couldn't they have told you?''

''Well, I don't know. I suppose they did the best they could.''

He turns away, then faces me. I see a different smile. ''It did take me a time to get used to it here but now I think you couldn't find a finer place.''

Most older people live in apartments or homes. Emile Kahn lives in a large apartment on the west side of New York. People always ask him why he needs an apartment that size and he answers he doesn't, but if he moved to a smaller place he'd have to pay more money since his apartment is rent-controlled. I understand his predicament since I am in a similar one.

Terry Pettus lives in a houseboat, a home he's lived in for many years. We sit in his living room, surrounded by the lake while boats pass by. I am lulled by the lap lap sound of the water moving against the houseboat. In this community right in the center of Seattle, Washington are 440 houseboats all hooked up to a legal moorage site, with all the city advantages, telephone, lights, special sewage and a country atmosphere; lovely gardens, neighbors that care and look out for one another.

But are there many older people here? Terry Pettus, in his early seventies, says, unfortunately no. Many of the older residents were forced out because of high maintenance and the increased price of moorage. The older people who remained didn't have to rely on their social security but managed to save some money.

And then there are the street people. It used to be that you'd find them in any large city, those who literally make their home on the streets, sleep in doorways, sprawled on sidewalks, sometimes making their way into abandoned buildings. Now they can be seen in smaller towns. Often they're alcoholics, or people who've lost touch with reality or older people who are less frightened on the streets than in their homes.

I knew one of the street people quite well. His name was Happy and in his wheelchair he would hang around our neighborhood. He had one leg missing, was always swathed in all kinds of cloths. Sometimes in the winter he'd disappear for a while and then I'd think he died. But he'd magically appear. We'd always stop and talk with him, my three sons, me, the people in the neighborhood. We'd give him money. Sometimes we'd buy him beer.

He told me he was once a baseball player, had been in business, didn't want to live with his only son and preferred being out in the open. A few times he lost his balance and fell out of the wheelchair and we had to call the police. They were always sympathetic, understanding. They knew him well. He'd become the neighborhood character. They backed his story. He was a well known professional baseball player, had had a successful business, was a college graduate. He always had a smile on his face, some interesting story to tell. But in the summer the flies would surround his festered leg which was partially missing and the decaying smell was hard to take.

One time he stopped me and my family when we were on our way to the beach. "I'm sick," he said. We offered to get an ambulance but he said no, he didn't want to go to the hospital. He was afraid. This time he wasn't smiling. His skin was ashen. I said, "Happy, what do you want me to do for you?" Nothing, he said. "What do you want, Happy?" I want to die, he said. I want to die.

We did call an ambulance and he was taken to the hospital. The police said that he was admitted four, five times a year, that they would clean his festered wound, feed him, bathe him and then release him, that his son had given up on him.

I always looked for Happy, whenever I left my apartment. I found myself going blocks out of my way just to make sure he was there. At first when he wasn't around it upset me. It was always winter when he disappeared. Where he went none of us knew but suddenly when the weather warmed Happy was there.

I've since moved from the neighborhood so I don't see him any more but there are so many others like him, women, men, and all of it makes me wonder.

Happy avoided hospitals but even those of us who aren't street people avoid them. I have one friend who turns an unusual shade of green as soon as he sees the front door. So it comes as a surprise to me to find that Doris Cavanagh has been making the hospital her home for close to a year and a half.

A firm believer in destiny, this to her is her destiny. She talks about falling, being immobile, then walking again but it is all very vague. She does manage to walk to the bathroom to take a shower and takes a brief walk through the corridors before lunch. She says she put all her papers in order before coming to the hospital, and since being here has sold her home. This is where she plans to spend the rest of her life.

"You know, my dear, they tried to get rid of me and send me to Elco, to the nursing home, but I wouldn't go. I felt that I'm as much entitled to having treatment in the hospital as other people. I have lived in Winnemucca 36 years. And then in Elco, who would visit me?"

I am absolutely amazed at her attitude, her lack of depression and ask her what accounts for this seeming happiness. "Oh my dear," she says, "I learned to be happy a long time ago. When I die I want three days of celebrations, wine and drinking. I want my casket put on top of Winnemucca Mountain." For the first time she laughs out loud. "I'm going to come back and haunt the people who were unkind to me."

Eileen Glassford, who calls Gibsons Landing her spiritual home, didn't wait till she retired to move. At the age of 40, when she was widowed, she decided to winterize her home here, a home she's known since childhood.

"Always, even as a child I felt the happiest here. An interesting story is that the Indians here had a custom. When a woman was pregnant and the baby was due she would go out into the woods all by herself and deliver the baby. She would take the umbilical cord and put it in a wee basket and put the basket under a big tree or rock and that would be the spiritual home for the baby."

But not all people have or know they have a spiritual home. Some change location for other reasons. Friends of mine who retired moved from New York to Hallendale, Florida to enjoy the warmth, the lack of rushing, the company of people their own age

in a congenial atmosphere. It turned out the way they expected
and they loved it.

An older friend of mine tried the same thing and came back
hating it. "My God, it's like one enormous old age home. Who
wants to be with older people morning, noon and night. You can
have it."

I receive a letter from a friend whose husband, ten years her
senior, convinced her to move to a retirement village similar to
Green Valley. Unlike the Evanses she is unhappy there. A loner,
who's worked independently all her life, she feels she doesn't fit.
"Everybody is so friendly and lovely but I just want to be left by
myself most of the time. I'm trying to be friendlier and do what
others do, for Bill's sake, but it's very trying and I have a feeling
I'm fighting a losing battle. If ever I felt like an oddball it's here.
Everybody seems so happy and here I am with my long face."

Some people do change their habitat but most do not. The most
unusual change I found was that of Celia, an avid cosmopolite,
who changed her way of life totally. She lives as a member of a
commune, the only older member at Seven Trees.

Sitting outside in glorious surroundings I ask her why more
older people are not attracted to communal life. Celia says, "They
won't give up television. They won't give up private bathrooms or
air conditioning."

What makes a woman like Celia come to a commune? Married,
later widowed, with two sons, a well known editor, she says, "It's
what I always envisioned. People working together, lush vegetable gardens, communal projects, children's center. There are
three things I always wanted to do when I had leisure time:
reading, sewing and eating and all three are here. Seven Trees like
all places has its faults and I'm a pessimist about the probabilities
but an optimist about the possibilities. That's the thing to say
about Seven Trees. The probabilities are here and we're always
working to improve them."

The philosophy at this commune is that of B. F. Skinner, the
behavioral psychologist. Simply stated, the practice here is that

everything is free, food, clothing, room, everything, but the people living here pay by doing work and this work is called labor credits. Everybody must work a certain amount of hours a week. There is no sex discrimination and all jobs are on an equality basis. In the children's house as well as in the kitchen I saw both women and men. Auto repairs and mechanical work were also shared equally.

We sit in Celia's room which is small but extremely well organized. There she has the memorabilia of her lifetime, some from her many trips to Europe, books signed by authors who know her, old linens that belonged to her grandmother. She tells me that when she visits her friends in the cities it is like going to "the fleshpots of Egypt."

"Living here means I can't take a long bath in a bathtub since the house that has the baths is too far from here and I have to walk to and fro so it isn't worth it. I just shower when I'm here but when I visit my friends I sit and sit in a good hot tub."

The days I spend with Celia are unbearably hot, one of the worst heat waves, there is absolutely no way to avoid the heat. Her room has a fan which means she has rushing hot air, but I suppose it is better than nothing. Celia, at 70, says she feels old, complaining that she tires very easily, doesn't have the strength or energy she once had.

The oldest person on this commune is 44, the next oldest in her thirties but most of the residents are in their twenties. This she feels may have something to do with her feeling old, not having somebody her own age to communicate with. She says she doesn't expect to be alive ten years from now but this doesn't bother her. "Look, I've lived a marvellous big life. I've travelled, I've lived all kinds of lives. And I love it here. Of course I have friends that wouldn't understand this way of life, the lack of conveniences, but for me it's marvellous."

"Celia, what do you think happens after we die?"

"Nothing. When I'm sewing and I put my needle in here and put my thimble on top of it because that's the way my mother did, that means my mother isn't dead. The Latins had a wonderful saying which goes something like this: as long as you're on the lips of people you're alive."

"I spoke to a woman recently who believed in destiny or predestination. Do you?"

"Not really. We make our own lives. I could have done different things with what I had. I could have done more, but that was up to me. You see I was very lucky working with such famous people. Think of the marvellous company I've had, the brilliant minds."

The sun is beginning to set and a golden glow moves over the grass. We sit for a long time, past twilight. Silver stars blink through a blackened sky. I watch the silhouette of Celia.

"I don't have nice long hours to talk with people as I did with you, Bonnie. It's wonderful to speak of ideas and books and philosophy. I miss that. The people here are lovely, as you can see, but so young. They're not finished people. But look at how lovely it is."

She smiles. "When I'm off the reservation, when I'm outside, I get cantankerous about what goes on there that I don't like. Locks on the door, finding a place to park, being afraid to go out alone. Bonnie, I've done things alone all my life but I don't believe I could go out alone in the evening anywhere but here."

She talks of sharing, not having to worry about money, not having to look for her keys or pay bills. Or live in fear.

CRIMES AGAINST THE ELDERLY

Annabelle Smith is a shut-in. Her physical condition makes her a victim. Her age makes her a victim. That she has had two husbands and two children is of no help. Her daughter is dead. Her son wants no part of her. Her niece and nephew are busy with their own family but they do write on occasion. They've also made some effort to take Annabelle Smith to their home on holidays but she says timidly that it would be an imposition because her diet is limited.

She lives in a retirement hotel on Pike Street, a seedy section of Seattle Washington. The room costs $60 a month. She has a two-burner stove, one burner works, a very small refrigerator, a bed, a dresser, a table and one chair. She doesn't have a telephone because she is hard of hearing. A nun who knows her arranged for me to meet Annabelle Smith. She told her the exact time I would be there so she wouldn't be afraid to open her door. She has reason to be frightened. She has been mugged a number of times.

There are so many locks on her door that it seems to take her forever to open it. All this time she is excusing herself, asking me to be patient. A lovely smile greets me, a warm hug. I am treated like a friend. I take my coat off, then am sorry I did, because the room is cold. But I don't make any effort to put it back on. She touches my face. "My, aren't you a nice type person. Didn't it turn nasty today, dark and a cold wind."

There's no place for me to sit except the bed so I decide on the floor. She looks at me in wonder. "Oh my, you're so agile. I can't do anything."

I don't know what to ask her. I can't bear the thought that I will say anything to make her unhappy. Yet she sits quietly, her arthritic hands folded in her lap. I ask her how long she's been in the hotel and she tells me it's been three years.

"I hope you weren't upset by the filthy halls. This is the fifth couple that have this place. I guess they try to keep it clean. You wouldn't get me to use the rest room in the hall. There are so many dirty people here."

I know that an aide comes to help Annabelle so I try to get her to talk about it. I learn I am mistaken, that she did have an aide but let her go because the only exercise she gets is in making her bed and straightening her room. When she is inactive her body stiffens and she becomes immobile.

She is 86. How does she shop? How does she get food to eat? A volunteer comes sometimes and takes her in a car but they generally come when she calls and since she doesn't have a phone she can't call. She leaves her apartment once every few weeks to purchase food and once a month she takes a bus to another part of town to cash her social security check.

Why don't you go in the neighborhood?, I ask. "I was robbed here. I'd just gone to the store to get my check cashed and buy some groceries. I'm slow walking because I have arthritis so I take my time and I'm awkward opening· doors. There was this young girl. She was outside the store and she helped me to the hotel and then she helped me open the door to the lobby. Then I got this feeling inside because she followed me to my door. She said to me, do you have change of a quarter, so I reached in my purse to give her change and she grabbed my purse. She was such a nice looking girl, dressed so well. She ran away and I yelled HELP, HELP and the couple next door heard and they came out and called the police. When they came I gave a good description but I was pretty upset and the police said do you want to go to the hospital and I said no, I'll be alright. I'll take a pill. It wasn't too long before the police came back. They caught her and got my money but the purse didn't come back to me till later because she'd thrown it into a building a few blocks away."

What kind of a life did Annabelle Smith have before she grew old? She married a man who left her after her second child was born. She worked all her life, mostly as a waitress and had to leave the care of her children to other people. She married another man who also deserted her. Still she managed to save enough money to buy a modest home. When she finally paid for it her children were grown and gone.

What kind of daughter did Annabelle have? Kind, loving. But she died twenty years ago. She has not seen her son in over fifteen years and the last time she heard from him he wrote asking for money. She doesn't know where he is, if he's alive.

She sits huddled in her chair, the tears streaming from her eyes. "I pray for him all the time and hope and pray he understands. What he said to me the last time was terrible. I did the best I could for him. I worked at everything and anything."

Still she would have children again, saying she loves them. "I see them out my window, all colors, all sizes." The tears flow. "If my son hates me I don't understand it."

I try to change the conversation. We speak of changing neighborhoods. She talks of how the neighborhood she lives in has changed, how she's afraid to walk along the streets. She doesn't want to continue living there. "I'm hoping and praying the good Lord will help me make a change. He's been good to me so far and I'm sure he will again."

I ask her what she does with her days. Her tears are replaced by a giggle. "I'm a person who can find more things to do. My second husband used to say to me, Annabelle, you can just think and find more things to do than any person around." Then sadly, "I can't walk now, I used to love to walk so much. I would go with a woman who lived near me and we would go down to a senior club together. It's just a wonderful place for elderly people. We would have lunch there everyday and there was a card room. I never had much time for cards. I was so busy working. But they were so nice to me there. They were such lovely people.''

She bends over in her chair and reaches toward me. ''Maybe you shouldn't sit on the floor. Bugs are everywhere. You see they don't sweep in the hall. They haven't for weeks. I sweep outside my own door but I can't do it for others. I haven't the strength.''

Still I sit while she speaks of the people who live in the hotel, of the woman who goes around all day through the halls in her nightgown, others who frighten her. She sighs, ''So many things happen to older people. You don't know until you get old. I'm afraid now.''

As I start to leave she asks me when I'll visit her again and when I say I'm leaving Seattle the next day she touches my face. ''I was hoping you'd keep coming to see me. I feel good talking to you.'' Such a deep sigh comes from her small body. ''Will you write me? I love to receive letters.''

''I will Annabelle.''

And I do.

In Denver I ask Judge Otto Moore, 80, why so much crime is commited against the elderly. He claims it is a breakdown in family life, a breakdown in our appraisal of morality and the spirit of rebellion which started in the sixties on the college campuses, and that most of the crimes against older people are commited by teen-agers. I disagree.

''These are not the same kind of teen-agers who rebelled. They were fighting for principles.''

''Yes, but it's a carry over from the lack of discipline in family, the lack of influence of the church on the young, a lack of opportunity to make a living which was presented to me as a boy.''

Because there is so much crime against the elderly, the District Attorney's office, where Judge Moore works recodifying and redefining the crimes against the people of the State of Colorado, decided to hold seminars and meetings, teaching old people how to prevent being victimized. "Some of the weirdest confidence games you ever heard of come across my desk and it's invariably some older person whose life savings have been ripped off by some confidence person. They're just more gullible than other people."

I ask if older people can safely go out at night in Denver and the answer is, "It depends on the neighborhood but we don't advise it. We say, don't go out alone."

Commissioner Alice Brophy feels differently. As a speaker she often tells her audience, "I too am a senior citizen. I have some of the same problems you do. I refuse to abdicate and turn the streets over to the criminals."

She says she is a product of the depression so that taking cabs is often difficult for her and as a result she often walks in neighborhoods where she probably shouldn't, but is never fearful.

At the California Legislative Council for Older Americans I meet with Coordinator Frances Brown, a dynamic woman in her seventies who insists our system breeds crime. "If you put two and two together you get four. Unemployment causes crime. Here in San Francisco we've already spent a million and a half dollars playing cops and robbers, when that million and a half could have been used to create jobs for young people. We should open the universities and have free tuition. We need full employment for the young so they won't have to fear, so they won't have to mug the elderly."

Stella and Margaret are old-time friends who live in Brooklyn, New York. Until recently both went out to functions, to the theatre and to visit friends at night. Stella, 73, who's been mugged, rarely goes out at night now and when she does she's not alone. "People ask me how can you stay home every night. But I'm so busy during the day I don't mind."

Margaret does attend functions at night and often alone. She too was mugged and suffered a broken finger. Her husband, a reverend in his seventies, was stabbed in front of their home but it stops neither one from going, together or alone.

STELLA: I was at a marvellous dinner recently and the speaker was marvellous but I was so aware of the time I couldn't get the full flavor of the speech. I ran all the way home from the subway and my heart was pounding so. I have hypertension and anything can throw me off. I thought, this is foolish. It isn't worth the tension. Years ago I'd go by myself. I would go to meetings and afterwards we'd all sit till two in the morning and then take a subway and never think anything of it.

BONNIE: What do you think is responsible for the crime against the elderly?

STELLA: The young.

MARGARET: The young.

STELLA: That puzzles me most because most of the old people they attack are without funds.

MARGARET: They stole years ago. They took food from pushcarts and candy stores. But I think they rob the old people because they're weaker and now in the big cities there's not the same kind of neighborhood feeling where people not only felt the responsibility for their own kids but other kids.

STELLA: Years ago grandparents were important in the home and the children respected them.

MARGARET: Today they're learning their values not from grandparents or parents but from TV which is ridden with violence. I also think it was the closeness people had years ago. Now something can happen to you and people look and don't move, either because they don't care or they're afraid. I think all our crime has to do with alienation. There's an economic base but its mainly alienation.

STELLA: You're told to be isolated.

MARGARET: Keep to yourself. Keep your possessions safe.

STELLA: Isolate from yourself and everybody.

MARGARET: I'm not going to give up going at night. I understand Stella that you're all alone but there are some things I want to go to so badly I'd rather live with the fear.

STELLA: (sighing) Do you know, this fear of going out at night has changed our way of life.

In Chicago I find a 75-year-old woman who was raped a year ago. I think if I live to be 100 I'll never forget the expression on her face, the way her hands shook as she spoke with me, the unbelievable embarrassment she showed as if she were somehow responsible.

A woman who had been widowed for 25 years and hadn't had sex in all those years, she was accosted in the elevator of her building at knife point. Her assailant forced her to open her apartment door, brutally attacked her, the knife never leaving his hand. Sodomy they call it, fellatio they call it, but I call it murder. Aside from her closest friend I am the only one who knows. She did not tell her daughter or her sister who's also in her seventies. She didn't call the police or the Rape Squad. She was too embarrassed to tell anybody.

All of it is vague, a nightmare that will never leave her for the rest of her life. She remembers lying in a pool of her own blood, too frightened to move. She doesn't remember how long she lay there but she does remember that she didn't leave her apartment for a long time, afraid to go out and also afraid people would know what happened from looking at her.

She now lives with her friend and refuses to leave the apartment unless she's with her or somebody else. She agrees to talk with me because she hopes in telling her story it will help other women.

"I say to myself over and over again, why did I go in that elevator alone? Why didn't I wait? But all the whys won't change what happened. You can't know what I feel inside, you can never know and I pray to God you never will. Why did he pick on an old woman like me? What kind of hate does a man have in his heart to rape an old lady? I used to say to my granddaughter, sweetheart don't wear such tight jeans, don't go without a brassiere. You're just inviting trouble but look at me. Go, look. I'm an old lady."

She begins sobbing. Her friend holds her, soothing her, smoothing her hair. I sit in my chair, not knowing what to do, what to say, feeling sick to my stomach and the sick feeling stays with me for days.

I call my mother long distance. She keeps saying horrible,

horrible, over and over again. But should I write it?, I ask. "Listen Bonnie, you can't just write an upbeat book about us. Everything is important."

And then there is a long pause. I ask, "Mom, are you there?"

And she tells me the story of a woman she knew quite well who'd been raped. She lived in a slum and was frightened so she moved to a well-protected building but her apartment was on the first floor facing the rear and didn't have bars on the windows. She called management demanding bars but they said it would ruin the appearance of the building. She tried over and over again without success. A few weeks after she moved in a man broke through the window and raped her and robbed her of every penny. She never even heard him come in. Unlike the woman in Chicago she immediately contacted the police who came and drove her around in a squad car. The rapist was apprehended.

"Mom, did she talk to you?"

"Oh yes, she talked. She kept saying I never thought it could happen to me. I'll never get over it as long as I live. I have nightmares every night. Bonnie, she was beside herself. I couldn't talk to her as I'm talking to you. It was terrible. You know she was such a lively woman, so young for her age. She was a beautiful dancer and she played bridge and was very active in the senior center. She was vivacious, do you know what I mean?"

My mother saw her many times after the rape and she'd always say to my mother, Mary, I'll never get over it. She stopped going to the senior club. She stopped dancing. She stopped all her activities. My mother tells me, "She just gave up. The spark had gone out of her and she just went downhill. She kept saying, Mary I'll never get over it." And she didn't.

Two months later she went shopping in a supermarket, walked out with her packages and collapsed. An ambulance took her to a hospital. She'd had a stroke. My mother went to visit her. After that she visited her in a nursing home where she will spend the rest of her life.

"Bonnie, it sickened me. Overnight this beautiful woman turned into a little hunched up lady. Everything was drained out of her. She was just a hunched up old lady. She was so active and alive and alert. And those bastards now have bars on the window. Now, when it's too late."

"I don't know what to say."

"Bonnie, it's so horrendous that I can't even talk about it. It horrifies me to even mention it. It makes me suspicious of all men. I just look at them with a jaundiced eye. Those monsters don't give a damn, young, old. They have no respect for anybody."

My mother. Mary Bluh. I remember her telling friends who didn't go out alone at night, "What are you, a baby? I go everywhere alone. I'm not afraid of anything."

Three years ago she stopped going out alone. She refuses to be a prisoner in her home but when she goes out it is always with somebody and when she goes home she either takes her friend to her home or they go to the friend's home.

In a small town in Montana a couple tell me that for the first time they lock their doors, something they never dreamed they'd do. So far nobody's been mugged but there have been house robberies. An elderly couple nearby were victims as well as a few others. "Not too much mind you but enough to make you cautious. We was taught to mind and a lot of kids today aren't taught that. I'd kick the wadding right loose from them if they was my kids. I don't want you to get the wrong idea. We don't have muggings like they do in Butte or Billings." Locking the doors for the first time is something I heard in many small towns.

In Winnemucca, Nevada, just as I'm leaving to get the bus, an old man yells his wallet's been stolen at the bus depot.

In New Orleans I speak with Albirdie, 72. "I just think about living, living, living and I don't let anything worry me. But sometimes it gets to me. Then pretty soon it goes away. The reason I say that is, in February I had my purse snatched from me

right in front of my door. I had valuable jewels in it and I thought I
didn't want to live anymore because I thought everything was
taken from me.''

For two months she was very upset. She just couldn't believe it
happened to her. ''Throughout my working years when I bought
something for myself I thought it was worthwhile. A two-carat
diamond ring, a watch. Security. The next thought I had and
that's what pulled me through was, I'm lucky to be alive. And
that's how I feel now, lucky to be alive.''

The irony is that often older people in the worst situations,
people like Annabelle Smith or those who live in slums and are
constantly afraid of being victimized, won't leave their areas even
when the opportunity arises.

Tom Guznick, 25, one of the young people who is not only
concerned for older people but devotes all his time to them, has to
convince them to leave their homes for a cost-free holiday at a
Senior Vacation Home.

Tom is with The Little Brothers of the Poor. Among their many
services to the old, which includes transportation to hospitals,
houses of worship, shopping and delivering hot meals daily to
people who are homebound, are two vacation homes which they
run. ''Many people are afraid to leave their homes for two and
three weeks so one of the activities is to take the people to the
vacation homes for one day. Some are scared of a new experience
but many are frightened of being robbed while they're away, so
for some it is a good idea to take them for one day so they can see
what the vacation home is like and to show them when they get
home that everything is alright.''

Whether crime against the elderly is due to economics, alienation or changing morals, one thing is certain: these crimes are
escalating at a rate that is frightening. These people could be our
grandparents or parents, our uncles, our aunts and eventually
ourselves. If you live long enough you're bound to get old, like it
or not. So, you who read this, whatever your age, if you're
horrified by this as I am but do nothing about it, you're absolutely
guaranteeing your own victimization.

CHANGES

It is impossible to write a book about older people and not think about change. Many of the people I spoke with have lived through depressions, four wars. They've gone from horses to automobiles, dirt roads to complex highways, railroads to jets. More important, the values they lived by are now being questioned. The extended family which they depended on is rare and they've had to adjust to a mobile society. Where marriage and family once reigned supreme they now see all kinds of coupling. How do they feel about changes?

Sari Dienes, when asked if she thinks people change through the years, answers, "There is nothing in life but change. Even while people sit they change. Whether they know it, whether they don't know it, they change. They might change so slowly that you cannot recognize it."

I also remember her words "you have to accept change and go with it . . . I think one of my successes in aging is, I'm not resisting."

Terry Pettus believes change is taught like a fairy-tale. "For instance, they got married and lived happily ever after. They got into a changed situation, a new situation came into being and they were able to adjust to it and find a great richness or they may end up getting divorced. Now both of these things are good for those people. So it's the dialectic of the question. I think people should recognize that when you change your situation you bring a new situation into being. That new situation will very likely have negative and positive aspects."

A new situation is inevitable when you get older. You suddenly realize you have less time to do everything. Perhaps what was important is no longer important or maybe more important. I myself am no longer putting things off. I kept saying I'd stop smoking but procrastinated and then I began thinking I may not reach old age if I continue smoking. So I stopped. I'm also studying languages, something I always said I'd do and I'm studying the piano, something I always wanted to do. I now look at life differently, thanks to the people I've spoken with, like Catherine Van Bibber who tells me, "I think you become more honest with yourself. Yes. You could develop more courage when you get older, in saying what you think, particularly after you're retired and you don't have to make an impression on anybody anymore. I enjoy being retired for that reason. I value honesty with self more than anything. I think that lots of people who are perfectly honest, who wouldn't lie to you, fool themselves, and that always irritates me."

"Were you concerned how people thought of you years ago?"

"Oh yes. I used to care terribly. That's the one thing that changed. And I used to be awfully fussy about my clothes. I'm not anymore. And I wanted to be sure and say the right thing."

I ask when that changes and am uplifted by her answer. "I would think in my fifties when I felt more secure and more sure of myself."

Enid Allen says, "It's gotten so I can say to my friends you can kiss my capital A, whether it's a man or a woman. I don't know what's done it. I guess I'm with the times. People speak more freely and you never know about people today. Let me tell you a funny story. There was a woman next door to me. She was 65, a real nice person. We shared the same bathroom and we got friendly and one day my son called me and I was all excited. I'd opened the bathroom door and there was a man taking what they call a leak and I said to my son, the woman next door has a guy there. And he said, what do you care if she has a guy? I said, if she keeps him in her room she can have a hundred there but when I open the bathroom door and the guy is taking a leak . . . Ooooo, he said. He came right over and got me out of there.''

She bursts out laughing. ''Oh honey, everything has changed.''

But more older people are concerned with the lack of concern, the lack of caring.

At the Plains Hotel in Cheyenne, Mildred G., 91, tells me that years ago everybody was interested in one another. Everybody was ready to help. ''I think it would be hard to replace many of the older people. We cared and, don't you know, life was simple then. My sister and I used to take walks across the prairies, go to a hill, come to the top and there would be a neighbor on the other side, so we would visit.''

Marjorie sits with her friend and lover Anita, talking of the changing world, how people don't have time to enjoy life. ''And they don't give a hoot about their neighbors. Everything today is a money-making scheme. When I was a kid we made our own toys and we had one dress-up dress. Today they have a dress for every occasion and everything that's made is to attract the young.''

Livia Beauregard agrees that everything is made for the young, with little or no thought about older people. ''I'm always screaming at the shoe department. I say there are women like me who will not wear the funky shoes and the platform wedgies and who have to wear low heels because the feet give out.''

In North Platte at the RSVP office I speak with Martin, in his late sixties, who tells about his concept of change. ''Have you ever been to the Grand Canyon? You stay there for maybe three or four hours and you gradually see the colors change. It goes clear on from one color to the other. It's losing the old and picking up the new. So I guess our lifestyles are gradually changing that way. We're losing something as we get older and gaining something and we accept what is probably the best for us.''

Bryna Singleton believes she is no longer the person she was and that getting older has helped. ''I think when I was younger I expected too much and was afraid I might disappoint myself. I finally decided that I shouldn't care about always being perfect and to allow my mistakes. Really, everyone is doing the best they know how in view of the circumstances of their life. Your life, after all, is a reflection, from the time you were born up till now.''

But Eileen Glassford doesn't agree. She feels we're born with a certain type of id and that directs your life. ''I've always been a slaphappy cheerful person so my life has always been cheerful. I don't honestly think I've changed that much. I also believe that if you've lived to the age of 25 or 30 and you're not sensitive you'll never be sensitive no matter what you try to do. It's part of your personality. I don't mean sensitive about your person but to other people.''

I tend to think that often people change with the times. I also agree with Margaret who maintains people were closer years ago, that now people don't move to help others either because they don't care or are afraid. I'm not so sure people have stopped caring. Perhaps the changes have become so horrendous that some of us have turned off, to protect ourselves from falling apart emotionally.

Isabelle Van Frank feels we remain very much the same kind of person throughout life. She explains, ''Our judgement hopefully matures but fundamentally we're the same.''

''Isabelle, what were you like as a child?''

''I was very sensitive to suffering as many children are and the first vivid memory I have is that my mother and I were going somewhere and there was a long line of men waiting and I said to my mother, what are they waiting for and she said that's a bread line. They're waiting for something to eat. They're hungry. I couldn't understand why, when there was so much food in the nearby markets. You could see the markets from where they were in the line and I wondered why, and I'm still wondering why there should be such poverty.''

I agree with Isabelle. I agree with so many of the people I've spoken with because I think we all carry many conflicting ideas and thoughts inside ourselves. To get them all together is the trick; to be able to see the changes and know which changes are going to make this world better and which will only harm us. Being too frightened to help somebody, an older person, for instance, may end up badly (I'm speaking of the victim) but if we all do nothing we'll end up with a world of victims.

Dr. Alfred Bayne smiles warmly, puts his arm around me when I ask about change. "Why, everything has changed in the last decade. For instance, you're here talking with me which is a good experience. It wouldn't have happened twenty years ago. And just look at this beautiful center and all the senior centers that have sprung up all over. There are now Departments on Aging and second careers for seniors, which weren't possible years ago. We need the virility and the vitality and the daring and imagination of younger people but we need the experience of older people and the world is beginning to recognize that." To change and to recognize that old and young must work together.

I ask Alf Bayne what has changed in his personal life. He answers that he still walks briskly, swims, rides his bicycle, even though it is against his doctor's order, and maintains a large vegetable garden.

What has changed? He smiles broadly. "I can't run any more but why should I run? I don't find any need to run. Let's put it this way. I'm older but water seems just as wet to me, the sky looks just as blue as it ever did and I still get pleasure from spending a day such as we did. Come back and visit us. You're always welcome."

Change brings on a different response at the RSVP offices in North Platte where Martin says marriage has changed for older people, that often when they get married today the woman loses her social security, so they're just living together. "I have no objection to it personally because I think two people in their seventies aren't going to get in any kind of trouble."

Margaret talks about changes that should be made. Packaging for one thing. She is annoyed that packaging caters to the family and often ignores the single person. "We have no desire to eat two pounds of one thing. We'd like a change."

Anna feels portions for seniors in restaurants are unrealistic. "Regular portions are too large because most of us have cut down on our meals and the children's portions are too small."

Margaret turns to her and laughs. "I did try the child's portion. I went into a restaurant and I said I'm a senior citizen and I want a child's portion and they went and brought it."

Anna complains about transportation, a major complaint of people living in small towns who no longer drive. Although many of the towns have buses that run during the day hours of the week, they rarely have buses at night or during the week-end. She believes money should be allocated for buses so that older people won't feel deserted on week-ends. Many complained that since they no longer drive they cannot get to churches and synagogues on the week-ends. I don't know why the synagogues and churches can't keep track of their older people and make it a point to see that the younger ones pick them up and taken them home.

I believe Margaret speaks for many of the people I spoke with in middle America when she says, "Oh years ago things weren't as complicated and we made the most of what we had. I remember on Sunday having no one to play with, getting up on the haystack in the hot sun and looking at the clouds and wondering what they were composed of, where they were going and so forth. Or watching the cows and trying to figure out why the cow had this or didn't have that and what she was going to do. We didn't have electricity in our house and that isn't necessary, I feel. We just became accustomed to it. I didn't know what an orange was, only to see it at the church at Christmastime. I was 20 years old before I ate an orange. I can tell you how to make sausages. I can tell you how to make candles and I can tell you how to make soap. I'd hate to think that I missed the period from the wheelbarrow to the space age. I am a product of all of it and how many people can say that? Not you, Bonnie."

No I can't.

There are other changes. Some are inflicted by others.

Lorna B of the Melrose Plantation in Louisiana speaks of the way it was years ago. "Mr. G. Docker used to ring the bell for the slaves to go to work. They didn't have watches or clocks then. If the women wouldn't go with the men and work in the fields, he'd take them outside and whip them. I saw that."

"But you weren't around during slavery."

"I know that, Bonnie. We was freeborn but the people, they was under the bell just like slaves. It wasn't slavery times 'cause they freed the slaves but plantation people lived like slaves. I saw them whip the women. Then we went to the law and told and they was made to pay a fine so they quit whipping the women."

Lorna, born in 1884, talks of years ago, of the changes. "Oh, things was so different. I had a sewing machine, the kind you work with your feet. All the neighbors, when they wanted something sewn, they came to me. We didn't get no pay then. We did favors. Nobody had money. Poverty was among us. I was twelve, thirteen years old. Cotton was king then. We got five to ten cents a pound for picking cotton. Things was so different. I been working since I was a child. But the kids today, the parents go on welfare and the kids don't do nothing. They go to the gas station where my daughter is and she says to them, you gonna pick pecans and they say no. They're trifling. They get everything too free."

Reverend Cornelius Jones, the oldest person interviewed, tells me things have definitely changed. He was born April 21, 1861.

"I was born in slavery times. I was four and a half when freedom come. Mr. Lincoln, he signed the emancipation. That was December 1865. My momma and poppa, they was slaves on a plantation. If the emancipation papers hadn't of come I'd of been sold. I wouldn't know where my momma and poppa would be."

He talks of how his parents told of slavery, telling him how lucky he was to have been young when the changes took place.

Still some changes come too late. Reverend Jones never had the opportunity to go to school. He worked taking care of children for 25¢ a day when he was a child himself "and then I didn't get the money. My momma and poppa got it. Then when I was 11 years old I got me a job as a water boy right here in Chicago. I come here with the people who was putting up the 'El' and we would come down State Street through mud and water.''

Birdi, in her late seventies, has worked as a maid most of her life. She talks about the changes for blacks, how they weren't allowed to vote years ago.

''How long are you voting, Birdi?''

''Oh I don't know. It must be in the fifties when I registered. You know today how the politicians come round and want to know if you're gonna vote for them. And I say don't ask me to vote for you. One time you didn't want me to vote at all.''

She laughs, tickled, then turns serious. ''When they started, the way they treated us . . . Only a few people could vote, those that had a good education, and even they had a time to register. And what for? That was uncalled for. People are human. You're a human being but they think you're an animal. Some people treat you worse than animals. I went and registered because I should register. That's all. Things have changed alright but they's plenty of room for more changing.''

Many people spoke of advances in medical science but Helen Lindgren complains that too few doctors listen to what their older patients are saying. She told her own doctor, ''You should get all the sicknesses we have. Then maybe you'll be able to help us.''

And James Charles Mattison is bothered by the impersonal attitude. ''Years ago doctors knew you. Not today. I don't think much of them. I'm a better doctor myself. I can tell you what's happening in my body. My advice to the old people is to change your doctor if you're not making any headway. Don't hesitate.''

Frances Brown, when speaking for herself, voices the opinion of so many others. ''Changes? What changes! We now have Medicare which should be a good thing for older people but the truth is the doctors are making the money off Medicare and the old are being ripped off. I recently had minor surgery. I've been paying for Medicare since I was 60 and I'm 74 so it's the first time I had to ask for anything and still I paid 20% of the bill. Preventive medicine is what we need. This is what would save money in the long run but Medicare does not pay for this.''

I confront Professor Giovanni Costigan with the subject of changing. I ask if we've learned anything from history and does human nature change?

His answer: ''The chief conviction I've derived from a lifetime study of history is that on the whole mankind learns nothing. The French say the more people change the more they're the same. And this I'm convinced is true. I wish it weren't so. The fact that mankind has not learned the horrors of war is one example. In my own lifetime I've seen two world wars and the concentration camps which were far worse than either of the wars. Yet most people, above all young people, only want to forget. I don't blame them but they don't want to be bothered and the survivors often don't either so how can we learn from history when its dominant motive is to forget the lessons of history, or even worse, falsify them?''

''Before we continue, I'd like to point out that there has been a change in the language. You say mankind and I say humankind to include all people.''

''I say mankind simply because I've done it all my life but I agree with you. To speak of humanity is better.''

''Why don't you think we can change?''

''The reason we never change is because human nature does not change. In a short period you can see certain changes but in a large period all is the same essentially as it was before. I mean, it's useless to pretend that we've changed. One sees the ardor and enthusiasm of youth in every generation, my own in the past. We were going to change the world. Four thousand years of human beings fail but we're not going to. It's still worth fighting for but it doesn't come about in a single generation. While changes are being made, the same old humans will be at work, and to hold out messianic visions to youth is always to disappoint them and probably make them cynical so it's better not to do so.''

"I don't agree. I think without change there is little hope and we have to show young people that change is absolutely necessary for life and survival."

"I suggest you study history and if you do the lesson is inescapable. Human beings do not change. Now we can kill millions where before we killed dozens and unless human nature does change to control the atom bomb, then indeed we're doomed. I happen to have been very much influenced by Freud and if you have that approach the answer is that people's deepest nature is shaped by their experience in infancy. The mistakes you make when you are young you make for the rest of your life. It's probably impossible to change one's basic nature but one's ideas about the world, what one will do with this dynamic force which we have, one can change."

"Have your students changed over the years?"

"Oh indeed. There have been three periods in my own life when students have been more interesting than others. The students of the Depression, of the Second World War and those students reacting to the Vietnam War. But I often wonder about these people ten years later. You know the sayings of the sixties: 'Don't trust anyone over 30'."

"One thing that has changed is our concept of the family. So many of us feel the nuclear family does not work."

"Well, Ms. Bluh, would you wish the abolition of the family?"

"I would like to see an extended family where every person is responsible for everybody, rather than a biological family. I think the old are suffering because of this. Why must we care for only the old who are blood relatives when we're all related in human feelings?"

"Is it because we're brought up this way or because in one's family there is a most powerful emotional tie?"

"I think it's pure conditioning."

"Undoubtedly there are changes but it doesn't essentially change human nature in the end. There are more older people living today than ever before but the main problem is that of extinction. Aggression seems to be instinctual."

"I don't think so, Professor Costigan. I think we're taught aggression. We're rewarded when we compete, when we have power, when we have money. I believe in a totally different society where aggression would not be rewarded but cooperation would, we would have totally different people. It's the way society is set up. Values are not instinctual. They're taught."

"But I can't help wondering if some people don't have, by instinct, the desire to wield power over others. It seems to me, I think you wouldn't agree, that this is the result of biological innate qualities and I think if you did institute a society in which competition was limited to the minimum the same old tendencies would appear. The strong would dominate the weak."

"But I believe it is the weak who dominate the strong."

"You mean they *should*?"

"No, I mean they *do*. Professor Costigan, when I speak of the strong I'm not speaking of some power-hungry person but one who has strength of character, strength of conviction and does not bend to the mass consciousness. The weak often latch on to the strong, never really absorbing their values. They use and drain them and eventually attack them for their very strength. I also think that people who are weak inside often appear as overly powerful people to compensate for their weaknesses."

"I absolutely agree but these are the people who wield power."

"Only because we allow them to. Professor Costigan, I have three sons. I did not allow any war toys or aggressive games in our home. They weren't permitted to go to war movies or watch violence on television. I took them on anti-war marches and other marches and the heroes and heroines in our home were people of peace, of principle. Now they're definitely all different but all do not fight physically and never did and none believe in war."

"I do not wish to sound cynical but if they have children, what will they be like? How will they react to this permissive and gentle environment."

"Gentle is not necessarily permissive. It was not a permissive home."

"Alright. I accept your correction but how will they react. The failure of civilization is in not transmitting their best qualities to the next generation. The problem of civilization is how to civilize the barbarians that every new wave of infants has by nature. Admiring you as I must, my question is still open. Will that be continued through the next generation?''

"One never knows but I hope so. Still, as a humanitarian I had to do it.''

"I admire your admitting that, because most people would reject the possibility. I think however much we may differ in our views of human nature, our goals for humanity are the same. You are writing about the old, about my generation. This is only part of the problem. The main problem is the danger of extinction of all people, young and old. You use the word humanitarian. I think this word embraces all humanity. Christianity, Judaism, Buddhism, Muslim, these will never become universal terms. They're not. They're partisan and sectarian. William James talked about the moral equivalent of war. What we need is a moral equivalent for organized religion and this can only be world humanism.''

The above is but a portion of my dialogue with Giovanni Costigan. It was he who made me realize that often when you're focusing on one thing, such as the problems of aging, you lose sight of the larger problem, that the way we view older people is but a reflection of the total society. We value competition, we value aggression, we value people who are pushing their way upward and if this is the case how can we value people who are no longer *in there*? The message through our lifetime is to hang in there, no matter what, because if you stop, this society is not going to recognize your existence, even if it is the society that forced you out.

Perhaps it is not the older people who have outlived their usefulness but the system itself.

WIDOWS AND CHILDREN

Life has a strange way of circling itself, only to come back to another beginning. Most children grown up, get married, have children, the children leave, get married, have children, the circle moves. And you who have taken care of your children, whose children have been dependent on you, then become suddenly in some way dependent on your children.

Earl Guillot speaks angrily. "The trouble with old people is that they have nobody. Even your own kids don't want you. If I don't go to my kids I'd never see them. The biggest fear is loneliness. Look, my kids can bust their butt going to a football game, but they can't make it to see my wife and me for a half hour." His wife feels differently. She refuses to visit them.

Helen Lindgren lived in New York. Her daughter was so anxious to have her live near her that she literally found her an apartment, helped her to move to Denver. They are different in temperament but close in family feelings.

In Chicago I speak with a 70-year-old widow who spends every week-end with her children. She groans. "Between the barking of the dog, the noise of my grandchildren, the constant ringing of the telephone, my daughter's nagging that I should be doing something and my son-in-law's staring at the television set, the best part of the week-end is when they take me home."

Would she rather spend her week-ends at her own home? No, she says, anything is better than being alone.

When I first took the trip in 1975 in search of older people, my

119

destination was Los Angeles. Strange the feeling I had. Am I going home again or am I imagining there is such a place? The people I knew over twenty years ago. The hospital where I gave birth to my first two sons. The studio where I first taught dancing. The theatres where I acted, directed. Los Angeles, a place I couldn't wait to leave. Days of sun that addled my brain and now I'm rushing in a car wondering.

My friend Marilyn Kimmel stands at the door. When I left California it was Marilyn who took me to the airport. Our children were babies. Now, no longer younger, not yet old, I stand in the middle of my life waiting, knowing the reality of old age is coming closer to me.

I visit people I know from that time. Some are friends' parents, others are people I knew in New York who moved to California, relatives of relatives, people I once knew, if I ever knew anybody, if anybody ever knows anybody.

Clara Greenberg. I know her since I was seven. She was a very close friend of my mother's. She picks me up at Marilyn's, drives me to her apartment where we talk of the old days, of today, of Allan, her son who died last year when he was 47. Allan, my first love at age seven, who passed love notes to me on the kitchen table where we were supposed to be doing homework. It scared me when Allan died. I'd lost somebody I loved. I realized if Allan could die so could I. That scared me even more.

She tells me that when her husband died it was terrible for her but when Allan died she was inconsolable. I ask her if she sees much of her other son. "Oh sure, he's wonderful to me and the kids are so considerate. I see Allan's kids when they come home from college on vacation. If I didn't have the kids I don't know what I'd do. Not that I demand from them. You know me, Bonnie. Their life is their life."

Clara works as a volunteer three days a week in a hospital, shops for shut-ins her own age and older. She is a self-appointed good will ambassador. I ask her what else she does with her time.

"Oh I find things to do."

"Like what Clara?"

"I straighten the apartment and I go for a walk or I visit a neighbor. I have one upstairs who's a shut-in, poor thing."

"Clara, are you happy living here?"

"What do you mean here? Are you talking about New York?"

"Well partly that and partly your apartment seems so far away from everything. I can't see living in the valley. You won't drive your car anywhere but close by and it seems so isolated."

"Where should I go? There's no place to go. I could never go back to New York. Why would I want to? My son is here and all my grandchildren. As for this apartment, you know I've had it for years, even when you lived here. If I moved I'd have to pay a fortune."

I remember when Clara first moved here, how she cried for New York, for her sisters and brothers, her friends. How changed her statement, "What do I have in New York?"

Her life is her past, the past of a wife and mother. "I had 33 years with Harry, 33 beautiful years that I wouldn't trade for anything. I'm left with beautiful memories and a heritage."

She smiles at me but her eyes hold no warmth.

Clara takes me to the apartment of a woman she's adopted. Kitty says a brief hello, then sits dejectedly. Clara asks her if she's blue.

So softly I can barely hear she says, "I don't know. I just feel like crying and I tell you the truth, I'd like to take something and put an end to my life."

Clara is annoyed. "Don't talk like that."

"I've never been like this. I was always such a happy person. My sister said, Kitty I don't know how you live like this. You used to be such fun."

Kitty is past 80. Her marriage of 63 years ended last year when her husband died. She complains her days are empty, she can't seem to eat and the only time of day she looks forward to is early evening when her only son calls.

"I have a wonderful son. He calls me at the same time every

night. Saturday is the worst day for me. It's so lonely. All my friends are gone. My husband was the last to go and it's awfully hard to make friends at my age. If I went to a senior citizens home I'd be in a room all alone. They'd ring the bell for lunch and a bell for dinner and that's all it would be."

She claims the biggest problem when you get older is worrying. "I worry about my kids. That's all I think about, my son and his wife. I worry all the time. Like today I'm in a state of panic. My son didn't call last night and I got so worried. I called him and he was so annoyed with me. He said mother I'm not a little boy anymore. But I'm lonely, I said. Well then find somebody, he said to me. But how can I? Untie me from your apronstrings, he said. I'm a big boy now. I'm 65 years old mother."

I ask Clara why she thought Kitty would be good for my book. "Well, isn't she typical?" she answered.

Mattie. She moved from Boston when her husband died, moved to be close to her daughter and her daughter's family. That's when I first met her, when she came here at the age of 54. Now 74, she is retired from work, devotes most of her time to the senior center where she lives. Is she happy here?

"Well, of course. It's my home. Where else would I live? I have my daughter, my darling grandchildren. I would be miserable if I couldn't see them."

"Mattie, do you still have friends in Boston?"

"Of course I do but it isn't the same as your children. There's nothing in life compared to that."

But I know she only sees her daughter once a month. When I ask if that's enough she answers, "Bonnie, I can't say. She has her own life and you know me. I never interfere. My only wish is for her happiness."

Celia and I sit under a tree at the commune. When I ask about her children a strange smile plays on her lips. "Margaret Mead said some years ago, wait till women find out they don't have to have children. Women must learn to be independent of their children. I know I had to free myself. Now I can say I have nothing to look forward to with my children. They no longer interest me and believe me the first time I said it with tears.''

Marshall LaRue says his heart feels good when he's with his grandchildren, that they give him the most joy. But a woman at a senior center in Nebraska says, "You know how the grandchildren are. When they're little they think you're wonderful but when they get older they just seem to outgrow you.''

A man in his eighties. "You'll find out soon enough. When they're young it's Ma this and Pa that because they need you, you see. But when they get older they can't even remember your phone number. Well, let's not discuss it. It's too damned depressing.''

Katarine, 69, lives at the Little Sisters of the Poor Nursing Home in Phoenix. We enter the dining room where candles are lit, flowers are on each table. There's wine. A volunteer plays the piano during dinner. It is Thanksgiving. Katarine and I are having a light evening meal since the dinner was served in the afternoon, a dinner Katarine didn't have since she spent the day with one of her sons and his family. She will spend Christmas with her other son and his family. When she speaks of her sons she says, "They only owe me general respect and love because both of my sons are adopted. We took them home from the hospital when they were babies. They didn't ask me to take them.''

An enormously vivacious woman, she works as a secretary in the nursing home where she's lived for two years. Why does she live here? She says she can't live alone.

In Katarine's room I see photographs of her sons, of her grandchildren. She talks of how close they are, how they disapproved of Katarine's decision to go to the nursing home. "But now they feel it is the best thing I did. They see how happy I am.''

I spend a sleepless night. I can see the nuns are dedicated, that if you have to go to a nursing home, surely this is one of the best. But Katarine was not an exception there. There were others like her, others that spoke and paraphrased her statements with one exception. Their children were not adopted.

I wake up in the middle of the night with my Grandma Anna's words coming at me. "A mother can take care of nine children but nine children can't take care of one mother."

In San Francisco, I speak with Ginarn Lao, an 84-year-old man who spent most of his life in China and, now retired, works full time as a volunteer for the Self-Help Center in Chinatown.

"Mr. Lao, I always hear that the Chinese people take care of their old. Is this still true?"

"Not here. No, it is not the same. At the Self-Help Center we are helping the older people. We are paying visits to them. Their own children don't have the time to visit. I don't know why. You know before my father died, every Sunday we all come to pay respect. We don't live in the same place but we travel and bring the children along to pay respect to their elder, my father."

"Are you saying that part of the culture is lost here?"

"Some might retain it but personally I think very few, very few. I feel very sorry for them. So many of these old people are so lonesome here. It's a pity. It makes me sad when I visit them. I'm really taking the part of their children. It is a sad picture for me because I am a very old type of Chinese in this respect."

The Indian Resource Center suggests I go to San Xavier Mission where Maria Rooz, a woman in her eighties, lives. The mission stands white and imposing. I walk from the immaculately kept San Xavier Mission to dirt roads, covered with broken bottles, empty soda cans. The stucco houses are rundown. My feet kick dust into the hot dry air. Dogs bark, clothes are hung on lines. I am directed to the home of Maria Rooz.

The house is in better condition than most. The man who opens the door says, yes, she lives here. Yes, the old one. I am asked to enter. The man goes into another room and within minutes is back with Maria Rooz in a wheelchair. Both her legs are missing. Her hands are folded quietly in her lap. She stares at me through intense dark eyes.

What do you want to know? she asks, but when I do ask, she

remembers little. She does remember she was born near the Mission, that she had an older brother and sister. There was another little girl but she died. She is vague about her own marriage and speaks only of her childhood.

In this house she lives with her granddaughter and grandson-in-law and their new baby. The man goes to the rear and returns with the baby whom he places on the floor. The old woman's face beams as she follows the child's movements. Lined crevices deepen as she grins at me. "See our baby. Pretty." And then from nowhere. "I am going to a nursing home tomorrow. To the Sisters of St. Joseph."

It is hard for me to respond. All I can see is my own grandmother in the nursing home. The baby makes gurgling sounds. "Isn't she pretty?" Maria says.

"Yes."

"You see, I lost my legs. It is hard for my granddaughter and her husband now that they have a baby. It is too hard for them. They say I am very old, 80-something but I don't know. Old people don't keep their ages."

A woman enters the room, looks at me, then away. The old lady introduces her as her niece, explaining that she is the one who takes care of her. We sit silently while the football players run across the screen, the man sits mesmerized, the child crawls on the floor. Maria Rooz sits patiently waiting for me to say something. I don't know what to ask a woman who's going to a nursing home the next day, a woman who has lost both her legs. So I ask about her life. She tells me she worked as a cook for a hospital, as an assistant seamstress. She smiles. "I like to sew. This is the thing I like best."

The man turns away from the TV and without a word wheels the old lady away. I wait while the baby crawls on the floor. The man enters, saying she was tired, and once more turns to the football game. In the kitchen the niece is opening up two cans of soup. She speaks without looking at me.

"She's going to a nursing home tomorrow. People will criticize so we say nothing. They don't know how hard it is to take care of her. We told nobody because of what they'll say and then they will all want to visit her here and it will be too much.''

"Does anybody visit her now, her children?''

"No. Nobody comes to see her.''

"Why?'' I ask.

The woman looks over at me. And shrugs. I feel uncomfortable, like an intruder. I leave.

1975. At a senior center in New Orleans I speak with two women. Augustine was born in 1886. Albirdie in 1903. They are mother and daughter.

Two years ago when Augustine's second husband died Albirdie left her home in Chicago, her only daughter and grandchildren, sold all her possessions and came to live in New Orleans to be close to her mother who was then 87. She is ambivalent about this move.

Her mother talks about her childhood where she was shifted from relative to relative, how badly she feels that of the four children she birthed only one is still living. Albirdie.

Her daughter says, "The only thing that's bugging her now is she's lonely losing her husband after 56 years.''

"That's right, Albirdie. Loneliness, and you can't do for yourself. As long as you can navigate and do things for yourself it's beautiful. But I don't do so bad. Other people say I'm old. I say how old is old. As long as you can see up and you don't go down and you're not senile you're not old.''

She teases her daughter because she won't fly, talking about her first flight when she was 76 years old. She says she's happy her daughter decided to come back home. Albirdie no longer considers New Orleans her home. She stays because her mother refuses to move to Chicago. Two years ago, in 1973 when she was 70 she tried to find work here. All she could find was a job as a waitress, which she took.

"There is so much more age discrimination in New Orleans. It was very humiliating for me to work for $35 a week when I was making $35 a day in the needle-trade industry in Chicago. Being a waitress was hard, very hard, and I said if I continued working on this job I wouldn't be able to enjoy my social security. Now I can keep all the money I earn because I'm past 72 but because of my age I can't get anything decent to do. I think it's a sin. They push the people off at 65. You still want to work but they won't let you. I'm not tired yet and I know if I was in Chicago I'd get a job. They don't sit on you about your age."

Her mother joins in. "Honey, it's cruel now. The time is mean. It's a different world. The elderly people, they push them aside. Oh you're old, that's what you get. But I have no regrets. I counted up some time and I got joy and I got tears."

Albirdie and I decide to go for a walk. She kisses her mother, says she'll see her later. We walk along the waterfront, enter the open market where we buy fruit. Rows and rows of fresh vegetables sit on the stands.

"This is not my home anymore but my mother doesn't like it when I say that. She says you were born and raised here. I miss my grandchildren. How will they remember me if they don't see me more than once a year. I sold all of my things or gave them away and bought second hand furniture just to be near my mother. But what is there for me? I'm just doing it cause she's my mother. I don't know. I always thought when I got social security I'd be able to enjoy life, to travel, see the world. I thought it would be easy but now I'm hog-tied."

We walk on. She shows me the New Orleans of her childhood. Then, "She's strong, you could see that. She's got a good memory. No senility there. But she keeps saying every night, I'm dying, I'm dying. She'll live to be one hundred. She isn't satisfied unless she's complaining."

Yet Albirdie is quick to add if she weren't there to take care of her she'd have nobody. She speaks of nursing homes, telling me it would be pure murder to put her mother in a home. "She'd die there. I could never do it. After all, she is my mother."

I stand on a streetcorner after Albirdie and I part and ask an older man, "What's most important as you get older?"

"Somebody to love you and take care of you. My son is good as gold and I'm not bragging either. If I lose him I lose everything. He's the only thing I have. My wife died. That was seven years ago."

A man walks over, listens. "Watcha doing, getting his history?"

The first man reflects. "Music is important too. I'm a piano player, did I tell you that? And I still have this Dixieland band. That's right. Even at my age. I'll bet you couldn't guess how old I am. Guess. Go on."

"73?"

"You're pretty close. I'm 76. As I get older I get more lonesome. Am I blue. That's a song. I wish I had a piano here. I'd play it for you. If it weren't for my son I don't know what I'd do. We live together, did I tell you that?"

The second man says, "You've said enough. Now it's my turn."

And without taking a breath says, "I'm 70 years old is that ok? I retired years ago when I had a nervous breakdown. I like it here in New Orleans. I go to a senior center every day. The man you spoke to, he plays the piano there. You didn't think I knew him, did you? I go home every night, stay home and do nothing. I never had kids so I don't have sorrow and I don't have joy. Did I tell you enough?"

Before I get a chance to answer he's gone.

It was surprising how many single women and men said they didn't regret not having children and how many who did have children expressed disappointment in them. Then there were those, who after extolling the virtues of their children, finally changed their tune.

In a small town in Nevada, Myrtle, 76, "I'm tired of it, just tired of it. All those years of taking care of them and now I feel I'm not strong enough to do things for myself. Why don't I just do what I want? Why can't I convince myself? Why am I always doing things I don't want to? My family, for instance, thinks I need company. They think I'm lonely. I don't get lonely. I don't want them to think they have to come here to keep me company.''

My mother puts it differently when speaking of the children of her contemporaries. ''They think they do us a favor by calling us and asking us to come over. We're not sitting home waiting for a call. Many times we go because it's expected of us when actually we prefer to do other things.''

''Mom, aside from children, what's it like being a widow?''

''The trouble with society is that everything is in two's. A woman alone has to be a very strong character to overcome the prejudice of one person by themselves. There's a tendency to look down on a widow alone.''

Some widows learn to live alone, to become a one. Others don't.

This is the story of Sadye. She died on a Sunday night. A sudden death. She'd just been released from the hospital and after undergoing a number of tests was told she was fine. There was nothing wrong with her.

She had two fears. One was cancer because she'd dropped quite a bit of weight and had difficulty eating. They ruled out cancer. She feared a stroke. She suffered from headaches and dizziness and two and a half years ago she had a minor stroke. They said it was not apt to occur again. Something about one weak blood vessel that had been activated. Tests were done, brain scans, whatever doctors do in hospitals. They ruled out stroke. The medical diagnosis: Sadye was a woman with an emotional problem. She was tense, nervous. She needed psychiatric help.

The doctors asked her all their medical questions. What they didn't ask was how a woman of 70, whose husband has recently died, who's been so well taken care of she can't balance a checkbook, can't drive a car, survive? To get anywhere in her neighborhood except for the local synagogue she had to take a bus, then a train. Sadye had never done this. She was transported by car by her husband. How does a woman who's led a comfortable middle-class existence cope when she realizes her money's run out, that she cannot live on her social security, that she is forced to sell the house she's lived in for 35 years, to move to a strange neighborhood.

To Sadye, the family was everything. She lived for her husband, her two sons. But her husband was dead. Her sons, devoted as they were, and they were devoted, had their own lives. Life had meant being a wife, a mother, a woman who took great pride in her home.

She began to realize she was preserving what even she knew had died, was finished for her. And as she saw, she deteriorated. Her dream life of husband, children, home, family, was just that, a dream. Her brothers and their wives moved to Florida but Sadye stayed put. She did not have the strength to move she said. Last year she told me, "Bonnie, I'm at the stage in life where nobody needs me and I need everybody."

Sadye died tonight of causes unknown. The doctor who took care of her refused to sign the death certificate. He stated that when he dismissed her from the hospital four days earlier she was a healthy woman. I cringe when I think of his stupidity.

Sadye died of causes unknown. Perhaps it was a massive stroke or a heart attack. Does it matter? It does matter, however, that her doctors took her case so lightly, that the day before, her son had to plead with one of them to talk to her, give her some comfort. The doctor's answer was simple. It is in her head. She's fine.

I am not a doctor but I will perform my own autopsy. Sadye died from causes well known. She died because there was nothing left for her. She died because her life was over. She died because she was taught to be a wife, a mother, a good hostess, a charming woman. There was no husband left to care for, no children to minister to, nobody to serve and be charming to. And she wasn't capable of changing.

I weep for you Sadye. The only way I can make sense of your life is to write about you and say what I feel. You were a victim. It was not your fault. It was not your fault.

GETTING OVER THE TRAUMA

My father Morris Bluh suffered for over four and a half months with leukemia. Most of that time he was hospitalized. My mother stayed at the hospital from early morning until they literally threw her out. The manager of the catalog department in Sears, she was forced to quit in order to stay near my father. She was 63 and hadn't planned on retiring.

When my father died my mother was worn, saddened, bewildered even though she knew it was coming. Her work was finished, her husband dead and she was going to have to face a life alone. Her sister-in-law immediately took charge and within weeks my mother was whisked to Europe. I remember her saying to me before she left, "What am I going to Europe for?" She was so confused that she actually left without taking her passport and was held in custody in Portugal for 24 hours until it was sent to her.

But that trip did help. She was in different surroundings, moving from place to place, without a chance to think too much about what had happened. I don't know if this is good but it seemed to work for my mother.

How do others handle the trauma?

In Vancouver there is 97-year-old James Charles Mattison. He has been married twice. Both wives died, the second one three years ago, when Charlie was 94. "It was difficult," he says. "When I love I'm very sentimental and I love sincerely so when my wives passed away it was heartbreaking. The first one wasn't so bad but with my last wife the sorrow in my heart was something terrible. I couldn't shake the remorse. I couldn't get rid of it. It's a terrible thing. Going through the remorse, uncontrollable remorse. You can't do anything for it. I couldn't do anything. Couldn't sleep at night and just weep weep weep knowing deep down in my intelligence that she's out of her worry and her sickness, that she's better off. There's just no consolation, there's no words of consolation that can remedy it. It's there and it's got to wear off. It takes time.

"The other day I went to both my wives' graves and I put flowers there. There was the old man, me, putting flowers on both his wives' graves. That's something you could put in your book. But that remorse. Oh boy it hits hard and it's a serious matter. You can call that very important because I couldn't shake it."

(He did. There's more about James Charles Mattison in the Over Ninety Section.)

Living near the sea has always been a dream of mine. Not so for Berta and Terry Pettus who moved from an apartment in Seattle to a houseboat 35 years ago. The dream was ideal in many ways. Both the Pettuses shared the same views, the same kind of life, all the household tasks. He shows me the portrait of her on the wall and says, "In 1965 this tragedy. Berta, who'd never been sick a day in her life, had a stroke."

She spent many weeks in the hospital, months in a convalescent home and then Terry brought her to their houseboat. "Berta was a real fighter. She'd had a massive stroke. The doctor said if it wasn't for her determination she would have never walked again. By God, she wouldn't settle for that wheelchair and pretty soon she was on crutches and then pretty soon she managed without them. The tragedy is it was a stroke that affected the left side of her brain. She had to face the fact that she couldn't speak. Oh she could talk but it wouldn't make sense. She was 60 years old at the time. There are three things we loved to do. Walk, read and talk, and all of them were taken away from her. I thought of that ESP and I'm more or less convinced there's something there. There's something to this nonverbal communication if peopler are as close as we were."

Five years later his wife died and Terry Pettus went into a deep depression. He explains, ''I always thought of myself as a fairly strong person. We'd had our ups and downs and our lumps. When my mother and father died I felt awfully close to them and it was a terrible blow to me but nothing compared to this. I really had to fight with myself for two years to overcome a despondency that was so strong. It was awful, just awful.''

''Even though she'd been so sick for those five years?''

''Bonnie, I rationalized. I realized that any grief I felt was pure selfishness. It is the most selfish emotion people can have, there's no question about it.''

''What did you do Terry, to fight this depression?''

''There was no way to fight it and even now I don't know of any good way. Booze. I had to stop drinking. I was always a social drinker but you drink under those circumstances and it doesn't do a thing for you, I can tell you. I can now drink again but for more than two years I wasn't very pleasant.''

''Didn't you have any friends that could help?''

''No. I can intellectualize but the days were hard to describe, the dark dogs. You can't rationalize it. You just have that miserable feeling and you have to fight it and talk to yourself and it took more than two years for me to do that. Now I don't have the unpleasant memories of her illness. I say goodnight to her, goodnight to her picture. I live in this home with all the wonderful things she loved and we collected. I'll tell you I thought I was a little wacky until I heard George Burns talk on TV about Gracie and he was describing how he tried to get over Gracie's death. Usually I don't listen much to TV but I kept listening to this and he said finally he started sleeping in Gracie's bed. I got up that night and felt morose. It was one of those miserable rainy nights. I don't know why I awakened but I felt so damned miserable. I moved over to Berta's bed and I've slept in it ever since.''

He talks of their life together, of the egalitarian relationship they had. ''There's nothing glamorous about housework. It is just plain goddamned hard work. I'm going to be rough about it. I think all men ought to be made to do it at the point of a gun. It's miserable work. Berta and I always shared. It wasn't my coming home and sitting on my ass. She worked the same as me. Oh you didn't tangle with Berta. If I'd have walked in or tried to get away with doing nothing I'd have been cured of that in one evening. I was lucky to have that kind of wife."

"You talked about feeling close to your parents. Would you tell me about them?"

"My dad was a minister with socialist leanings, christian-type socialism, so I was exposed at a very early age to quite a lot of ideas. I would say this, we were encouraged to read and make up our own minds. My mother refused to live in the parsonage, insisting our home was separate from the church. I appreciate my upbringing and God knows Freud wouldn't get very far with me on the question of your parents doing all sorts of horrible things to you. I had nothing but the greatest fondness for them. I felt I was very fortunate.

"Bonnie, you're writing about old people. I watched the tragedy of old people when my father died. My mother had died a few years before. I'll never forget the day my dad fell and broke his hip and had to go to a nursing home. It was a good nursing home but still a nursing home. I remember the last afternoon I went out to see dad and we were talking and finally he looked up with a smile and said, Terry I'm just too tired to talk. Well Bonnie, if you listen to me you'll know the Pettuses are all very verbal. Goddamn we can talk and you know I had a cold clammy feeling coming over me. It was such a sweet affection I had for him and I said alright daddy I'll go. When I got home the nurse called and told me he died. So I'm happy he went that way."

"Terry, Berta died seven years ago. Would you consider getting married again?"

He takes me by the hand, shows me the things she treasured, the artifacts, the books, the artwork. "We were married 41 years. We had so many things together. I'm not unmarried."

We look at Berta's picture together. "I'm not unmarried."

OVER NINETY WITHOUT YOGURT

My great grandmother Bluh lived to be 102, maybe more. We're not quite sure when she died. It was the Second World War and in Budapest, where she lived, Hitler's troops were rounding up the Jews. My cousin who saw her last in 1940, when she was 100, told how people came from all over to listen to her. A university graduate, a woman who, he says, was curious about everything and exceptionally versed in all sorts of matters, she was not hard of hearing, did not wear glasses.

On my mother's side, her father Joseph Steinberg lived to be 93 and he was vital, alive, with good sight and hearing till the end. At 85 he married for the third time.

I'm very fortunate. All my grandparents lived beyond life expectancy but as I write I'm beginning to realize that one can get carried away with statistics, life expectancy among them.

A story I adore is one told to me a number of years ago. A woman in her eighties was told by a clairvoyant that she had six months to live. She began to prepare for her death. She got weaker and weaker as time went by. On the day she was to die she put everything in order, got into bed and waited for the end to come. The next day, to her surprise, she was still alive so she promptly got out of bed and began living again—which is what happens when you look at a statistic. You're supposed to live to 72 or 73 and if you're 65, why get into anything when there isn't too much time left. Why struggle, why learn, why battle, why anything? Why? Because statistics may not have your name attached.

It certainly didn't have Joe Smith's on the form, even though he had suffered a heart attack many years ago.

For all of you who are too young to know, Joe Smith is one half of the famous vaudeville act, Smith and Dale, an act that took them around the world, to all the major theatres. Their Doctor Kronkite routine was seen on the Ed Sullivan show, at the Palace Theatre, where they worked with Judy Garland, in many other theatres for decades and last on the Barbra Streisand show in 1967. When David Frost asked them to work on his show in 1971 Smith told him no. He was worried about his friend Charlie Dale's memory and tells me, "We left when we were tops. I didn't care what money they offered. It don't mean a thing. The money never did mean a thing to me anyhow."

We sit in Joe Smith's room at the Actor's Home in New Jersey. The walls are covered with photographs, awards, mementos of a lifetime. From his window you can see the beautiful grounds, the trees and clouds and sky. "Charlie and I first came here in 1962 when we put on shows and finally I said to Charlie, 'Charlie when we retire I'm going to come here. I like it because there's people I know and all.' So when Mabel, my second wife, passed away in '67 I came here. Then Charlie lived in the apartment on West 55 Street. After Charlie's wife died in '69 I stayed with him for a while and finally Charlie said, 'Joe I wanna come with you. I wanna live there'."

He joined Smith at the Actor's Home in 1970.

The partnership began in 1898 on the lower East Side of New York when they were 14- and 16-year-old kids known as Joe Seltzer and Charlie Marx. They discovered each other when their rented bikes collided and both landed on the ground.

Joe says, "I took my wheels and started to walk to the corner where I'd hired the bike and as I was walking I happened to look back and Dale was following me so I said, 'Who are you following' and he said 'I'm not following you. You're walking in front of me'.''

They continued their dialogue in the store. The owner said they reminded him of Weber and Fields, a famous vaudeville team of that time. "See, he got a kick out of us, so he offered us a tandem at no cost so we could get acquainted."

This was the beginning, not only of an act, but a friendship that lasted a lifetime.

Joe Smith talks of the good old days, of quitting school when he was 14. The fifth child in a family of thirteen, his parents didn't complain. "My father was a tailor. He was very artistic but what did he have? And I mean, my brothers worked and nobody had anything."

He talks of the beginning of Smith and Dale, how they worked anywhere just to break in the act, of how they went on one night stands in a horse and sleigh. The act was called The Imperial Vaudeville and Comedy Company. Later they were known as the Avon Comedy Four and finally as Smith and Dale.

"People ask me who my favorite comedian is and I always say my partner. He was the funniest guy that I knew. He used to break me up. The theatre, meeting new people, keeps you going. You'd have fun, you'd be with some of them for maybe three months in vaudeville on the Orpheum time and in a show over a year. You'd meet different people and that kept you young. I'm 93 just last month on February 16. I don't know how fast the time is going. You don't feel it. You just go with the times and as long as you go with the times, you're with it. And you pray to God to keep you healthy. You can't move fast because if you move too fast you're liable to fall. I found that out. I found out a lot of things but at the same time you have to be very optimistic. I look at the clouds, I look at the forms of the clouds and I say to myself, this is God, nobody could do this, nobody could build this, the trees and the grass, nobody could do this. God is the only one."

He talks of his life now, of the enormous correspondence he

keeps up, of the time spent at the neighboring high schools where he speaks and does vaudeville routines with the students and faculty, of the friends he has at the Actor's Home.

I ask him about *The Sunshine Boys,* if it was really the life of Smith and Dale.

"No, it isn't our life. Neil Simon said that when he wrote the show he had Smith and Dale in the back of his mind, so it's nothing but a paraphrase of us."

"What about the Doctor routine?"

"Not ours. It was a different thing entirely. Dinah Shore called me from Hollywood and she said, 'Joe, I want to get permission to use a few of your Dr. Kronkite routines for my show' and I said alright. So I was sitting here one afternoon looking at her show and when she opens up Neil Simon is sitting there with Benjamin, the fellow who played the nephew. And she blows me a kiss and says 'thank you Joe' and they read some of our stuff. I knew that she was going to put on the routines but I didn't know with whom."

He tells me he's seen the play a few times because his friends are often in it, that not too long ago he was invited to sit on the dais when a dinner was given for George Burns and Walter Matthau who did the movie version. Simon was on one side of the table and Smith was on the other. "I wouldn't go to him and say hello. I never met him. Now I think he should have come over to me. Don't you think so? Well, what am I going to do? You can use what I said, Bonnie, but just say it wasn't our life."

Throughout my time with Joe Smith much of his conversation centered around his life in show business and always his friend Charlie Dale. He reads a poem he sends to his friends who reach the age of 80 and then a poem he wrote especially for Dale:

Over seventy years together
It's a great age we've lived in.
From the streetcar to the jet plane,
from Strauss to Irving Berlin.

Over seventy years together
but it seems like yesterday.
From the Old Atlantic Garden in the Bowery
we shared each other's sorrows
and we shared each other's joys
in all phases of show business
since we were a couple of boys.
Over seventy years together
as close as two peas in a pod
and the only one that could separate us
was God.
With a bond that never tore.
And if God is only willing
we'll make it more and more.

He turns to me. "That was what we said at the finish of the act."

"It's more than a marriage, isn't it, Joe?"

"Now Charlie is buried at the Woodlawn Cemetery and we have a stone and on the stone it says Smith and Dale with a line underneath, Joe Marx and Charlie Seltzer. Now, how long can you be partners? That's for eternity. There you are. We were together and we'll be together."

Driving through Louisiana I see the sun bouncing off the bayous. Fingers of light stretch toward the sky. The sulphurous smell is all around, lulling me into a dreamy state. I turn into the Melrose Plantation just as my car makes a strange sound and stops. A group of black workers sit in a round circle of grass. I get out of my car. "Does anybody know where Clementine Hunter lives?"

"Sure," a woman answers. "Everybody round these parts knows where Clementine lives."

"I've run out of gas."

"It sure look like it." And the group bursts out laughing goodnaturedly.

Somebody with a truck appears and I am taken to the nearest gas station where I am given a can of gas and told I can pay when I come back. Back at the station I speak to the owner's mother who is in her late sixties, who tells me her mother who's in her nineties lives across the road from her in the house she's resided in for 50 years.

"Soon as you get finished talking to Clementine you come back here. Mama would love talking with you."

She is stooped over, gathering wood for the fireplace even though it is very hot outside. She eyes me suspiciously when I ask if she's Clementine Hunter, reluctantly invites me in when I explain about my book. In her kitchen we sit. Ms. Hunter's hands are folded in her lap, waiting.

"Can I ask how old you are?"

"I guess I'm about 90, 92. I guess so but I don't know 'cause when my mother died they didn't tole us our age. I tried to get the priest to find it but he said they didn't have no book so I have to guess my age."

She's lived on Melrose Plantation most of her life, went to school for two years, says she didn't learn anything so she quit. When she was older she picked cotton on the plantation, earning 50¢ for every 100 pounds she picked. After she married and had children, she continued picking cotton. She can't remember when, but some time during her adult life, a woman who'd spent summers on the plantation painting left her paints with Clementine Hunter. I look on her walls and notice there aren't any of her works hanging there. I ask what she paints.

"Just scenes. Pecan picking, cotton picking, wash days and little things. I just paint anything I see but I can't look at nothin' and paint it. It come out of my head."

"Clementine, I came here because I heard you're famous. I wish I could see your paintings because I hear they're beautiful."

She beams. "I guess they is. I got paintings everywhere I guess. I mix the colors myself, any color that come to my mind. I feel pretty good when I paint cause all the energy is in your head. You don't have to worry 'bout it or think 'bout it.''

While we're talking there is a knock at the door. A white woman enters, says, "Why Clementine, we didn't know you were sick. I heard you were in the hospital. My! I just dropped by to see if you have any paintings I could buy.''

"Don't have any. I been sick.''

"That's too bad, Clementine. I'm sorry to hear that.''

"I been in the hospital up in Nachitosis.''

"I didn't know that, Clementine. What was wrong? Was it the arthritis?''

"I don't know. They were just checking on me.''

"Are you from a museum?'' she asks me.

"No. I'm writing a book about older people.''

"Well, Clementine is real famous in these parts. A lady from the Metropolitan Museum was here about a month ago looking at the paintings they have down by the church. Clementine, when do you think you'll have some paintings?''

"I don't know. Can't say.''

"Well, I'll just run along and some day when you have some paintings I'll come back.'' The screen door closes.

"Clementine, do you know who Grandma Moses is?'' I ask.

"They say she's a painter. Somebody say to me that they bring me one of Grandma Moses pictures for me to see but they ain't brought none here. I never did go to no museum. I never saw other people's paintings when I was young. But today you could see paintings everywhere you go 'cause everybody's painting now. Everybody.''

I ask again if she can remember when she started painting. She seems deep in thought. "I didn't start when my children were married. I know that. I didn't paint when my children was small. I was busy working in the field.''

"Who took care of your children?''

"They took care of themselves. I put them in the field, set 'em down.'' She pauses, then says, "They say Grandma Moses paints pictures with snow. We get snow here in Louisiana but I never paint it. I never paint nothing but just what come to my mind. I can't do like other people, go look at this, go look at that. I can't. I don't believe in it. Can't. I just wait till it come in my mind, then I mark it and paint it."

"Do you ever paint your family?"

"No, I never paint any of them. I paint little children sometime. All my paintings is colored. I paint all colored. I don't paint no whites and I only paints when I feel good. Well, I don't know anymore 'bout my life."

I tell her I'm going to speak with the 94-year-old woman up the road. "I knows her. They nice people." Then her eyes penetrate mine. "Why you talking to all them old people? Why you writing all them old people?"

"Because I think it's important that their voices are heard."

She smiles at me for the first time. "I likes children but I always like best to be with people older than me. It look like they can tell me what I can't tell them, you see. They're older and they know more than me and I be glad to talk with them."

"How do you feel about getting older, Clementine?"

"Well I'm glad long as the Lord let me live. That's the way I is. Just got to live my life. My grandmother, she was 110. And she wasn't walkin' with no cane, she didn't wear glasses or nothin'. What killed her, she mashed her big toe and she got blood poisoning. She wasn't sick or nothin'. Well, that's about all I know."

Lorna B., 94, greets me warmly. "I have a dream that I would be picked up by somebody and they would realize my memories and make something of them, just like you are doing."

Her story is about her life on the plantation, her ancestors who came from Ireland, France and Africa, her quitting school when she was 12. Her mother, who she was told had died, was taken to a mental institution where she lived until her death. As the oldest she had to take care of her father, her brothers and sisters. We talk about Clementine Hunter and how she picked cotton when she had little children.

Lorna says, "Clementine told a story about how she would give birth to her babies and a week later she was out picking cotton. She had five babies. Well, I picked cotton too but when I gave birth to the babies I always stayed put, took care of myself and of course we didn't do it for others. We did it in our own place. We was independent. We had cows, had our own milk, took care of our children. I used to get so tired straining milk I thought will the time ever come, and the time has come where we have to buy the milk."

Lorna goes back and forth in time. She speaks of outhouses, how she boiled water for her children's baths, of doors without screens, the mosquitoes coming in droves from the bayous. Of the malaria her children had, of draughts and floods in the area. She speaks of the first time she voted.

"That's so straining for us to know we're under such evil people. I would like an honest man to be president. The best we had was Kennedy. They say when he died it was raining weather and the trees all wept. I liked him. He was for the people. And Robert was wonderful. I saw him on TV. And I loved the man that went on the hill and dreamed a dream. Martin Luther King making all those walks, and Robert, he had his coat on his shoulder. I think of that all the time."

She also thinks of her marriage to what she calls "a fine looking man, a different man from most men. He didn't ramble around, he didn't drink, didn't smoke. So many girls marry those trifling men. A man, they say he depends so much on the woman. The doctor I went to for my arthritis, he had me on a high table with a needle sticking in my shoulder and he says, you women, you just kills the men. They ain't no truth to that. We women know what the truth is. But my husband was a good man."

Lorna, with her bad arthritis, picked eight pounds of pecans today from her own trees.

On her 90th birthday her eight children came from all over the United States and Canada and gave her a big party which was covered by the local newspaper. But the one daughter who stays near and she calls her backbone is Kitty, the woman I met. "All my children are good" she says, "but there is only one Kitty."

A religious woman, she goes to church every day and tells me when she dies she's planning on a large funeral. "Well I tell you, Bonnie, this is the way I feel about it. I got me some money. Not much, but what can I do with it now? I give it to the church and I love to play bingo but what else can I do with the money? So I bought me a mausoleum and I'm paying for it every month. I want me one beautiful funeral. My children, they're all doing just fine. Living on their own. So what am I going to do with the money?"

She stands at the door, asks me to call when I get back to my hotel so she won't worry, shaking her head, comparing today to the day when she was a young woman, "Things are so different. I lock my door now. We never locked them years ago."

Every month The Little Brothers of the Poor holds a birthday party for the people born that month. It is the custom to have the oldest person there blow out the candles. Today it is Reverend Cornelius Jones, age 116, the oldest living person in Chicago.

He takes a deep breath, blows the candles out with help from Catherine who works with The Little Brothers. Happy birthday, she says. Thank you sweetheart, he answers, moving his hand over the tablecloth for his champagne. It is then I discover that he is almost totally blind. When I speak with him he has difficulty hearing. But none of this dampens his spirit. He is paid court by the people at this party so I have to catch him between congratulations. He sits tall and acts as if he's used to this attention. And he is. A few weeks ago his birthday was celebrated at City Hall.

He grins at me. "I didn't do nothing there. I just let the mayor see me. What are you writing, sweetheart, something for a newspaper?"

Reverend Jones was married seven times. His wives gave him

fourteen children. All are dead, his wives, his children. He doesn't believe men should live alone, teases the woman next to him, saying he would marry her if she would have him.

She laughs. "Isn't he the limit?"

"If she wants me I will."

Rather than live alone or go to a nursing home he lives with a couple. He attributes his long life to his religion, his respect for all people and for minding his own business. He became a minister in his early twenties, cannot read the Bible but claims to know it by heart and begins quoting from it when people interrupt with their congratulations.

A woman. "Can I shake your hand? I never met anybody 116."

Another woman. "Reverend Jones, you sure look good for your age."

"Come closer, sweet baby. I don't hear so good."

A man asks. " He's 89, no?"

When told he's 116 he stares. "How much?" Then bursts out laughing. "They forgot about you already. Now you can live as long as you want."

Cornelius Jones says he never dreamed he would live to this age and adds, "I didn't know what was in the storehouse but I never had no worry in my head. Don't believe in it. I just takes things as they come."

What advice would he give younger people? "Nothing. You can't tell them nothing. They know everything and think you don't know nothing. You can't tell a child nothing nowadays. If you gonna try and tell them they say we don't want to hear you. We gonna do what we want."

James Charles Mattison was born in London in 1880. He has children, grandchildren, great-grandchildren and now a great-great grandchild four months old. He laughs. "They're coming from all directions."

A widower who lives with one of his sons, he proudly boasts he does his own cooking, his cleaning and laundry by hand. "I do the gardening too. I love flowers and all that stuff." He's full of stories, of days gone by, of his childhood and remembers everything in minute detail. He talks of the balls they had, how they promenaded and then waltzed around a large ballroom. "The music was delightful. All the waltzes we'd do and the two-step and oh it was wonderful. You would be there in a dream dancing with a girl beside you and you'd have a chance to make a date. Now they dance a mile away from each other and they call that dancing.

"There were canoe trips and hiking through the woods and going on a Sunday with your best girl to the parks just taking in the beautiful sights of nature. Oh the winters were delightful and you could see the roses growing all over, all afield in the winter gardens. Then they put up all those KEEP OFF THE GRASS and NO WALKING ON THE GRASS signs. I thought that terrible and I formed a group. We argued that grass grows quickly, that people should be able to go on the grass and enjoy it." The signs are gone now.

How does James Charles Mattison feel about being 97? "Well I don't feel old but only the other day I made a remark. Why, I said, I'm walking like an old man. I have a few ailments but nothing in particular. I get a little tired but then I suppose that's my own fault in a way because I overdo. I danced here the other day and some of them said I dance better than the rest of them. I still like to dance and as a matter of fact one of the women here proposed to me. She was younger, but I said no, nothing doing. I couldn't take the responsibility of looking after another wife. And another woman sitting near said the idea of you saying you can't take the responsibility. Why it's us women who look after the men. You don't look after us at all. So I said the mistake of old people is they start something, they get into something . . ."

He studies me, his eyes crinkled into a smile. "You've heard of the law of sequence, eh? The law of sequence is this, you start something, out of something comes what you least expect and that's the blooming thing I'm trying to tell you."

After mourning his second wife's death for two years he

decided to take off by himself to see his father's birthplace. He was 96. "I jumped on a plane and got in all kinds of mixups. My son was so afraid I'd get into trouble." He can't stop laughing. "I'm more afraid of him looking at me thinking I'll get into trouble than he is of me."

His son gave him a letter of introduction to the Salvation Army in London but when Mr. Mattison got there he discovered all the rooms he could afford were filled. This didn't faze him since he was planning to go to York anyhow. The Salvation Army gave him the train schedule and off he went. "But wherever I went people were watching me. They must have told them I was coming and so they were looking out for me, but they scared the life out of me. I met this old feller coming back on the train and he said to me, well was it worth it? And I said to him, not in my condition, not with all those people trying to help me."

"But Charlie, how many people take off for Europe when they're 96?"

"I don't know, but they should. What an adventure. Why some feller in London asked me to go to a football game with him. All the people treated me fine. I'll tell you something funny. I hadn't been there more than one hour when people were coming up to me asking where this place and that place was."

Charlie Mattison travelled all through England on trains, to every small village. Did he get tired? "No. I was having too much fun. You know I never get lonely now because I can sit for hours and hours and laugh when I look back and I can cry when I look back. Oh, I've got great memories."

How does he feel about old people? "We're still looking after ourselves, we old people. Believe me, we're not dead. We're on the job looking after ourselves. We still have our social lives here at the Vancouver Center, meeting one another in friendly spirit and all that kind of thing. They're nice people and I'm very glad that the government maintains these centers and keeps these things going. We want as many as we possibly can get for the old people. But it's the young I worry about. Vancouver is not like it was. It's a big city now and I don't know where the young people are meeting each other, how they're getting along or what they're doing."

When I ask to what he attributes his good health, he tells me he doesn't think much of doctors, that he advises people to learn about their own bodies. "Why doctors don't even know about life. We had a group come here one night to advise us old people how to live and I told the doctors there, 'I'll tell you something you don't know. There are a lot of habits we're in. When we walk we start off with the right foot usually. Why don't we start off with the left foot and give the brain machinery a chance to exercise, to move ourselves around a bit, to change things around?' "

One of his theories flips me out. He claims that when he was living in Montreal there was a candy factory nearby and for 2¢ he bought a big bag of broken candy. "Well from that time to now I've been very fond of candy, very fond of sweet stuff. Now this is my theory about cancer. In your flesh there's cancer germs, there's all kinds of viruses staying there just waiting to be triggered into action."

I tell him I don't understand.

"My flesh is too sweet. That's my point. A sweet flesh is not what cancer cells want."

"But, Charlie, there's a theory that sugar is responsible for heart attacks."

"I know that, but you can control heart conditions by other means but you can't control cancer. It may sound ridiculous but there it is, that's my theory. Of course I'm going to live as long as I can. I'm aiming for 100 now. Whether I'll be taken away before that time I don't know but I think I will make it."

"Charlie, what changes would you like seen for older people?"

"Of course you know money is a big problem. I'd like to see the government spend more money on senior housing. They should build everything that's necessary all under one roof: proper doctors who understand old people and their bodies, stores, library, entertainment, everything. There should be transportation that would take the people out, not have everything the way it is, scattered all over the place. That makes it hard for the old people. Now look. I know an old lady who went to a home. She died an unhappy woman. When the family took her out for a day she didn't want to go back to the nursing home. We shouldn't have places like that. I dread going into those homes. Let them build good housing for us. They should do it. They spend all that money on going to the moon and you can't even breathe the air up there."

James Charles Mattison gets that wonderfully mischievous grin before he tells another story. The people have all gone home. The only person left is the porter who is waiting for us to leave. We walk out together.

"Did you tell me you were staying at English Bay?" he asks me. I nod. "You would have loved it years ago. I'd go out on a Saturday afternoon and there wouldn't be a soul around. I'd have the whole beach to myself. You'd go down to Stanley Park and you'd go to the beaches down at English Bay, where you're staying and you could have the whole beach. It was lovely to go picnicking and it was lovely to go across to the North Shore. Did I tell you about the adventure I had going up Grouse Mountain with my friends? We had quite an adventure. It was 1905. We reached this body of water and went out in punts when an oarlock broke and everybody was laughing but they didn't realize the seriousness of the situation because they couldn't see the rapids and then Myrtle . . . ."

Ten years ago, when Peggy Daniels was 84, she took a jet for the first time in her life and loved it. When she decided to visit her niece in California two years ago her son was upset that she was going alone and arranged for his son to go with her. She loves her grandson but decided this year when she went she wouldn't tell a soul and travelled by herself.

She also didn't tell anybody she was being released from a rest home today. Peggy Daniels, who was never in a hospital until she was 85, had to go to one recently because she fell down a flight of stairs in her home and broke her pelvic bone. Her son wanted her to come to his house but she decided, no, she'd rather be alone.

"I think the most important thing is taking care of yourself. I would like to do that as long as I can. The rest home was really nice, as clean as clean can be. And you have to dress to eat your meals but I don't know. I wouldn't want to live there. I thought how awful it would be to live in a home like that."

She explains her life was a simple one. Married when she was 42 to a widower who had a son, she never had any children of her own. She's spent most of her life in the town of Three Forks, Montana. I ask if she is religious and she says no.

"I'm not really affiliated with any church. I belonged to the Free Methodist Church when I was a child and when I got older I went to the Methodist Church. In the hospital they asked me what I was and I said I'm Episcopalian."

"Are you?"

She bursts out laughing. "No, but I'm thinking of it. The Episcopalian minister came to see me every day in the hospital and when he had to leave for Pennsylvania he sent me a dozen roses. Maybe I should belong to some church but I haven't gotten around to it. I believe we have only one God and I certainly don't believe in purgatory."

"Do you think of death, Peggy?"

"I do get confused sometimes when I read about it. I was going to tell you about this friend of mine. She was 93 and she owned this hotel and she was a jolly person. Last week I got a letter from her niece that she'd passed away and her body was to be cremated. I wonder about that. I never thought about that before but I do now."

"How did you feel about older people when you were twenty?"

"Oh they were old. They were really old."

"And at thirty?"

She laughs. "I began to think I was getting old then."

"Do you have friends your age?"

"Who would there be in this town? I think I am about the oldest person here."

"How does it feel?"

"I don't notice any difference. I just received a letter from my niece and she's looking forward to my visiting her again. I'm planning to go to California soon. My doctor says I'll live to be 100 but I'm not so sure I want to."

"What's most important to you, Peggy?"

"Getting the world settled. There's a lot of things I'd like to see straightened out. No more wars. I'd sure like that."

"What qualities do you look for in people?"

"I like honesty and for people to be jolly. In friendship and marriage you need to be companionable, to enjoy the same things and be able to do them together. I was always ready to go and do things my husband liked."

She talks of her childhood, living on a ranch with her parents, how she rented a house with friends in Three Forks when she was in her thirties, clerking in a store, the first car she rode sixty years ago.

"I guess I liked it all. Where does it go? Bonnie, I think it was a year ago when I received so many cards on my birthday and I said if people would read them they'd think I was a saint, they would think I have wings sprouting. So many people ask me if I felt older as I was getting older. The past couple of years since I had arthritis I've slowed down but that's improved. I don't believe in taking medicines, not even vitamins. I guess I've been lucky."

"One more question. Do you care what people think of you?"

Her face lights up. "I think when you reach my age you should be able to do what you want."

The director of the center in Cheyenne, Wyoming says everybody calls her doc. She is a pathologist who was born in 1887.

"Jenny, what do you think of the new lifestyles?"

"You mean sexually, psychologically or intellectually?"

"Sexually."

She grins at me. "I think we're going to have to accept it. It seems to be in full swing right now. People are just living together and if I were young I suppose I would live with someone too. You have to accept the heartbreak whether you're married or living with someone. Look at all the people who get divorced. Women, you know, have more sexual desire than men and I guess they always will. I think to a certain extent we are cheated sexually, don't you?"

"Yes."

"Naturally you would. That was rhetorical because I can see you're a bright woman. You have to take life with a sense of humor. If you always look down all you'll see is the ground. If you look up you'll see the sky and you'll learn to look up to things."

A man walks over. "Hi, doc."

Her smile is contagious. "They call me doc. I'm a doctor to them."

He winks at me. "I've been trying to get sick for years but haven't been able to make it. Well, so long doc."

"I have many degrees, one in biology and one in biochemistry. Did they tell you I'm a pathologist? When I first came to Casper to work in the hospital they didn't even have paving on the streets."

"Jenny, what is the most important thing in your life?"

"Kleenex, right now," she says blowing her nose and laughing at the same time. "I believe in premonition, do you? I get feelings. I can't explain it. I could be thinking of you and you could be hundreds of miles away and you'll call me. They call it ESP and although I don't know anything about it, I know it happens."

"Could you tell me about your family, if you think they influenced your life?"

"I'm not proud of them but it's like a brand you can't take away. My grandfather bought and sold slaves like you do cattle. My grandfather on the other side was just as bad. He was a German baron who killed people with a sword when he didn't like them. My family was one of the first colonists. They claim we were the scum who came over and I'm ashamed to say I believe it. It seems history always repeats itself. We always had slaves and I don't believe in that."

"How do you feel about aging?"

The question strikes her funny. "Well, you can't change it. I want to stick around and pester people for a while."

"What could be done for older people, Jenny?"

"Well, in Cheyenne it's transportation. It's very difficult for old people to get around. And then there's always the lack of money when you get older. Your income is cut next to nothing. I take care of all kinds of small ailments gratis of course and I'm glad to help."

"Are you religious?"

"I'm not an atheist but I'm not religious. I never did have time for religion. One of the main things for older people is to enjoy life. I don't care who anyone is as long as they have a happy outlook. I'm a regular guy. I like to dance and I don't mind a couple of drinks once in a while."

"How did you feel about old people when you were younger?"

"An old person was somebody who had little spirit and zest for life. I felt like that when I was young and I feel the same now. We're all different and to lump us all together is as silly as lumping all young people together. Gertrude Stein said a rose is a rose but that's not true. There are roses and there are roses and even roses from the same family are different."

"Do you have any desire for sex?"

"Of course I do. I'm not dead yet."

THE SURVIVORS

The voices of doom have bothered me all my life. They come at all ages but seem to accelerate for people as they get older. How many times have I heard, when you're young you can survive anything.

A friend of mine, Hank Weiss, a pilot in the Korean War, crashed to the earth in his jet. In the hospital they said he wouldn't survive. But he did. Then the same medical authorities said, ok he survived but now he'll be a vegetable the rest of his life. For one year they patched up his broken body so he could sit in a wheelchair forever.

Hank had other ideas. He began researching, trying exercises, different diets and on and on. The following year he began walking. When I met him, a year after that, he was playing tennis every day, living a normal life. He silenced the predicters of doom.

The tragedy about the doom carriers is twofold. First of all your guess is often as good as theirs, and secondly, vulnerable people tend to believe out of fear and helplessness. And if you believe, anything can happen; negative or positive, it usually does.

There is no doubt that certain physiological changes take place as one gets older. People do get strokes and heart attacks and they do break bones. But this is not the end and in some cases is a new beginning. A stroke is not a death sentence. Nor is a heart attack.

Some people when they hear of some catastrophic disease or event say, "Let's not talk about it." Others, like Dr. Alfred

155

Bayne, say, let's discuss what we'd do if this should happen to us, which is what he did with his nurse. When he suffered a stroke while taking care of a dental patient she knew exactly what to do.

He talks of his stay in the hospital, of his stay in intensive care. "I'm inclined to think there are people who go off into the world and die. They wish it on themselves and I think you can wish yourself health as well. I don't know how far this goes but I think it helps if you help yourself along."

He tells me a story about his roommate, a man who also had a stroke and was completely out of it. Before Dr. Bayne left they put the man in a wheelchair. Dr. Bayne was also in a wheelchair ready to be dismissed. The superintendent asked him if he would talk to the man. "She said to me, you'll get no reaction but try." She put the two wheelchairs close together. I got real close, looking him straight in the eyes and I could see he was getting it and I said, 'Don't despair my friend. You're going to get well.' Now, he was considered a hopeless case. Two months later he walked out of the hospital."

Although he was able to help others, he himself suffered from depression. On the way to the North Vancouver Senior Center, where he and Violet are members. Alfred Bayne talks about it. "I'd wake up at night in a cold sweat and pray I would die. It was a terrible depression."

Violet adds, "He was a very changed person, unlike himself, different, a worry wart, gloomy. Somehow or other it penetrated his head that nobody could help him. I've noticed it time and time again. Depression is the biggest problem for the patient and the family. You see a person you've known for years suddenly change and it's very frightening."

"I thought everybody was against me."

"Even me, his wife. And kids and everybody and when he came out of it . . ."

"It was overnight. I had a conversation with myself, to tell the truth. I figured out I was the culprit and I was the only one that could do it for me and I discovered I'd been living in a fog."

Vi shakes her head. "A dark fog."

"Yes Vi, it was a gloomy fog anyway."

Violet turns to me. "We were visiting a friend and she said, why do you let him sleep, why don't you make him do things? Then a year later she was in the same boat and she understood."

As he parks the car, Alf Bayne says, "Bonnie, I look at life as a long street, a country road through streets and cities that you've never been through before and you don't know these areas but when you pass through them you know them. Then you can speak with authority."

We walk toward the entrance. "Alf, how long did it take you to get over this depression?"

"It took me pretty near two years. Eighteen months would be more like it. I might still be in it yet if it hadn't been for Vi's understanding."

He didn't go to a therapist but feels if he had it might well have speeded up the process.

The spirit that helped Alf Bayne recover is the same kind of spirit he's had all his life. His fight for a new senior center stems from a compassion he's always had for older people. His mother lived to be 100, his father was in his middle nineties.

"I remember one day, having dinner with them when I was in my fifties and it suddenly struck me. These people are special, they've got something. They said something to me, you see, that stirred me. From that time on I became interested in senior citizens and as time went on I became one."

He is disturbed by the myths we've accepted and believes most of the people perpetrating these very myths are those around 40 and 45, who suddenly realize their own approach to old age and become terrified. According to Dr. Bayne, this is where the education must begin and that's what he and others are working on. "I love talking to groups of people of that age and telling them, 'You're scared to death of approaching old age. You're approaching the best part of your life and if you approach it intelligently and with the proper attitude, every year you live on is worth two or three or four of what you lived in the past as far as getting that much more out of life'."

Dr. Alfred Bayne's stroke has made him appreciate life more, see everything with a fresh new outlook. We eat lunch. He takes me through this lovely senior center while Violet is busy elsewhere. We look at the paintings of the students, which pleasures him. He talks of his wife.

"Vi was just a beautiful Irish beauty, but she's just as beautiful today or more so to me, although a younger person might not see it compared to what she was but I see something now that wasn't there before. I see things I didn't see years ago or maybe even yesterday. Every year, every day that I live it becomes more distinct. My eyesight may be failing but my perception is improving."

I spend the most delightful day with Alf Bayne. We go from subject to subject and finally to the variance in aging. He claims the mind can deteriorate due to nutritional and chemical deficiencies which could be supplied, as insulin is supplied to diabetics. He believes in Vitamin E and has been taking 800 units a day for 31 years. When I tell him I also take the same amount he smiles warmly, says "Good for you. It shows you're smart. Bonnie, you know older people learn a little slower but they learn better. They remember more and this forgetfulness is a hoax. I've forgotten lots of things but it's because I don't want to remember."

Depression seems to be a big problem for older people who've suffered strokes and heart attacks. One man told me he never thought of his stroke after he had it and continued on with his acting career, but he was the exception. Others went through what Violet Bayne calls a dark and gloomy period but they survived.

In June 1974 when Esther Goldmacher was 71 years old, she was rushed to the emergency room of a Manhattan hospital with a heart attack. For seven days she was in an intensive care unit. The next six weeks was spent in the hospital. When she came home she was told to do very little. And she was frightened. A widow, whose only living relative in New York is her daughter, who also has a heart condition, she was forced to rely on friends.

Her fear slowly left and within six months she was walking over a mile a day, going dancing. When her friends showed concern she shrugged, "You only live once. What is the life? You live a year more or a year less. I want to enjoy myself. I don't give a damn for nothing."

Eleven months later she was back in the hospital, this time for a facelift. She'd lost forty-nine pounds on doctor's orders, claimed the skin hung on her face. "I looked like a 100-year-old woman. I couldn't stand to see myself anymore."

Her heart attack stirred memories she wanted to forget, about her life in Germany, how she and her husband and daughter fled the Nazis and went to Ecuador, a climate that proved bad for both husband and daughter. Their hearts were affected and in 1952 they emigrated to the United States. Less than a year later Esther's husband died of a heart attack.

She says "I'm a very nervous person because of my life. My mother died in a gas chamber. You know Treblinka?" She starts to talk of the Nazis, then changes her mind.

During dinner the conversation turns to the negligence of doctors. "The first doctor wasn't careful. I got the pain a year before in my back and I couldn't lift my left arm. He wouldn't see me, just said drink water and sit down. If you don't feel better come to my office. But then the pain is gone. For me, that was the first heart attack, a mild one, but a heart attack."

She looks at me, her eyes sad. "Bonnie, I tell you something. I don't know what's happening to me. Sometimes I think somebody pushes me. Go here, go there and then I go and I'm satisfied. I'm not happy anymore. I tell you I've changed since my heart attack. All my life changed. Everything is different. I had a facelift but I don't know why. At my age it's crazy, right? Sometimes I get up in the morning and I hear music and I start crying. I cry sometimes and I don't know why. I cry for nothing, no reason."

"I cry for no reason too Esther, sometimes. I think a lot of people do but they don't talk about it."

She hugs me. "Why should you cry. You're young." Then, "See how young my body is. It didn't wrinkle like my face. I exercise every day." She raises her arms above her head, stretches, then bends down and touches her toes. "Do you do that, Bonnie?"

I laugh. "No and I never could. I'm great at leaps."

I watch my friend Esther show her exercises. I am very saddened by the person I see, a different Esther from the one I knew.

This dialogue was done in July of 1975, thirteen months after her heart attack. Two years later, the Esther I see is completely back to the person she was. She feels marvellous, looks marvellous and says, "I look at my life with so much joy. It is difficult to explain but for me it is like I was given a second life."

Back in 1945, when Joe Smith was 61 years old, he and his partner Charlie Dale did a show with Martha Raye. The day after the closing show, in his hotel room, Smith passed out. He stayed in the hospital for some time, was told he couldn't smoke again.

Today he wears his third pacemaker and claims the most priceless human possession is peace of mind. "I worry sometimes but I'm what you'd call an opti-pessimist. I coined that word. I tell somebody that everything is fine. Don't worry about anything, you'll get over it, when I might have a pain myself."

He bursts out laughing. "But I went through life with operations and all. I had gall bladder, kidney problems and appendicitis. And now I have emphysema and have to have this contraption." He points to a machine in his room.

Joe Smith is a survivor, no doubt about it. After speaking with him and a number of other heart attack victims, all of whom were smokers, I've given up cigarettes, this time for good.

Rose Schlessinger was another heavy smoker. Six years ago, when she was 63, coming home from my mother's house, she felt faint. The next day she went to her doctor who took a cardiogram and told her to go to the hospital immediately. She stayed for six weeks.

How has it affected her? She accepts it as a fact of life, nothing more. The cigarettes were given up. Three weeks after leaving the hospital she was back at work.

She talks of the experience. "When my doctor said, can you get to the hospital and I asked if I could drive and he said no, I want you to take a cab immediately, I said, don't panic. You'll be alright. The funny thing is I'd just gotten over a broken arm. My husband had broken his hip and here I had this broken arm. We'd go for walks, my arm in a sling and him on crutches and people looked at us to see who did what to whom."

She laughs, then says, "Bonnie, this has always been my philosophy. Don't pamper yourself. Get right back on the job. I always look at the bright side of things. I always did."

Rose, recently retired, belongs to a senior center. She does yoga, exercises, dancing. She does everything as always, without fear, feeling life is meant to be lived.

And then there are Paul and Mary Large who've survived everything but their own prejudices. As a week-end guest in their home in Texas, I admire their will to live but not their bigotry which permeates the air they breathe, their home, their southern Baptist church where I am greeted warmly by the parishioners, am then told by the preacher that I am an infidel. I must admit they are very fair in their prejudices. All people other than Baptists are going to hell. We all need to be saved, so it isn't just an attack against Jews but I would say Jews and blacks are pretty much at the top of their hate list.

Between them they've survived heart attacks, strokes and dizzy spells. They are in their early nineties and their only answer for being saved is God who loves all Baptists.

My mother broke her leg in 1976, the first week in September. I was on vacation and my kids agreed with my mother that I shouldn't be notified. So it came as a tremendous shock to find her in the hospital. Worse was the news that she might lose her leg. The visiting hours don't start until the afternoon but I sneak up early in the morning. It is the first time I've seen her since the accident. She has been on intravenous feeding, is aware she has a multiple compound fracture but unaware she may lose her leg.

When she sees me her face lights up. We hug and kiss each other. "Bonnie, you don't know how good it is to see you."

She tries to be cheerful throughout the day, but we both know what she's thinking. My grandmother started with a broken hip, then another fall, another break, then the nursing home. She cannot believe this is happening to her and says finally, "When I think of the mountains I've climbed, all the things I've done, to think this could happen on stairs."

After the cast was on for a few weeks and it was agreed she would not lose her leg they started her on therapy. The first time is very traumatic. She has a cast up to her hip that pinches the skin. She's frightened which is unusual for her. She tells me the therapist asked her to walk holding on to the bar. She tried and did but somehow the experience started a flow of tears. The slowness, the helplessness, the reality that she's learning to walk again. The therapist yelled at her, called her a baby.

The second time in therapy they decide on crutches. The third time they decide crutches are not for her. She's too old they say. She's not learning fast enough. They try her on a walker. The therapist, my mother says, is abusive, not just with her but with everybody. Fight back, I yell. Insist on crutches. You'll be limited with a walker. You'll learn.

She says she can't, she feels old for the first time in her life.

I visit her often. And am infuriated by her acceptance of everything, even when it isn't good for her and she knows it. I have a few run-ins with her doctors whom she didn't choose (she was an ambulance case) but were assigned to her. She begs me to stop, says that I'm causing trouble. Fight back, I yell. "I can't, don't you understand. I'm helpless here. I'm in pain. What good will it do to antagonize them?''

But something happens after five weeks in the hospital. She is now moving faster on the walker. She is encouraged and not so helpless as she thought. She makes demands on one doctor and is euphoric. She puts me in hysterics when she reenacts the scene in mime. She also decides to hell with the dumb rules and lets me cut and wash her hair while her friend Rose keeps guard at the door so the nurses won't enter.

Six weeks later I take her home or try to. She's been dismissed but the papers have not been signed by her doctor. After waiting close to an hour I sneak her down the elevator in a wheelchair past the emergency room and out into the street. Kenn, my son, who's been alerted, rushes toward us and together we roll her at breakneck speed and get her quickly in the car. Nurses are screaming, what are you doing? Take off, I tell Kenn. And he does, a fantastic smile on his face.

I nonchalantly wheel the empty chair back into the hospital. A man screams about the rules, how she wasn't checked out. The nurse from the floor who was invisible all morning becomes a real person. "Where is the patient?" she screams. "She's gone home," I smile. "She can't have. We didn't sign her out."

I move out the door and walk to the next street where a smiling Kenn and Mary wait.

It is April of 1977, seven months after my mother broke her leg. She's had three new casts put on. She moves with the walker, pleads with me to travel further for this book, a trip I've been postponing, waiting for her cast to come off. "Go," she says, "will you go? You're making me nervous. I'll be fine. My friends will take care of me."

But her depression hasn't lessened, she is unbelievably vulnerable and it frightens me. For the first time I see her differently. My mother, who's never discussed sickness, dwells on her leg. Will she walk again? Will she ever be the same? Will she ever teach dancing or dance again? I force the issue. "You're thinking of grandma."

"Alright, so I'm thinking of her. It's true. Once you break a bone it's the beginning of the end, if you're older like me."

"That's ridiculous. Grandma got dizzy and fell. She was having those strokes. That didn't happen to you. Besides she lived for over 30 years after she had the first stroke. You fell because of negligence, of faulty stairs. It could have happened to anybody and you know it. Your leg will heal. You're a healthy woman."

"I'm not a kid."

"So what."

"So we don't know if I'll walk again."

"You are walking with the walker."

"I don't call that walking."

"If you know you'll walk again, you will."

The second week in April I decide to take the trip. I meet with Mary Herrick in Chicago who broke her hip seven years ago when she was 75 and is still running from meeting to meeting. In Denver I talk with Helen Lindgren about my mother. She says, tell her not to worry. "Tell her she'll be fine. I broke my ankle when I was close to 80."

Even with the cast on, Helen took a trip to Europe with her daughter but admits it was the first time in her life she really felt sorry for herself. "For the first time I felt old. It didn't get better when the cast was off. I had to carry a stick and I thought, how awful if I have to walk around like that for the rest of my life. I mean I never felt age as pitiful as I did that time. Feeling that I'd never be able to walk again."

Helen Lindgren no longer uses a stick, exercises twice a day and goes for long walks. "Tell your mother the depression goes away. I know."

In San Francisco I speak with Isabelle Van Frank whose 93-year-old husband broke his leg last year. "The doctor didn't think he'd ever walk again but you know Alex, he wouldn't listen. He was walking in less than three months."

She tells me that after seven weeks in the hospital Alex was going crazy. The doctor suggested a nursing home for him but their daughter was furious. She converted one room into a complete hospital set-up and they all took turns taking care of Alex Van Frank. "What really impressed me was my grandson. He was supposed to go to Mexico and cancelled the trip. He said we're all responsible for grandpa and I want to do my share."

The story is utterly amazing to me because I spent time with Alex and there was no way to tell he'd broken a leg and here he was 92 when it happened.

A book I read by a leading authority states if you break a bone and you're older, forget it. This certainly wasn't true of the people I met.

Jean R. who teaches yoga at a senior center in New England broke her leg when she was 68. It was the worst experience in her life since physical activity was the most important thing to her. "I would lay in the hospital day after day with the most unbelievable depression you can imagine. My friends came, trying to console me, but nothing helped. I was inconsolable. The doctor told me I had to be realistic, that I would be able to continue with my life but doing yoga would be out of the question. Continue with my life? My life was yoga. Well, perhaps that's an exaggeration. I do have other interests but it threw me. I thought, my God, this is the beginning of old age, something I'd never thought of before."

The depression lasted during her hospital stay and didn't leave when she went home. "Here I was, with a cast on my leg, up to my hip, unable to do the simplest tasks. I must have cried more during that period than I cried in my entire life. Then one day a good friend came and got angry with me. She said I can't stand coming to see you. I never realized what a defeatist you are. Stop pitying yourself. So you can't do yoga. So what? When she left I started meditating and then I said no, I will not take any doctor's ultimatum because that's what it was. I will be well, I will be well. I'm positive healing begins with the mind."

One year later Jean was back teaching her students. One thing her experience taught her was that people accept the voice of authority.

"Had I listened to this doctor I would probably never have attempted teaching again. How can any person know what another person is capable of? The most horrible thing about aging is believing what others tell you about yourself. You can't learn, you can't do physical activity, you can't do this and that. It's true, I can't do what I did at 20 but then I can still do more than many 20-year-olds who never participate in any physical activity."

"What would you advise older people to do when they have fractures?"

"To keep their spirits up, set a goal and stick to it. It's important to keep a positive image of yourself at all times, particularly when you're older. Now this may sound strange to you but there are times I'm glad I broke my leg because it taught me something invaluable. That you can overcome much in life and now when I see older people who have fractures, when I say you can do it and they say I can't, I tell them about myself and it gives them courage."

YOU ONLY DIE ONCE

My father died when he was 67 years old. I lied to him when he asked me if he was dying. We all did. I pretended everything was fine, that he was going to get well. Now when I look back I don't know whether it was to protect him or me or perhaps both. Or maybe it was just my own fear of death. But because of it I never really found out what kind of a funeral he wanted, what he thought about euthanasia since his deteriorating body took him away from life and most importantly what he thought about death.

I feel I was wrong in not discussing this with him. Unfair. Yet, if it were happening today how would I handle it?

Death is a difficult subject for me. I find it difficult to think of, much less discuss. With older people I found myself taking deep breaths, preparing speeches, then rationalizing it would be cruel to discuss death, funerals, etc. But it was painfully apparent that the fears I had were strictly my own and that the fear of death seems to have little to do with age, but where you're at in your own life.

Folmar Blangsted in Los Angeles, a well known film editor, is writing a book about his life. "Being a Dane you think about death. I call this alleged book of mine *The Not So Melancholy Dane* because you know who the melancholy Dane was. Hamlet, of course. And many years ago, as a matter of fact, shortly before my first wife died, I willed my body to UCLA because first of all I feel that, if through this kind of gesture, I can be useful to medicine, conceivably benefit somebody, say a student to become a good surgeon, I made a contribution. Instead of making undertakers and florists rich. Because I sure as shooting don't believe in funerals. There isn't going to be any in my case. I think it is the worst kind of barbarism, this business of preserving bodies.''

Lois Palmer uses the same word, barbarous, firm in her belief that all cemeteries should be plowed up and used either as public parks or as vegetable or fruit gardens, depending on their location.

Owen Evans agrees that donating your organs to medical science and then being cremated is the only way. "I'm not an atheist or an agnostic. I was brought up in the Unitarian church. When I was a kid they closed the church in the summertime and said go up in the mountains and have a picnic because you're closer to God there than any place else. Well, certainly you're closer to God in nature than you are in church or Sunday school.''

But what does death mean to older people? The religious people had no problem with this question. All was up to God who was waiting for them. Some used the expression they'd be going home. Others like Mr. Blangsted had different views.

''You know nothing. You don't even know that you're not. That to me is the most comforting state that one can find oneself in. There is nothing. I don't have to worry about heaven or hell or all those other multiple things like being reborn because I don't believe in it so I'm not afraid to die. By the same token I don't want to die because there are so many things that I enjoy and I don't want to exist without being able to do these things. Now my wife had an uncle who had a stroke. This poor man sat in a wheelchair. He couldn't clean himself. He couldn't perform natural functions without help. And he sat there and clung to life. I cannot understand that.''

In New Orleans, Marshall LaRue feels people should live as long as they can, no matter what condition they're in. "A person never wants to die,'' he says. "I've seen it too many times. Like my poor mother used to say, oh I wish I'd die, all that trouble and this and that going around and when she got real sick you didn't hear no more about that. They just tell you that when they're strong. When they get weak and pooped out they don't want to die no more."

"Are you saying it's better to be bedridden?"

"It's best to be alive regardless. Bedridden or not, no money or whatsoever. It's still best to be alive. Even a worm or cat or anything, a little animal. They like to live all they can."

Folmar Blangsted believes people are afraid to die because "Over the generations we have been programmed to believe in eternal punishment for sins committed so people are afraid to die because they have been threatened by their priests who have achieved power by saying you cannot get into heaven without my key. I ain't gonna open it for you unless you do what I say and if you don't do it I also have the authority to send you below. So people carry these fears around."

Professor Giovanni Costigan believes that all cultures, regardless of their differences, have a fear of death. "The fear of death is universal. Each culture has its own method. Most people from the beginning have refused to recognize the fact of death, I mean, the neolithic ancestor of ours many thousands of years ago saw the fact of death and denied it. He pretended there was an after-life and people have been pretending ever since. Religion institutionalized it. The desire for immortality as Freud would say is from the unconscious, which recognizes no limit to itself, so how can it die."

Terry Pettus does not believe in reincarnation, maintaining it takes more ego than he has. He tells me he tries to understand infinity, often when he's just going off to sleep.

"Try it sometime. Infinity, no end. I think of this enormous universe, this great power and I wonder why it would be concerned about a speck on a speck on a speck. You know, a personal god. Whatever it is, it isn't a very orderly universe. It's very destructive. No I don't need the belief of a life after death. It would give me no consolation. As a matter of fact the idea of living forever would be the most cruel thing. Because life has meaning, you see, and I think if most people would analyze this they would have to admit death is nothing to be afraid of. I find the most distressing thing is when I see young people die who haven't had a chance to live. But if it wasn't for death, life wouldn't have any meaning. It's because we know consciously that life has a span that gives it a parameter, a meaning.''

On the subject of funerals the responses were surprising. More than half the people I spoke with hadn't made any will and many others had filled out standard forms but didn't leave instructions for burial. Many had family plots and were leaving everything up to their families. At least one-third of the people were religious and wanted an old fashioned funeral with flowers and all but more said they preferred people send donations to their favorite charities. A small percentage, approximately 10%, wanted to be cremated.

Howard Shoup. ''I've said it for years and I don't know if I'd take it back. I used to say it campy as we say in show biz that I want to go back to Dallas to the family plot and I want the flowers never to stop. I don't want to be ashes thrown over the Pacific Ocean. I don't think that's very religious somehow. I don't think I'm going to change that. Lots of flowers.''

And Lorna, 94, was paying for a mausoleum and Doris Cavanagh wanted her casket put on top of a mountain with three days of celebrations.

Euthanasia brought another response. I was surprised at how many people never thought about it and said they couldn't voice an opinion. Many didn't know what it was. However, most of the people who had thought about it didn't believe in prolonging life if there was no hope. But some hesitated when it came to taking a life.

Helen Evans. ''People should make their own choices about life and death and when they can't their families should be able to decide.''

Owen Evans. ''I don't think you should inject air into their veins because in effect this would become murder. But I do think there's a line some place. Who's going to define it I don't know.''

Helen. ''People talk about God. This is against God but it's people that keep people alive. It's people who rigged up the machine, who discover and administer drugs, so that logic doesn't make sense to me.''

The word euthanasia is derived from the Greek and means ''good death.'' The Euthanasia Educational Council in New York has prepared ''A Living Will,'' which gives individuals the rights over their own life and death, providing they have a doctor who will go along with it and live in a state that does not consider euthanasia illegal.

A doctor in Boston who chooses to be nameless tells me he's watched patients more dead than alive. ''Yet we say they are living. What's worse is watching the families being sucked of their life savings when everybody knows there's no hope.'' Yet he refuses to take a life but admits he does as little as he can to keep them alive.

Dr. Charles Still talks about a patient in a sanitarium who was 99 years old, who had been mentally incompetent for 25 years. ''In that period of time he'd never had a digestive disturbance, never had a cold. He'd break a window and it would be 10 below zero. He'd sit there with the cold wind blowing on him. He bankrupted his family. Just keeping him there, keeping him alive bankrupted them. It's very difficult to justify this.''

Yet he too admits he couldn't take a life. When I protest about prolonging the life of a nonfunctioning person and giving awards to those who kill on the battlefield he answers, ''There are a lot of paradoxes that exist, things that are very difficult to justify.''

Celia feels it indecent for old people to stay alive and contribute nothing. ''Here in this commune I think it applies particularly. I have a whole lot to give to these people and I've given a great deal. When the time comes I'm going to take my pill. I'm going to decide when I've had enough. It will be up to me.''

But Howard Shoup feels differently. ''I was taught by my

grandmother never to mingle in human destiny so I could never decide things like that. But if it were me? I love to dance and go to parties and have fun and feel young. But if I were bopped over the head or hit by lightning or something and were lying in a coma for four months and the doctor said he's never going to come out of it, I would like for the family to tell the doctor to go away and do nothing for me. To act as if it were natural which is what they do so often with important people. If it were me I'd like my sister to say, oh don't let Howard lie there like a dead fish year in and year out.''

Eileen Glassford says she believes in God's good time. ''I don't believe in using things to keep an incapable person alive. My husband was a respiratory cripple for the latter part of his life and sometimes he used to say to me, when he was having this terrible pain, why don't you let me go. Rationally, I would quite agree with him and then he would go into a coma and, boy, my subconscious would spring forward and I would have him out and under an oxygen tent in no time. Rationally I believe in euthanasia but emotionally I don't.''

Marta Torrens discusses a woman of 80 who's dying. ''I don't know how many years she's been swallowing pills. Doctors are so insensitive. This woman has been made a carcass with her mind clear. No. Let me die. Let me weaken up. Let every part of me die at the same time.''

Catherine Van Bibber says she hasn't made up her mind but is afraid euthanasia might be subject to abuses ''and people are so quick to make up their minds that there is no future for somebody. I've seen too many cases.''

And Charles Raymond says he believes only God has the right to take a life but when I question how he'd feel as a vegetable he looks at me for some time, then says, ''I have said to my wife if I had terminal cancer don't put me in the hospital. Put me in the bedroom. Don't kill me but don't give me anything that will prolong what is inevitable. Ok, I'm not going to take a pill and I'm not going to take a knife. I don't believe in that, alright. But if it comes down to cold economics, once it is proven by the medical profession that the chips are down, you don't use experimental drugs or anything else and a person is perfectly right in saying I don't want to be touched. But I wouldn't sign a statement that would give anybody but God the right to take a life."

A nurse in Denver. "I don't know how I'd feel if it were my husband. I'm 68 and he's ten years older. If it were me I'd rather die than be a vegetable. I've seen so much in the hospital that I would have to say yes, I do believe in euthanasia, but only in hopeless cases."

A doctor in San Francisco. "This is really a tough problem especially for a doctor and for the family, for that matter. Often the patient is so far gone they aren't capable of making any decision and the family is so traumatized they vacillate back and forth. I think as far as I'm concerned personally, I would feel that I should have a choice and I would hope that if any of my family were in the same situation they would have a choice. In my own father's case he got to the point in his physical existence where he was in excruciating pain and he had nothing in the future to look for. I'm sure he could have been kept alive longer than he was but neither my sister nor I felt that he should be and that was his choice as well. Like me he was a doctor and we were personal friends of the attending physician. I'm now 73 and still practicing. I feel strong physically and mentally but if something should happen. . .My physician has questioned me about this and he knows what I want. As for me, I wouldn't want to make the decision about taking the life of a patient and I wouldn't unless it was their wish."

LIFE AFTER DEATH

I remember vividly a story that a man told me after the Second World War. He was fighting at Normandy and was terribly frightened when suddenly his grandmother appeared and told him not to worry, that she'd watch over him. Two weeks later he received a letter that said she had died a week before she materialized on the battlefield.

I think everybody has heard these stories. I myself have had a number of personal experiences, always with older people who died, the first being my grandfather Charles Bluh. I was 16. I was in a tight sleep dreaming about something, what, I cannot remember, when suddenly a coffin appeared in my dream and in it was my grandfather. I woke up shaking and for some reason looked at the clock on the dresser. I found out the next day that he'd died at the exact time I saw him in my dream, in his coffin.

Catherine Van Bibber tells me her father told a story she's thought about. A country doctor, he was attending an ill man who'd had many strokes. "He had been in a coma for a week or more and my father was sitting beside him, waiting to see if he'd regain consciousness before he died. He opened his eyes and was perfectly rational and he said to my father, Armfield, I saw your mother yesterday and she asked me how you are."

I've heard so many stories like that, it makes me wonder. My grandma Anna Fox Steinberg was also in a coma but before she died she said perfectly clearly, I see my father. He's waiting for me.

175

Eileen Glassford, when we discuss death, says she thinks of it and hasn't any fear. "It would be a new experience, exciting, the ultimate experience."

"What do you think happens after we die?"

"I haven't the vaguest idea but it would be interesting to find out, wouldn't it?"

"I'm not sure."

"I'll tell you a very interesting experience. About two years ago I had a massive operation and I was under an anesthetic for over three hours. I had a very beautiful vision. I was walking through a field of wildflowers and it was so clear that I was identifying each of the wildflowers as I walked through. And my wee dog that had died about three years before was at my heels and my husband was standing at the end of the field. It was a beautiful thing and I thought when I came to, I wonder what anesthetic that is. I'm going to become a junkie." She laughs.

"And when I got back I told my doctor about it and he said we hesitate to put older people under anesthetic for any length of time because nearly everyone that is very close to death has a very beautiful vision. I read an article in a magazine. This woman had a great golden glow but mine was very specific and it was almost this passing over. It seems, if you aren't satisfied with your life on this globe, you just follow the vision and drift away, which intrigued me very much. It is a very common thing apparently among old people who are close to death."

I had a very different experience. I had major surgery a few years ago and I felt I was being pulled elsewhere and I had to fight to pull my body back. It was very frightening and I remember that I was using all the strength I had and it seemed to go on forever.

Edgar Cayce was a phenomenon. As a medical diagnostician who needed nothing more than the names and addresses of patients to pinpoint what was wrong with them physically, he helped thousands of people.

His work is carried on at the Association of Research and

Enlightenment (A.R.E.) in Virginia Beach, Virginia, where over 14,000 readings are available to physicians, psychics and the public. Here people come from all over the world to attend lectures, seminars, study, etc.

I sit outside, on the beautiful A.R.E. grounds with Gladys Turner who worked with Edgar Cayce as his secretary from 1923 to 1945, the only secretary hired to keep records of his readings and his work.

She talks about this. "He would lie down and put his hands over his solar plexus and he would look at the ceiling and his eyes would get sort of glazed. You could see his eyelids flutter and then he would start heavy breathing. You could see his chest rise and fall. It was at that time the suggestions were given to him by his wife. She was there all the time. The three of us were like triplets."

Cayce gave two one-hour readings a day. Most of them were given over the phone, then typed and mailed to the people. I ask Gladys about life after death. She says in some of the readings they speak of a baby being an old soul, old in experience on the earth. "The readings indicate that all souls were created at once. We're all the same age but some can be older in experience. Some have been here many times. And I feel age is not what makes you old. It is the way you live and think."

Gladys Turner's life readings show many past lives. But the four incarnations she's working on now have a bearing on her present life. One life was in the lost continent of Atlantis. Another in pre-history Egypt. "A lot of information that came from Cayce's Egyptian and Atlantis readings is now coming to light. The flood of Noah, according to the readings, was the second deluge of Atlantis, which was about 10,000 BC. There were three big upheavals and the second one was Noah's. And according to the readings there were prehistoric periods where women ruled."

Gladys Turner believes she's coming back again and claims we apparently keep coming back until we fulfill the purpose for which we came into earth in the beginning. "We choose to come in and it is said we come from God and have to go back to God, you know, back to the oneness which we chose to leave in the first place.''

As for predestined death. ''The statement made by Mr. Cayce in one of the readings was that even God doesn't know what a person will do until they make up their own minds and then when they do you can see the end of it. Even prophesies can be changed if people change and go in another direction. It makes the result different.''

She claims this applies to nations as well.

Gladys Turner says she is freer now that she's older. Once quiet and very concerned about how people saw her she is outspoken. ''I'm having more fun now. Of course my work may have helped me change. The fact that Mr. and Ms. Cayce died and their son Hugh Lynn and I were left to carry on could have made the change.''

However, in 1973, overloaded with work, she became ill with a nerve and muscle disease. She tried everything to overcome this but nothing worked. ''Then one day I had what you'd call a religious experience. I had been complaining to myself and to everybody, I can't do this, can't do that. All of a sudden I realized if I couldn't do any of these things ever again I would still have a purpose. I could still use my mind to think and pray and be at one with God, without being up and doing and running around, doing all these things maybe somebody else could do just as well. I began to get better as soon as I realized this.''

Since then she has trained people to do more of her work. She feels the responsibility and urgency of getting all of Cayce's work out but is now feeling well.

What would her life have been like if she hadn't met Edgar Cayce? ''I probably would have gotten married and had a household of children and been very much caught up in my own little group. I think without this work which gave me a broad scope I would have just been in my little family group in the community. I would have been very closed in, I would have been very. . .what is the word. . .narrow.''

Edgar Cayce was 67 years old when he died in 1945. He was overloaded with work, deluged with urgent requests for help, partly because of the war. He was concerned about both his sons who were in the service. During the year that he was ailing he received approximately five hundred letters a day. He went from two readings a day to six and eight readings, which he knew was unhealthy. Gladys Turner tells me that Edgar Cayce knew he was going to die.

"Gladys, I notice the expression here is passed over. Is it because you're passing over to another dimension?"

"Yes."

"Why don't people just say die?"

"Well we do say that about Edgar Cayce. Hugh Lynn brought that up one time, when people were saying Edgar Cayce passed on. He said he died. Actually the physical body dies. It doesn't mean your soul dies."

"Do you believe in funerals, Gladys?"

"No. My first husband and I willed our bodies to medical research. Mr. Cayce said cremation is a sanitary way. And there's not much danger of being held on earth if your soul is freed. You can't burn the soul."

I complain that the library has categories for everything but aging. Ms. Turner says she has kept tabs on readings for older people which will eventually be catalogued.

"There was a lot of advice given to people who were older, sort of urging them to be proud that they have all this experience behind them. That it's something you should look forward to rather than dreading."

Every other week a group of people come to the home of Glady Moon Jones for what she calls a cross between a seance and group therapy. There is no money exchanged. Ms. Jones does not go into a trance but feels vibrations when she's reaching some person from beyond.

My coming together with Gladys Moon Jones was rather odd. I

was driving with a friend and for some reason we couldn't get out of the Washington area. Either the car stalled or we lost all sense of direction. We finally gave up and stayed outside Washington for the night. I cannot say what prompted me but I found myself talking about Albert Einstein. The conversation perplexed my friend but not more than it did me. I couldn't seem to stop myself. The next day I went to a service station because the car was behaving so strangely. I told the owner casually that I was writing a book about older people and he immediately suggested Gladys Moon Jones.

At her home she insists it was Einstein who got me lost, who directed me to the service station, that it is Einstein who communicates with her every day during her morning meditations, through automatic writing. "Einstein began writing through me marvellous things but I kept saying, Mr. Einstein, I don't know anything about this and as for your $E = MC^2$, it doesn't mean anything to me. I can't understand it.

"He said, do not worry. What is important is the atom bomb was a grave mistake. Rewrite my old equation as mind-energy equals thought-manifestation, that everything you see is a manifestation of thoughts. It was the mass thoughts of war that produced the atom bomb. Now multiplied thoughts of peace can change the world."

She goes into another room and returns with the automatic writing. "I can read you what he wrote to me about the atom bomb from the spirit world. He said this is the worst thing that ever happened, but bound to happen sometime somewhere. It has kept the world from holocaust so far, but that sitting on a world devastatingly explosive is a bitter business causing people to deteriorate morally."

Reading from the papers she says, "Einstein tells me, think of what total destruction of your planet will mean from our viewpoint. Souls will be catapulted out into the dimension where we are now. It will be crowded with unprogressed unawakened entities who will have to be nourished to a consciousness of being. They will have to be awakened so that they can review their lives and plan their goings on. To have billions of unawakened souls propelled instantaneously into the beyond will create a great problem. Believe me, we worked hard taking care of the thousands of soldiers who came out suddenly.''

Albert Einstein says that he is working hard with other scientists trying to reach the leaders of the world. He also insists there will be a new discovery which will change the world and even the person on the street will know about it. ''He tells me they are going to have communications from some star, maybe in another galaxy but the discovery will not come from our planet. He's given me a whole other series of stars, the pulsars, the black holes and the ghost stars to study.''

Gladys Moon Jones is certain that there is life after death, that we come back to work out our past lives. She believes we are here to experience and, no matter how bad the experience, it is there for the progress of the individual.

Both her uncle and mother were clairvoyants. She tells me her uncle was able to put one finger on a table and the table would twirl around on one leg. She calls him remarkable. ''After the doctor pronounced him dead my uncle said to him, don't be in such a hurry and then just as he died he sat up and said, 'Why, father!' He saw his father who'd been dead for ten years.''

Ms. Jones' mother went into a coma for three days, after suffering a paralyzing stroke. She stayed by her bed, certain her mother would do something as she always told Gladys she would go over consciously. ''For three days she couldn't say a word because her throat was paralyzed. Suddenly she took a deep breath and on the exhalation said, perfectly clearly, *now*. She did it a second time, then a third time and died.''

Gladys stood looking at her mother's face when she heard her laugh. ''She said 'Gladys you're looking at me. I won the bet.' And then I remembered that about five years ago my mother thought we ought to go to some neighbor's funeral and I said 'No, I'm not going to any funeral on a hot day like this. In fact I'm never going to any funeral again. I just don't believe in them. I'm not going to look at any dead people. I won't even look at you after you're dead because I want to remember you alive.' I saw the hurt in her eyes and she said, 'Yes you will. You'll look at me because, after all, you came out of my body.' So there I was standing looking down at her body and thinking I came out of it and she laughed and said, 'Well you're looking at me.' I laughed and my brother said, 'Gladys what's the matter?' And I told him. Then he said she said something meaningful to him too.''

When Gladys Moon Jones lectures on design in art and life, she tells her audiences that all the experiences they have are thought to be the true things that happen but it is the person's attitudes toward these experiences that matters. ''The way you recreate your past by your attitude and the way you create your future and the way you work with all these experiences, that is the design in life.''

To her life after death is just a continuance of that design.

OLD AGE IS BIG BUSINESS

Old age has become big business. Over twenty years ago the first Senior Center was opened. Now there is hardly a city, town or village that doesn't have one, in some form or other.

In 1961 the U. S. Senate set up a Special Committee for Aging. Now, every state has its Office on Aging, every city its Department on Aging. There are grants to be had; Titles I, II, III, VII, etc. etc. etc.; money to be made.

There are senior newspapers and magazines and theatres and camps. There are Meals on Wheels, Dial a Friend, Foster Grandparents, the American Association for Retired Persons (AARP), the Retired Volunteers Service Program (RVSP). There are Continuing Education for senior adults, Foster Homes for Adults, Day Care Centers, Retired Housing, Nutrition Programs and these are but a few.

Some of the programs are excellent. Some are not. But either way, in most cases the chief beneficiaries of these programs are not older people themselves but those hired to help the old.

Terry Pettus discusses this. "All these programs for the aged, whether good, bad or indifferent. . .you've already made a whole group of people whose entire careers depend on it. It's like the war on poverty. How in hell can you expect the government to eliminate poverty when they would eliminate their own jobs? They have a vested interest and we create this."

He is adamant in insisting that old people should run their own programs and feels the only solution is to make the recipients a part of the administration. "Otherwise you create a bureaucracy.

Who knows better than the old people, but you see we don't do it.''

He deplores the fact that old people are now having their choices made by others. ''After all, they are the people who all of their lives made decisions for themselves, all the things we piously say about them. Then we consign them to the dump heap. Age is a chronological situation that is going to happen to everybody. You can always escape it by dying. But a certain percentage are not going to escape and that's that.''

Terry Pettus claims he alternates between bitter anger and pity for the way we treat old people and although he believes all his fights cannot end in Utopia ''it sure as hell is going to improve a lot of things. Imagine a life where people can be free to expand themselves. What the human spirit, old and young, is capable of we only know by seeing what the rare ones have done.''

Max McCarthy in San Francisco calls himself an agitator. He complains that the Commission on Aging is supposed to service senior citizens but what it does is control them. ''They get a lot of money and put forth their programs but the senior centers, for example, don't have that much say. These programs are planned by the so-called experts and they think they're doing a lot but they're not doing anything. If people can't do something for themselves they're not free. Now that people are older and retired they should have the time and opportunity to do a little thinking for themselves. But at the senior centers, if anybody tries to do that they're immediately pounced upon.'' He believes seniors are brainwashed, accepting the fact that their time is taken up from the minute they enter these centers until they leave.

Max McCarthy, 80, is an artist, concerned with a creative environment for the old. His wife Jean, also an artist, disagrees. She feels environment has little to do with it and that the senior centers attract the kind of person who is content to do little. She turns to her husband. ''Some of our greatest people were in the wrong environment but they managed to rise above it.''

"But Jean, environment is not a place. Environment is people too, you know. You find all kinds of conditions in a place because of the different people in it. You can be in one place with the wrong people and that's your environment. You mix with other people and you're in a different environment. I would like to see people controlling their own destiny instead of other people controlling it. We get a lot of propaganda to keep the status quo. People don't want to see any change come about so our energy is spent in trying to keep the status quo. In that respect the younger generation is not so influenced."

But what of the young people who run programs, who run senior centers? The Santa Monica Senior Center is a one-story building facing the Pacific. I visited in December 1975. The woman who was in charge is 68 and had to retire last year because of her age. She didn't want to. Neither did the members of this center. The 19-year-old-girl who replaced her is adorable, they say. They also say, "Tell us how can a young girl like that know how we feel? Why should she be expected to know? She sits in the office waiting for members to come to her."

The previous director helps the young director who is very open about her feelings. "I have a lot to learn. I make mistakes." She is insecure in this position, anxious to do the right thing but admits she hasn't the vaguest idea of what the right thing is.

Betty Elkin, the former director, is a trained social worker, who has spent her life working in recreation and with seniors. The programs she planned were geared toward the members, to benefit them physically and mentally. Although she is retired most of the members still act as if she were in charge. They talk to her of sickness, loneliness. Ms. Elkin says, "Some of the people live in four walls, one room with nobody to talk to. You have to listen or they'll go crazy. The answer of course is to get them interested in coming here. Everybody has something they can be interested in. Nobody's a blah."

A woman stops me. "It was wonderful when Betty was the

director. She was one of us. It's a disgrace that they made her retire, a disgrace.''

In a large western city a man, 31, runs the senior paper. He has received grant money for three years. His qualifications: He previously worked for Parks and Recreation. This is a quote. ''I started a paper in New Orleans in 1969. The newspaper started out of my own boredom.''

Why a newspaper for senior citizens? ''I had a number of close relatives who were older people and I was at a place where it was able to happen. I started the paper within the Parks Department and that was very limiting. Then I applied for a grant under Title III of the Older Americans Act and the first year I got a $47,000 grant and it has been clicking ever since.'' That first year he was 28.

The people who work for him are called senior aides, earn minimum wage and are not experienced newspaper people. The woman who is associate editor is a former nun, 72 years old. She has spent her entire lifetime teaching in Catholic schools. My interview with her made me wonder why she was chosen. A woman well versed in Catholicism, she is totally oblivious of the needs of seniors unless they happen to be reactionaries like her.

In a large senior center in Los Angeles I meet with the director who tells me I will be eligible to join when I am 50. The director himself is not eligible since he's 31. But he believes everyone is young because a group of women, all deep in their seventies, are admonished when they ask to speak to him, ''Girls, girls, you must not interrupt. Come back later when I am free.''

A woman talks about this director. ''He's a boy, a disgusting macho but what can we do? They hired him so we're stuck with him. We don't choose the director. We don't even choose our activities.''

Then there's the other side. Older people who work with their own age groups.

Louise Markham was born in 1893. In 1958, when she was 65,

she was retired from the YWCA. A former employee was hired to open a senior center in California and asked Ms. Markham if she would join her. She was delighted with the opportunity and moved all her belongings from the east to the west coast. She has now worked with older people for 19 years and claims, "People who work in settings like mine are the specialists on aging. We are the people concerned with the older people. We are the people who scorn the bingo parties, the bridge parties, who want to see people developing their potential."

She talks about younger people who work with older people. "It's difficult for them. They tend to be patronizing and over-protective. They definitely underestimate the mental capacity, the physical capabilities, and fail to understand that old people are still evolving, still trying to find themselves in the same way that younger people are and this is what makes life good. There is no zest in being alive unless you are still exploring some potential within yourself."

We talk of the media view of older people and discuss "Over Easy," a show both of us have seen. Louise Markham did a survey of 120 people over 65 and not a single person thought the television program representative of older people's educational level, academic level or entertainment level. "It was cheap show business. The media image is unfair. Either it's the nursing home people or some ridiculous stereotype."

I meet Isabelle Van Frank in her home in Berkeley. Her involvement with the elderly goes back twenty years when she realized there wasn't any budget for senior citizens and the programs they had were less than adequate. She was outraged that the directors were mostly young men who had taken physical education and had been working with children. "The Recreation Department thought they should do something for the old folks and they should be commended for seeing there was a need but they had no understanding of the need. They turned it over to these young men who gave older people the same programs they gave five year olds."

As a result she and three other people formed a group that was first called The East Bay Coordination Council of Senior Citizens. She was president for fifteen years. During that time she visited many senior centers. "It was appalling. They didn't let the elderly do anything. They couldn't discuss anything that was controversial because they were afraid they would get their blood pressure up and I said it was good for people to get their blood heated once in a while. I used to say there was an invisible sign over the doorway. 'Think not as ye enter here.' When I went from one group to another to try to educate, and to discuss things, there was always a small group that would correspond but the majority of them were interested in bingo and cards. I think most people who were attracted by and large were people who didn't have the opportunity to explore themselves and develop other interests. I think you'll still find people like that but not as many. I would say more interesting people are coming to these programs."

She compares the programs years ago to her childhood. "I used to say when I was in kindergarden we made endless chains with colored strips of paper and in these recreation programs they were making these little ashtrays. Endless, one ashtray after another and they colored these and that's what they called arts and crafts. Here were these adults having their decisions made for them by these young people. Of course it is much improved today and there are still bingo and card programs but apparently some people are satisfied with it."

Isabelle Van Frank is not satisfied with the way older people are treated and as a speaker airs her grievances. At a recent conference she talks of people insisting we add dignity to the life of elderly persons "and now dignity in death. How can there be dignity in death when one is reduced to a life of deprivation, malnutrition, worry and despair, all the terrible consequences of such deep, devastating poverty?"

She went on to talk about the $13,000 raise Congress said they needed for their survival when their salaries were $44,000, excluding fringe benefits. She continues. "Well, I think most of us here would be glad to demonstrate how we could survive on that $13,000 alone.''

She complains that millions of dollars are spent on programs to help older people ''but this older person feels that actually there are many young people who are helped to a greater extent than those for which these programs are planned. These are the people who are getting the jobs, administrating programs under Title II, Title III, Title XX and all the other titles.''

She feels the word ''advocate'' is overused, that there are so many advocates telling the elderly what to do and what not to do. ''They forget that these old people were the former leaders of yesterday. They were the business leaders, making policy and now because we've become 65 or 70 we're not capable of making our own decisions. Under Title III we advise but they don't have to listen to our advice. Personally I feel we had more influence fifteen years ago. I know a lot of elderly don't agree with me but I think we've been pushed into the advisory role rather than a policy-making role.''

The next time I see Isabelle we walk arm in arm along upper Broadway. She is distressed that so many of her relatives in New York are ailing, that her sister is in a nursing home. She believes older people should be taken care of in their own homes, rather than warehousing them to institutions and has been working on a solution for some time. Ms. Van Frank and a group have tried to get more day care centers for seniors but have not succeeded because the lobbyists for nursing homes are powerful. ''All we asked was for a few but they felt two this year, three next year. Empty beds in nursing homes means they don't make money.''

She continues. ''If I say to my sister I saw A, she'll say who is A? But if I say you know B and C are A's children she'll say, 'of course, how are they?' A lot of old people don't remember certain things but is that a reason to put them away?''

She believes researchers have done a lot to perpetuate the stereotypes of aging but they don't point out that by far the greatest number of us are no different from younger people.

"Researchers, even the most outstanding gerontologists who are recognized authorities always talk as if the problem of aging applied equally to all older people and, as you know, Bonnie, it's only a small percentage of the elderly who are completely dependent on others."

Frances Brown talks about a conference she went to in Denver, sponsored by the Western Gerontologist Society. "They were supposed to help the elderly. In what way I don't know. It's basically policy, it's basically training, it's basically BS. The basic concern today is health insurance and when we said you didn't mention it they said they're only concerned with policy. They're not an action group. They should know that policy is not enough. You have to have action with it. What's policy to a person living on a fixed income? To me it was like being in a classroom again. I don't believe in young people telling us how to live. We know how to live. What old people have to have are their rights. I said to them, why are you taking old people by the hand? They're capable."

She shakes her head angrily. "Experts! When I was leaving, one older person said, 'let's have less experts and more action.' The thing is the young people take over and that's not good. We have to do for ourselves. We're of age."

But Isabelle Van Frank, who's been a member of The Grey Panthers since the early seventies believes the strength of the movement is young and old working together. And there are young people who work with the old, groups such as The Little Brothers of the Poor.

Unfortunately the average younger person can't see that aging has much to do with them. What's worse is the older persons who deny their age. I'm beginning to parade my wrinkles around defiantly. When I hear statements such as "I'm growing younger every day," I retort with, "well, I'm getting older every day."

And while I continue to age, many of my contemporaries have magically become my juniors. Some have shed as much as eight years. They think it's great. I think it's dumb.

I agree with Alice Brophy who says age must be brought out of the closet. A woman who's worked in the field of aging for over 30 years until she herself has become one of the two million older people residing in New York, she says, "Not talking about your age is like denying your religion. I think some day we'll accept the beauty and dignity and graciousness of age. Most of us don't talk of senility as we used to. If a kid takes an exam and at age 21 freezes, you don't say she's senile. But if you ask an older person a question, somebody who goes through life in a pedestrian way, where every day is the same as the next and he or she doesn't know if it is a Friday or a Tuesday, why should they?"

As the Commissioner of the Department on Aging she states, "I've always enjoyed older people. They're not necessarily wiser if they weren't wise when they were young, and aging doesn't add anything to their stature, but I think the experience of older people is a value we underestimate."

I also agree with that statement and, like Terry Pettus and Isabelle Van Frank, fail to understand why older people are not running their own programs. Why aren't the younger geriatric workers and gerontologists working as consultants rather than the other way around? The other way around seems ass backwards to me. If I want to find out what a blind person feels I'm not going to ask a sighted authority on blindness; I'll ask blind people themselves.

There's also a matter of money. So many of the older people working in the field of aging either earn a pittance or nothing. My mother is a good example. She's been teaching dancing for years as a volunteer for which she is well qualified and should have been paid. And now she is on the advisory board for senior camps (VASCA) and again is not being paid. But the younger workers are the paid experts.

One person who does not believe in volunteerism is Katherine Porsant, 71, who teaches physical fitness to senior citizens at the 92nd Street YW-YMHA in New York. A retired physical education teacher, she has been working with older people for the past three years. Her students are absolutely amazing. I join their exercise class and klutz along. They cheer me on.

"You can do it. We can and look how much younger you are."

I shrink a couple of inches. "I guess I'm in lousy condition."

"We couldn't do it either at the beginning." Apparently they couldn't. Ms. Porsant has developed a class using her own techniques to fit the student's needs. The exercises she gives loosens up their joints, helps them to limber up. She believes exercises can begin at any age but that it is extremely important to work up gradually.

When I ask about people over 65 who are exercising for the first time I get a surprising answer. "These are good people to work with because their muscles are flabby and not set so they are not musclebound in any way."

I ask her to talk realistically about changes in the physical body. "There is a gradual aging process that begins at 30 which varies somewhat with the individual. Changes do take place in the circulatory, respiratory, muscular and organic systems of the body. But elasticity of the muscles and good circulation of the blood can be improved through continuous exercise. Many of us assume that deterioration is synonymous with aging and many of the elderly just sit and wait for the symptoms to develop. My belief is that people can feel just as good in their later years as in their youth, provided they work to retain their health."

As a person who did voluntary work for years while my husband earned money I realize how demeaning that can be—not the work—in a society that considers monies earned as a measure of who you are. The implication in working for nothing is painfully obvious.

Katherine Porsant continues. "You know, Bonnie, there could be a desire to teach but you can teach all wrong, which many people do, and this does not benefit the students at all. I think it important that we have qualified teachers and that we should adequately compensate them."

I agree with Katherine. But who are the volunteers? Go to any organization that uses volunteers and you'll find a large percentage of women. They don't need the money, we are told, and besides it is for a good cause. Certain things never change. As people get older and retire you'll find more widows doing voluntary work than widowers. Why? They don't need the money, they have time and it is a good cause. Money is what men earn and causes are often what women proudly work for.

Then there are men who work after retirement and get paid less than they're accustomed to. Victor Stern, 90, is a good example. After working all his life in his own business, then retiring at the age of 70, he decided to go back to work a few years ago. His wife had died and he felt lost. "There was a tremendous void and I needed some commitment. I was hired as a senior aide, which has to be the lowest category here at the magnificent salary of $2.50 an hour." Although he's contributed a great deal to the Department on Aging, his salary is not about to rise much.

Mr. Stern is just one of the many senior aides who work throughout this country. Some like Victor Stern work because they want to, but more work because their social security is inadequate. The point is that these adults who've lived, experienced, and amassed knowledge are being paid what a kid just out of high school earns.

Old age has come of age. It is definitely big business. Take Medicare. Now that we have Medicare, doctors can jack up their fees and they do. A book should be written about this subject alone.

From my own experience as a member of a hospital plan, the first question I hear when I enter a hospital or a doctor's office is, "Do you have a medical plan?" Then I'm sure some white-coated individual goes into a computerized room, figures out what the plan pays and charges accordingly. Patients blindly think they're getting off cheaply but they're not. Everybody benefits but the patient. Well over half the people I spoke with complained about their doctors.

Isabelle Van Frank. "I went to a doctor. I'm so down on them. I asked him about my hearing and my eyes and the only answer he had, and he's a big shot in the field, was well I can't run as fast as I used to so why should you see as well. I was hoping for some comfort and he couldn't understand.''

Not every doctor is unconcerned. Dr. Charles Still in Scottsdale, Arizona has worked for years on the Governor's Advisory Board dealing with aging. ''I think the biggest problem is the impersonalization that's taking place. Medicine has gotten so scientific and mechanized that so often the one thing older people are trying to get, a personal relationship, is wiped out. They have a problem they want to discuss, they don't necessarily want to discuss it with a nurse, and when they find that they're not getting the service they need they often go from doctor to doctor. Of course I know from a doctor's standpoint it can be a great time waster but on the other hand this is one of the chances that an older person has to eliminate their worries, a chance to talk it out with somebody who will listen to them and give them sound advice.''

I ask Dr. Still why doctors were more concerned with their patients years ago. He answers, ''I think part of this is a time element. More patients are being seen today but on the other hand, those who really need the time, like older patients, are not getting it. Another big problem is that an older person often doesn't know where to start to find out what's wrong with them and they'll go to a clinic and maybe see seven or eight doctors, and feel they are not in the care of anybody, or when they leave they don't have any information. Not enough doctors give the patient the information needed. And the patient will still feel something is wrong but not know where else to go. They feel that they have no one who is really interested in their case. I've had patients come to me and say, 'When I go to Doctor So-and-so he always sends me in for so many tests.' Others say, 'Every time I go they do the same thing.' Or they'll say, 'I've had some trouble thinking lately so they'll do a brain scan and if I go back three months later they'll do exactly the same thing. And when I get through I feel like I've got nothing out of it.' A lot of them feel that they've just gotten on a merry-go-round."

"Dr. Still, can you tell me why some older people are healthier than others, aside from the obvious genetics."

"I think the genetic factor is important and I also think the challenge of living is important. Older people minimize their aches and pains when they still have a challenge, something that intrigues them. They go ahead and do it and this in turn generates more energy. So I think, in the main, something that they really are vitally interested in is a very important thing. Because if they lose the challenge they seem to go downhill. There are an awful lot of sick people that are healthy. They have diseases but they're healthy because they're going to go ahead and lead their lives and do as complete a job of it as they can. And there are other people who have minor infirmities, minor diseases that control them the rest of their lives.

"I have patients that have a minimum amount of problems and make a maximum amount of noise about it and affect their whole family because of it and affect their whole life because they're not interested in anything else. They focus their whole lives on their aches and pains. It is really hard to figure out why some people are this way but it's true."

He believes that couples who are dependent on one another are in for problems when they get older. A good solution is to separate periodically, for a month or so, which is what Charles Still and his wife do. The biggest problem for him when his wife is gone is eating. He says he loses his enthusiasm for cooking after a few days and resorts to the can opener or cold cereal. He feels if he were left alone he would eat lunch at a senior center, for the company as well as the food.

"As far as nutrition is concerned you have two factors. One is sociability. It's hard to eat alone. The other is finding the desire to prepare meals."

"Yes, but it's one thing when you go to a center for a meal because you want to be with people, and another when you don't have enough food and it's your only decent meal."

He agrees and is concerned with those who are having difficulty making ends meet. He claims they are eligible for supplemental social security (SSI) but often aren't aware that they're entitled to benefits. "They don't have the educational background to begin with or they've lost their glasses or can't see anymore or they're not aware. They need to be helped and we do have information referral centers but they have no idea of where to go and we don't always reach these people."

The high suicide rate among the old disturbs him as does alcohol which he feels is another form of suicide. "There are a lot of older people who get a quick pick-me-up from a couple of shots of liquor. Three or four shots sometimes kills their appetite and they get to depend on the liquor too much. Some of the retirees are plagued with a real alcoholic problem."

Dr. Still who spends most of his time in health planning these days says, "We spend millions of dollars in administrating programs but what about people who are in dire need and have no way of getting money? I've been out to meetings where three to four hundred people go to hear the Governor talking about what we're doing for the older adult or a Senator gets up and tells what they're doing. Yet I mingle with the crowds and I hear some old gentleman standing there saying, I need $20 a month more to live on, and what'll I do?

"This is what's so disturbing about our planning for older people. There isn't enough flexibility. Nothing to take care of the immediate situation."

AFTERTHOUGHTS

There are some 23 million people over 65 in the United States. By the year 2000 this number is expected to increase to 32 million. If the present birth rate continues, old people will be 12.2% of the total population of about 260 million. However, if the birth rate should continue to decline, the over-65's will represent close to 13% of a total population of about 246 million.

The 1978 statistics show that 18.7% of the married couples had an income of over $15,000. 20.2% had incomes of $4,000 to $6,000. The $2,000 to $4,000 range was a little over 11%.

Of the widowed, divorced and those who were never married, 8.4% had an income of over $10,000. 19.8% were in the $4,000 to $6,000 bracket. Some 26% had from $2,000 to $3,000. And 10.5% were supposed to live on a shocking $2,000 and under.

It doesn't take a genius or even a mathematician to see that a significant number of older people are expected to live below the poverty level. What the statistics don't show is that those who earned more money during their lifetime are being rewarded with higher social security payments. Those who earned the bare minimum can get as little as $114.30 a month, which means that poverty actually perpetuates itself.

These statistics aren't mere numbers. Behind every number is a face, a human being, somebody who's spent over 65 years on this earth. Numbers are easy to deal with. What isn't easy is to realize that while you're reading these figures there are some old people who aren't getting enough to eat.

However, statistics can change. It isn't a statistician that makes changes but people. If enough people dislike a statistic they can make things happen.

Since I started this book, the retirement age upped from 65 to 70 when a bill was signed by Congress in March of 1978. This is fine but there are people who are not ready to be retired at 70. I also believe that the main issue is not that of retirement. It is the way we view older people that makes these laws and practices possible, and our stereotyping of old people as silly, infirm, feeble, forgetful. These word-pictures really reflect our own attitudes rather than what old people are like and perhaps more our refusal to face our own eventual old age—a cruel insensitive joke, played on ourselves.

Attitudes are often hard to change. Some older people perpetuate the stereotyping; they cannot accept that they are growing older. One woman yelled at me, "You know what's wrong with you. Your attitude is all wrong. There's no such thing as old. It's all in your head."

A musician with the Senior Concert Orchestra refuses to tell his age even when I protest that as a member of this orchestra he must be retired. His answer: "I don't act my age. I'm as young as any twenty-year-old kid."

Another man: "I don't have friends my age. I don't know any old people. They bore me."

A very wrinkled woman in her late sixties: "My oldest friend is in her forties. I never bothered with old people. What person my age could swim the way I do? I'm energetic. Everybody thinks I'm in my forties."

She's kidding herself, and what's worse she's negating her life experience.

Folmar Blongstad: "Sometimes I look in the mirror and say, oh my God, that old man can't be me. I see the big furrows, the turned down corners of my mouth, which is exactly the way my grandfather looked, by the way, and it is a surprise.''

I take a long hard look at my own face, the face that's taken me time to get used to. It's not the face of the girl, of the young woman, of the mother who raised three children. It's the face of a middle-aged woman who's lived, who's experienced, who's lived through very conceivable emotion. It's a face that shows all of this, lined like hell, and I like it. It's a middle-aged face that's on its way to old age and all of my life, good, bad, indifferent, is etched there. And when I see those offensive TV commercials that promise to take the lines off older faces I feel like screaming back at the set, ''Nobody's going to take my life from me, because wiping the lines from my face would be like wiping away who I am.''

I love that about an older face. You can't hide who you are any longer.

But there are truths that hurt. Alice Brophy says, ''You don't want to get old in a society that feels old isn't important. You want to be accepted, not rejected.''

Madelaine Massenoir: ''You see the point is, the whole society suffers when they say how awful it is to be old. It's all over the place and you know that. So you can't help being tainted by this a little. You can't help absorbing some of that.''

It's tragic that even the old sometimes reject themselves— sometimes.

Many things have changed in my own life since I started writing this book. My three sons, Craig, Kenn and Brian, who lived with me, are now on their own. This brings old age closer to me for I am no longer a vital part of the family in a living situation. I am alone. And I like it.

Many things have happened since I started this book. My grandma Annie, age 95, died. Let me tell you about Anna Ziegler Bluh. She was placed in a lovely nursing home by a doctor who said it was best. This doctor was in his forties and hadn't spent one day of his life in a nursing home. But he knew it was best.

Let me tell you about my grandmother. We would come, my

father and me, sometimes together, sometimes separately. We would bring her special things that she loved. We would take her in a wheelchair outside into the sun. We would talk to her, always avoiding the truth, never allowing her to express her fears. All of us, so honest, my mother, my father, me, sitting there with masked lies covering our faces. In our honesty we were unbearably cruel. She would plead with us, looking with those beautiful eyes. "Take me home, please take me home. I'll be good. What did I do wrong? Tell me what I did?"

You grew old, grandma. You committed the crime of growing old in a world that has little respect or feeling for the old. You had a few hours of senility in a twenty-four hour day. You had bones that were brittle and broke. We couldn't take care of you, grandma, unless we gave up our lives so instead we let you give up yours.

Let me tell you about my grandma Annie. During the time she was at the nursing home her only son, my father, died. My mother went to see her often but she carried on so, asking for my father that my mother stopped going. And when I went I pretended my parents were on vacation. I didn't see her as often as I should have. The nursing home was in New York and I lived in Philadelphia, then later in Europe.

Annie became blind, partially deaf, totally bedridden. She ate baby food, stayed in bed. All of this happened the year I was in Europe. The first time I enter the nursing home after returning, when I ask how she is, I am told by a nurse that she's very healthy, that she had the flu and recovered beautifully. "What a strong healthy woman. The doctor says she has a heart like a young woman. They don't make people like that today."

I am infuriated. "What good is her young heart if she's totally bedridden and you won't even let me take her out into the sun?"

The nurse is annoyed. "Well she is old, you know. How old is she anyhow?" She goes to the files.

"Don't bother looking it up. She's 92."

She stares at me. "Well, what do you expect at 92?"

"I expect you would have let her die from the flu, not help a woman whom I love continue being a vegetable."

"Is that so?" she says.

I cannot speak anymore and rush to the elevator to visit my grandmother. I hold her hand, talk to her, wonder if someday somebody will be holding my hand, saying what they think are soothing words, words I cannot hear. I realize that less than 4% of older people end up in institutions. Will I be one of them?

The day they called me to say my grandma died my first emotion was one of relief. Because the truth is she died seven years ago, the day she was placed in the nursing home.

You who read this, this isn't a story. It's the truth, not only my truth but yours as well. And the bed that Anna Ziegler Bluh vacated may be your bed one day. That's if you live long enough, and there are still so few alternatives. But there are alternatives. There should be more day care centers like El Rinconcita. Foster Homes for Adults is an excellent alternative. There should be community responsibility, an awareness of the old who live in our neighborhoods and do not have families nearby. I agree with Isabelle Van Frank that most old people could and should be taken care of in their own homes. If neighborhoods became aware, and synagogues and churches, we could alleviate many of the problems of the old, including making safe neighborhoods, which affects us as well.

If each individual gave two hours a week we could lessen so much loneliness and suffering and we could eliminate much of the segregation of old and young which is largely responsible for the discrimination.

We could join the Grey Panthers to work for a better old age for people living it now and, in time, ourselves.

So many questions since I began this book. I question younger people's attitudes, especially those in the media who continually give us either ridiculously silly old people or those who are infirm. It might be a real awakening if they stopped to think that the portrait they're showing will one day be attributed to themselves, that 20, 30 or even 40 years from now they will have people looking at them in the stereotypical way unless they start doing something about it now. Because we're all going to get old, hopefully. And that old person you see on television or perhaps your mother, father, your grandparent, a co-worker, that person with wrinkles, with the slower walk, that person that annoys the hell out of you, will be you.

I think of my own life. My mother walking with my grandmother, annoyed because suddenly she wasn't walking fast enough, her eyes searching for the sky in utter impatience. Years later, me, walking with my mother, wanting to sprint and having to walk slower because she couldn't keep up and my eyes starting for the sky and stopping halfway there, remembering my mother's look of years ago. And now, my personal stab. Always walking faster than my kids and now my kids moving those long legs of theirs past me and my rushing to keep up.

Well, we all get there.

But when is old old? It starts when you're young. It's the time when you should keep your body in shape, when you should pay attention to daily exercise, to a good healthy diet, to developing many interests that will follow you through life, It's the time to take a good look at older people, not with disdain but with an eye toward your own future. And what's wrong with that future? What's wrong is the way we're taught to look at it.

When is old old? Old is when you give up, when you accept the stereotype of that forgetful, doddering, inactive, infirm, enfeebled, senile, useless, silly person.

Our society scorns older people partly because of what Dr. Alfred Bayne calls a fear of our own old age, partly because we are segregated from older people, and any group we're segregated from appears peculiar—and anything that is seen as peculiar is undesirable—and partly because older people are not the major buyers. They don't buy the big appliances, the cars, and are not the consumers they once were.

And it is that same consumerism that fosters wrinkle-free

people in order to sell mountains of cremes and oil and cosmetics. If old becomes beautiful, they're out a lot of money.

But what is old?

An old person is just a young person grown old. The feelings, the dreams, the desires are always there. Old people are just like you. Like you the people in this book were once embryos, a fetus, a baby, a child, a youngster, an adult and finally an older person. They like you are yesterday's children.

I wrote this book because I believe everything is possible, that change is made first by opening the doors with words. But words haven't any power other than to activate. It's up to you, the reader, to make changes a reality. The point is, life is living and that you can do at any age.

A FEW OF MY FAVORITE PEOPLE

Although it's usual to end a book with afterthoughts or some other title that says finished, a book never finishes any more than life.

Originally the book was a group of word-portraits. When the form changed some of my favorite people were left out. I am hoping that, like me, when you read something you're absorbed in, like a good friendship, you don't want it to end.

This section is for those of you who don't want this to end, about people who have the timeless and beautiful spirit of age.

At 10:00 A.M. I pick her up in what she calls her little house, which is a narrow house in the middle of Soho in New York. We drive to her other house in upstate New York, a co-op where artists live. To live there, one must be recommended and Sari Dienes (pronounced Shari Deens) was recommended by her friend, the composer John Cage.

At midnight I listen to her sing in the bathtub. I sit in her sole room, painted footprints of Sari on the floor. Her mouse-o-leum faces me. It is a plastic shrine encasing a dead mouse on top, two pieces of burnt strudel underneath, surrounded by burnt paper, and at the bottom is a bird that killed itself against her window. I hear Sari this morning, "Isn't that the most valiant mouse you ever saw?"

The mouse's tail is up in the air, its head high.

"It looks like a lion to me," I say.

She laughs. "I'm so glad you said so."

205

Five minutes after I meet her, driving past the lovely changing fall leaves she turns to me and says, "The spirit has no age." At that point I realize that discussing age with Sari Dienes would be pointless. She is right. The spirit has no age, nor does nature; and Sari Dienes is her art is herself is nature.

That morning. We arrive at Stony Point and she shows me the grounds. Long pieces of burnt wood, all the things civilization has thrown away, earth things and human-made things are her shrine. I see her Mt. Fuji. A green plant sits in the center. "Somebody brought me that fern because they said it looks like my hair and you can see how its grows so marvellously." Her Rock River is literally made of rocks.

After struggling with the tape recorder and complaining about machines she answers, "The flower and the machine and you and I and the stars, there is no real difference. You see the Zen people said that thousands of years ago, that I am stone and the flowers, and now science has proven that everything, everything in the world, is made of the same substance, the moon and all the stars and you and me and cheese."

Inside her house we eat lunch. She says, "I will give you things to eat that you've never eaten before. I'm a very inventive cook." And she is.

Sari speaks of time, lost years. "You will never catch up and there's nothing to catch up to anyhow. If I don't feel like doing something I don't do it. I think it pays to give in. It's one of those good things. You bend with the wind. You don't piss against the wind. But women haven't any choice at all. Our piss goes wherever it goes."

When we speak of art and I say I think it transcends time she disagrees. "No it cannot go beyond this time, because you are this time. This moment is everything. There is nothing else but this moment. Wherever you are, this moment is the full thing and I don't think you can transcend it. Art gives form to express the moment."

Sari Dienes was born in Hungary. She didn't study art until she was 30. A student of Ozenfant in Paris, she became his assistant. In 1939 she came to the United States, got stuck here because of the war and then decided to stay.

Her work has appeared in shows with Calder, Man Ray, Louise Nevelson, Motherwell, Dali, Lipschitz, Pollock, Ernst and others. She has had one-woman shows, taught art and recently a film was made about her life and work. Still at times she has been forced to go on welfare. I ask her if I can write about this.

"Yes. I was on relief for years. I didn't choose to be an artist. It chose me. I have to do this. I can't do anything else. This is my life. Alright, so I don't make any money. I don't make a big success of it but this is what I have to do. And alright, so I have to go on relief."

Sari has taught art for many years but gave it up when she realized art cannot be taught. "Because art is like life. You can't teach life to anybody. You can inspire them, you can give them certain ideas about what it is about, but you can't teach it." She feels it is equally impossible to help people, saying that once this was her great thing, this desire to help everybody.

We sit and sip campari and soda. "Bonnie, there's no way of making anybody happy. People have to do it themselves. We have to do it ourselves. You can be a great help but you can't make people happy. I'm helping more people nowadays by not helping anybody. Not trying. Now there's another thing I always say. Don't try. Just do. If I'm good to somebody it's not because I'm trying. I feel that way and I do it. There are many people who say, oh but I try to be so nice to you. I say don't try because if you try you are going to fail. Either be nice to me or leave me alone." We have talked through the afternoon. We have dinner. I see photographs of Sari from the time she was two years old. A lifetime of photographs, of experiences that make Sari Dienes the person she is.

She opens the door to a pouring rain. "Oh how lovely," she says. "I think I'll put on my African hat. Do you like it? Oh and will you be warm enough, Bonnie?" I put on a pair of her socks, borrow a coat and we walk into the wet dark night, a flashlight showing us the way. She speaks to me in French. I say, "I don't speak French well."

"Oh you don't. That's too bad. That was something Picasso said. It meant I am not looking for anything. I am finding things. It is the same thing. You have goals, you have expectations, that means you are searching. You have to find things. I thought, well that's an arrogant statement. Then I realized later that it was my arrogance. This is the real marvellous thing to do. You have a goal. You are limiting yourself. You are looking for something and you can't see what there is because you are looking for something that might not be there at all. You will miss the things that are right there. All the things you could find you miss mostly when you are looking for so and so and so and so. You miss all the marvellous things that are around you."

She tells me that when she was younger she was greatly irritated and bothered by all sorts of stupid things. "Irritation and worry are the two things that are anti-life. They don't serve any purpose. You can be concerned, you can be interested, you can be upset, you can be angry. But irritation and worry, which people spend so much energy on, is really an absolutely negative luxury, especially when you are older."

It is the following day and still raining when we get into the car. I tell her rain is my favorite weather. She says, "That's very nice because you see there's this wonderful Oriental saying. Every day is a wonderful day. Every day is a beautiful day and it doesn't matter if it rains or snows. Even when you're miserable it's a wonderful day. To be able to accept that is a great thing. Marvellous. Even if you are miserable, you are suffering, you are sick. . ."

What gives Sari Dienes her enormous vitality, what gives her the energy to work every day? "If you don't press and don't push, don't force yourself, you don't get so tired. And you have to know your limitations and have to accept these limitations and sometimes of course there is no limitation at any age. You can go a whole hog. You work and you don't sleep and you don't do

anything else. You go on and on and on and on and on because it is
in you and has to come out. But it doesn't really exhaust you. You
get tired, you know, but it is a good tired."

Reading me her poetry as I drive back to the city, poems she
wrote in the forties she says, "Everything I am today was already
in those poems. Zen says you don't learn anything from Zen. You
already have it in you. And of course I think everybody does
have it but we don't listen to what we have, you know. It is very
difficult to hear ourselves or listen to ourselves or understand
ourselves unless we are free to do that, unless we are freed from
all kinds of junk."

"Do you feel freer as you get older?"

"Oh yes, definitely. I could never speak like this ten years
ago."

Sari Dienes was born in 1898.

In New Orleans, Livia and Brent insist I speak with Birdi, their
maid. Brent says, "She'll tell you about plantation life. It will be
marvellous for your book."

Birdi sits on a stool, studying me. She isn't discussing plantation life, she isn't discussing anything. Her eyes are on me, her
ears on a TV soap opera. Her annoyance is apparent.

"Don't ask me about the life of plantation. Mr. Beauregard tell
me, 'Birdi you tell that writer lady about the life of plantation' and
I said, 'listen I never worked on no plantation. Poppa had his own
farm and he hired people to work with him.' Child, I don't know
why you want to speak with me. I ain't done nothing, believe me.
That's why I stay like I am. I left New Orleans. I went to New
York. I lived there just like I live here."

Birdi was born on December 17, 1893. The only work she's ever
done is housekeeping. "Light housekeeping," she says emphati-
cally. "And when I first come to New Orleans I didn't know too
much about that." She shakes her head. "I don't have anything
in my past life to tell you."

"Birdi, do you think you'll ever retire?"

"Oh I will if they would just leave me alone. See I got a broken foot and they got me working with a broken foot.''

Her ankle has an ace bandage on it.

Brent enters. ''Birdi, stop this foolishness. You know what will happen to you the day you stay home.''

Birdi breaks up laughing. ''Look at the way you're dressed in front of the lady. Go put some clothes on.'' Brent exits. She shakes her head. ''In my day a man wouldn't be seen in front of a lady without a shirt on.''

I ask her if she's really unhappy working. She smiles broadly. ''Oh it keeps me going. I tease him because they keep me working but it's not them. I work because I want to. Long as I'm able and not sick.''

''Birdi, do you feel differently now that you're older?''

''Just the same. I don't worry. Life is too short to worry about anything. Just like you see me today you find me tomorrow. The same way. I ain't gonna add no worry or take no worry.''

She tells me she has never been in a hospital, that the first time she took off from work was when she hurt her foot. She never remembers her family being sick either.

''My momma was older and she wasn't sick far as I can remember but when the time come she just died. My father too. They didn't make anybody tired. My two brothers, they was the same thing. One got up in the morning, went on his daily walk and he took a heart condition and died that day. The other was coming home and he took sick on the street. At least somebody take him in the car and brought him to my house. Two hours and he was gone. That is to say, nobody would linger long enough to say they're tired.''

Birdi came to New Orleans from the country when she was 18. Since she'd only gone to the eighth grade she decided to go to night school to get her certificate. She married, never had children of her own. But when her sister and her husband died in an auto accident, she raised their four children. Of the four, two went to college. She says, ''That was a hard pull. Four children. Well, they got something that nobody can take away from them. They all got something and they can take care of themselves. Anyway that's all I know. There's nothing that I could say that would be a shock.''

"Birdi, I don't want a shock.''

"I can tell you I'm glad I'm here. That I can tell you. And like I told you, I don't let anything worry me. If nothing worries you, you'll make it. That's why I say, long as the children are working for themselves I have nothing to worry me and they're going to do what they want anyway. They go when they're ready. They make their own money. So what. What I got to do. They don't belong to me.''

"Do they appreciate what you did for them, Birdi?''

"Oh yes, oh yes they do. It's a laugh with the little bit of money I was making, to take care of them.''

"Can I ask how much money you earn?''

"How much money I make now? Nothing.''

"Nothing?''

She laughs. "What I earn I call nothing. When I was able to make money they wasn't paying nothing. Now that they're paying I'm too old to get some. I work a little here, a little there. I make enough money for me to live off. I draw my social security and I can make all the money I want because I'm past 72. I been working for Livia 28 years, ever since she come to the city. That's one of the reasons I haven't retired; on account of her. I like her and she likes me. We stick together, Livia and me.''

"What do you think of the world today?''

"We were just talking of it on the bus this morning and an elderly woman, she said to me, what will become of the world. I said that's what I'm thinking every day. People have no respect for one another. They wants something for nothing. They steal. They kill for that almighty dollar. That's why I keep a couple of dollars in my pocket. 'Cause if you don't have anything they're gonna beat you up. It's awful the way the people live. Not only here; everywhere. I was in the country last Saturday. They say they're selling dope up there just like they do in the city.

Everybody want that almighty dollar and nobody wants to work for it."

"Do you have family in the country?"

"There's nobody my age anymore. You see, all the folks I would know, they all gone. There ain't nobody. As we're sitting here talking I'm thinking back. What have I done that you could repeat and write up?"

"Birdi, everybody has something to say. Do you prefer people your own age?"

"Yeah, oh yeah. We speak the same language. What can I speak with the young folks? I'm going to a dance the later part of this month. I told one woman I want to see old people." She sighs. "I'm going to be the oldest one there. I still dance but I don't do the dances they dance now. You don't need a partner to dance anymore. I just go and watch the kids. I get a kick out of it." Another sigh. "People don't have no time for old folks."

When it comes to politics Birdi is very vocal. "People have been doing wrong things ever since there come a world. But right now they do anything they want and there's nobody to do anything about it."

Birdi, who has been voting since the fifties says "We never seen such politicians as these. They steal and do so many things. How can you put some of them in office? How you gonna have respect for people like that?"

She gets up, goes into the kitchen. "So now you better let me go and do my work. I know you got to do your book. I hope you can make something of it, because you deserve it. But you got the wrong somebody that don't have nothing to tell you."

"Birdi, I think what you've said is wonderful."

She smiles. "You do?"

"One more question and then I won't bother you. Do you think blacks are treated better today?"

"Well, some of them are doing better than they ever did but there's plenty of room to do better. This generation being the way they are, they're demanding and I don't think that's right. If you want anything work for it."

"But sometimes you aren't given the chance."

"I know that, girl."

"You have to have the power to make choices."

"But you see you don't have it because you don't have money in the first place. The blacks don't have any money and where you have to get your money from is from the white and some of them will give and some of them won't. We never had the opportunity to do anything. You look back in time, you go way back. You find everything that was on this earth the white had. Now how did they get it?"

"How?"

"How did they get it?"

"Birdi, you tell me."

"Girl, that's what I would like to know. I'm asking you now. That's always been the question. How did they get so much and us get so little?"

I call Howard Shoup, who as a major costume designer was up for the Oscar five times. I tell him I'm a friend of Betsy and Oliver Hailey's and we make an appointment.

Shoup, who is Betsy's uncle, tells me he met Oliver for the first time when the Haileys moved to California. "They called me up and I thought how great, the way you do with everybody in Hollywood who's young and new. Little did we know youth was going to take over. Over at Warner's where I was for 30 years the producers were in their sixties and seventies. The producers are now 30, barely 40."

Howard Shoup, born in Texas, moved to New York when he was 21. There he worked as a designer for Bonwit Teller and Hattie Carnegie. He'd planned to stay in New York but when his father became seriously ill he returned to Texas. A well-known clairvoyant in Dallas advised him to go to Hollywood. "Hollywood's calling you she said, and I said, 'Madame Raphael, what'll I do in Hollywood?' and she said, 'You'll find out.' "

He took her advice. In Hollywood he called Minna Wallis whom he'd met at a party in New York, not realizing she was the sister of Hal Wallis. Three days later he was working for Warner Brothers. Later he worked for MGM, then returned to Warners until he retired in 1970, when he was 72. "We no longer had contracts but worked from picture to picture. They didn't put me away when I was 72. They called me and said I was eligible for retirement. I would have hated it if the studio said, you're no longer eligible for work. I think I would have gone to court because they have 76-year-old actors, actresses and producers."

"Howard, how come so many older men are still playing romantic leads with younger women but they never give older actresses romantic leads with younger men?"

"Because we were all brought up thinking an older man can be romantic and chase girls but an older woman should never chase young men. Momma shouldn't go around with our college friends but Daddy could go around with the college girls and did. Not my daddy but daddies."

"I really resent it."

"It will change but now it would have to be a tragedy. They couldn't end up with her all festooned, riding in the Rose Bowl Parade, the two of them clutching each other because everybody would say, what a comedy."

Howard Shoup is one of the most marvellous storytellers, he talks about his experiences, the actresses and actors he's worked with, and periodically turns to me and says, "I know I haven't done a thing for your book. I'm supposed to be talking about age." Then, "I don't feel any age because in the studio age doesn't mean a thing. It's what you can do. So I never ask anybody about their age and it doesn't bother me."

"You never think about age?"

"Well at 50 I knew dern well I was middle-aged. I thought, what a milestone, but what do I care. I'm having fun so I forgot all about it. At 60 I thought, gee, people retire at this age but they've got to have a lot of money and I don't have anything because anybody in the movie industry spends more than they make. Well, there are a few who make fortunes. When I got to my 69th birthday I thought, well, that's a number you're ill-advised to celebrate so I thought I wouldn't tell anybody and of course my buddies had a party for me, everybody holding their sides laughing but me. 70 was a real milestone I felt and I dreaded it. August 29th is my birthday and it's not a season to celebrate. People are always away on vacation so I've rarely had parties or anything but I thought, I dread tomorrow. 70, I thought. But I got up and didn't even look in the mirror. I didn't feel one day older. I did the same exercises to see if I could reach the floor and I did. So what. Big deal. So on my 72nd birthday it didn't matter. But then I was at Fox, seeing some films for the Academy, and people said you're looking wonderful. They meant for my age. It almost sounds like you were in bed for years and you got up and you're still around. So I gave them sad sweet smiles and said, so are you.''

It would be impossible to write about Howard Shoup without relating at least one of his stories, this one beautiful to me because it shows agism when he was 38. He joined the army during the Second World War and nobody in his group thought he could make it through basic training since he was so much older.

''They said we'll help you, we'll cover for you somehow and I said, oh well, the good Lord will manage. My mother used to tell me not to worry. Well anyhow the day comes and it is alphabetical order and wouldn't you know I'm not only the oldest but the last in line. Well we had to climb up bunches of rocks that started falling down like an avalanche. We had to go over bridges that were breaking. We had to swing on to something or other. You climb to the top of a pole and you sit there until they tell you to come down. And the scareder you look the longer you sit, you know. And it kept going on all day and here I am running along with them and they'd wave and they couldn't believe I was doing all the things. So the last thing was a wall about eight feet high. It was curved and as slick as a bass's behind. You had to shinny over it and that was it. If you did it you were in. That was the end of the obstacles.

"Anyhow, here they all climbed over this thing and here I am the last one. So I run about five feet from the wall and stop. I think, you'll never make this thing. You're running too fast. So I go back and I run slower and I come a little closer and I think, no, you'll never make this because it's too high. You can't reach and jump that high and shinny or shimmy over or whatever it is. Anyway the third time I walked because I thought it was the running that did it. There were officers there, talking to each other and bored with the whole thing. And this lieutenant said, soldier what the hell's the matter with you. What are you waiting for? And I said, I'm waiting for somebody to help me over the damn fence. He went like this with his hands (cupped them). I stepped on his hand and leapt over the fence and I was in the Air Force. Well, the men all hollered and laughed and the other officers had to hold themselves back because the lieutenant was so embarrassed. He just did it automatically. It was just one of the most old-fashioned gestures in the world. And that night at the PX we were all laughing and giggling and somebody said what's the matter with you all. And they said, Shoup passed the obstacle course. But how!"

We sit in my hotel room, drinking wine, laughing and again I hear, "Bonnie, let's be honest. I haven't done your book one bit of good. I'm supposed to be talking about age."

"Ok, Shoupie, how do you feel about it?"

"It's just a state of mind and I don't care if people think it silly or shallow but I actually for days at a time feel young. I've learned to accept tragedy as fate, rather than, why me? And it keeps me young. I used to be told that when you start talking to yourself, your mind was going, you know, and I used to see people mumbling to themselves on the bus and I'd think, oh the poor little old man, he's lonesome. I was never lonesome one day in my entire life. I left home for the first time when I was 21. I loved my family. I missed them but I was not lonesome. I wanted whatever was outside that door. I must say I am a fatalist. I have just drifted along and had a ball.''

Howard Shoup likes people, who unlike himself, are married, have had children, grandchildren, people who've had a well-rounded life, have had their ups and downs. ''But I can't stand anybody who was happy in St. Paul or Kansas City all these years and just stayed there and when they got a vacation went four miles out to a country home. I like to meet celebrities but they're not much fun to sit down with, you know, because they're never going to tell the story of their lives. Never, never. It's been too tough.''

''Are you saying Shoupie that you're not telling the truth?''

''I'm not a celebrity. A colorful individual but not a celebrity. I never wanted to do anything else but design clothes and I was just lucky enough that it evolved into something that was respectable enough so the family could say, well, Howard is doing very well in Hollywood.''

We watch the sun set on the Hollywood Hills, the orange and red colors that rapidly drop into the sea. We walk to a nearby restaurant, sip some wine waiting for the food to come. Shoup turns to me.

''Now we'll talk about this age thing. Your face ages head on. It's there. It isn't going to change back you know. I feel young and I act young but that's as far as I can go. I face facts and pray for the future as I did when I was a child. I found out things about people that make them warm and close to me. You don't know how show biz is. You just meet everybody. How do you do and oh you're Shoupie, maybe we'll get together sometime. But I've never felt lonely. I have what so few people have. Music, books, memories. I can't stand people who say, 'I have lots of friends everywhere.' I doubt seriously they do.''

When Howard Shoup was invited for lunch at one of the studios he refused because Madame Raphael told him that when he left the studios, those gates would never open again. But he changed his mind when he was invited to a preview of a movie Oliver Hailey had written.

"I couldn't wait to go and I thought, being back at Warners after five years I would cry, you know, out of sentiment. So after the picture ended I sneaked out by myself to make the grand tour. The fronts of the old sets, the wardrobe didn't look the same. The restaurant didn't look the same. And when I went back there wasn't one soul in the whole room that I'd ever seen before except for Betsy and Oliver. Instead of being a broken valentine my heart just hardened."

His mood is shortlived. He turns to me and smiles broadly. "I loved life and I'm facing age because it's approaching, but with a smile."

In the town of Winnemucca, Nevada in the senior center where the director explains away the limited activities with "You have to work slowly here," I meet the most unlikely character.

He calls himself Portuguese Joe. With flowing white hair, flowing beard, colorful clothes, flamboyant in manner, he stands out like a sore thumb. And the people at the center look at him as if he were a thumb, floating around the area, one that will hopefully move on to another place.

That's what Portuguese Joe has done all his life. A former seaman, he loves travelling but now that he's older he needs an address where his social security checks can be sent. An oldtime socialist, he is aware that Winnemucca is far from liberal but exclaims, "Well I'm a liberal and they can't do shit about it. You can also put in your book I'm a whiskey head, a weedhead and I first came here 20 years ago." His laugh has the sound of somebody who has smoked a lifetime.

"Listen, they're reactionaries here. They don't like kids with long hair so I grew long hair. They don't like beards so I grew a beard. I'll tell you why I'm here. I have an apartment for $40 a month and this includes utilities. That's exceptional, even for this town."

His views on the red light district in Winnemucca are that every city should have them, for women as well as men. Society, he says, has put women down for their sexual desire, making them outcasts. Yet he believes if the society were different, more humane, there would be no need for prostitutes.

He rants about the way older people are treated. "We're ripped off continuously. Take a small thing like barbers. They want $2 to $2.50 here. We have to pay the same for everything but we don't have the money. Your establishment don't give a damn, they don't give a shit. The most critical thing, not only for elderly people but for everybody, is socialized medicine. They're knocking off the old people with the bills. Those doctors are a bunch of crooks. They don't care if you're old. They're doing better with Medicare than we are."

Portuguese Joe rolls a cigarette, pauses, reflects, "You think it strange that I'm here but I'll tell you. I think every progressive should go amongst people who are not progressive and do whatever they can to change their minds. It's hard but I've changed a few. They should go out like the Christians do and carry the word. Do missionary work in progressive thoughts because the establishment doesn't suffer the perils of this society. They reap the rewards on the backs of the underprivileged and the underpaid and the elderly. You put that in your book."